Collaborative/ Therapeutic Assessment

A Casebook and Guide

Edited by

**Stephen E. Finn
Constance T. Fischer
and
Leonard Handler**

WILEY

John Wiley & Sons, Inc.

This book is printed on acid-free paper. ♾

Copyright © 2012 by John Wiley & Sons, Inc. All rights reserved.

Published by John Wiley & Sons, Inc., Hoboken, New Jersey.
Published simultaneously in Canada.

Library of Congress Cataloging-in-Publication Data:

Collaborative/therapeutic assessment / edited by Stephen E. Finn,
Constance T. Fischer, and Leonard Handler.
    p. ; cm.
  Includes bibliographical references and indexes.
  ISBN 978-0-470-55135-6 (pbk. : alk. paper)
  ISBN 978-1-118-16866-0 (ebk)
  ISBN 978-1-118-16864-6 (ebk)
  ISBN 978-1-118-16865-3 (ebk)
  I. Finn, Stephen E., 1956– II. Fischer, Constance T., 1938– III. Handler, Leonard, 1936–
  [DNLM: 1. Psychological Tests. 2. Personality Assessment. 3. Psychotherapy—methods. WM 145]
  LC classification not assigned
  616.89′075—dc23
                                                                                      2011029119

Printed in the United States of America
10 9 8 7 6 5 4 3 2 1

Contents

Preface   vii

About the Contributors   xix

  1 **Collaborative/Therapeutic Assessment: Basic Concepts, History, and Research**   1
Stephen E. Finn, Constance T. Fischer, and Leonard Handler

PART I: Assessments of Individual Adults

  2 **Therapeutic Assessment of a Dissociating Client: Learning Internal Navigation**   27
Judith Armstrong

  3 **Therapeutic Assessment of Depression: Love's Labors Lost?**   47
Marc J. Diener, Mark J. Hilsenroth, Thomas D. Cromer, Frank P. Pesale, and Jenelle Slavin-Mulford

  4 **Collaboration in Neuropsychological Assessment: Metaphor as Intervention With a Suicidal Adult**   69
Diane H. Engelman and J. B. Allyn

  5 **Collaboration Throughout the Assessment: A Young Man in Transition**   93
Constance T. Fischer

  6 **Therapeutic Assessment for a Treatment in Crisis Following Multiple Suicide Attempts**   113
J. Christopher Fowler

7 Using Therapeutic Assessment to Explore Emotional
Constriction: A Creative Professional in Crisis   133
Jan H. Kamphuis and Hilde de Saeger

8 Therapeutic Assessment Involving Multiple Life Issues:
Coming to Terms With Problems of Health, Culture, and
Learning   157
Hale Martin and Erin Jacklin

9 Collaborative Assessment for Psychotherapy: Witnessing
A Woman's Reawakening   179
Patrick J. McElfresh

10 Therapeutic Assessment of Severe Abuse: A Woman
Living With Her Past   199
Carol Groves Overton

PART II: Assessments of Children, Adolescents, and Young Adults

11 Therapeutic Assessment of an Adolescent: An Adopted
Teenager Comes to Feel Understood   225
Marita Frackowiak

12 Collaborative Storytelling With Children: An Unruly
Six-Year-Old Boy   243
Leonard Handler

13 Rorschach-Based Psychotherapy: Collaboration
With a Suicidal Young Woman   269
Noriko Nakamura

14 Collaborative Assessment of a Child in Foster Care:
New Understanding of Bad Behavior   291
Caroline Purves

15 Therapeutic Assessment With a 10-Year-Old Boy
and His Parents: The Pain Under the Disrespect   311
Deborah J. Tharinger, Melissa E. Fisher, and Bradley Gerber

16 Collaborative Assessment on an Adolescent Psychiatric
Ward: A Psychotic Teenage Girl   335
Heikki Toivakka

PART III: Special Applications

17 Therapeutic Assessment Alternative to Custody
Evaluation: An Adolescent Whose Parents Could
Not Stop Fighting   357
F. Barton Evans

18 Therapeutic Assessment With a Couple in Crisis:
Undoing Problematic Projective Identification via
the Consensus Rorschach   379
Stephen E. Finn

19 Case Studies in Collaborative Neuropsychology: A Man With
Brain Injury and a Child With Learning Problems   401
Tad T. Gorske and Steven R. Smith

Afterword: Forward!   421
Constance T. Fischer, Leonard Handler, and Stephen E. Finn

Author Index   427

Subject Index   430

Preface

Collaborative/Therapeutic Assessment (C/TA) is the term we use in this book to refer to multiple closely related approaches to psychological testing that are variously called individualized assessment, Collaborative Assessment, therapeutic assessment (lowercase), Therapeutic Assessment (uppercase), Therapeutic Model of Assessment, Collaborative Therapeutic Neuropsychological Assessment, Rorschach-based psychotherapy, projective counseling, and dynamic assessment. We will define and draw distinctions among many of these approaches in Chapter 1 and give a brief history of the field. We will also review research about these methods, which continues to accrue at a rapid pace. The remainder of the book consists of 18 case examples of C/TA from practitioners (including us) in four different countries. The chapters are divided into three sections: Part I concerns C/TA with adult individual clients; cases in Part II illustrate C/TA with children, adolescents, and young adults; and Part III contains cases illustrating special topics in C/TA, such as Collaborative Therapeutic Neuropsychological Assessment (CTNA), therapeutic assessment in a child-custody situation, and Therapeutic Assessment of couples. Within each section, the chapters are arranged alphabetically by the first author's last name. In a final chapter we discuss commonalities among the cases and make concluding comments.

The clients written about in this book include adults, children, adolescents, couples, and families with many different types of backgrounds and concerns. All clients' names and identifying information have been greatly altered to protect their privacy. The authors/practitioners include longstanding colleagues and young professionals, some of whom were former students of ours. All assessors necessarily adapted the basic concepts and practices of C/TA to their different settings, clients, and theoretical backgrounds. Readers will readily see that there is no single way to undertake C/TA, and that they already engage in various of these practices, and can easily tailor others for their own use.

This case study project was designed as a *teaching* text, and every chapter contains clearly labeled *Teaching Points* throughout its pages. Different authors have located these teaching points in different ways. We believe these points will be useful to graduate students and seasoned professionals alike. As we edited one another's and our contributors' work, we found ourselves continuing to learn about the ways in which creative, respectful, and well-trained professionals can use psychological tests to help clients and important people in their lives achieve new ways of thinking and being in the world.

Although the terminology used varies, all of the approaches represented in this book share the notion that psychological assessment is a serious enterprise, involving a special kind of professional relationship, and that it has the power to illuminate and affect people's lives. As we read through these chapters, we found ourselves moved and inspired, and we experienced a range of emotions: awe, sadness, excitement, hope, envy, and gratitude. Our hope is that you will find these accounts equally moving, and that if you do, you will help spread the word about the potential therapeutic power of psychological assessment.

OUR PERSONAL CONTEXTS FOR THIS BOOK

We strongly believe that all behavior occurs within specific meaningful contexts. Therefore, we decided it would be responsible and most likely meaningful to readers to give information at the beginning of this book about our personal contexts and how they shaped us. We now share three first-person accounts of our involvement with Collaborative/ Therapeutic Assessment.

Connie Fischer

Prelude to entering graduate school in psychology

I majored in political science and minored in philosophy at the University of Oklahoma, where I also took a social psychology course from Muzafer Sherif, whose research took place in everyday life settings.

His discussions did not involve explaining findings in terms of causes and constructs, but rather addressed the actual interactions of observed people (e.g., the Robbers Cave experiment with kids at summer camp). Unsurprisingly, I was also impressed with Kurt Lewin's experiments, which involved people in their usual settings responding to various conditions (e.g., grade-school youngsters being taught by teachers told to be authoritarian, democratic, or laissez-faire).

While at OU, I earned a secondary schools teaching certificate in social studies and did my student teaching in Oklahoma City. While teaching an honors senior world history course, a student asked who had set up the French class structure of bourgeoisie, aristocracy, journalists, and so on. I said that I was sure that no one designed that system. A student asked me if I had noticed mud huts on a road on the way into Oklahoma City from Norman. When I nodded, she said that the corner hut with chickens pecking in the dirt for corn seed belonged to her grandfather. She told us that her father was the president of a First National Bank in town, and she said that she thought that her own family showed that although we have a certain kind of class system, it is not like the permanent caste system of India.

Knowing that in this large school, many of the students did not know one another's families, I did a class experiment in which I pointed to one student at a time in the first row and asked for a show of hands regarding which salad dressing probably was favored in that student's home, then for another row of students I asked how many cars were owned by the family, and so on. Then I pointed to each student in a row and asked whether that student would go to college (all were academically qualified). We agreed both that no one had set up this structure and that many students would break out of it. Two days later I was told to report to the Superintendent of Schools, who informed me that my job was to teach facts, not to teach students to think, which was dangerous for them.

Graduate school

So I decided to apply to graduate schools in psychology, with the goal of earning a Master's degree. I thought that I would be terrifically mature by then and would have found my answer as to whether I might be dangerous to students. And if I determined that encouraging students to reflect was not dangerous, I would have the authority of a graduate degree (which was true then). I chose the University of Kentucky, which listed lots of courses about "learning." Of course they turned out to be about rats, not people, but I became fascinated about psychology, especially social psychology. I eventually changed my concentration to clinical psychology, with the thought that I might find a way to work with communities in what I thought of as "preventative mental health." Besides, there were no jobs except as professors for social psychologists, and I certainly did not want to be a professor! Clinical psychology at the time was practiced almost exclusively in child guidance centers and hospitals, and I didn't want to do that either. So here I am, with a 45-year history of being a professor and clinical psychologist!

My UK program was heavily experimental and psychoanalytic (and a strong program that has served me well). But it was my four-year traineeship at the Lexington Veterans Administration neuropsychiatric hospital that allowed me to add what today I call "collaborative" explorations with patients both in therapy and testing. Also I was able to observe and interact with the patients in hallways, the canteen, and on their wards and on outside walkways. These experiences grounded my attending to contexts of comportment. Many of my supervisors had come to this hospital because the German emigrant phenomenological psychiatrist, Erwin Straus, was in residence. In my last year of classes, despite earning A's in all practica and clinical courses, my faculty assigned me a grade of C in my last diagnostic testing course because they noted from the two-way mirror that: (1) I was inefficient in test administration (I put my pencil down on the left side of my body, requiring that I cross my body to pick it up); (2) when I saw that the just-admitted 19-year-old, who had suffered a first psychotic break, was frightened by the giggling and talking seeming to come from the mirror, I explained that the mirror was indeed a window through which my teachers were watching to see if I was giving the tests correctly. I had been told not to talk with the patient, just to test. Criticisms three through six were similar, and convinced me that I would never practice in the way I had been taught, which I believed undermined patients' sense of agency and confidence.

Career

Anyway, with my new PhD, I wound up at Duquesne University, whose psychology department was bringing in members who would work together to develop philosophical foundations and clinical and research methods that were explicitly appropriate to humans' aspects that exceeded physiological and learning history (the dominant paradigm at the time). We now call our approach "human-science psychology" (in comparison to its companion natural science psychology). Our early philosophical sources were European existentialism and phenomenology (e.g., Heidegger). I was assigned to teach the "testing course," which no one else wanted to teach but was necessary if our students were to be eligible for licensure and to land jobs. This unwelcome assignment turned out to be a blessing. Together, over years, besides learning standardized administration, testing research, and so on, the students explored ways to carry out individualized assessments and report writing. My book *Individualizing Psychological Assessment* (1985) was based on my lecture notes and my ongoing list of suggestions to students about their reports. We did some testing in clients' homes, we learned to write without constructs, to describe in terms of observed action and clients' discussions with us. Clients read and wrote comments on our reports.

My early journal manuscripts, about writing reports to be read by clients and their helpers, were quickly and emphatically rejected, variously as unethical (patients would be injured by hearing about their pathology) and unprofessional, and even as dangerous to our profession (without our jargon, we would seem to be ordinary). One editor instructed me never to submit to his journal again. I suspect that no one read the full papers, where I provided excerpts that did not tell clients that they had underlying homosexual or aggressive drives, and so on. Reviewers could not imagine writing in ways that clients could understand and that would not be overwhelming.

Eventually, I found my way to the Society for Personality Assessment, whose members are engaged multiply in developing and researching tests, teaching assessment, and in the practice of therapy and assessment. I think that SPA members' openness to my presentations was largely due to their multiple involvements in assessment. Some years after publication of *Individualizing Psychological Assessment*, which both Steve Finn and Len Handler had read, we introduced ourselves to each other and then often organized symposia, learning from each other. For example, I borrowed Steve's practice of asking referred clients what they might want to learn for themselves from the assessment, and I borrowed Len's Rorschach postinquiry question, "And if this mushroom could talk, what would it say?" and much more; ours has been a mutually profitable journey.

Steve Finn

My interest in personality began while I was an undergraduate at Haverford College. My advisor and mentor, Douglas A. Davis, taught a course on Harry Stack Sullivan, and I found it fascinating. But it was later, as a graduate student at the University of Minnesota, that the power of personality assessment grabbed me. In 1979, my first year there, we students took basic courses in personality assessment and clinical psychology from some of the great personality psychologists of our times, such as Auke Tellegen, Paul Meehl, and James Butcher. The summer of my first year, I did a practicum in the adult psychiatric unit of Hennepin County Medical Center (HCMC), and during my very first assessment, a client underwent a huge transformation following a feedback session I gave about his Rorschach. (I have written about this case in my book, *In Our Clients' Shoes*, 2007). I was moved, awestruck, and curious.

I remember speaking to my professors at the university about what I had witnessed. They commented that they had heard about clients' appearing to get better as a result of an assessment. "Has anyone studied this or written about this phenomenon?" I asked. "Not that we know of," they replied. And so I decided that I wanted to be the person who figured all this out! I had many more impressive experiences during my internship and fellowship at HCMC, under the supervision of three extremely wise and capable clinical psychologists, Ada Hegion, Kenneth Hampton, and Ziegrieds Stelmachers. All three helped me begin to think through the underlying therapeutic mechanisms of psychological assessment.

After I received my PhD, I was hired as a faculty member in Clinical Psychology at the University of Texas at Austin, in part because I agreed to teach the "testing course." I remember spending weeks preparing my first lecture for this course, which I titled "An Interpersonal Model of Psychological Assessment" in a deliberate nod to Sullivan. Over the next nine years, I continued to read, do research, and experiment with how to make psychological assessment therapeutic for clients. A student of mine, Mary Tonsager, collaborated on a study for her Master's thesis of the therapeutic effects of a specific method of giving MMPI-2 feedback to clients (Finn & Tonsager, 1992). This was the first published controlled study showing that psychological assessment could lead to significant changes in clients' symptomatology and self-esteem.

A very important event during this period was my discovery of Connie Fischer's book, *Individualizing Psychological Assessment* (1985/1994). A friend had recommended the book to me, and I remember staying up all night reading it the night I checked it out of the library. I was astonished, inspired, and excited that someone had so fully developed an assessment model that spoke to me. I read and re-read Connie's book and all of her articles that I could get my hands on. I studied transcripts of her interactions with clients, and I began to incorporate many of her ways of involving clients as active collaborators. I found that Connie's methods greatly increased the therapeutic power of the assessments I was doing in my small private practice.

In 1993, I was hungry for time to fully test out my emerging model of psychological assessment, which I named Therapeutic Assessment. After much consideration, I resigned my full-time position at the University of Texas to open the Center for Therapeutic Assessment in Austin, Texas. I remember being scared about whether I could earn enough money to support myself, so I did one of the only things I could think of for marketing. I went to three of the most successful psychotherapists in town, took them out to lunch, and volunteered to do an assessment for free with one of their most difficult therapy clients. All accepted my offer, and within months, word had spread, and I had more referrals than I could possibly handle. Initially, I had one part-time employee (Mary Tonsager). Nine months later there were seven full-time psychologists working at the Center, and we had a nine-month waiting list for assessments.

Over the next 7 to 10 years, my colleagues and I collaborated in developing the methods of Therapeutic Assessment for adult clients, child and adolescent clients, and couples. We did hundreds of assessments with clients who had many different types of life difficulties, and we became known for consultative assessments, in which we worked with clients and psychotherapists who felt they were stuck in their work together. This was an exciting and rich time, and I was also fed by my involvement with the Society for Personality Assessment (SPA). There I finally met Connie Fischer, whom I had long admired, and found her to be open, approachable, and encouraging of my work. I also heard papers by Len Handler and Caroline Purves and recognized them as kindred souls. I organized symposia and workshops at SPA, APA, and the meetings of the International Society for Rorschach and Projective Methods to bring us all together and help us learn from each other. International meetings helped me find colleagues in many other countries who thought about psychological assessment in similar ways, and gradually an international community has evolved.

My last 10 years have been devoted to a mixture of clinical practice, writing, research, and training others in Therapeutic Assessment. My colleague at the University of Texas, Deborah Tharinger, spearheaded a research project on Therapeutic Assessment with children and adolescents that has been extremely productive and that helped refine the methods of TA with these populations. In 2007, I published *In Our Clients' Shoes: Theory and Techniques of Therapeutic Assessment*, and this has led to more invitations to present around the world. I established a website on Collaborative/Therapeutic Assessment (www.therapeutic assessment.com), a training institute (the Therapeutic Assessment Institute), and I cofounded the European Center for Therapeutic Assessment at Catholic University in Milan, Italy. These days I am concentrating on how to train clinicians in the methods written about in this book. I am still disheartened by many poorly written traditional psychological assessment reports that I come across in my clinical practice, but the tide seems to be turning. Recently, it seems the world is increasingly ready for Collaborative and Therapeutic Assessment.

Len Handler

I've told this story many times, but each telling varies as to the time it took place. Let's just say that I met Connie Fischer and Steve Finn about 15 years ago, at an annual meeting of the Society for Personality

Assessment. They were sitting at a hotel restaurant table, sharing a bottle of good wine. Steve asked whether I would like to join them, and I did so, eagerly. Soon our conversation led to my assessment approach, after which, to my surprise, both Steve and Connie remarked that what I was really doing was therapeutic or collaborative assessment. I felt welcomed and pleased that there was a place for me in the assessment world—one that now made my approach legitimate. I no longer felt that I had unsystematically diverted from the only "correct" scientific assessment approach, based on standardized assessment procedures.

We agreed that the wine was good and that adherence to a standardized approach was often not helpful to the client and might even be harmful. I shared with them the problems patients often had when I conducted assessments at two Veterans Administration hospitals, and the ways in which I tried to make the assessment process less painful. In my previous assessment experiences, I had been asked not to deviate from standardized methods, but I continued to make changes nevertheless.

It was important, I recognized, to provide support, direction, and sequential feedback to the patients. For example, I asked one inpatient the first item of the Similarities subtest, "How are an orange and a banana alike?" He looked at me, obviously troubled, and said, "They're not alike." According to the directions for the Similarities subtest of the 1955 Wechsler Adult Intelligence Scale (WAIS), the examiner was to tell the patient how the two fruits were similar, if the patient did not give a correct answer. No hints were to be given after that. The patient continued to say the subsequent items were not alike, and would have failed the subtest if we had continued in this fashion. I told the patient that there were no tricks in these questions; there really was a way in which the two items were alike. Given this reassurance, we went back over the items and the patient achieved an excellent score.

When I used this example in assessment class many years later, I was chastised by some students for varying from standardized procedure who believed that the patient should be given a score of zero for that subtest. The class discussed my approach, which was to continue to assure the patient that there was "no trick here," and that there really was a way in which these pairs of items were alike. I asked him if we could go back over the items, and he agreed to do so. We no longer had any problems with suspicion. The patient was able to lay aside his suspicion after only mild reassurance and would probably be able to function outside the hospital, with just a little bit of support and assurance. In retrospect, the patient's initial suspicious reaction was a natural reaction, because he was a newcomer to the hospital ward and his history included situations in which he had been "hurt" by friends and family members. He shared these events with me later in our relationship. At that point I was learning how to be "as" the patient, so I could learn to know what he was experiencing. I was delighted by the results of "knowing" the persons I was testing, and in most situations the patients seemed like they enjoyed "knowing" me.

To mention a metaphor that many of us have adopted (thanks to Steve Finn), from *In Our Clients' Shoes*, the "shoes" metaphor has been very helpful for me and others to experience what it's like to feel, think, and have other aspects of inner experiences. I am not talking about empathy, which is an external stance, experienced by a person about *another* person. According to *Webster's Dictionary* (1953), *empathy* is defined as "Imaginative projection of one's own consciousness into another being." Rather, I mean "intimate contact with the internal life that makes the [assessor] *the same as his [her] patients*" (Bouchard & Guérette, 1991, p. 388). Perhaps that is why Jan Kamphuis, in his chapter (in this volume), stated that he simply does not forget his TA clients. There is usually some personality aspect or a life situation expressed by a client that is or was also mine at some time, as well as theirs. I remember most of the veterans I tested at the two Veterans Administration hospitals, so long ago, and have still kept their reports in my files.

Becoming aware of the client's experience of his or her daily work and family relationships helps me to be better connected with the client. All the while I am learning from him or her, for example, what it was like to be a *mailman*, and sometimes imagining that *I* am a mailman. I remember that patient, whom I tested almost 50 years ago, and the initially unexpected (to me) stresses he faced, sorting or delivering the mail. For him the post office was a minefield, filled with associates who were dangerous if he interacted with them. Yet, he trusted me; I began to feel it was, indeed, a minefield and we were both cautious in our discussion—until "he-me" found the other employees were less and less harmful and eventually were even safe.

In another area, I have always been fascinated with various aspects of narrative therapy and the importance of stories in a child's (and in my own) life. I also spent many years studying children's play. I made up stories for my children, especially on long trips. The more unusual the stories were, the more the kids liked them. Even today, Greenberg, the flying pig, is with us in our home. So it seemed natural that we should draw and tell each other stories. Yet, in doing therapy with children, many of the stories did not seem to have dynamic meaning. One frightened child was unresponsive until I asked her to draw—not a person or a tree or a family, but to my amazement I suddenly chose "a make-believe animal." I found that stories generated with that approach were rich with emotions, be they positive or negative, and helped me understand the fantasy world of a child.

I decided to collaborate with the child and to respond with my own story, one that touches the soul of the child and mine as well. Children have shoes to be in, just like adults do. So I listen to the child's make-believe story and I respond with my story, one that gives the child a message that says, "I understand." In some cases my story is affiliative for the child, and for some, the message is one of strength or protection. My choice of a story that answers a child's need can often be seen as the child begins to participate in what has now become "our" story.

I'm happy that I stopped, those many years ago, for a glass of good wine, with Connie and Steve. Our relationship has been fulfilling.

REFERENCES

Bouchard, M., & Guérette, L. (1991). Psychotherapy as a hermeneutical experience. *Psychotherapy, 28,* 385–394.

Finn, S. E. (2007). *In our clients' shoes: Theory and techniques of Therapeutic Assessment.* Mahwah, NJ: Erlbaum.

Finn, S. E., & Tonsager, M. E. (1992). Therapeutic effects of providing MMPI-2 test feedback to college students awaiting therapy. *Psychological Assessment, 4*, 278–287.

Fischer, C. T. (1985/1994). *Individualizing psychological assessment*. Mahwah, NJ: Erlbaum. (Originally published by Brooks/Cole.)

Webster's new collegiate dictionary. (1953). Springfield, MA: G. & C. Merriam.

Wechsler, D. (1955). *Weschlser Adult Intelligence Scale (WAIS) manual*. New York, NY: The Psychological Corporation.

About the Contributors

J. B. Allyn, MBA, specializes in creative and technical writing and editing in the field of psychology. For many years, she has collaborated with Diane Engelman in writing therapeutic stories for assessment clients. She also wrote the forthcoming book *Writing to Clients and Referring Professionals About Psychological Assessment Results: A Handbook of Style and Grammar* (in press). She is affiliated with the Center for Collaborative Psychology, Psychiatry, and Medicine in Northern California.

Judith Armstrong, PhD, is a Clinical Associate Professor of Psychology at the University of Southern California and in private consulting practice. Her research on the assessment of trauma based on disorders and traumatic dissociation includes developing the Rorschach Trauma Content Index and the Adolescent Dissociation Experiences Scale. She is chair of the APA Trauma Division Task Force that created the first clinical guidelines for trauma assessment.

Thomas D. Cromer, PhD, is a staff psychologist at North Shore University Hospital Long Island Jewish Medical Center in Manhasset, NY. He has presented and published research regarding early psychotherapy processes and therapeutic alliance, as well as patient personality characteristics and their relationships to psychotherapy outcomes.

Hilde de Saeger, MA, is a clinical psychologist who works at the Viersprong, a psychotherapeutic center for people with personality disorders, in the Netherlands. She is currently working on a doctoral dissertation about the effects of Therapeutic Assessment on people with severe personality disorders. She is a member of the Therapeutic Assessment Institute.

Marc J. Diener, PhD, is an Assistant Professor in the Clinical Psychology Program at the American School of Professional Psychology, Argosy University, Washington, DC. His research program focuses on personality assessment as well as psychotherapy process and outcome. He has presented and published research in the following areas: attachment, psychotherapy technique, psychotherapy outcome, application of meta-analytic methodology, self-report and performance-based measures of personality, and clinician training. He also maintains a part-time independent practice.

Diane H. Engelman, PhD, cofounded and codirects the Center for Collaborative Psychology, Psychiatry, and Medicine in Northern California. She is a neuropsychologist in private practice, specializing in collaborative, individualized therapeutic assessment and assessment-informed psychotherapy. Other areas of focus include the psychological aspects of medical illness and patient empowerment. She has cowritten dozens of therapeutic stories used as intervention with assessment clients and the article "The Three Person Field: Collaborative Consultation to Psychotherapy" (2002).

F. Barton Evans, PhD, is a clinical and forensic psychologist and Therapeutic Assessment practitioner. He lives in Asheville, NC, where he works at the Asheville Veterans Administration Hospital and is Clinical Professor of Psychiatry at the George Washington University School of Medicine, Washington, DC. He is the author of *Harry Stack Sullivan: Interpersonal Theory and Psychotherapy* (1997) and coeditor of the *Handbook of Forensic Rorschach Assessment* (2008).

Stephen E. Finn, PhD, is the founder of the Center for Therapeutic Assessment in Austin, TX, a Clinical Associate Professor of Psychology at the University of Texas at Austin, and Director of Training at the European Center for Therapeutic Assessment in Milan, Italy. He is the author of *A Manual for Using the MMPI-2 as a Therapeutic Intervention* (1996) and of *In Our Clients' Shoes: Theory and Techniques of Therapeutic Assessment* (2007).

Constance T. Fischer, PhD, ABPP, is Professor of Psychology at Duquesne University, Pittsburgh, PA, and is in part-time independent practice. She authored *Individualizing Psychological Assessment* (1st edition 1985/1994; 2nd edition in press), coedited *Client Participation in Human Services* (1978), and edited *Qualitative Research Methods for Psychologists* (2006). She has published widely on collaborative assessment and on psychology as human science—a companion to psychology as a natural science. She is a past President of APA's Divisions 24 and 32.

Melissa E. Fisher, PhD, received her doctorate in School Psychology from the University of Texas at Austin. She is currently completing a postdoctoral fellowship at the Texas Child Study Center in Austin, TX in cognitive-behavioral therapy and neuropsychological assessment. Her research interests include the prevention and treatment of depressive and anxiety disorders in youth.

J. Christopher Fowler, PhD, is a senior psychologist and Associate Director of Research at The Menninger Clinic, Baylor College of Medicine, Galveston, TX. His clinical and research interests include complex treatment-resistant psychiatric disorders, borderline personality disorder, psychological assessment, and suicide.

Marita Frackowiak, PhD, is a licensed psychologist in private practice at the Center for Therapeutic Assessment in Austin, TX. She is a founding member of the Therapeutic Assessment Institute and a Lecturer at the University of Texas at Austin. Dr. Frackowiak is certified in Therapeutic Assessment with adults, children, adolescents, couples, and families. She lectures internationally on Therapeutic Assessment and offers consultation to clinicians wanting to learn Therapeutic Assessment.

Bradley Gerber, PhD, received his doctorate in School Psychology from The University of Texas at Austin. He is currently completing a postdoctoral fellowship at Children's Hospital Boston and Harvard Medical School in pediatric psychology. His areas of research interest include evidence-based interventions, psychosocial treatment for children with medical illnesses, and the role of therapeutic alliance in treatment.

Tad T. Gorske, PhD, is Director of Outpatient Neuropsychology in the Department of Physical Medicine and Rehabilitation at the University of Pittsburgh School of Medicine. He is the first author of *Collaborative Therapeutic Neuropsychological Assessment* (2008), which describes a client-centered method of providing feedback from neuropsychological test results based on Collaborative/Therapeutic Assessment and Motivational Interviewing.

Leonard Handler, PhD, ABAP, is Professor Emeritus at the University of Tennessee, where he served, periodically, as Director of the Psychological Clinic and as Associate Director of the Clinical Training Program. He is a past President of the Society for Personality Assessment (SPA). He was given the Martin Mayman and Bruno Klopfer awards from SPA. He is a coeditor of two texts, *Teaching and Learning Personality Assessment*

(1998) and *The Clinical Assessment of Children and Adolescents: A Practitioner's Handbook* (2006).

Mark J. Hilsenroth, PhD, ABAP, is a Professor of Psychology at the Derner Institute of Advanced Psychological Studies at Adelphi University, Garden City, NY. Dr. Hilsenroth is the primary investigator of the Adelphi University Psychotherapy Project and devotes his energy to teaching, one-to-one mentoring in psychotherapy supervision and research, as well as his own clinical practice. His areas of research interest are personality assessment, training/supervision, psychotherapy process, and treatment outcomes. He is currently the Editor of the journal *Psychotherapy*.

Erin Jacklin, PsyD, is the clinical director and founder of The Catalyst Center, a collaborative assessment and psychotherapy practice located in Denver, CO. She was also cofounder of the Colorado Assessment Society in 2006. Dr. Jacklin specializes in utilizing psychological assessment as a therapeutic tool in her practice.

Jan H. Kamphuis, PhD, is Professor of Psychology at the University of Amsterdam, The Netherlands, and a licensed clinical psychologist. Supported by a Fulbright scholarship, he completed the clinical psychology program of the University of Texas at Austin (1991–1997) and trained at the Center for Therapeutic Assessment. He is Fellow of the Society for Personality Assessment and was recently officially certified in Therapeutic Assessment. He has published extensively on clinical assessment and on personality pathology.

Hale Martin, PhD, is a Clinical Associate Professor in the Graduate School of Professional Psychology at the University of Denver, CO, where he teaches and supervises psychological assessment, emphasizing Therapeutic Assessment. He is also the director of the Colorado Center for Therapeutic Assessment and a member of the Therapeutic Assessment Institute. Dr. Martin cofounded the Colorado Assessment Society in 2006. He is coauthor with Stephen E. Finn of *Masculinity-Femininity and the MMPI-2 and MMPI-A* (2010).

Patrick J. McElfresh, PhD, is program coordinator and a postdoctoral fellow in the Childhood Depression Treatment Study at the University of Pittsburgh's Western Psychiatric Institute and Clinic. He is also Adjunct Professor in Psychology at Chatham University, Pittsburgh, PA, where he teaches introductory and personality assessment. A mentee of Constance Fischer, Dr. McElfresh aims to continue practicing and researching Collaborative Assessment in private practice. He is also currently investigating qualitative research approaches for the Rorschach.

Noriko Nakamura, MA, is codirector of the Nakamura Psychotherapy Institute in Tokyo, Japan, founded in 1998, and a former Professor of Clinical Psychology at Soka Graduate University in Tokyo. She is a founding member of the Japanese Rorschach Society for the Comprehensive System (JRSC) and currently serves as its president. She has been involved in the International Society for the Rorschach and Projective Methods (ISR) since 1988 and has been serving as vice president since 2008.

Carol Groves Overton, PhD, received her doctorate from Temple University in 1990. She is the former director of the partial hospital program of Hahnemann University Hospital in Philadelphia, PA. In 2001, Dr. Overton received the Martin Mayman Award from the Society for Personality Assessment for distinguished contribution to the literature in personality assessment. She is currently in private practice in Washington Crossing, PA.

Frank P. Pesale, PhD, is a recent graduate from the clinical psychology program at Adelphi University, Garden City, NY. His research interests are in psychotherapy process and outcome. He has presented and published research in the following areas: psychotherapy technique and process, psychotherapy outcome, personality assessment, and research training.

Caroline Purves, PhD, has completed assessments in Canada, England, and the United States. She developed some nontraditional ideas about the form on her own, only to discover later the more formal collaborative/therapeutic assessment models, which she embraced with enthusiasm. As well as private practice, she supervises assessment and therapy at WestCoast Children's Clinic in Oakland, CA.

Jenelle Slavin-Mulford, PhD, received her doctorate in Clinical Psychology from the Derner Institute of Advanced Psychological Studies at Adelphi University, Garden City, NY. She is currently completing a postdoctoral fellowship at the Massachusetts General

Hospital and Harvard Medical School, Boston, MA, in psychological/ neuropsychological assessment. Her areas of research interest include personality assessment, training/supervision, and psychotherapy process and outcome.

Steve R. Smith, PhD, is an Associate Professor and Director of Clinical Training in the Department of Counseling, Clinical, and School Psychology and consulting psychologist to the Department of Intercollegiate Athletics at the University of California, Santa Barbara. He conducts research on therapeutic neuropsychological and personality assessment, diversity issues in assessment, and performance enhancement training with athletes.

Deborah J. Tharinger, PhD, is a Professor in the Department of Educational Psychology at the University of Texas at Austin, a Licensed Psychologist, and Director of the Therapeutic Assessment Project (TAP). Along with Stephen Finn and a group of graduate students, she is studying the efficacy of TA with children, adolescents, and their parents. She has published and presented extensively in this area. Dr. Tharinger is also a founding member of the Institute of Therapeutic Assessment.

Heikki Toivakka, PsL, is a licensed psychologist in the Department of Adolescent Psychiatry, Tampere University Hospital, Tampere, Finland, where he conducts collaborative assessments and family therapy with adolescents and their families. Mr. Toivakka is the President of the Finnish Rorschach Association for the Comprehensive System, and he also teaches family therapy. He has presented around the world on his work with collaborative assessment.

Collaborative/Therapeutic Assessment: Basic Concepts, History, and Research

STEPHEN E. FINN, CONSTANCE T. FISCHER, AND LEONARD HANDLER

WHAT IS THE HISTORY OF COLLABORATIVE/ THERAPEUTIC ASSESSMENT?

Until relatively recently, psychological testing has been thought of exclusively by most mental health professionals as a way to diagnose psychological disorders and plan treatment interventions. Finn and Tonsager (1997) described the goals of this traditional "information gathering model" of assessment as

> a way to facilitate communication between professionals and to help make decisions about clients. By describing clients in terms of already existing categories and dimensions (e.g., schizophrenic, IQ of 100, 2–7 code type on the MMPI-2), assessors hope to convey a great deal of information about clients in an efficient manner. Also, such descriptions are the basis for important decisions, such as whether clients are mentally competent or dangerous, whether they should receive one treatment or another, be granted custody of a child, hired for

a certain job, or be given publicly funded special education services. Given the inherent uncertainty involved in such weighty decisions, clinicians and researchers have long emphasized the statistical reliability and validity of their assessment instruments; these characteristics allow one to make nomothetic comparisons (i.e., generalizable across persons and situations and used by a number of clinicians) between a particular client and similar clients who have been treated in the past or studied in research. (p. 378)

However, as early as the middle of the 20th century, some American psychologists were experimenting with ways of using psychological assessment to promote therapeutic change, by engaging clients in discussing their responses to psychological tests. For example, Harrower (1956) devised a method she called "projective counseling," in which clients discussed their own Rorschach percepts and projective drawings with their assessor/therapists to help them "come to grips, sometimes surprisingly quickly, with some of [their] problems" (p. 86). Similarly, Jacques (1945), Bettelheim (1947), Bellak, Pasquarelli, and Braverman (1949), and Luborsky (1953) all advocated having clients self-interpret their stories to the Thematic Apperception Test (TAT; Murray, 1943) as a way to bypass "resistance" and promote insight.

In recent years, these early efforts have been superseded by various highly developed models of psychological assessment, which we are broadly calling Collaborative/Therapeutic Assessment. Let us trace some of the major models encompassed by this term.

Fischer's Collaborative, Individualized Assessment

Constance Fischer began in the 1970s (e.g., 1970, 1971, 1972, 1979) articulating a coherent model of psychological assessment grounded in phenomenological psychology, which she at times called *collaborative psychological assessment* (1978), *individualized psychological assessment* (1979, 1985/1994), or *collaborative, individualized psychological assessment* (2000). At that time, Fischer regarded collaborating with clients as a major means of individualizing the assessment process, so the descriptions and suggestions were about this person in his or her life context. She regarded collaboration as therapeutic in process; she also regarded much of standardized testing practice as objectifying the test taker.

Fischer (2000) defined the major principles of her approach as:

1. **Collaborate**: The assessor and client "co-labor to reach useful understandings" (p. 3) throughout the assessment, which are constantly revised in a hermeneutic, interpersonal process. "The client is engaged as an active agent" (p. 3) in discussing the purposes of the assessment, the meanings of her or his own test responses, useful next steps, and the written feedback that results at the end of the assessment.

2. **Contextualize**: Clients are not seen as "an assemblage of traits or even as set patterns of dynamics" (p. 4), but rather as persons "in lively flux" (p. 4). Their problems are explored in the context of their lived worlds, "from which they extend, grow, and change" (p. 4).

3. **Intervene**: The goal is "not just to describe or classify the person's present state but to identify personally viable options to problematic comportment" (p. 5). Although Fischer clearly differentiated between assessment and psychotherapy in her early writings, she always was clear that a goal of assessment was to assist clients in discovering new ways of thinking and being.

4. **Describe**: From the beginning, Fischer eschewed the use of "constructs" such as traits or defenses to explain clients' behavior and advocated the use of thick descriptions in written reports, using clients' own words whenever possible, to help assessors and the readers find their way "into clients' worlds" (p. 6).

5. **Respect complexity, holism, and ambiguity**: Assessors should "respect the complex interrelations of our lives; they do not reduce lives to a variable or to any system of explanation. The goal is understanding rather than explanation" (p. 6).

Fischer hoped that readers of her assessment reports would recognize the clients as described, but would come to see them in new ways. She hoped to capture the many contradictions that each one of us embodies, rather than oversimplifying our complex ways of being.

Fischer's work was important in providing an eloquent and coherent exposition of a new paradigm of psychological assessment. In addition, she also pioneered many innovative practices that are now widely used within the Collaborative/Therapeutic Assessment (C/TA) community. Finn (2007) and others mined Fischer's writings and adopted such techniques as (1) writing psychological assessment reports in first person, in language that is easily understood, and then sharing them with clients; (2) asking clients for comments at the end of an assessment, which are then routinely shared with readers of the assessment report; (3) writing fables for children at the end of an assessment, which capture in metaphor the results and suggestions resulting from the assessment; and (4) engaging clients in "mini-experiments" during psychological assessment sessions (e.g., retelling stories to picture story cards to help clients discover new ways of approaching typical problem situations).

Fischer continues to teach, advise, and write about her approach to assessment, as well as the overlap between C/TA and qualitative research. Fischer published an early, now classic, empirical phenomenological study (Fischer & Wertz, 1979). She published qualitative studies she undertook because of their relation to C/TA, for example, *Toward the Structure of Privacy* (1971) and *Intimacy in Psychological Assessment* (1982).

Fischer's method and philosophy are illustrated in this volume in her case example (Chapter 5) and also in the case written by McElfresh (Chapter 9), who is one of Fischer's former students.

Finn's Therapeutic Assessment

Finn (2007) defined Therapeutic Assessment (TA; capital "T" and "A") as a semistructured form of collaborative assessment originally developed by him and his colleagues at the Center for Therapeutic Assessment in Austin, Texas, and later refined on the basis of ongoing research and practice. From the outset, Finn wanted to explore psychological assessment as a brief therapeutic intervention. He initially focused on how to make feedback from psychological assessments therapeutic, and based his techniques and theory on results from a series of studies (e.g., Schroeder, Hahn, Finn, & Swann, 1993) with his colleague at the University of Texas, William Swann, Jr., the developer of self-verification theory (Cf. Swann, 1997). This research led to the distinction made in TA between what is called "Level 1, 2, and 3" information resulting from an assessment. That is, Finn and colleagues discovered that clients found assessment feedback most impactful and therapeutic when they were first presented with information that was close to their current self-schemas, then with information that was mildly discrepant from these schemas, and finally with information that was highly discrepant from the ways they already thought about themselves (Cf. Finn, 1996, 2007, for further exposition of this principle).

As explained in a later book (Finn, 2007), Finn then began to focus on the role of other steps in the assessment process in helping clients change, and he deliberately incorporated many of Fischer's techniques and underlying principles after he encountered her work and the two of them began collaborating. Basically, Finn discovered that if you wanted to make psychological assessment therapeutic, it helped greatly to engage clients as collaborators. This fit with Swann's self-verification theory, which posited that clients' self-schemas would be more amenable to change if clients were actively involved in revising the ways in which they viewed themselves.

Finn was also interested in teaching collaborative assessment to his graduate students at the University of Texas and in doing controlled research on this topic. Thus, he began to standardize many of the techniques developed by Fischer (and later, Handler) into series of steps that could be taught in an orderly fashion. These steps included (1) gathering "assessment questions" from clients at the beginning of an assessment about what they hoped to learn about themselves; (2) involving clients in "extended inquiries" of standardized tests, after a standard administration had been completed; (3) "assessment intervention sessions," in which assessors planned assessment "encounters" near the end of an assessment during which clients would discover information that was emerging from the standardized sessions; (4) closing "summary/discussion sessions," in which clients' assessment questions were addressed according to the Level 1, 2, 3 schema mentioned earlier; (5) sending clients letters instead of reports at the end of an assessment; and (6) holding follow-up sessions several months after the close of a psychological assessment, during which clients and assessors continued to discuss and process the experience of the psychological assessment. This structure is not seen as fixed or absolute, however. Finn has repeatedly emphasized that it can and should be altered to fit each client and setting, and that the well-being of the client always takes priority. The study by Finn and Tonsager (1992) was the first to test this method as a therapeutic intervention, with positive results (more below).

After he left the University of Texas to found the Center for Therapeutic Assessment, Finn was largely free to travel and present his semistructured model of collaborative assessment around the world. Many psychologists first heard about collaborative assessment and about Fischer's seminal work through Finn's presentations. This happened about the time that managed care providers started greatly restricting psychological services and particularly, psychological assessment services, to clients in the United States. All of these factors led to a surge in interest in the therapeutic potential of psychological assessment, and many new applications and much new research ensued. We will review this research shortly.

In recent years, Finn's work and thinking has centered on connecting TA to other important therapeutic models, such as attachment theory (Finn, 2011d), Control Mastery Theory (Finn, 2007), and intersubjectivity theory (Finn, 2007). He also is attempting to integrate theories of Therapeutic Assessment with recent research on infant development and neurobiology (Finn, 2011a, 2011b). Finn's theory and model are illustrated in his own case example (Chapter 18) on Therapeutic Assessment with couples, and in the chapters by Kamphuis and de Saeger (Chapter 7) and Martin and Jacklin (Chapter 8); Kamphuis and Martin are former students of Finn.

Therapeutic Assessment With Children (TA-C) and Therapeutic Assessment With Adolescents (TA-A)

Finn and his colleagues at the Center for Therapeutic Assessment conducted TA with children, adolescents, and their families from the start. TA with children and adolescents was viewed as a family systems intervention, and involving parents/caregivers as collaborators in the assessment was always seen as essential (Finn, 1997). It was not until 2003, however, that these methods were formally studied. Around this time, Finn paired with Deborah Tharinger to form the Therapeutic Assessment Project (TAP) at the University of Texas at Austin. This collaboration has resulted in a series of articles describing steps in the semistructured model of TA-C, including engaging parents in their children's assessment (Tharinger, Finn, Wilkinson, & Schaber, 2007), having parents observe their children's assessment sessions (Tharinger, Finn, et al., in press), using family sessions as part of child psychological assessment (Tharinger, Finn, Austin, et al., 2008), giving feedback to parents at the end of a child assessment (Tharinger, Finn, Hersh, et al., 2008), and writing fables for children at the end of an assessment (Tharinger, Finn, Wilkinson, et al., 2008). TAP also published a pilot study of TA-C (Tharinger, Finn, et al., 2009). Recently, Tharinger has begun to publish articles from their study of Therapeutic Assessment of adolescents and families (Tharinger, Finn, Gentry, & Matson, 2007).

The cases by Frackowiak (Chapter 11) and by Tharinger, Fisher, and Gerber (Chapter 15) utilize Finn's and Tharinger's model of Therapeutic Assessment with children and adolescents. Frackowiak trained with Finn after receiving her PhD and was one of the early supervisors on the TAP project.

therapeutic assessment

Finn (2007) has suggested that the term "therapeutic assessment" (lowercase) be used for the work of those psychologists who aim to positively impact clients and important others around them via psychological assessment, but who do not use the semistructured model developed by Finn and colleagues, and may or may not use collaborative methods beyond that of giving feedback to clients. In a much-cited article, Finn and Tonsager (1997) contrasted therapeutic assessment with the traditional "information-gathering" assessment model on multiple dimensions, including their (1) goals, (2) process, (3) view of tests, (4) focus of attention, (5) view of the assessor's role, and (6) what they considered to be an assessment failure. This article is still relevant today.

The work of Armstrong (Chapter 2), Fowler (Chapter 6), and Overton (Chapter 10) are good examples of therapeutic assessment. Fowler is a former student of Leonard Handler.

Handler's Therapeutic Assessment With Children

Another person who uses the term "therapeutic assessment" to describe his work is Leonard Handler. Although Handler has written and presented about his collaborative assessments of adults (1996, 1997, 1999), he is best known for his innovative work using collaborative assessment methods with children. For example, Handler developed a set of creative probes to be used with children (and some adults) during extended inquiries of the Rorschach, such as "If this mushroom could talk, what would it say?" Handler also refined collaborative storytelling methods with children (e.g., Mutchnik & Handler, 2002), and invented a now widely used method called the Fantasy Animal Drawing Game. In this method, the assessor first asks the child to draw a "make-believe animal that no one has ever seen" and then to tell a story about the animal. The assessor listens for the message the child gives in his or her story, and then sends a message back by telling a subsequent portion of the story. Handler summarized this and other child collaborative assessment methods in an influential chapter in 2006. He and his students have also published many important case studies and research studies on uppercase Therapeutic Assessment (Peters, Handler, White, & Winkel, 2008) and Therapeutic Assessment With Children (Smith & Handler, 2009; Smith, Handler, & Nash, 2010; Smith, Nicholas, Handler, & Nash, 2011; Smith, Wolf, Handler, & Nash, 2009). Handler has also traveled the world in recent years, presenting workshops on his innovative methods.

Handler's therapeutic assessment with children is illustrated in Chapter 12, including an extended example of the Fantasy Animal Drawing Game. Toivakka (Chapter 16) also writes about using this method with a hospitalized psychotic adolescent.

Hilsenroth's Therapeutic Model of Assessment

A former student of Handler's, Mark J. Hilsenroth, has made substantial contributions to the development of Collaborative/Therapeutic Assessment through a series of studies and articles concerning what he calls the Therapeutic Model of Assessment (TMA; Ackerman, Hilsenroth, Baity, & Blagys, 2000; Hilsenroth, Ackerman, Clemence, Strassle, & Handler, 2002; Hilsenroth & Cromer, 2007; Hilsenroth, Peters, &

Ackerman, 2004). Basically, Hilsenroth's research demonstrated that collaborative psychological assessment leads to better therapeutic alliance between assessors/therapists and clients than does traditional information-gathering assessment, and that this advantage in alliance influences compliance with recommendations for treatment, and persists into psychotherapy long after an assessment. Although initially, Hilsenroth referenced the work of Finn and Fischer as the origin of his model, the article by Hilsenroth and Cromer (2007) clarifies that the TMA approach is somewhat different. As they explain, "in a TMA the assessors are committed to: (a) developing and maintaining empathic connections with clients, (b) working collaboratively with clients to define individualized assessment goals, . . . and (c) sharing and exploring assessment results with clients" (p. 206). Great emphasis is placed on relationship building, on feedback at the end of the assessment, and on clinicians using clear, emotionally arousing language with clients and using their counter-transference to help clients become aware of problematic cycles of relating with others.

The case by Diener, Hilsenroth, Cromer, Pesale, and Slavin-Mulford (Chapter 3) represents an excellent example of the Therapeutic Model of Assessment and summarizes major features of this method.

Collaborative Therapeutic Neuropsychological Assessment

In 2008, Tad Gorske and Steven Smith published their book, *Collaborative Therapeutic Neuropsychological Assessment*, in which they applied principles of therapeutic assessment to adult and child neuropsychological assessment. Again, although the authors were inspired by Fischer and by Finn, they also credit other influences, such as Motivational Interviewing (MI; Miller & Rollnick, 2002). Collaborative Therapeutic Neuropsychological Assessment (CTNA) differs from other forms of therapeutic assessment in that testing assistants are often used in collecting standardized test data, which makes procedures like extended inquiries more difficult. A great deal of effort is placed on rapport building at the beginning of the assessment and on presenting feedback via techniques of MI so as to overcome "resistance" on the part of clients. Chapter 19 by Gorske and Smith provides two case examples of CTNA, one with an adult brain-injured client and one with a child with learning difficulties. Diane Engelman and J. B. Allyn also write about integrating neuropsychological assessment into C/TA in Chapter 4.

Collaborative Assessment

Of the various terms encompassed by C/TA, collaborative assessment is perhaps the most general. As mentioned earlier, Fischer (1978) sometimes referred to her work as *collaborative assessment*, and many individuals who were inspired primarily by her now use this term to describe their assessment practices. There are also several other writers who independently developed practices similar to those of Fischer and Finn, and who now call their work collaborative assessment (Cf. Purves, 2002; Engelman & Frankel, 2002; Nakamura & Nakamura, 1999). Finn (2007) suggested that the term collaborative assessment be used when assessors strive to reduce the power imbalance typically found between assessor and client in traditional assessment, and to involve clients in multiple phases of an assessment, including "(a) framing the reasons for the assessment, (b) observing test responses and behaviors, (c) discovering the significance of those responses and behaviors, (d) coming up with useful recommendations, and (e) drafting summary documents at the end" (p. 5). It might be useful to say that collaborative assessors place more emphasis on *understanding* than on *transformation*, whereas those calling their approaches Therapeutic Assessment or therapeutic assessment appear to prioritize client change. As discussed earlier, however, therapeutic assessment almost always uses collaborative assessment techniques, and collaborative assessment may be inherently therapeutic.

One group of assessors who tend to call their approach collaborative assessment and who have done much to extend C/TA to traumatized, underprivileged populations are the psychologists at WestCoast Children's Clinic (WCC) in Oakland, CA. Caroline Purves (Cf. Chapter 14) has long had an association with WCC, and Barbara Mercer, the assessment director, is an active member of the Society for Personality Assessment. Finn has served as a consultant to WCC for many years and has done a great deal of training with staff. Recently, WCC psychologists have started publishing about their work, and this has greatly highlighted the complexities of using C/TA with clients from other cultures, races, and socioeconomic backgrounds (Finn, 2011c; Guerrero, Lipkind, & Rosenberg, 2011; Haydel, Mercer, & Rosenblatt, 2011; Mercer, 2011; Rosenberg, Almeida, & Macdonald, in press).

The cases by Engelman and Allyn (Chapter 4), Fischer (Chapter 5), McElfresh (Chapter 9), Nakamura (Chapter 13), Purves (Chapter 14), and Toivakka (Chapter 16) are all examples of collaborative psychological assessment.

WHAT ARE THE COMMON FEATURES OF COLLABORATIVE/THERAPEUTIC ASSESSMENT?

In all this variety, are there common elements that define the core of C/TA? We believe there are. The following features are not mutually exclusive.

Respect for Clients

Finn (2009) has said that respect is a core value of Therapeutic Assessment, and Fischer mentions the word often in her writings. The collaborative practices and principles of C/TA are—in many ways— operational definitions of respect for clients. C/TA practitioners treat clients as they would like to be treated in a similar situation, generally (1) providing informed consent at the beginning of the assessment and asking clients what they wish to learn, (2) recognizing that clients are "experts on themselves" and involving them in making sense of their test productions, (3) working with clients to find personally viable ways of handling typical problem situations in new ways, (4) always providing clients with comprehensible feedback at least by the end of an assessment, and (5) acknowledging clients' active participation in all written documents resulting from the assessment.

A Relational View of Psychological Assessment

Similarly, all C/TA practitioners recognize that clients' coming for a psychological assessment is very different than their coming for a blood test or x-ray. Psychological assessment is seen as an interpersonal event, and the relationship that develops between clients and assessors is recognized as paramount in making sense of what occurs during the assessment. In general, C/TA practitioners acknowledge the vulnerability of clients in the assessment situation, and they try to minimize any unnecessary discomfort for clients. Some anxiety will inevitably be present for most clients, but even this is acknowledged as normal given the import of many assessment situations.

A Stance of Compassion and Curiosity Rather Than Judgment and Classification

In general, C/TA practitioners seek to understand rather than to judge or classify. They bring curiosity about the ways that human beings adapt to difficult situations, and they try to make sense of puzzling, offputting, and even obnoxious behaviors. Their goal at the end of an assessment is to more fully understand clients in all their complexity, rather than to summarize them in several terms. C/TA can be used to diagnose clients if this will be helpful, but it rarely is the major goal of C/TA. Even assessments with a diagnostic focus can incorporate collaborative/ therapeutic interaction.

A Desire to Help Clients Directly

All clinicians practicing C/TA seem to share a common desire to use psychological assessments to help clients directly—not just by providing helpful information to other decision makers. For this reason, C/TA of any name always involves sharing and checking impressions directly with clients. Furthermore, there is an emphasis on making this feedback useful, relevant, memorable, and enriching for clients, even if the client is a child (hence the frequent practice of writing feedback fables for children).

A Special View of Tests

C/TA practitioners love and are fascinated by their tests; they view tests as powerful tools to help them understand clients' inner worlds and dilemmas of change, and as opportunities for discussion with clients about their ways of being in the world. Finn (2007) coined the term "empathy magnifiers" to reflect his view of psychological tests as helpful tools that help assessors get "in our clients' shoes." Fischer (1985/1994) often writes about tests giving access into clients' lived worlds, and says that life always has priority over test scores. She speaks of test scores as being our tools and results as being our revised ways of understanding and being of help to clients.

Flexibility

C/TA practitioners follow traditional professional boundaries in conducting psychological assessments, but they are more willing to stretch their practices when it will serve the purposes of the assessment, such as by conducting a home visit as part of an assessment (Fischer, 1985/1994). Also, clinicians practicing C/TA use psychological tests in standardized ways, but they are willing to modify test administration practices at times to help understand clients' test responses, or when doing so helps clients identify alternative ways of approaching typical problem situations. Many C/TA practitioners show amazing creativity in their use of psychological tests with clients.

WHAT DOES RESEARCH SHOW ABOUT COLLABORATIVE/THERAPEUTIC ASSESSMENT?

Outcome Research

Table 1.1 shows a summary of existing outcome research related to Collaborative/Therapeutic Assessment. Two types of studies are listed: group comparisons (e.g., Finn & Tonsager, 1992) and time-series analyses (e.g., Aschieri & Smith, in press). Both types of research are useful in showing that a clinical intervention is effective (Borckardt et al., 2008). As you can see in the table, at this point C/TA has been shown to have positive effects with outpatient and inpatient clients facing a variety of difficulties, and with adults, children, adolescents, and couples. To be sure, many of the samples in these studies are small, long-term follow-ups are generally lacking, and all findings would benefit from replication. Still, the evidence is accruing that C/TA can be very helpful to clients and their loved ones.

Table 1.1   Benefits to Clients Documented in Controlled Research on Collaborative/Therapeutic Assessment

Type of Benefit Shown (Type of Client)	Research Studies Where Documented
Decreased symptomatology and increased self-esteem (adult outpatients)	Finn & Tonsager, 1992; Newman & Greenway, 1997; Allen, Montgomery, Tubman, Frazier, & Escovar, 2003
Increased hope (adult outpatients)	Finn & Tonsager, 1992; Holm-Denoma et al., 2008
Better compliance with treatment recommendations (adult outpatients)	Ackerman, Hilsenroth, Baity, & Blagys, 2000
Better therapeutic alliance with subsequent psychotherapist (adult outpatients)	Hilsenroth, Peters, & Ackerman, 2004
Better outcome in borderline patients receiving Manual Assisted Cognitive Therapy (adult outpatients)	Morey, Lowmaster, & Hopwood, 2010
Decrease in distress, increase in self-esteem, and decrease in emotional reactivity (college students identified via prescreening as maladaptive perfectionists)	Aldea, Rice, Gormley, & Rojas, 2010
Decreased self-criticism, anxiety, and improved relational functioning as demonstrated in a time-series design (outpatient 21-year-old traumatized woman)	Aschieri & Smith, in press
Increased emotional control, self-efficacy, and energy, and less fear and anxiety as demonstrated in a time-series analysis (outpatient 52-year-old traumatized woman with metastatic cancer)	Smith & George, in press
Better alliance, cooperation, and satisfaction with treatment, lower distress, and increased sense of well-being (psychiatric inpatients)	Little & Smith, 2009
Decreased number of suicide attempts and days of hospitalization (suicidal VA outpatients)	Jobes, Wong, Conrad, Drozd, & Neal-Walden, 2005
Decreased symptomatology in children and their mothers; increased communication and cohesion and decreased conflict in families; mothers have more positive and fewer negative feelings about their children (latency-aged outpatient children and their mothers)	Tharinger, Finn, Gentry, Hamilton et al., 2009

Table 1.1   (Continued)

Type of Benefit Shown (Type of Client)	Research Studies Where Documented
Symptomatic improvement and improved family relationships in latency-aged boys with Oppositional Defiant Disorder (boys with ODD and their parents)	Smith, Handler, & Nash, 2010
Decreased externalizing behavior and improvements in family functioning as demonstrated in a time-series design (outpatient 9-year-old boy and his parents)	Smith, Wolf, Handler, & Nash, 2009
Decreased symptomatology and depression, and increased self-esteem in distressed adolescents (adolescents screened as depressed in high school)	Newman, 2004
Better compliance with treatment recommendations in adolescents admitted to emergency rooms for self-harm (adolescent outpatients)	Ougrin, Ng, & Low, 2008
Improvements in the relationships of married couples "stuck" in couples therapy	Durham-Fowler, 2010

A recent important publication adds to this assertion. Poston and Hanson (2010) conducted a meta-analysis on 17 published studies of psychological assessment as a therapeutic intervention. The overall effect size for therapy outcome variables was $d = .423$, considered a medium effect size (i.e., of moderate clinical significance). Furthermore, not all of the studies examined used a collaborative or therapeutic assessment approach, and there was evidence that adopting this approach greatly increased efficacy. Poston and Hanson concluded:

> Clinicians should . . . seek out continuing-education training related to these models [of therapeutic and collaborative assessment]. Those who engage in assessment and testing as usual may miss out, it seems, on a golden opportunity to effect client change and enhance clinically important treatment processes. Similarly, applied training programs in clinical, counseling, and school psychology should incorporate therapeutic models of assessment into their curricula, foundational didactic classes, and practica. (p. 210)

Poston and Hanson went on to assert that their findings had implications for mental health policy:

> ... the results indicate that competency benchmarks and guide-lines for psychological assessment practice should be revisited to make sure they include key aspects of therapeutic models of assessment. Furthermore, managed care policy makers should take these results into account, especially as they make future policy and reimbursement decisions regarding assessment and testing practices. (p. 210)

In our minds, the research by Poston and Hanson goes a long way in demonstrating the contributions that C/TA can offer to clients and to psychological assessors. This research strengthened our resolve to publish this case book, so that psychological assessors and graduate students can view C/TA in action.

Process Research

Besides Poston and Hanson, other researchers have examined process variables in psychological assessment to answer the question, "What aspects of psychological assessment promote therapeutic change?" Let us review a few of these.

Collaborative Versus Noncollaborative Feedback

Multiple studies have compared the relative effectiveness of "inter-active" versus "delivered" test feedback—that is, whether clients are actively involved in discussing and processing feedback presented to them from psychological tests (Goodyear, 1990, provided a review). In general, clients rated collaborative feedback as more satisfying and more influential than feedback that is unilaterally "delivered" by an assessor with minimal client involvement (e.g., Hanson, Claiborn, & Kerr, 1977; Rogers, 1954).

Ordering of Information in a Feedback Session

Schroeder, Hahn, Finn, and Swann (1993) examined Finn's assertion that feedback to clients is most therapeutic if it is presented in accordance with clients' current self-schemas. They found that college students receiving feedback on normal-range personality traits rated the feedback as most positive and influential if they were first given feedback that was congruent with their self-views and then presented with information that was slightly discrepant from their self-views. These effects persisted over a 2-week follow-up. This study provided partial support for Finn's (1996, 2007) "Level 1, 2, 3" schema in giving feedback to clients.

Written Versus Oral Feedback

Lance and Krishnamurthy (2003) compared three groups, each with 21 clients, receiving collaborative feedback on their Minnesota Multiphasic Personality Inventory–2 (MMPI-2) profiles according to Finn's (1996) method. One group received only oral feedback, one only written feedback, and one group received both oral and written feedback. Clients in the combined feedback condition reported that they learned more about themselves, felt more positive about the assessor, and were more satisfied with the assessment than did clients in the other two groups.

Family Sessions in Therapeutic Assessment With Children

One advantage of time-series designs is that they allow researchers to look at the process of change in regard to an individual client. Smith, Nicholas, Handler, and Nash (2011) tested the assertion by Tharinger, Finn, Austin et al. (2008) that family sessions in Therapeutic Assessment With Children (TA-C) are often crucial turning points in psychological improvement of children. A 12-year-old boy with social difficulties and low self-esteem was tracked as he and his father progressed through a 12-week Therapeutic Assessment. Consistent with theory, the family session appeared to be the tipping point in psychological improvement.

Providing Individualized Feedback via Fables to Parents and Children

Tharinger and Pilgrim (in press) studied the effects of incorporating one element of Therapeutic Assessment With Children—giving feedback through individualized fables—into traditional neuropsychological assessments. The research involved 32 children and their parents being assessed in a traditional neuropsychology practice because of the children's academic difficulties, inattention, and socio-emotional difficulties. Half of the children (the experimental group) were given individualized feedback fables following the standard verbal parental feedback. Half (the comparison group) were given their fables later, after they and their parents completed the research outcome measures. Children in the experimental group reported a greater sense of learning about themselves, a more positive relationship with the assessor, a greater sense of collaboration with the assessment process, and that their parents learned more about them through the assessment than did children in the comparison group. Parents in the experimental group reported a more positive relationship between their child and the assessor, a greater sense of collaboration with the assessment process, and higher satisfaction with clinic services than did parents in the comparison group.

CONCLUSION

Collaborative/Therapeutic Assessment refers to a family of psychological assessment approaches, all of which aspire to help clients and their important others achieve new understandings and find new ways of dealing with typical problem situations. C/TA developed out of the recognition by practicing psychologists that assessments conducted in a collaborative and respectful manner can be immensely valuable to clients, their families, and mental health professionals. Interest in C/TA is growing, and evidence is mounting for its efficacy and utility with a variety of clients in different contexts dealing with varied psychological problems. Still, noncollaborative assessment remains the predominant paradigm in the United States and in the rest of the world.

Just as clients have difficulties envisioning new ways of thinking and being, so do psychological assessors who are trained in traditional assessment often have problems imagining what C/TA looks like in action. Hence, we now turn to 18 case accounts of C/TA. We hope these will serve as invitations to readers to incorporate more aspects of C/TA into their own practices.

REFERENCES

Ackerman, S. J., Hilsenroth, M. J., Baity, M. R., & Blagys, M. D. (2000). Interaction of therapeutic process and alliance during psychological assessment. *Journal of Personality Assessment, 75*, 82–109.

Aldea, M. A., Rice, K. G., Gormley, B., & Rojas, A. (2010). Testing perfectionists about their perfectionism: Effects of providing feedback on emotional reactivity and psychological symptoms. *Behavior Research and Therapy, 48*, 1194–1203.

Allen, A., Montgomery, M., Tubman, J., Frazier, L., & Escovar, L. (2003). The affects of assessment feedback on rapport-building and self-enhancement processes. *Journal of Mental Health Counseling, 25*, 165–181.

Aschieri, F., & Smith, J. D. (in press). The effectiveness of therapeutic assessment with an adult client: A single case study using a time-series design. *Journal of Personality Assessment.*

Bellak, L., Pasquarelli, B. A., & Braverman, S. (1949). The use of the Thematic Apperception Test in psychotherapy. *Journal of Nervous and Mental Disease, 110*, 51–65.

Bettelheim, B. (1947). Self-interpretation of fantasy: The Thematic Apperception Test as an educational and therapeutic device. *American Journal of Orthopsychiatry, 17*, 80–100.

Borckardt, J. J., Nash, M. R., Murphy, M. D., Moore, M., Shaw, D., & O'Neil, P. (2008). Clinical practice as natural laboratory for psychotherapy research. *American Psychologist, 63*, 1–19.

Durham-Fowler, J. A. (2010). *Therapeutic Assessment with couples.* Unpublished doctoral dissertation, University of Texas, Austin.

Engelman, D. H., & Frankel, S. A. (2002). The three person field: Collaborative consultation to psychotherapy. *The Humanistic Psychologist, 30*, 49–62.

Finn, S. E. (1996). *A manual for using the MMPI-2 as a therapeutic intervention.* Minneapolis: University of Minnesota Press.

Finn, S. E. (1997, March). *Collaborative child assessment as a family systems intervention.* Paper presented at the annual meeting of the Society for Personality Assessment, San Diego, CA, as part of a symposium, "Collaborative assessment of children and families," S. E. Finn (Chair).

Finn, S. E. (2007). *In our clients' shoes: Theory and techniques of Therapeutic Assessment.* Mahwah, NJ: Erlbaum.

Finn, S. E. (2009). *Core values of Therapeutic Assessment.* Downloaded from www.therapeuticassessment.com on June 1, 2011.

Finn, S. E. (2011a, March). *Implications of recent research in neurobiology for psychological assessment.* Address given to the annual meeting of the Society for Personality Assessment, Boston, MA, upon receipt of the Bruno Klopfer Award.

Finn, S. E. (2011b). Journeys through the Valley of Death: Multimethod psychological assessment and personality transformation in long-term psychotherapy. *Journal of Personality Assessment, 93,* 123–141.

Finn, S. E. (2011c). Therapeutic Assessment "on the front lines": Comment on articles from WestCoast Children's Clinic. *Journal of Personality Assessment, 93*(1), 23–25.

Finn, S. E. (2011d). Use of the Adult Attachment Projective Picture System in the middle of a long-term psychotherapy. *Journal of Personality Assessment, 93,* 427–433.

Finn, S. E., & Tonsager, M. E. (1992). Therapeutic effects of providing MMPI-2 test feedback to college students awaiting therapy. *Psychological Assessment, 4,* 278–287.

Finn, S. E., & Tonsager, M. E. (1997). Information-gathering and therapeutic models of assessment: Complementary paradigms. *Psychological Assessment, 9,* 374–385.

Fischer, C. T. (1970). The testee as co-evaluator. *Journal of Counseling Psychology, 17,* 70–76.

Fischer, C. T. (1971). Toward the structure of privacy: Implications for psychological assessment. In A. Giorgi, W. F. Fischer, & R. von Eckhartsberg (Eds.), *Duquesne studies in phenomenological psychology* (Vol. 1, pp. 149–163). Pittsburgh, PA: Duquesne University Press.

Fischer, C. T. (1972). Paradigm changes which allow sharing of results. *Professional Psychology, 3,* 364–369.

Fischer, C. T. (1978). Collaborative psychological assessment. In C. T. Fischer & S. L. Brodsky (Eds.), *Client participation in human services* (pp. 41–61). New Brunswick, NJ: Transaction Books.

Fischer, C. T. (1979). Individualized assessment and phenomenological psychology. *Journal of Personality Assessment, 43,* 115–122.

Fischer, C. T. (1980). Privacy and human development. In W. C. Bier (Ed.), *Privacy: A vanishing value* (pp. 37–45). Bronx, NY: Fordham University Press.

Fischer, C. T. (1982). Intimacy in psychological assessment. In M. Fisher & G. Stricker (Eds.), *Intimacy* (pp. 443–460). New York, NY: Plenum.

Fischer, C. T. (1985/1994). *Individualizing psychological assessment.* Mahwah, NJ: Erlbaum. (Originally published by Brooks/Cole.)

Fischer, C. T. (2000). Collaborative, individualized assessment. *Journal of Personality Assessment, 74*, 2–14.

Fischer, C. T., & Wertz, F. J. (1979). Empirical phenomenological analyses of being criminally victimized. In A. Giorgi, R. Knowles, & D. Smith (Eds.), *Duquesne studies in phenomenological psychology* (Vol. 3, pp. 135–158). Pittsburgh, PA: Duquesne University Press.

Goodyear, R. K. (1990). Research on the effects of test interpretation: A review. *The Counseling Psychologist, 18*, 240–257.

Gorske, T. T., & Smith, S. (2008). *Collaborative therapeutic neuropsychological assessment.* New York, NY: Springer.

Guerrero, B., Lipkind, J., & Rosenberg, A. (2011). Why did she put nail polish in my drink? Applying the Therapeutic Assessment model with an African American foster child in a community mental health setting. *Journal of Personality Assessment, 93*, 7–15.

Handler, L. (1996). The clinical use of figure drawings. In C. Newmark (Ed.), *Major psychological assessment instruments* (pp. 206–293). Boston, MA: Allyn & Bacon.

Handler, L. (1997). He says, she says, they say: The consensus Rorschach. In J. R. Meloy, M. W. Acklin, C. B. Gacono, J. F. Murray, & C. A. Peterson (Eds.), *Contemporary Rorschach interpretation* (pp. 499–533). Mahwah, NJ: Erlbaum.

Handler, L. (1999). The assessment of playfulness: Hermann Rorschach meets D. W. Winnicott. *Journal of Personality Assessment, 72*, 208–217.

Handler, L. (2006). Therapeutic assessment with children and adolescents. In S. Smith & L. Handler (Eds.), *Clinical assessment of children and adolescents: A practitioner's guide* (pp. 53–72). Mahwah, NJ: Erlbaum.

Hanson, W. E., Claiborn, C. D., & Kerr, B. (1997). Differential effects of two test-interpretation styles in counseling: A field study. *Journal of Counseling Psychology, 44*, 400–405.

Harrower, M. (1956). Projective counseling: A psychotherapeutic technique. *American Journal of Psychotherapy, 10*, 74–86.

Haydel, M. E., Mercer, B. L., & Rosenblatt, E. (2011). Training assessors in Therapeutic Assessment. *Journal of Personality Assessment, 93*, 16–22.

Hilsenroth, M. J., Ackerman, S. J., Clemence, A. J., Strassle, C. G., & Handler, L. (2002). Effects of structured clinical training on patient and therapist perspectives of alliance early in psychotherapy. *Psychotherapy: Theory/Research/Practice/Training, 39*, 309–323.

Hilsenroth, M. J., & Cromer, T. D. (2007). Clinician interventions related to alliance during the initial interview and psychological assessment. *Psychotherapy: Theory, Research, Practice, Training, 44*, 205–218.

Hilsenroth, M. J., Peters, E. J., & Ackerman, S. J. (2004). The development of therapeutic alliance during psychology assessment: Patient and therapist perspectives across treatment. *Journal of Personality Assessment, 83,* 331–344.

Holm-Denoma, J. M, Gordon, K. H., Donohue, K. F., Waesche, M. C., Castro, Y., Brown, J. S., . . . & Joiner, T. E. (2008). Patients' affective reactions to receiving diagnostic feedback. *Journal of Social and Clinical Psychology, 27,* 555–575.

Jacques, E. (1945). The clinical use of the Thematic Apperception Test with soldiers. *Journal of Abnormal and Social Psychology, 40,* 363–375.

Jobes, D. A., Wong, S. A., Conrad, A. K., Drozd, J. F., & Neal-Walden, T. (2005). The collaborative assessment and management of suicidality versus treatment as usual: A retrospective study. *Suicide & Life-Threatening Behavior, 35,* 483–497.

Lance, B. R., & Krishnamurthy, R. (2003, March). *A comparison of three modes of MMPI-2 test feedback.* Paper presented at the Midwinter Meeting of the Society for Personality Assessment, San Francisco, CA.

Little, J. A., & Smith, S. R. (2009, March.) *Collaborative assessment, supportive psychotherapy, or treatment as usual: An analysis of brief individualized intervention with psychiatric inpatients.* Paper presented at the annual meeting of the Society for Personality Assessment, Chicago, IL.

Luborsky, L. (1953). Self-interpretation of the TAT as a clinical technique. *Journal of Projective Techniques, 17,* 217–223.

Mercer, B. L. (2011). Psychological assessment of children in a community mental health clinic. *Journal of Personality Assessment, 93,* 1–6.

Miller, W. R., & Rollnick, S. (2002). *Motivational interviewing: Preparing people to change.* New York, NY: Guilford Press. (Original work published 1991)

Morey, L. C., Lowmaster, S. E., & Hopwood, C. J. (2010). A pilot study of Manual-Assisted Cognitive Therapy with a Therapeutic Assessment augmentation for Borderline Personality Disorder. *Psychiatry Research, 178,* 531–535.

Murray, H. A. (1943). *Thematic Apperception Test manual.* Cambridge, MA: Harvard University Press.

Mutchnick, M. G., & Handler, L. (2002). Once upon a time . . . : Therapeutic interactive stories. *The Humanistic Psychologist, 30,* 75–84.

Nakamura, N., & Nakamura, S. (1999). The method and therapeutic effectiveness of RFBS (*Rorschach Feedback Session*). *Japanese Journal of Psychotherapy, 25*(1), 31–38. (In Japanese.)

Newman, M. L. (2004). *Psychological assessment as brief psychotherapy: Therapeutic effects of providing MMPI-A test feedback to adolescents.* Unpublished doctoral dissertation, La Trobe University, Melbourne, Australia.

Newman, M. L., & Greenway, P. (1997). Therapeutic effects of providing MMPI-2 test feedback to clients at a university counseling service. *Psychological Assessment, 9*, 122–131.

Ougrin, D., Ng, A. V., & Low, J. (2008). Therapeutic assessment based on cognitive-analytic therapy for young people presenting with self-harm: Pilot study. *Psychiatric Bulletin, 32*, 423–426.

Peters, E. J., Handler, L., White, K. G., & Winkel, J. D. (2008). "Am I going crazy, doc?": A self psychology approach to Therapeutic Assessment. *Journal of Personality Assessment, 90*, 421–434.

Poston, J. M., & Hanson, W. M. (2010). Meta-analysis of psychological assessment as a therapeutic intervention. *Psychological Assessment, 22*, 203–212.

Purves, C. (2002). Collaborative assessment with involuntary populations: Foster children and their mothers. *The Humanistic Psychologist, 30*, 164–174.

Rogers, L. B. (1954). A comparison of two types of test interpretation interview. *Journal of Counseling Psychology, 1*, 224–231.

Rosenberg, A., Almeida, A., & Macdonald, H. (in press). Crossing the cultural divide: Issues in translation, mistrust, and co-creation of meaning in cross-cultural therapeutic assessment. *Journal of Personality Assessment.*

Schroeder, D. G., Hahn, E. D., Finn, S. E., & Swann, W. B. Jr. (1993, June). *Personality feedback has more impact when mildly discrepant from self-views.* Paper presented at the fifth annual convention of the American Psychological Society, Chicago, IL.

Smith, J. D., & George, C. (in press). Therapeutic Assessment case study: Treatment of a woman diagnosed with metastatic cancer and attachment trauma. *Journal of Personality Assessment.*

Smith, J. D., & Handler, L. (2009). "Why do I get in trouble so much?": A family Therapeutic Assessment case study. *Journal of Personality Assessment, 91*, 197–210.

Smith, J. D., Handler, L., & Nash, M. R. (2010). Family Therapeutic Assessment for preadolescent boys with oppositional defiant disorder: A replicated single-case time-series design. *Psychological Assessment, 22*, 593–602.

Smith, J. D., Nicholas, C. R. N., Handler, L., & Nash, M. R. (2011). Examining the clinical effectiveness of a family intervention session in Therapeutic Assessment: A single-case experiment. *Journal of Personality Assessment, 93*, 149–158.

Smith, J. D., Wolf, N. J., Handler, L., & Nash, M. R. (2009). Testing the effectiveness of family Therapeutic Assessment: A case study using a time-series design. *Journal of Personality Assessment, 91*, 518–536.

Swann, W. B. Jr. (1997). The trouble with change: Self-verification and allegiance to the self. *Psychological Science, 8,* 177–180.

Tharinger, D. J., Finn, S. E., Arora, P., Judd-Glossy, L., Ihorn, S. M., & Wan, J. T. (in press). Therapeutic Assessment with children: Intervening with parents "behind the mirror." *Journal of Personality Assessment.*

Tharinger, D. J., Finn, S. E., Austin, C. A., Gentry, L. B., Bailey, K., Parton, V. T., & Fisher, M. E. (2008). Family sessions as part of child psychological assessment: Goals, techniques, clinical utility, and therapeutic value. *Journal of Personality Assessment, 90*(6), 547–558.

Tharinger, D. J., Finn, S. E., Gentry, L., Hamilton, A., Fowler, J., Matson, M., Krumholz, L., & Walkowiak, J. (2009). Therapeutic Assessment with children: A pilot study of treatment acceptability and outcome. *Journal of Personality Assessment, 91,* 238–244.

Tharinger, D. J., Finn, S. E., Gentry, L., & Matson, M. (2007). Therapeutic Assessment with adolescents and their parents: A comprehensive model. In D. Sakllofske & V. Schwean (Eds.), *Oxford Press handbook of psychological assessment of children and adolescents.* New York, NY: Oxford University Press.

Tharinger, D. J., Finn, S. E., Hersh, B., Wilkinson, A., Christopher, G., & Tran, A. (2008). Assessment feedback with parents and pre-adolescent children: A collaborative approach. *Professional Psychology: Research and Practice, 39,* 600–609.

Tharinger, D. J., Finn, S. E., Wilkinson, A., DeHay, T., Parton, V. T., Bailey, K., & Tran, A. (2008). Providing psychological assessment feedback to children through individualized fables. *Professional Psychology: Research and Practice, 39*(6), 610–618.

Tharinger, D. J., Finn, S. E., Wilkinson, A. D., & Schaber, P. (2007). Therapeutic assessment with a child as a family intervention: A clinical and research case study. *Psychology in the Schools, 44,* 293–309.

Tharinger, D. J., & Pilgrim, S. (in press). Parent and child experiences of neuropsychological assessment as a function of child feedback by individualized fable. *Child Neuropsychology.*

PART

I

Assessments of Individual Adults

2

---=>◆<=---

Therapeutic Assessment of a Dissociating Client: Learning Internal Navigation

JUDITH ARMSTRONG

CLARISSA'S DECLINE

I first saw Clarissa, age 37, through the eyes of her referring psychiatrist, Dr. Stevens, an expert on the treatment of dissociative disorders to whom she was referred after cognitive therapy for posttraumatic stress disorder (PTSD) had failed to impact her symptoms. Dr. Stevens described her as having psychologically unraveled over the past three years to the point that if the flood of her ever-increasing symptoms was not staunched, she would soon require inpatient treatment. He said there were times when she didn't sleep, and her speech raced so fast that she was unintelligible. Only moments later, she would become logical and impress him with her insight and control. He was unwilling to diagnose and medicate her until he knew more.

Clarissa reported a trauma background, and there was no question in Dr. Stevens' mind that she also dissociated. At moments during their sessions, she would freeze midsentence and stare into space with a terrified "deer in the headlights" look. She complained of finding herself driving on the freeway not knowing where she was, and in her words, "looking at the world through a frightened child's eyes." She worried about becoming a drag on her friends and her husband. With the former, she often felt a sudden need to be comforted like a baby. Her friends held her in their arms until they ran out of patience. Her husband complained that he never knew what to expect when he came home from work: a companion who was almost aggressively seductive, one who was oversolicitous, or one who drew away from him with fear and paranoid accusations. Clarissa, who had always been so healthy, now had a body that was wracked with pain from head to toe.

Dr. Stevens also told me that despite Clarissa's crumbling defenses, there were signs of the past strengths and the fighting spirit she once had. Before her downward trajectory, she had led an adventurous life filled with world travel and entrepreneurial business success. Her relationships, while unsteady, had been rich and often long lasting. A beautiful woman with a sensual but waiflike manner, she drew people toward her and was never at a loss for company.

Clarissa told Dr. Stevens that from the ages of 7 to 10 she was fondled with deep finger penetration by the minister at her church school for girls as he drove her back to her home from school. This was something she always remembered, and she and her classmates discussed it together since he also fondled them. She had successful therapy in adolescence for depression, drug use, and suicidality. Her therapist didn't ask about trauma, so Clarissa never discussed it with her. She did confide in her boyfriend, who responded in a sensitive way that Clarissa also found healing. All was going well in her life until three years previous, when a series of trauma-related events occurred. First, her old classmates decided to file a class-action lawsuit against the minister and church and asked Clarissa to join them because she seemed to remember more about her abuse than many of them did about theirs. She agreed to help them out of loyalty, but only as a witness, not a plaintiff. She then tried to contact her old boyfriend, only to find out that he had committed suicide recently while he was abroad. Two years before, her beloved father, the parent who encouraged her intellectual and career development, suddenly died. Recently, she told Dr. Stevens that between the ages of 11 and 16 her father watched her as she showered. He stood outside the shower stall and masturbated and explained that she calmed and satisfied him as her mother never could. Clarissa had a dream about her father after he died, a dream that continued to torment and unhinge her. He spoke to her and told her that he loved her and he wasn't sorry for what he did.

MY THOUGHTS AS I APPROACH CLARISSA

Teaching Point

Clarissa's story is a good example of the fact that there is more to trauma reactions than just PTSD. Assessing the full range of trauma-related symptoms becomes crucial for treatment planning (Courtois, Ford, & van der Kolk, 2009).

Untreated trauma disorders can develop over time in a seesaw of emotional flooding, denial, and dissociative numbing, and the life costs of all these reactions. A sufferer at first may be depressed or anxious, then move to a period of avoidance in which she turns to drug use or masks her sorrow with anger, then come to a point where she feels nothing, not even love. All of this can take a toll on her health (Weissbecker & Clark, 2007). She may seek addictive painkillers and repeated medical interventions for both the health costs of trauma and the bodily expression of her hidden inner pain. Based on her psychiatrist's description, Clarissa was in the "flooded" stage of trauma characterized by a loss of the ability to regulate one's emotions and navigate smoothly from one cognitive-emotional state to another. This is why, when Clarissa's therapist requested an assessment for diagnostic clarification, he also wanted to learn about her coping strengths. He knew that unless her coping could be mobilized and strengthened in treatment, her underlying diagnosis would remain unclear. Even more important, further uncovering of trauma would lead to more flooding and psychological decline (Ford, Courtois, Steele, van der Hart, & Nijenhuis, 2005).

Unlike repression in which a memory is lost, Clarissa also suffered from both too much and too little memory. She existed in that characteristically dissociative in-between state of knowing and not knowing what was tormenting her mind. She remembered, but because she also veered abruptly between her cognitive-emotional states, her ability to hold onto and reflect on what she remembered was impaired. Thus, she and her therapist did not yet know what triggered her loss of logic or what repaired it, what made her need to be comforted as a frightened child or push others away, and what role experiences of past abuse were still playing in her mind.

OUR COLLABORATIVE RELATIONSHIP BEGINS: SAFETY AND CONTROL FIRST

Teaching Point

In trauma the environment becomes dangerous, unpredictable, even deadly. One's ability to affect what happens is minimal at best, and one's body and mind and the lives of those one loves can be invaded, maimed, shamed, or even lost forever. Trauma is not a rare phenomenon. In fact, after a period of natural distress and anxiety, the majority of people recover from a traumatic experience and get on with their lives (Breslau, 2002). A negative outcome is more likely when a social support system is not available to give understanding and comfort and when the trauma is repetitive, occurs during the developmental years, and involves betrayal of trust (Pearlman & Courtois, 2005; Freyd, 1996). In such cases, the sense of external and internal helplessness often lingers. This is why something that seems mundane, Informed Consent to the assessment procedure, becomes crucial for safe and ethical trauma assessment.

Clarissa was so charmingly helpless that it immediately brought out the maternal in me. I knew that I needed to carefully watch my boundaries for such things as the amount of time I gave her. I also needed to guard against "overhelping" her, like her friends who held her like a baby, or I'd just be reinforcing her helplessness (Dalenberg, 2000). Fortunately, Clarissa's own reason for agreeing to a collaborative/therapeutic assessment told me that she was pretty tired of feeling helpless. The "burning question" she wanted her assessment to answer was, in her words, "How do I shift from a problematic state? How do I heal it?" Her response to my question about what she most feared learning from our assessment brought up an underlying distrust of therapy that she then discussed with her therapist. She was afraid she'd find out she had dissociative iden-tity disorder (DID), because another therapist she went to before her cognitive therapist had assigned her this diagnosis. In a clear case of malpractice, that treater had given names to Clarissa's abruptly chang-ing emotional states and then suddenly terminated treatment when Clarissa suddenly became so furious with him that he was frightened for his safety.

Teaching Point

The burning question and feared answer portions of collaborative/therapeutic assessment are particularly vital in trauma assessment because they enable the psychologist to pick up hidden coping competen-cies and reinforce these in their interactions with the client.

I was impressed by Clarissa's honesty about her explosive anger. I told her that we first needed to learn about her dissociation because it had once helped her by calming her but had now gotten out of hand. We agreed that during the next week she would keep a "dissociation diary" in which she'd write down her thoughts and feelings when she dis-sociated without worrying whether they made sense or not. Her next homework would be to write down what happened just before she dis-sociated, including the ideas, feelings, and physical reactions she had. I assured her that once she discovered what trauma reminders set off her dissociation, they'd begin to lose their power over her. The following is a brief excerpt from Clarissa's first dissociation diary, which she entitled "Possible Clues That I am Dissociating:"

I get cold. I don't care if I am bleeding or anything that might happen. I have no sense of feeling. No one means anything to me; I can't feel what they're saying. I yearn, but from very far away. I have made people scared of me but I don't know why they are so scared. Sometimes I feel like I am very little, that other people terrify me and that the world is too much. Too fast, too intense.

We now had clues to help us check in on her condition as the assessment progressed: cold, emotional deadness, fear, sense of distance, and anger. I also told her to alert me if the speed and intensity of our assessment was becoming too much for her.

DIPPING INTO THE DISSOCIATIVE WHIRLPOOL WITH STRUCTURED AND SEMISTRUCTURED PERFORMANCE TESTS

The Dissociative Relational Field

The signs of traumatic dissociation are subtle but powerful. Dissociation both expresses and hides itself in our clients' silences, their sudden changes in topic that cut the thread of their narrative, in their shifts in posture and grimaces that reveal their body pain, in their bursts of crying that surprise them because they don't feel sad. Fortunately, dissociation is "catching." If it weren't, we assessors might never understand what was happening within our dissociating clients. This means we must also be attuned to our own bodies, our empathetic sense of dizziness as we become aware that our client has entered a light trance state, our empathetic amnesia when we suddenly forget a question we wanted to ask, our momentary inattention when we "come to" and realized that the theme of our client's narrative had so abruptly shifted that we don't know what the conversation is all about.

☞ Teaching Point

When we are so attuned, we can then ask our clients a simple but powerfully effective question, one that helps them begin to monitor themselves: "What's happening now?"

Clarissa and I Begin Our Exploration

We started by looking at Clarissa's traumatic and dissociative symptoms through the lens of the Trauma Symptom Inventory (TSI; Briere, 1995). We then put her symptoms into the context of her larger personality functioning with the Minnesota Multiphasic Personality Inventory–2 (MMPI-2; Butcher et al., 2001).

Clarissa's Tr(auma) Summary Scale on the TSI at $T = 71$ suggested that she met the diagnostic criteria for PTSD. Her highest Clinical scale was Dissociation (DIS $T = 87$). I knew I needed to approach the subject of dissociation particularly sensitively with Clarissa. My dissociative-disordered clients had taught me that dissociating made them feel "crazy," so they assumed other people would see them as crazy too. It was possible to speak about such things if the listener didn't act surprised, change the subject, or look nervous. Then the clients felt less ashamed, less like someone from "another planet."

Clarissa's MMPI-2 presented the clinical challenge that Dr. Stevens faced. Her elevated F validity scale ($T = 75$) was not unusual for trauma survivors, because the scale contains many trauma and dissociation symptoms (Carlson, 1997). Her elevated Response Variability scale (VRIN $T = 74$) suggested that she went into different cognitive-emotional states while answering the test items. Clarissa later told me that one reason for this was that answering the questions made her body hurt as much as her mind, and she was trying different ways to relieve this pain. Her Clinical scale pattern traced out the anger, cognitive disarray, and emotional instability (Psychopathic Deviate $T = 87$, Paranoia $T = 78$, Depression $T = 75$, Schizophrenia $T = 87$, Mania $T = 71$) characteristic of the traumatic flooding and affect regulation problems seen in those with developmentally based abuse (Briere & Armstrong, 2007). Of special concern was that Clarissa endorsed having recently considered killing herself. Her elevated Mania scale suggested that she had the energy to carry this out despite her depression, just as she once had done during the emotional turmoil of adolescence.

After she completed the tests, Clarissa said she felt "shaky" and would be talking to her therapist that day. Nonetheless, she let me know that she wanted us to discuss the test findings at our next session, rather than waiting until her assessment was finished, so she could begin to work on her problems now. If I was going to help her navigate through the shoals of her shaky mind, promoting her safety and sense of control in our relationship would have to be a priority for us both.

At our next session, Clarissa came in smiling and looking much more confident. She politely but firmly requested that I show her the MMPI-2 printout and explain the meaning of each scale, which I did. I was worried about jumping prematurely to a "Level 3 interpretation" (Finn, 2007), so I went over each subscale with her and encouraged her to give me examples of how it fit, or did not fit, her experience. The Bizarre Experiences subscale that substantially elevated her Schizophrenia scale consisted of flashbacks and an associated sense that she was losing her mind. The distrust of others and overreaction to criticism so evident in her Psychopathic Deviate (Pd) and Paranoia (Pa) scales was marked by her angry sense of betrayal and fear that everyone knew that she was a truly bad, permanently damaged woman. Clarissa was not at all dismayed by the findings—quite the opposite. She told me with a joyful smile, "It's like a mirror of how I feel!" She said the MMPI-2 helped her "feel real . . . I saw my low self-esteem and [pointing to these scales alongside the low Masculinity-Femininity scale that marked her unassertiveness], there's a part of me that doesn't express itself." She admitted having suicidal thoughts that she had begun to discuss in therapy, but she assured me that she didn't plan to actually kill herself. I wasn't so sure. I hoped that the angry part of Clarissa that didn't express itself to her and others didn't harbor more serious suicidal thinking.

Clarissa calmly took notes as we talked about the test so she could think about things later and discuss them in therapy. I told her that she looked different, more confident and organized today. She smiled and explained that she was proud because she had discovered a trauma reminder and then it disappeared, leaving her feeling more in the present. This discovery concerned the origin of her changeable reactions to her husband's homecoming after his workday. Her dissociation diary helped her realize that the smell of exhaust fumes as his car entered the garage reminded her of her minister's car and brought back the complex feelings she'd had when he sexually abused her there. Clarissa explained that although she remembered the incidents with her minister, she had never thought of them as abuse until she discussed them with a friend who was a plaintiff in the lawsuit. It was only when she saw the pain in her friend's face as she listened that "I started to feel how I felt [sic]. Up until then I thought it was normal. When it was happening I just went away from myself." Clarissa added that the same surge of unnerving feeling occurred when she recently told her therapist about her father watching her while she showered.

I began to sense Clarissa's loss of focus as she told me this. Her eyes now looked unfocused, and her voice became a monotone, making me think she was "going away" from herself now. I asked her to check in on how she was feeling. She replied "fine," in a clipped, emotionless voice. I asked her if it was okay to ask her a bit more about how she was doing. She hesitated and then agreed. I explained that the best way to deal with dissociation was to slow down her reaction (Kluft, 1993) and check in with her body, because I thought it now held her feelings. Clarissa told me that her back had started to ache and her head too with some of my questions. When I asked her to do another check-in, she smiled and told me she felt good and excited because she was able to be honest with me, but that a part of her felt anxious when I asked her to check in. She paused and added that she thought she'd done enough this session and didn't want feedback on the TSI. We agreed to end, and Clarissa looked quite pleased. "It felt good to tell you to stop," she said. "I need to say 'stop' more in therapy when things become too much for me. I didn't get to do this when I was growing up."

Exploring Clarissa's Feared Answer

Dr. Stevens told me that Clarissa's reasoning was becoming more organized, both in treatment and in her outside life. Clarissa had started a trial of mood-stabilizing medication but remained determined to build up her coping skills so she could be medication free. Despite Clarissa's treatment progress, she would become disorganized and dissociative whenever the topic of her father watching her shower came up. Dr. Stevens wanted to forewarn me that he thought there was more to that story than they both knew now. Recently, Clarissa told him she felt nauseous and like throwing up whenever they discussed her father, and she recalled having had an eating disorder during adolescence. This made Dr. Stevens wonder whether oral sex had been involved in the shower incidents.

Dr. Stevens was also worried about Clarissa's ability to tolerate the SCID-D, despite her determination to proceed. They had agreed that she would check in with him after our assessment session was over. I remembered that Clarissa's earlier experience of being diagnosed with DID was linked with having a psychologist invade her mind by naming her "parts," and in doing this, taking ownership of the narrative of who she was.

Clarissa came into the next session wearing a cap. She told me she was ready to begin, took off her cap, and shook her head to free her hair as we started our Structured Clinical Interview for DSM-IV Dissociative Disorders–Revised (SCID-D-R; Steinberg, Rounsaville, & Cichetti, 1994). One benefit of this standardized semistructured interview is that discussing dissociative symptoms tends to evoke them. Thus, both the client and assessor can see the problematic behavior in action during the interview. Clarissa gave me many examples of forgetting. For example, she thought she didn't know how to tell time but recently realized that this was because she "spaced out" and then came to herself to find that hours had passed. She thought that during some of those lost hours she was cleaning and putting things away. She explained that when she was anxious and "felt dirty," cleaning and organizing the outside world calmed her, although she later forgot where she put things. Lately, she "awoke" to find she was cleaning at 4 a.m. Could this be part of her sleep problem?

☞ Teaching Point

Clarissa asked me to repeat my SCID-D-R questions several times because she forgot them. Amnesia is so easy for assessors and treaters to miss when it is ongoing like this, because the client has amnesia for the amnesia and, thus, can't report it. Gently pointing out her forgetting led to a discussion of Clarissa's ongoing amnesia in therapy.

Clarissa also described feeling depersonalized: "I feel like I'm in a bubble I'm creating where I can't get to myself or other people and

I feel numb. It makes me feel crazy. I want to be present." This sense of anguished numbing, this lonely distance from themselves and the world, often makes dissociative-disordered clients feel more emotionally dead than depressed. Clarissa's derealization symptoms consisted of feeling at times that her home was foreign to her. However, Clarissa did not show or report the alterations in identity characteristic of a dissociative disorder. Instead, she reported the confused identity and sense of inner dividedness that is characteristic of developmentally based dissociation (Liotti, 2004).

I told Clarissa that while her SCID-D did not suggest DID, it did suggest she had a serious dissociative disorder, Dissociative Disorder Not Otherwise Specified (DDNOS). I explained that her dissociation caused her to be confused about who she was, because in so many ways she was hidden to herself. Clarissa nodded and said, "It makes me feel vulnerable and scared and, I think, suggestible too because I don't know who I am. Sometimes I feel like killing off my confusion, it gives me a headache." Fear, anger, body pain, and suicidality all were so muddled in Clarissa's mind that it was no wonder the emotional numbness dissociation brought her was as relieving as it was maddening.

I had been observing Clarissa's behavior as she answered the SCID-D questions. She looked quite angry at times and took frequent, long bathroom breaks. After we completed the SCID-D, I asked her whether this was her way of coping with the feelings the interview brought up. Clarissa smiled and said she went to the bathroom because she wanted the time and privacy to go into an emotional state that would help her answer my questions. For example, going into an angry state helped her deal with the fear that some of my questions brought up. She then paused and told me that she was thinking about the time she frightened the therapist who gave names to her emotional states. "He scared me and I needed to get angry to get out of there. Even now sometimes my friends will say I look angry when I'm not. I'd just better let them know I'm scared so we can discuss what's going on between us." Clarissa put her hair up and her cap back on. Aware that I and my SCID-D had a role in her fear and anger today, I added that maybe she had had enough of letting her hair down with me for now. Clarissa laughed and agreed.

OPEN-ENDED PERFORMANCE MEASURES: NEARSIGHT, FARSIGHT, AND INSIGHT

Much was happening in Clarissa's treatment with Dr. Stevens. She told him she now remembered that her father didn't just watch her from outside the shower, but he came inside and made her orally copulate him so he could have a good night's sleep. Clarissa's increasing nausea apparently had been her body memory of this act. This body memory went away when the full memory of what it was connected to returned.

Clarissa came into the "projective" test portion of our assessment looking harried but still proud. She told me she was doing body check-ins to help herself when she remembered upsetting things and had discovered that she often had complex, mixed feelings about memories, which she now could take into account. I encouraged her to do check-ins after each test so we could think together about her reactions. I would be giving her two tests made up of visual images, and I knew that images could provoke the disjointed narratives that characterize a "traumatic thought disorder" (Armstrong, 2002). What I would be looking for now would be Clarissa's ability to draw back from her turmoil and become more analytic and affectively distant. This ability distinguishes clients with a dissociative form of trauma disorder from those with a borderline or psychotic spectrum disorder (Lanius et al., 2010).

I first gave Clarissa the Thematic Apperception Test (TAT; Murray et al., 1943) to help clarify how her past trauma affected her views of her relationships now (Westen, Lohr, Silk, Gold, & Kerber, 1990). I became worried as I listened to her stories. So many of them involved heroes who killed themselves because of their sense of dissociative disconnection from themselves and from any sense of life meaning. However, after the test was over, Clarissa decided to work on relating her TAT stories to her life. Her reflections on these stories gave both of us hope that she wasn't ready to give up on herself. Following is one of her TAT stories and her comments on it as she and I explored the lingering psychological effects of her father's sexual abuse. It would provide fertile ground for our feedback discussion.

> (Card 1: showing a boy looking at a violin) "This boy was given the gift of a violin by his father, but he's thinking he'd rather be

outside playing. His father is very attached to him, and he wants him to be better than he is. The boy knows that playing violin will hurt his neck. He swallows himself up (Clarissa swallowed hard here), and twenty years later he becomes the good violinist his father is proud of. But the boy isn't proud, he's disconnected. So he kills himself. Is it self-indulgent to be here?"

I asked Clarissa why she thought it might be self-indulgent. She told me it was because her husband wasn't very psychological minded, so he could be very critical of her treatment. "If my husband says something hurtful, I swallow myself. Wow, look at what I just said. Then I get manic or depressed if I don't deal with the fact that I get upset."

Teaching Point

While Clarissa was still too far away from her hidden feelings of anger to see them as more than "upset," she could use her dissociative distancing from emotion to gain self-insight. Here, Clarissa helped us both understand that her traumatic confound of swallowing semen and swallowing anger was one of the factors that made her look so bipolar at times.

Clarissa plunged into the Rorschach (Exner, 1985) with energy, but her inability to navigate a smooth course between the varying emotions, physical sensations, and thoughts that these blots evoked was brought into clear relief. Various of her Rorschach test scores were characteristic of people with dissociative disorders (Brand, Armstrong, Loewenstein, & McNary, 2009). Clarissa's approach to the test was intellectual and obsessional. She thought about her feelings (e.g., $EB = 11{:}8.0$), but she thought about them in such detail that they became overwhelming (e.g., $Lambda = .09$). Her dissociative distancing from her emotions enabled her to be insightful ($FD = 3$) and largely accurate in her perceptions ($XA\% = .71$), but her vulnerability to being flooded with depressive and angry emotions could distort her perceptions and reasoning ($DEPI$ or Depression $= 5$, S- or distorted anger $= 4$, $WSum6$ or distorted reasoning $= 27$). No wonder her thinking could become so scattered. Yet her ability to work with others, as seen in the working alliance she had with Dr. Stevens and me, was also evident on this test (*COP* or Cooperative Movement = 3). One of the developmental benefits of dissociative amnesia is that it enables traumatized children to preserve a safe place for love within their wavering mindset.

Teaching Point

Clarissa's Traumatic Content on the Rorschach further illustrated this seesaw of immersement in, and distancing from, her traumatic past. The Traumatic Content Index (TC/R; Armstrong & Loewenstein, 1990) is made up of the sum of Morbid, Aggressive, Anatomy, Blood, and Sex responses divided by the total number of test responses. While no test can validate the existence of an external event, a growing body of research on the TC/R (Kamphuis, Kugeares, & Finn, 2000; Smith, Chang, Kochinshi, Patz, & Nowinski, 2010) indicates that a cutoff of .30 and above warrants further clinical attention to the possibility of a trauma-based disorder.

Clarissa's *TC/R* was .30. The content of her responses was not at all surprising given her history. For example, on the first card, following a series of commonly seen and well-organized responses, Clarissa suddenly drew back. She described seeing two gargoyles gazing down from the top of a church door with an obsessive, aggressive look in their eyes. The look had something to do with the devil, and it freaked people out because it meant they were up to no good.

Like many dissociative-disordered people, Clarissa's insight was both profound and shallow. Traumatic intrusions brought her too near to her past to think about it clearly, but being dissociatively distanced from her feelings left her too far from her experience to, as she put it earlier, "feel how she felt." We would see this seesawing perspective in action when I brought up the topic of her significant Suicide Index (*S-CON* = 8) at our final feedback conference.

FEEDBACK SESSION: SLOWING DOWN NEAR THE SUICIDE BARRIER

Dr. Stevens helped us all see how the findings played out in their treatment and in Clarissa's daily life. We were working smoothly as a team until I brought up the issue of her significant Rorschach Suicide Index

(S-CON = 8). Because Clarissa had endorsed suicidal items on all of her tests, Dr. Stevens and I believed that we would be able to discuss her suicidality together as well. I showed her the Index (as always, she demanded to see the test printouts) and described each element of the score, asking for her feedback. Clarissa looked astounded. In a firm voice, she told me that the findings were just plain wrong, because she wasn't suicidal. Then, probably responding to the equally astounded look on my face and on her therapist's face as well, she smiled kindly and added that all of the other test findings were very helpful, but this one was just plain wrong. Struggling to find a way for her to just begin to incorporate the finding, I pointed to one of her Traumatic Content responses, a scar that was partially healed but still leaked blood (Card VI). I asked her whether this might be telling us that the body and emotional wounds she had endured growing up still leaked so painfully at times that she was willing to do just about anything to stop the pain. Clarissa could agree with that.

Now Dr. Stevens knew he had to approach the suicide issue with care. Despite her verbal statements about her misery, her TAT stories, and her test item endorsements, Clarissa hadn't yet connected to the depths of her anger and despair. She was rightfully focused on becoming emotionally stronger so that she could take a closer look at herself without falling apart once again.

FOLLOW-UP: CLARISSA'S GIFT

Clarissa and I met for our follow-up session 18 months later. She had been busy reentering the workforce and then went on an extended vacation with her husband to renew their relationship. Dr. Stevens had told me that she was no longer taking mood-stabilizing drugs, and she saw him less often now.

Clarissa looked healthy and confident, if somewhat tense, when I saw her. She explained that her schedule had unexpectedly become packed, but she wanted to tell me about her progress because she thought she had discovered some techniques to deal with dissociation that could be used by others who wanted to stop dissociating. She said that when she dissociated, she recognized it and knew she was keeping a secret from herself. She decided to tune into her body whenever she found herself dissociating, a ritualized version of the check-ins we did together. She did yoga-like balances while recognizing and then accepting the thoughts and feelings she was having. "I need the kinesthetic connection to organize my attention. Then I feel and understand my thoughts and this stops my dissociation." She carried this learning into her therapy so she could recognize the negative thoughts about herself that promoted her dissociation during her sessions. "I decided to do a divorce ceremony with Dr. Stevens whenever I had thoughts like I'm not good enough and no one loves me. I realized these were just thoughts, not me. They were things I had gathered from my family and my life. They were thoughts I married that I should never even have gone to have coffee with!"

Clarissa had become more assertive with her husband. She confronted him whenever he called her weird by telling him she was proud of being weird, and it was one of the reasons he loved her. He agreed and turned the word "weird" into a love compliment after that. Clarissa wasn't "swallowing herself" in her marital relationship anymore. Her husband felt freer to be more direct in return by explaining how the ways she tried to be helpful and supportive often put him down. Clarissa was starting to make contact with her hidden anger.

Clarissa came in early the next day to complete the same tests she took earlier and wondered if we could have our feedback session very soon afterward. I agreed because I appreciated how anxiety provoking a feedback session can be when one has been very psychologically ill. Pride is often mixed with memories of past shame for a long time afterward. Nonetheless, Clarissa seemed in an unusual rush. I waited to see why.

Clarissa's new test findings supported her emotional progress, but she had to work a bit to help me see this. It was true that on the TSI none of the symptom scales were significant, including dissociation. Also, none of her MMPI-2 clinical scales were elevated. However, I became concerned when I saw her MMPI-2 validity scales. Her "F" (psychological distress and disturbance) was down, but now both the "Lie" and "Superlative Presentation" validity scales were significant. Fortunately, Clarissa seemed to have predicted this result because she had attached a note to the test. In it she wrote that while she realized people can be dishonest, she wanted to let me know that she wasn't in denial about her negative thoughts. She knew she had marked many of the items as false, but that wasn't because she didn't have the thoughts. It was just that when she had them she no longer focused on them and allowed them to rule her life. Clarissa had not only taken the MMPI-2, she'd done an accurate interpretation of it. In addition, she alerted me to the valuable role of attention control in combating dissociation.

We met shortly afterward to discuss the findings. Clarissa's first question was whether or not the Rorschach still said she was suicidal. It didn't. Clarissa said she wasn't surprised, but she wanted me to know that it wasn't until about 6 months after our original feedback session that she found out how depressed and suicidal she actually was. She explained that she wasn't able to feel her depression before that because of her dissociation, and of course she couldn't work on it until she felt it.

It had been a difficult emotion to face, but only then could Clarissa begin to transform her past in a way that opened her up to a future. Her reworking of the TAT story of the boy with the violin (Card I) was a good example of this. The boy was still disappointed with his present of a violin, but now he paused to see if he could find something positive in what he had been given instead of just jumping to a reaction. He decided that the violin had beautiful wood. Perhaps then he could use the violin to create new music he did like. "So it's not like his parents saying he had to do something but an ardent wish from the boy himself to give the gift new meaning." Clarissa also transformed the leaking wound (Card VI) in her earlier Rorschach into a healing image. It became a Native American ceremonial totem staff. "It's got a complicated shape but it's not fragmented. It's a complicated inner design where the sides match up," she explained.

I didn't want to wound Clarissa's pride in the progress she had made, but I also didn't want to deny a problem that was evident. Not only did she look tense but, despite her statements about how much slowing down had helped her stop dissociating, our follow-up had been rushed due to her other schedule priorities. Her tests further suggested that she was highly anxious. For example, she endorsed anxiety symptoms on the MMPI-2 and TSI and had anxiety-related scores in her Rorschach (e.g., Y—diffuse shading = 4). I shared these things with Clarissa at our feedback session. She smiled and said she was afraid I'd make her come clean; she was very nervous about something and had been trying not to think about it. Almost immediately after she had set up our follow-up sessions, she had found out she would soon be called to the witness stand. Her friends' lawsuit against the church was moving forward—the lawsuit that had led to the revelation of all the pain she had been hiding from herself for many years. I asked if she knew exactly when she'd be called. She said, "tomorrow morning." No wonder Clarissa was trying to keep a lid on her anxiety! We agreed that she would call me after she testified to let me know how things went. Before she left, Clarissa added with a sly smile that something she learned from our assessment had made her a key witness. She had turned the tables on me. Now it was I who was waiting for our final assessment feedback.

Clarissa called the next afternoon to give me feedback. She reminded me that it was during our assessment with the SCID-D that she first talked about her need to put the external world in clean and neat order whenever she felt she was a mess inside and also how she then forgot where she put things for long periods of time. She remembered this when she found out she'd be testifying and realized that she probably saved all of the sexual letters the minister had written to her. But where had she put them? After some searching, she discovered piles of them intact in a box in the back of a closet. She discovered she'd also kept her copies of the photographs he had taken of her as he abused her. She told this to her old friend, who then told her lawyer, who then contacted Clarissa and told her that she wanted her to come to court as the first witness and to bring the box along with her. The lawyer predicted that when the defense attorneys saw what was in the box, the case would settle immediately. Clarissa told me that's exactly what happened. Dissociative obsessiveness, when it is recognized and harnessed, can sometimes have its rewards, including helping to heal others. For this insight, I thank Clarissa.

REFERENCES

Armstrong, J. G. (2002). Deciphering the broken narrative of trauma: Signs of traumatic dissociation in the Rorschach. *Rorschachiana*, XXV, 11–27.

Armstrong, J. G., & Loewenstein, R. J. (1990). Characteristics of patients with multiple personality and dissociative disorders on psychological testing. *Journal of Nervous and Mental Disease*, 178, 448–454.

Brand, B. L., Armstrong, J. G., Loewenstein, R. J., & McNary, S. W. (2009). Personality differences on the Rorschach of dissociative identity disordered, borderline personality disordered, and psychiatric inpatient. *Psychological Trauma: Theory, Research, Practice and Policy, 1*(3), 188–205.

Breslau, N. (2002). Epidemological studies of trauma, Posttraumatic Stress Disorder, and other psychiatric disorders. *The Canadian Journal of Psychiatry, 47*(10), 923–929.

Briere, J. (1995). *Trauma Symptom Inventory (TSI)*. Odessa, FL: Psychological Assessment Resources.

Briere, J., & Armstrong, J. G. (2007). Psychological assessment of posttraumatic dissociation. In E. Vermetten, M. J. Dorahy, & D. Spiegel (Eds.), *Traumatic dissociation: Neurobiology and treatment*. Washington, DC: American Psychiatric Publishing.

Butcher, J. N., Graham, J. R., Ben-Porath, Y. S., Tellegen, A., Dahlstrom, W. G., & Kaemmer, B. (2001). *Minnesota Multiphasic Personality Inventory–2: Manual for administration, scoring and interpretation (rev. ed.)*. Minneapolis: University of Minnesota Press.

Carlson, E. B. (1997). *Trauma assessment: A clinician's guide*. New York, NY: Guilford Press.

Courtois, C. A., Ford, J. D., & van der Kolk, B. A. (2009). *Treating complex traumatic stress disorders: An evidence-based guide*. New York, NY: Guilford Press.

Dalenberg, C. J. (2000). *Countertransference and the treatment of trauma*. Washington, DC: American Psychological Association Press.

Exner, J. E. (1995). *The Rorschach workbook for the comprehensive system*. Bayville, NY: Rorschach Workshops.

Finn, S. E. (2007). *In our clients' shoes: Theories and techniques of Therapeutic Assessment*. Mahwah, NJ: Erlbaum.

Ford, J. D., Courtois, C. A., Steele, K., van der Hart, O., & Nijenhuis, E. R. S. (2005). Treatment of complex posttraumatic self-dysregulation. *Journal of Traumatic Stress, 18*(5), 437–447.

Freyd, J. J. (1996). *Betrayal trauma: The logic of forgetting childhood abuse*. Cambridge, MA: Harvard.

Kamphuis, J. H., Kugeares, S. L., & Finn, S. E. (2000). Rorschach correlates of sexual abuse: Trauma content and aggression indices. *Journal of Personality Assessment, 75*, 212–224.

Kluft, R. P. (1993). The treatment of dissociative disorder patients: An overview of discoveries, successes and failures. *Dissociation, 6*, 87–101.

Lanius, R. A., Vermetten, M. J., Loewenstein, R. J., Brand, B., Schmal, C., Bremner, J. D., & Spiegel, D. (2010). Emotional modulation in PTSD:

Clinical and neurobiological evidence for a dissociative subtype. *American Journal of Psychiatry, 167*(6), 640–647.

Liotti, G. (2004). Trauma, dissociation, and disorganized attachment: Three strands of a single braid. *Psychotherapy: Theory, Research, Practice, Training, 41,* 472–486.

Murray, H. A., et al. (1943). *Thematic Apperception Test: Manual.* Cambridge, MA: Harvard University Press.

Pearlman, L. A., & Courtois, C. A. (2005). Clinical applications of the attachment framework: Relational treatment of complex trauma. *Journal of Traumatic Stress, 18,* 449–459.

Smith, S. R., Chang, J., Kochinski, S., Patz, S., & Nowinski, L. A. (2010). Initial validity of the Logical Rorschach in the assessment of trauma. *Journal of Personality Assessment, 92*(3), 222–231.

Steinberg, M., Rounsaville, B., & Cicchetti, D. V. (1994). Structured Clinical Interview for DSM-IV Dissociative Disorders–revised (SCID-D-R).Washington, DC: American Psychiatric Press.

Weissbecker, I., & Clark, C. (2007). The impact of violence and abuse on women's physical health: Can trauma-informed treatment make a difference? *Journal of Community Psychology, 35*(7), 909–923.

Westen, D., Lohr, N., Silk, K., Gold, L., & Kerber, K. (1990). Object relations and social cognition in borderlines, major depressives and normal: A Thematic Apperception Test analysis. *Psychological Assessment, 2,* 355–364.

CHAPTER

3

Therapeutic Assessment of Depression: Love's Labors Lost?

MARC J. DIENER, MARK J. HILSENROTH, THOMAS D. CROMER, FRANK P. PESALE, AND JENELLE SLAVIN-MULFORD

CONTEXT OF REFERRAL

Presented Issues

"Joy" was a 30-year-old single, Caucasian female who sought therapy after a recent and sudden end to the 6-month relationship with her female partner, "Amanda." Most essential to these recent relationship difficulties was the contrast that Joy noted between her own relationship style and that of Amanda. Joy explained that Amanda consistently experienced strong needs for emotional closeness and excessive expectations regarding time in the relationship. Joy, on the other hand, described herself as having more difficulty opening up to others emotionally, enjoying her time alone, and being particularly introverted.

This lack of interpersonal synchrony had recently come to a head with the progression of Amanda's hepatitis C. Amanda's condition had recently deteriorated, leading to further strain in their relationship as

47

she looked for increased comfort and attention from Joy. Conversely, Joy often felt herself backing away from Amanda emotionally.

As the tension in their relationship mounted, Joy felt that she needed time to better understand what was happening between her and Amanda. Amanda, however, demanded that Joy make a decision about their relationship one evening. When Joy could not do so, they agreed to stop seeing each other. Instead of feeling a sense of relief or clarity, Joy responded to the breakup with intense feelings of sadness, rejection, and self-doubt. After a few days, she composed a lengthy letter to Amanda expressing her feelings about their breakup and a desire to reunite, but she received no reply and later found out that Amanda had moved quickly into another relationship. Joy reported feeling hurt, increasingly rejected, and angry about these events.

In explaining her motivation for seeking services at this time, Joy pointed to this breakup and another area of her life in which she had been struggling. She explained that although she had been working as a physical therapy assistant for several years now, she had lost interest in the work and was considering alternative professions that she felt might be more academically challenging and might offer more opportunities for professional advancement. She reported being interested in going back to school, but she had experienced significant anxiety around this issue. Specifically, she explained that she became overwhelmed when trying to think about or plan this step, as she began to question herself and worry about the amount of time it would take as well as the nature of her future earning capacity.

Patient's[1] Background

Joy was born in Connecticut and moved with her parents and younger sister to Rhode Island at age 10. Joy's father was a retired plumber, and her mother worked part-time as a salesperson in a clothing store. Joy denied any complications of her birth and reported meeting her developmental milestones within appropriate limits. Growing up, Joy felt closest to her grandparents who lived downstairs, in particular her grandfather whom she remembers as "soft, happy, and affectionate." Joy noted that her

---

[1] In general, we use the term "patient" rather than "client," except in instances in which we cite the work of other authors who use the alternative term.

father drank excessively when she was younger, which could lead him to become verbally abusive to Joy and her mother. In addition, Joy remembered physical altercations that took place between her parents when she was between 5 and 10 years old. Joy reported that she would protect and shield her younger sister during these instances.

Joy described her current relationship with her parents as improved relative to her experience while growing up. She explained that she felt a bit closer to them and had started to become more expressive of her feelings. Joy noted that although she initiated some of these changes after the death of her uncle and grandparents, her parents began responding in kind. Joy reported that she visited her family about once a week. She described her relationship with her sister as close, noting that her sister served as one of her most important sources of social support.

Joy reported earning grades of A's in math and science and B's in social studies during school. Although she was placed in several honors classes during junior high, she began to doubt her academic abilities when she struggled in English. Joy stated that she experienced her first period of intense depression beginning around this time. She described herself as being quiet, reserved, and insecure since this period.

Joy earned an associate's degree in advertising and began working in the field. Soon, though, she became dissatisfied with her work and began taking classes at a community college in a variety of different subject areas. For several years, she worked in a group home for developmentally disabled individuals. Joy eventually earned an associate's degree as a physical therapy assistant and began working in a nursing home full-time.

Dynamic Flow of the Sessions

Although Joy presented initially for psychotherapy, her clinician discussed the option of conducting a thorough assessment before initiating formal psychotherapy. He explained that a detailed, comprehensive understanding of Joy's personality and background would provide a particularly useful starting point for their work and that the model of assessment utilized would be quite consistent with the aims of psychotherapy. Joy agreed to the assessment process and consented to participate in a research project on the psychotherapy process and outcome, in which all of her sessions, including the assessment process, were videotaped.

The initial session consisted of a semistructured interview in which the clinician and patient explored the presenting problems and their history, the patient's childhood and upbringing, educational and medical history, family history, psychiatric history, and relationship history. The desired outcomes of the initial meeting are to create an empathic relationship with the patient and collaborate to define treatment goals (see Hilsenroth, 2007; Hilsenroth, Peters, & Ackerman, 2004), explore factors contributing to the maintenance of life problems and potential solutions to these problems, as well as identify Core Conflictual Relationship Themes (CCRT; Book, 1998; Luborsky, 1984; Luborsky & Crits-Christoph, 1997). CCRT refer to repetitive patterns of interpersonal wishes, expected or actual responses from others, and emotional and behavioral responses of self that cut across a variety of relationship episodes narrated by the patient and/or are observed in the interaction between the therapist and patient. In the initial session with Joy, the therapist tentatively hypothesized the following CCRT: A wish to feel emotionally connected to another person that is often met with a harsh, rejecting response, leaving Joy despondent and self-critical with a renewed commitment to maintain her interpersonal distance from others.

The remainder of the initial session consisted of collecting an Early Memory protocol (Fowler, Hilsenroth, & Handler, 1995). This protocol asks the patient to describe eight earliest memories: earliest childhood memory, second earliest childhood memory, earliest memory of mother, earliest memory of father, earliest memory of first day of school, earliest memory of feeding or being fed, earliest memory of feeling or being "warm and snug," and earliest memory of a "special" object (i.e., transitional). These probes were developed based on Mayman's (1968) theory that early memories reflect dominant themes of an individual's object relations. Transcribed as follows are excerpts from several of Joy's memories.

When asked for her *earliest* memory, Joy responded as follows:

Joy (J):   My parents were fighting and my grandfather came upstairs . . . just to look what was going on. And my father kind of being verbally abusive to him and yelling, "go downstairs . . . mind your own business, everything's okay" . . . so obnoxious to my grandfather who is somebody that I was really close to.

When asked for her earliest memory of her *mother*, Joy responded:

> J: Probably being in the kitchen with an apron on, in the apartment upstairs that we lived in, and "get the things off the table." Critical, I remember criticalness from her.
>
> Clinician (C): (Query for what Joy was doing at the time)
>
> J: I was probably drawing on the table, and it was time for dinner and she wanted . . . "Get everything off the table. We have to clean up. Put those papers all in place." Kind of like making messes was a bad thing.
>
> C: (Query for Joy's response)
>
> J: I cleaned everything up. I was a little hurt because it was so important to me, and she kinda dismissed it.

Finally, when asked about her earliest memory of *feeding or eating*, Joy responded:

> J: My sister's birthday . . . eating hot dogs. I was in the backyard with a plaid dress on, and I was playing wiffleball with my cousin.
>
> C: (Query for what Joy was thinking and feeling)
>
> J: I was just having a good time. But I remember my mother being critical of me being such a tomboy . . . being in a skirt and yet wanting to do boyish things.

Several important themes emerged from these memories. Beginning with Joy's earliest memory as reflecting her self-representation (Fowler et al., 1995), she appeared to identify aggression as a reaction of a domineering and abusive paternal figure. Additionally, she seemed to consider paternal figures as scary, overpowering individuals who prevent the attempts of others to intervene in helpful and benevolent ways. Her earliest memory of her mother, suggesting an internal representation of her mother or maternal figures more generally, pointed to a disparaging and belittling object who failed to recognize or value Joy's own needs or desires. The earliest memory of feeding and eating, which assesses an individual's management of dependency, converged with the previously mentioned maternal image as reproachful, in particular with regards to nonstereotypical feminine interests. These themes were consistent with, and elaborated on, the initial relational patterns gathered during the first part of the interview and provided useful grist for the ongoing therapeutic assessment mill.

The second session consisted of an appointment for Joy to fill out several self-report measures, including the Brief Symptom Inventory (BSI; Derogatis, 1993), the Inventory of Interpersonal Problems (IIP; Horowitz, Alden, Wiggins, & Pincus, 2000), and the Personality Assessment Inventory (PAI; Morey, 1991). The examiner reviewed the instructions and made himself available should any questions arise. Joy completed the measures and agreed to meet again for a follow-up interview the next week.

The BSI revealed the following elevated scales: Obsessive-Compulsive (T = 78), Psychoticism (T = 78), Interpersonal Sensitivity (T = 71), Depression (T = 71), and Anxiety (T = 69). The elevated Obsessive-Compulsive scale suggested difficulties with decision making and unwanted behaviors of a repetitive nature (Derogatis, 1993). Although Joy scored quite high on the Psychoticism scale, examination of the specific items indicated primarily interpersonal difficulties rather than psychosis. These difficulties were consistent with the elevations on the Interpersonal Sensitivity scale, suggesting feelings of inferiority and interpersonal discomfort. Finally, the elevations on the Depression and Anxiety scales suggested tension, apprehension, dysphoric mood, and difficulties with motivation. Taken together, the BSI provided a fair summary of Joy's specific symptom distress as well as their potential connection to the interpersonal difficulties she had described during the interview.

On the IIP, Joy's elevation on the Nonassertive scale (T = 77) suggested deficits in self-esteem and self-confidence (Horowitz et al., 2000). These deficits, in turn, made it unlikely that she would express her wishes and needs to others. Instead, she tended to avoid socially challenging situations or ones in which she would need to wield influence on others. Her elevation on the Socially Inhibited scale (T = 67) pointed to fear of negative evaluation that could lead her to avoid full engagement in her social world. Her elevated score on the Cold/Distant scale

(T = 67) suggested her difficulties in forming intimate interpersonal connections and in expressing affection toward others. Overall, then, her IIP results highlighted her interpersonal difficulties with asserting or expressing her needs as well as developing more intimate connections with others, partially as a result of her fear of rejection or criticism.

Joy's PAI results indicated an elevation in only a single scale, Depression (T = 64). When considered in conjunction with her subscale scores (DEP-C with T = 64; DEP-A with T = 69; DEP-P with T = 55), her PAI results suggested deficits in self-confidence and hopefulness, difficulties with concentration and decision making, sadness, and general dissatisfaction with her current circumstances. These results converged with those indicated by the BSI and highlighted Joy's current dysphoria in the context of longstanding interpersonal patterns suggested by the IIP and the specific stressors associated with her recent breakup with her partner.

The third assessment session consisted of a follow-up clinical interview to cover areas of Joy's background and history that were not sufficiently reviewed in the initial meeting. During this session, the clinician assessed Joy for criteria of several relevant diagnoses, including major depressive disorder, dysthymic disorder, eating disorder, and avoidant personality disorder (American Psychiatric Association, 2000). Results suggested that Joy met criteria for Dysthymic Disorder[2] (overeating, hypersomnia, low energy, low self-esteem, difficulty making decisions), Eating Disorder NOS, Partner Relational Problem, and Occupational Problem on Axis I. Additionally, results indicated several features (restraint within intimate relationships due to fears of shame/ridicule, preoccupation with criticism and rejection, views self as socially inept, unappealing, or inferior) of Avoidant Personality Disorder on Axis II. She did not, however, meet sufficient criteria, 4, for an Axis II Avoidant Personality Disorder diagnosis.

The final assessment session consisted of a therapeutic, collaborative feedback session. A Therapeutic Model of Assessment (TMA) feedback session is based on the principle that "clients should first be given

---

[2]Although Joy did meet several criteria for major depressive disorder, she did not cross the threshold number of criteria required for a full diagnosis. Instead, results of the assessment suggested that dysthymic disorder more aptly characterized her functioning for some time, with recent mood exacerbation precipitated by the breakup with her partner.

feedback that closely matches their own preconceptions and then be presented with information that is progressively more discrepant from their self-concepts" (Finn & Tonsager, 1997, p. 380; Fischer, 1994; Hilsenroth, 2007; Hilsenroth, Peters, & Ackerman, 2004). In a TMA, psychological tests are viewed as "opportunities for dialogue between assessors and clients about clients' characteristic ways of responding to usual problem situations and tools for enhancing assessors' empathy about clients' subjective experience" (Finn & Tonsager, 1997, p. 378; Fischer, 1994; Hilsenroth, 2007; Hilsenroth, Peters, & Ackerman, 2004). The goal of the collaborative feedback session is to provide the patient with an alternative way of thinking and feeling about self and others, as well as to explore the factors that contribute to the clinician–patient interaction. In addition, patients are given the opportunity to probe these new understandings and apply them to their current problems in living.

Table 3.1 outlines a summary of clinician activities that have demonstrated significant relationships with positive alliance in initial interviews and psychological assessment (Hilsenroth & Cromer, 2007). Although these activities are useful *across* the different stages of an assessment, we review them here as they apply specifically to the feedback process utilized in Joy's assessment. All of the items in Table 3.1 are potential teaching points. However, for the purpose of the present chapter, we condensed several items and selected the ones that were particularly salient.

Table 3.1 Summary of Clinician Activities Found to Be Significantly Related to Positive Therapeutic Alliance During the Initial Interview and Psychological Assessment

Frame

Conduct longer, more involved, depth-oriented interviews

Adopt a collaborative stance toward client

Speak with emotional and cognitive content

Use clear, concrete, experience-near language

Focus

Allow client to initiate discussion of salient issues

Actively explore these issues

Clarify sources of distress

Table 3.1   (continued)

Identify cyclical relational themes

Facilitate client affect and experience

Explore uncomfortable feelings

Explore in-session process and affect

Maintain active focus on these related topics

Feedback

Review and explore meaning of assessment results

Provide client with new understanding and insight

Offer psychoeducation on symptoms and treatment process

Collaboratively develop individual treatment goals and tasks

Source: Reprinted with permission from "Clinician interventions related to alliance during the initial interview and psychological assessment," by M.J. Hilsenroth & T.D. Cromer, 2007, *Psychotherapy: Theory, Research, Practice, and Training,* 44, 205–218.

Conduct Longer, More Involved, Depth-Oriented Interviews

Joy's feedback and other assessment sessions each lasted approximately 2 hours. This significant period of time allowed her to work together with her clinician in a substantive way toward a deeper understanding of herself, her strengths and weaknesses, and the complex nature of her relationships. During the feedback session, a lengthy discussion of her relationship history with men and women ensued, including Joy's thoughts and feelings about which gender she dates. At one point, Joy noted her discomfort with the term *bisexual,* which led to the following interchange:

Clinician (C):   What about it bothers you?

Joy (J):   Just because there seems to be such a category affiliated with it.

C: Restrictive maybe?

J: Restrictive, yeah. When I was dating women, I felt like I almost had to closet my heterosexuality, because I would be judged. You know people would say, "She'll just run off and date a man when it's convenient."

C: And it seems like being judged by another person is really motivating for you, particularly when you consider the other examples we have spoken about.

J: Yes, it just seems to me another big issue in my life. As
     I'm talking about it, now things are starting to come up
     and make a little more sense . . .

This interchange led to an extended discussion of her relationship
and sexual history, coupled with the connections being drawn by Joy
between her feelings about this issue and larger patterns in her relationships. These types of interactions and meaning-making are more likely
to occur with a lengthier, more depth-oriented approach to assessment.

Adopt a Collaborative Stance Toward the Patient

Strengthening the therapeutic alliance involves fostering a more mutual,
collaborative relationship with the patient. In TMA, one way in which
this is accomplished is by inviting the patient to generate a set of referral
questions that he or she would like addressed via the assessment (Finn,
2007; Hilsenroth, 2007). In Joy's assessment, she expressed her interest
early on in helping her understand her difficulties in intimate relationships and in overcoming the obstacles to her professional growth.
Another way of facilitating a collaborative relationship involves engaging the patient in arriving at a mutually agreed-upon understanding of a
particular assessment issue. Take, for example, the following interaction
in which the clinician attempted to work with the patient to get a more
refined understanding of her relational patterns:

C: Have you noticed difficulty asserting yourself with other people or
     interactions with others?
J: Yes, most of the time I can't. A lot of the times automatically I do
     feel nervous or intimidated to speak to another person or let some-
     body know who I am.
C: So would you say that you expect a negative kind of reaction from
     others? Or is it something about how you feel yourself, something
     that is more independent of other people?
J: I think I feel like I'll be judged by the way I speak or the way I dress.
     Because I'm quiet, people misinterpret me and think, "I guess she
     thinks she's so wonderful." Sometimes I'm just fearful of exposing
     myself to new people.

C: You know that really fits in with that kind of core pattern we've been talking about—wanting to open up, get closer to people, but fearing that kind of critical, negative, or manipulative reaction. Does that seem right to you?

J: That's why I know that it's something I want to work on because it's uncomfortable. You know if I would just isolate myself and be totally at bliss and okay with it, that's fine, but I don't feel that way anymore. It's uncomfortable for me, and I want to be closer to people, and I want to change this thing about myself that I do, that's negative and self-destructive.

Rather than delivering clinical findings to the patient as a statement of fact, each element was offered to her in an open-ended and collaborative manner for her review, elaboration, and/or modification. Through this interchange, the patient seemed to increase her interest and motivation to work together with the therapist to try to understand and alter these patterns. This may have been a result of her feeling more like an active, valuable participant in the assessment and therapeutic process.

Speak With Emotional and Cognitive Content Using Clear, Concrete, and Experience-Near Language

This principle suggests that therapeutic communication should focus on thoughts and feelings using language that is easily understood by the patient, rather than more abstract and jargon-filled diction. In the following example, the clinician highlighted an internal conflict between a wish and fear in a way that resonated with Joy, elicited further relevant fears that impaired her ability to be in a close relationship, and led to identification of the characteristic ways in which she responded to such conflict:

C: It's almost like a paradox, because on the one hand you want to get close to someone else, to be able to trust them, but then it seems like you're afraid they will react in a way that is rejecting.

J: Yeah, and take some of my independence away. It's exactly like a paradox; on the one hand I want these nice things, but then I fight with myself on the other side.

C: So you kind of pull back.

J: I do.

C: And withdraw and isolate yourself, and that's specifically at a time when the other person is trying to get closer to you.

J: Exactly.

C: And you're trying to get closer. And you end up feeling hurt and disappointed.

J: Yeah, I feel pressure and disappointed in myself too. I get frustrated with myself for feeling the way I do. It's like you want a relationship, now you have one, and you can't let another person in. What's wrong with me?

Allow the Client to Initiate Discussion of Salient Issues and Actively Explore these Issues

This clinical activity also increases collaboration between the patient and clinician, while simultaneously facilitating the type of depth that is crucial for an effective assessment. At the beginning of the feedback session, Joy and her clinician discussed her expectations for how the session would proceed. Then, the clinician outlined the types of things they would be doing (i.e., putting together the things they had learned together over the assessment to sketch the contours of the upcoming psychotherapy), and emphasized how crucial Joy's input and engagement in the feedback session would be. The clinician asked Joy if she had any questions about the process. Joy said that she did not, although she hinted that there were some things on her mind that she wanted to discuss before jumping into the feedback session. At this point, the clinician decided that moving straight into the feedback would be counter-therapeutic, considering that Joy clearly had something important to discuss. Joy expressed some thoughts and feelings she had been having recently about her breakup with Amanda. As part of this discussion, the clinician worked together with Joy to explore these reactions in the larger context of Joy's relational history. In this way, Joy was able to set the agenda for an important issue with the help of the therapist focusing and broadening the exploration. The following interaction demonstrates the clinician's attempt to underscore the adaptive nature of Joy's initiation of the discussion:

C: As we're talking about these issues, I can't help but notice something that feels really important and different about how things started off today.

J: What's that?

C: Well, you were able to tell me that there was something that *you* needed.

J: Well, there was really something important that I wanted to talk about.

C: Yes, there was. You let me know that we needed to shift to something else instead of what I had planned. That's quite different from how you've done things in the past.

J: What do you mean?

C: In the past, you would have kept what you needed out of the picture, because what you need may not have been all that important. But it *is* important, and you found a way to tell me that. I think that what happened here, between us, is a really important step in doing things differently with people.

J: Maybe, but it's a lot easier here than it is out there.

C: That could very well be, but I'm also pretty sure that you would not have felt comfortable doing something like that when we first met. Something's beginning to change in you, and I'm hopeful that we can build on that in a way that moves you closer to getting more out of relationships than you've been able to so far.

Clarify Sources of Distress and Identify Cyclical Relational Themes

This principle suggests that the clinician work together with the patient in understanding precipitants, causes, and maintaining factors in patient problems, particularly as these problems manifest themselves in the repetitive interpersonal patterns that can come to dominate the patient's life. Consider the clinician–patient verbatim interaction cited earlier on pages 57–58, which dealt with the patient's pattern of withdrawing from others in fear of rejection or criticism, followed by the patient's emotional reaction of feeling hurt, disappointed, and self-critical. At this point, the clinician noted the following, which seemed to have sparked recognition in the patient of the ways in which her response to these patterns actually maintains them:

C: It's almost like compounding the pain that's intrinsic to it in addition to losing the relationship or moving away from somebody by beating yourself up about it.

J: Yeah, it just makes it worse, and I feel like I almost fulfill a prophecy for myself. The closer somebody gets, despite the fact that I want a relationship, I do things which make it inevitable that someone will be disgusted and pull away. So it's almost like I create the things that would push somebody away, and then I complain about them.

C: I think that's a really important point. It seems like you'd like to clearly see this pattern when it shows up and also to get a sense of how it's perpetuating itself.

Facilitate Client Affect and Experience, Explore Uncomfortable Feelings, and Explore In-Session Process

This principle highlights the particular importance of engaging the client's experience and expression of feelings in the session. Toward the end of the feedback session, the clinician raised the question of how Joy felt about initiating psychotherapy with him:

C: Let's talk a little about moving into a formal therapy stage of treatment. I'm wondering if you have any thoughts or reactions about us moving from the assessment process into therapy.

J: No, not really. Nothing in particular I can think of.

C: I think we may have touched on this last time. Do you think it may be difficult to talk about issues related to sexuality given that I am a man?

J: You know, when I met you before our first session, I thought it might be. It even crossed my mind, "Would I hurt his feelings if I asked for another therapist or something?" Maybe I will get into stuff which will make me uncomfortable, but that's not even going to be an issue because I feel comfortable with you. And I have already gotten into the things I thought were going to be difficult and they actually weren't. The bisexuality and the feelings and all that stuff that would have been the main thing I would have you know. I think it is a good thing that I didn't really specify what type of therapist I wanted.

C: But if you do feel, if you find something is uncomfortable or that it is difficult to raise an issue and talk about it, it is important you get the treatment that you need.

J: Yeah, so I think you know the tough parts. I think I kind of talked about it today. But, if anything else becomes difficult, I will try my best to express it.

C: Good. And we also touched a little bit last time on some of the things that we have seen come up in different ways that are difficult to discuss. Like in a relationship when you let yourself feel closer to a person. And we started to talk a little bit about that here in this relationship. We'll talk about a lot of really personal things. Have you had any thoughts about how that might affect our work?

J: It did cross my mind, like if things come up, it could be difficult to talk about, but I'll just deal with them when they come up. Nothing that's going to hold up the sessions or anything like that.

C: Any kind of hesitancy about revealing certain very personal things?

J: Honestly, no, because I think it's very important, especially here with you, to be as completely honest as I possibly can. You know, in these sessions, why come here and make things up? It won't be beneficial.

C: I think that makes a lot of sense, but we should also keep in mind that along with you wanting to be 100% honest, sometimes there are certain things that can have a very strong pull. Sometimes anyone can want to talk about something, but then when they start they can get pulled in a different direction.

Review and Explore Meaning of Assessment Results, Provide Client With New Understanding, and Offer Psychoeducation

This principle underscores the utility of working with the client to generate new ways of thinking about self and others based on the assessment data as well as the nature of the clinician–patient interaction. Many of the previously cited examples do just that—that is, explore what all the information and experiences generated in the assessment mean to the patient, and how to use that information to get a fresh perspective on difficulties for which the patient has sought treatment. More specifically, TMA recommends working "from surface to depth," meaning beginning with findings that are most consistent with how the patient already thinks about him or herself, moving next to findings that slightly rearrange the client's perspective, and ending with findings that significantly differ from the client's usual way of thinking about him or herself (Finn, 2007).

In the case of Joy, this translated into structuring the beginning of the feedback with results generated from the patient's responses to direct clinical interview questions and self-report measures. These discussions focused on relatively discrete symptoms and problems in mood, anxiety, and decision making, as well as interpersonal difficulties that were generally consistent with Joy's self-description during the clinical interview. Next, we moved to deepening the discussion of Joy's interpersonal patterns using results from the Early Memory protocol. Based on the discussion that ensued, the session covered a broad range of Joy's functioning. During this segment of the feedback session, the clinician underscored the interrelationship between the various areas as well as the repetitive, cyclical interpersonal patterns that seemed to encapsulate much of the discussion over the assessment sessions and ultimately explored how this pattern may come to include the therapeutic relationship as well.

Collaboratively Develop Individual Treatment Goals

According to this principle, the clinician should work with the patient to generate the desired outcome of the intervention. The latter part of the feedback session with Joy focused on this task. In particular, the clinician came prepared with several potential goals for discussion. Instead of assuming they would be amenable to Joy, the clinician suggested them as possibilities and elicited feedback about them. The following interaction details the clinician's suggestion of a particular goal, the patient's elaboration, and finally the clinician's broadening the patient's statements to suggest a goal with potentially more far-reaching consequences:

C: In addition, it seems we might also increase your understanding of both your professional and life goals. To help you clarify what you want and formulate more clearly where you want to go. Does that make sense as a goal?

J: Yeah, absolutely, and especially that one. You know, I've had self-help books and exercises. Even though that's a good thing, sometimes that can get overwhelming.

C: Like you are trying to do it all.

J: Do it all, and you know it's another chore like a homework assignment. I feel so pressed for time and I don't have the time to do these things. But yet, the thing that can really help me gets shoved off until the end of the day and I don't do it.

C: And I think you are hitting on another important part of that. Increasing the time focused on what it is that you want, what you enjoy or need. Decreasing the things that get in the way and what blocks you from getting what you want. I think that's an equally important part of that particular goal.

J: I totally agree!

The following patient-reported data provided a useful, evidence-based context for contextualizing the impact of Joy's collaborative feedback session. Using the Combined Alliance Short-Form Patient version (CASF-P; Hatcher & Barends, 1996), Joy's overall (Total) alliance score immediately after the collaborative feedback session was 6.7 (out of 7), her agreement on Goals and Tasks score was 7 (out of 7), and her Bond score was 6.6 (out of 7). Likewise, on the Session Evaluation Questionnaire (SEQ; Stiles, 1980), Joy's rating of the feedback session using the 7-value bipolar item describing the session as bad (score of 1) through good (score of 7) was a 7. Her Depth Index score on the SEQ was a 7 (out of 7). Overall, then, these results empirically demonstrate that the therapeutic assessment, and specifically the collaborative feedback session, was a particularly positive experience for Joy. During this time she developed a strong working alliance with the therapist, and their work in the context of this relationship felt particularly deep, powerful, valuable, full, and special for her (the constituent items of the SEQ Depth scale).

Assessment as a Catalyst for Psychotherapy

Following the assessment, the therapist and patient began formal therapy with once-weekly individual sessions. The beginning of treatment focused on helping Joy adjust to the loss of her partner and exploring repetitive relational patterns that continued to impact her. Specifically, the therapist and patient focused on the CCRT, which they had initially reviewed during the assessment, and which they continued to revisit as they explored additional relational episodes: Joy's wish to be able to trust others and open herself up emotionally met with significant opposition from her fears that others will respond in a rejecting and critical manner.

As a result, she withdrew from the relationship to protect herself, while feeling hurt and disappointed. Joy engaged actively in this exploration and demonstrated motivation to actualize her wish by discussing for the first time her sexual orientation with her mother. Joy noted that her mother was generally receptive to this discussion, despite Joy's fears to the contrary. Nevertheless, her mother seemed to shift soon thereafter to an attitude that was quite critical of lesbian relationships. This shift, and its impact on Joy, was then explored in the treatment. Around the same time, she took on a new part-time job in order to prepare herself financially for the career change she had expressed interest in when starting treatment. Joy eventually quit this part-time job and began making the career changes she wanted. During this time, treatment focused on helping her adjust to these changes, understanding their impact on her, and increasing her understanding of relational patterns that continued both at her new job and in the therapeutic relationship.

Early in treatment, Joy reported feeling increasingly depressed, overwhelmed, and anxious related to two particular events. First, Joy began attending a seminar to aid her in her career shift. The increased time demands and pressures added to her feelings of stress. In addition, participating in an academic environment stimulated some fears and concerns that she reported experiencing when she was previously in school. Treatment focused on helping her connect her emotional experience to relevant stressors, their personal meaning for her, and exploring potential solutions. The second incident was a family gathering that Joy attended. At this party, both her sister and cousin attended together with their respective, relatively new romantic partners. This augmented Joy's feelings of loneliness and isolation. Treatment explored the connection between this incident, its personal relevance to the patient, and her subsequent reaction.

As treatment continued, the therapist and Joy focused on changes Joy began to make professionally and the connections with many of the previously discussed relational themes. The sessions also focused on Joy's relationship with her mother, her desire for increased honesty and communication with her mother about her sexuality, effective expression of her frustration and hurt regarding her mother's criticisms, and the difficulties Joy envisioned in working toward those goals. Finally, treatment focused on the process of termination, how that process impacted Joy emotionally and behaviorally, as well as reviewing and consolidating the work that Joy had done in the sessions. At the final session, Joy expressed how grateful she felt for the space and time to explore and understand herself in a meaningful way; the positive and trusting relationship she had developed with a male figure (the therapist); and the significance of the attention paid to understanding, validating, and actualizing her needs and wishes. Joy became tearful as she talked about these feelings and their meaning for her. This was a poignant moment for both Joy and her therapist, particularly given Joy's past struggles with feelings of closeness and intimacy in relationships.

When Joy completed the treatment after approximately eight months, she met only a single criterion for a major depressive episode, and she no longer met criteria for dysthymic disorder, a clinically significant change. Her BSI scores were significantly lower than at assessment, with an Obsessive-Compulsive T-score of 61 (compared to 78 at assessment), a Psychoticism T-score of 58 (compared to 78 at assessment), an Interpersonal-Sensitivity T-score of 63 (compared to 71 at assessment), a Depression T-score of 57 (compared to 71 at assessment), and an Anxiety T-score of 52 (compared to 69 at assessment). Because T-scores have a standard deviation of 10, we can easily calculate a standardized difference score (d) to quantify the magnitude of change: For the Obsessive-Compulsive scale, $d = 1.7$; for the Psychoticism scale, $d = 2.0$; for the Interpersonal-Sensitivity scale, $d = 0.80$; for the Depression scale, $d = 1.4$; and for the Anxiety scale, $d = 1.7$. Using benchmarks provided by Cohen (1988), these effect sizes are all considered large, with most of them indicating a degree of change in excess of a full standard deviation.

Data from Joy's IIP completed at the end of treatment demonstrated a similar pattern of change: her T-score on the Nonassertive scale was 67 (compared to 77 at assessment; $d = 1.0$), her T-score on the Socially Inhibited scale was 56 (compared to 67 at assessment; $d = 1.1$), and her T-score on the Cold/Distant scale was 54 (compared to 67 at assessment; $d = 1.3$). All of these effect sizes are considered large, with each demonstrating a degree of change equal to, or in excess of, a full standard deviation.

Joy also completed the Patient's Estimate of Improvement (PEI; Hatcher & Barends, 1996). When asked about the helpfulness of therapy, Joy rated it as "9" (out of 9), indicating it was "very helpful." Joy indicated that she was "very much better" (a 9 out of 9) compared to when she began therapy; her original complaints or problems improved "very much" (a 7 out of 7); her feelings about herself "changed a great deal for the better" (a 9 out of 9); and her behavior "changed a great deal for the better" (a 9 out of 9) as a result of therapy. Finally, her overall alliance ratings on the CASF-P near the end of treatment yielded a 6.8 out of 7.

Taken together, these data suggest that Joy developed an initially strong alliance during her therapeutic assessment, which she experienced as deep and meaningful. Joy demonstrated robust improvement across many different symptom and interpersonal areas, and she found her treatment to be very productive, helpful in changing how she feels about herself, and, perhaps particularly salient, very useful in achieving positive change in the initial target complaints and symptoms. The usefulness of the therapeutic assessment appeared to reflect the impact of two related processes: (1) Joy developed a positive therapeutic alliance that laid the foundation for a strong relationship to continue during treatment (Hilsenroth, Peters, & Ackerman, 2004) and (2) the clinician and Joy developed a focus on identifying, exploring, and understanding her presenting problems in the context of her relationship patterns and history, a focus that continued to reap benefits throughout treatment. These gains initiated during the therapeutic assessment paved the way for a particularly rewarding, helpful, and meaningful treatment, which facilitated Joy's achievement of significant improvement in her target complaints, her mood, her interpersonal functioning, and her sense of self. Although the loss of a love relationship initially compelled Joy to seek therapy, the labor needed to lift her depression and create a more connected and fulfilled life involved finding a way to more authentically cultivate a love of herself.

REFERENCES

American Psychiatric Association. (2000). *Diagnostic and statistical manual of mental disorders* (4th ed., text revision). Washington, DC: Author.

Book, H. (1998). *How to practice brief psychodynamic psychotherapy: The core conflictual relationship theme method.* Washington, DC: American Psychological Association.

Cohen, J. (1988). *Statistical power analysis for the behavioral sciences* (2nd ed.). Hillsdale, NJ: Erlbaum.

Derogatis, L. (1993). *Brief symptom inventory.* Minneapolis, MN: NCS Pearson.

Finn, S. E. (2007). *In our clients' shoes: Theory and techniques of therapeutic assessment.* Mahwah, NJ: Erlbaum.

Finn, S. E., & Tonsager, M. E. (1997). Information-gathering and therapeutic models of assessment: Complementary paradigms. *Psychological Assessment, 9*, 374–385.

Fischer, C. (1994). *Individualized psychological assessment.* Hillsdale, NJ: Erlbaum.

Fowler, C., Hilsenroth, M. J., & Handler, L. (1995). Early memories: An exploration of theoretically derived queries and their clinical utility. *Bulletin of the Menninger Clinic, 59*, 31–52.

Hatcher, R., & Barends, A. (1996). Patients' view of the alliance in psychotherapy: Exploratory factor analysis of three alliance measures. *Journal of Consulting and Clinical Psychology, 64*, 1326–1336.

Hilsenroth, M. (2007). A programmatic study of short-term psychodynamic psychotherapy: Assessment, process, outcome, and training. *Psychotherapy Research, 17*, 31–45. doi:10.1080/10503300600953504.

Hilsenroth, M. J., & Cromer, T. D. (2007). Clinician interventions related to alliance during the initial interview and psychological assessment. *Psychotherapy: Theory, Research, Practice, and Training, 44*, 205–218.

Hilsenroth, M., Peters, E., & Ackerman, S. (2004). The development of therapeutic alliance during psychological assessment: Patient and therapist perspectives across treatment. *Journal of Personality Assessment, 83*, 332–344. doi:10.1207/s15327752jpa8303_14.

Horowitz, L. M., Alden, L. E., Wiggins, J. S., & Pincus, A. L. (2000). IIP: Inventory of Interpersonal Problems manual. San Antonio, TX: The Psychological Corporation.

Luborsky, L. (1984). *Principles of psychoanalytic psychotherapy: A manual for supportive/expressive treatment.* New York, NY: Basic Books.

Luborsky, L., & Crits-Christoph, P. (1997). *Understanding transference: The core conflictual relational theme method* (2nd ed.). Washington, DC: American Psychological Association.

Mayman, M. (1968). Early memories and character structure. *Journal of Projective Techniques and Personality Assessment, 32*, 302–316.

Morey, L. (1991). *The personality assessment inventory.* Odessa, FL: Psychological Assessment Resources.

Stiles, W. B. (1980). Measurement of the impact of psychotherapy sessions. *Journal of Consulting and Clinical Psychology, 48*, 176–185.

CHAPTER

4

Collaboration in
Neuropsychological
Assessment: Metaphor
as Intervention With
a Suicidal Adult

DIANE H. ENGELMAN AND J. B. ALLYN

The wounded child inside "Jackie" still saw herself as "bad," even though she was now 30 years old. Unmarried and well-educated, she had lived and worked overseas with little social or professional success. On her latest extended stay abroad, her disorganized work efforts triggered dramatic rejection by clients and coworkers. Fired for incompetency, she saw this as the latest in a string of relationship, academic, and work failures. Finally, she attempted suicide by taking pills and then slitting her wrists. When she did not succeed, she attributed it to again being "disorganized" and felt even more incompetent.

REFERRAL AND CONTEXT

Back in the United States, Jackie continued struggling to find direction for her life. Her therapist referred her for a neuropsychological assessment, seeking insight about Jackie's suicide attempt and her cognitive functioning. Because Jackie was obviously intelligent, her therapist wondered if ADHD or learning disabilities might explain her problems with both school and work.

The most significant issue in Jackie's background was her very difficult relationship with her mother, whom she described as having bipolar disorder. "I don't talk to my mom," she said, and then gave examples of her mother's behavior:

> When I was trying to learn long division in school, she screamed at me. Even now, I have trouble understanding math concepts or making change. Then, during college, I took a sabbatical. While I was gone, she wrote to the school, giving them a list of strange reasons why they should expel me. I guess when she attacked me, I felt I deserved it. Deep-down, I know I'm bad.

Jackie's father had not always been available to run interference for her, since his work frequently took him from home. He admitted that during Jackie's childhood he had abandoned and neglected her because he, too, was afraid of his ex-wife's (Jackie's mother's) rages. He also mentioned additional abusive actions his daughter had experienced at the hands of her mother, which Jackie herself had not mentioned in interviews.

Jackie asked three specific questions of the evaluation. About cognition, she asked, "Why am I so stupid? I can't remember directions or locations, like where I parked my car. I book reservations to the wrong airport. I look up a word five times and still don't remember what it means." Concerning personality, she wondered why she had such strong self-loathing, even while recognizing evidence to the contrary. "I must really feel stupid and hate myself to attempt suicide." Her third question focused on intimacy: "Why do I sabotage every relationship?" All of these questions were essential, historically loaded artifacts of the "old story" she had lived within all her life.

"The goal of therapeutic assessment is not just the collection of information *about* a patient/client, but rather, the assessment procedure itself is designed to be transformative" (Handler, 2007, p. 53). To encourage such transformation for Jackie, collaboration would be essential in gathering the details of her old story and making sense of them. She provided the bulk of the information, through interview, tests, and tasks, but critical pieces also emerged from interviews with her father and therapist. Later, a metaphorical story, written collaboratively by the assessor (Engelman) and a creative writer (coauthor Allyn), contributed another opening for understanding and interpreting Jackie's life experience. Facts, impressions, data, and metaphor combined to help us work toward changing Jackie's life story and redrawing the map of her life.

ASSESSMENT PROCESS

Dynamic Flow of Sessions

Each assessment is as unique as the individual client, whether conducting a complete neuropsychological evaluation or personality assessment alone. However, the sessions flow in a similar pattern, as follows:

1. *Initial Phone Contact* usually entails one or two calls. In Jackie's case, I (Engelman) spoke separately by phone with her and her therapist.

Teaching Point

An adult client who faced rejecting, frightening maternal behavior for many years will likely carry unresolved attachment issues. Comments and questions from Jackie's referring psychologist indicated that Jackie felt a lack of safety due to problematic attachment. To provide as much safety as possible throughout the assessment process, I carefully crafted word choice and order of testing and interventions.

2. *Gathering History* involves one or two sessions with the client and/or significant others. I interviewed Jackie, her father, and her therapist, individually.

Teaching Point

Based on longevity alone, an adult client will likely bring a more complicated biopsychosocial life history to the assessment. With a client such as Jackie, the complexity increases. I didn't know where I might find sensitive material and so proceeded carefully. Empathy and awareness established early in the process help avoid missteps.

3. *Administering Tests* generally requires several meetings for tasks, tests, and answering questionnaires. These meetings may be as few as two and as many as 12. Jackie completed the assessment in a month, meeting once a week for three hours each time.
4. *Presentation of Findings and Discussion* takes place in one or two sessions. Jackie and I met for one extensive session to discuss findings.
5. *Intervention* also requires one or two long sessions. For Jackie, two intervention sessions took place, one including her therapist.

I worked collaboratively with Jackie throughout the assessment, inviting her thoughts and feelings about the measures and process. I looked for signs of anxiety, upset, comfort, or pride. For example, following the Wechsler Abbreviated Scale of Intelligence (WASI; Psychological Corporation, 1999), Jackie beamed. Without being told so, she "knew that she knew" the answers, a significant issue given her concern about being stupid.

Teaching Point

Neuropsychological tests, tasks, and questionnaires are extensive and administered over a few to many weeks. With Jackie, who had recently attempted suicide, administering personality measures was a necessary first step in the neuropsychological evaluation. This step gave a snapshot of symptoms of depression and allowed me to screen for suicide ideation and lethality.

During many assessments, I may discuss findings throughout the sessions. In Jackie's case, however, her attempted suicide remained ever-present in the room during testing. On the Sentence Completion Series (Brown & Unger, 1992), she wrote, "Sometimes I wish *that I had succeeded in committing suicide*." Such signals alerted me and so, as a precaution, I carefully scored and integrated data from many of the measures before sharing with her what they might imply. Two other areas influenced my decision to discuss topics only briefly as we went along: (1) For accuracy, neuropsychological evaluation requires analyzing levels and patterns of performance as well as examining any signs that characterize a specific disease (Koziol & Budding, 2009); and (2) Jackie's vulnerability about her intelligence dictated that I have a sense of what *all* the findings suggested before sharing them. The decision to share less data with Jackie during the assessment required other methods of establishing essential connection with her. When she struggled with any measure, I reminded her that it was only one clue to her strengths and challenges, and I used self-examples of areas in which I perform less well. I also mentioned the concept of neurodiversity (Blume, 1998), which emphasizes the essential uniqueness of each person's brain due to both "hard-wiring" and environmental factors. These steps reduced her test-taking anxiety and encouraged a successful outcome of the collaborative/therapeutic process.

Teaching Point

Limiting immediate feedback/discussion is sensible in some situations and may be necessary with a client such as Jackie who has problematic attachment and a recent suicide attempt. Neuropsychological evaluation, too, demands analysis and integration to understand all its implications. Even in these cases, however, I sensitively explore the client's unique responses during the active phase of data collection.

Test Data

As I select measures for an assessment and make sense of the results with my clients, the following perspectives orient me, time and again: "Life events should be our point of departure into tests, and our point of return" (Fischer, 2000) and "Remember that our test data are our tools, not our findings" (C. T. Fischer, personal communication, July 2008). Because Jackie's questions and difficulties fell into the areas of both cognition and personality, I administered a full flexible neuropsychological battery. Measures in this type of battery cover several domains of brain function: (1) visual-perceptual-spatial; (2) language; (3) attention; (4) learning and memory; (5) executive function; (6) somatosensory; (7) motor; (8) motivational; (9) emotional; (10) social; (11) intelligence; and (12) achievement. To provide comprehensive information on aspects of brain-based functioning that might be implicated in Jackie's problems, each domain needed to be assessed. The 34 measures were the tools to help us toward our findings.

Overall neurocognitive test data suggested her impressive strengths in the areas of verbal intelligence (VIQ = 130; WASI; Psychological Corporation, 1999), academic abilities, and some components of executive function, the loosely defined collection of brain processes that control and manage other cognitive activities. However, relatively mild and subtle cognitive problems also surfaced in the areas of working memory, processing speed, concentration, and attention. Other aspects of executive function also challenged Jackie. These areas included inhibition, emotional control, shifting, initiating, planning and organizing, and monitoring tasks. Despite their subtlety in assessment findings, problems in these areas clearly affected her emotional and cognitive functioning. In comparing her scores with those of her peers, hers were absolutely adequate; but when they were compared to her overall assessment findings, and to reports of past academic strengths and weaknesses, her somewhat illusive brain-based challenges became clearer. These problems alone, however, did not account for Jackie's long-term cognitive difficulties.

In neuropsychological evaluation, one might attempt to draw a clear distinction between "neuro" and "psychology" (personality). However, the root word of *neuropsychology* is, after all, psychology, so personality should not be excised from the equation (A. Purisch, personal communication, March 2006). In Jackie's case, results of the personality measures uncovered areas that complicated her cognitive functioning and could be traced back to her very difficult childhood. Her life events, interviews, the Sentence Completion Series (Brown & Unger, 1991), the Minnesota Multiphasic Personality Inventory–2 (MMPI-2; Butcher, Dahlstrom, Graham, Tellegen, & Kaemmer, 1989), and the Personality Assessment Inventory (PAI; Morey, 1991) all identified problems with anxiety and depression. She was prone to worry, often feeling frustrated, irritated, angry, sad, lonely, and dejected, and she had poorly controlled impulses. The Rorschach (Exner & Erdberg, 2005), too, suggested depression. Morbid responses (4) indicated depressed mood, as reflected in her recent suicide attempt, and three indices were high: (a) the Depression Index (DEPI, 6), suggesting major depression; (b) the Coping Deficit Index (CDI, 4), indicating long-term trouble managing difficult emotions; and (c) the Trauma Index (Kamphuis, Kugeares, & Finn, 2000). Her Trauma Index was very high (.45) and supported by evidence of trauma in other measures, such as life events, interviews, Adult Attachment Projective Picture System (AAP; George & West [in press]), the Early Memories Procedure (EMP; Bruhn, 1989), the Sentence Completion Series, PAI, and MMPI-2. Other critical issues documented during the course of the assessment included overuse of alcohol, identity problems (PAI, Sentence Completion Series, interview), and low self-esteem, with sizable self-doubt (interview, EMP, MMPI-2).

On the EMP, Jackie described a time in her childhood when she had repeatedly lost belongings, and her mother's response was physical assault: "I recall feeling like the beatings would never end. As a child, I was always on alert for the next time my mom would lash out at me. I never felt safe." On the Sentence Completion Series, she wrote, "Our home life *was full of turmoil, anger, and abuse.*" Findings from interview, the Rorschach, and the AAP suggested problems resulting from (a) "early emotional deprivation"; (b) "insecure attachment"; and (c) "unresolved childhood trauma."

The most telling exploration of Jackie's situation came through the AAP. The final picture stimulus shows a line drawing of a child standing in a corner. Jackie's response in the following passage tells a story-within-a-story, laying bare the difficulties she has faced and painting a picture of trauma, abuse, and neglect.

🖎 Teaching Point

Unresolved attachment issues may be powerfully triggered by certain measures. After completing a protocol that brought out strong reactions in Jackie, I asked, "How was that for you?" Ensuing dialogue eased her discomfort, reduced her stress, and enabled us to better connect.

Jackie: Um. It's this kid who, who is *abused* by his mom. And, she's *about to strike him* because he broke a china figurine and so he's *putting his hands up in defense* and he is *afraid*, you know, really *afraid* of his mom's anger 'cause it can really be *out of control* and it seems like this time *it's gonna be really bad* and he's just kind of pleading with her . . . but he knows there's nothing he really can do and she . . . she's just *consumed by rage*, that's all she can feel, that's all she can see . . . she's gonna *beat him* until he's crying and sobbing and then, you know, she'll walk away and he'll slink in his room and just kind of *curl up in his bed and cry* [emphasis added throughout passage].

Results of the entire AAP disclosed the beatings that had emerged in the EMP, the Sentence Completion Series, and in interviews with Jackie and her father. In adulthood, Jackie's troubled relationships still manifested the disorganized attachment reflected in the AAP. Stephen Finn has observed that

> there is growing agreement in our field that early attachment experiences are related to many of the difficulties experienced by our clients and that when these difficulties are understood, they can be effectively addressed in psychotherapy. Many of us believe that the current integration of attachment theory, developmental neurobiology, and psychotherapy represents the cutting edge of clinical practice. (Finn, in press)

In addition to insecure attachment, Jackie's overall assessment results pointed toward (a) early deprivation, neglect, and abuse; (b) strong, unresolved trauma from the beatings; (c) long-standing depression;

(d) brain-based executive function problems; (e) affect management challenges with impulsivity (in part, from subtle executive dysfunction, but also from poor parental guidance); (f) self-image and self-concept organized around self-hatred; very low self-esteem and severe approach-avoidance with others; (g) massive, unresolved anger; (h) many difficult feelings, barely contained; and (i) reliance on alcohol as a way to cope with feelings.

Problems sometimes associated with childhood trauma include cognitive challenges with memory, attention, concentration, and learning (Courtois, Ford, van der Kolk, & Herman, 2009; Teicher et al., 2008). In addition, changes in the brain can occur after many years of depression and contribute to cognitive difficulties (Holtzheimer & Mayberg, 2008; Langenecker, Lee, & Bieliauskas, 2009). Anxiety and depression also add to cognitive deficits in areas such as concentration, attention, and memory (Holtzheimer & Mayberg, 2008; Stein & Rauch, 2008). Jackie showed problems with cognitive efficiency as well as low motivation, both of which are often brain-based, not volitional (Koziol & Budding, 2009).

I found several concerning areas in Jackie's personality functioning related to childhood trauma: (a) Hated by a parent, Jackie couldn't know it was her mother who had the problems; she decided that she herself was despicable, which led to long-term self-loathing; (b) with unresolved anger, she had cut off relations with her mother and never confronted her father for not protecting her; (c) low frustration-tolerance and reliance on alcohol both challenged her ability to cope with feelings; (d) assessment findings suggested that she, like many abused children, used dissociation as a defense mechanism to survive emotionally when she was abused (Dell & O'Neil, 2009); (e) her high Trauma Content Index on the Rorschach and multiple other measures pointed to major depression, alcohol overuse, and poor impulse control; (f) suicide remained an ongoing concern; and (g) under the influence of alcohol, Jackie was especially disinhibited and likely to show poor judgment or behavior.

SUMMARIZING WITH THE CLIENT

Before meeting with Jackie posttesting, I compared, contrasted, and looked for patterns in the data. I would explain those patterns to her in the sessions to follow, and we would jointly discuss what they might mean in the context of her life events and preassessment questions. The full range of measures would help me give Jackie insight into why she might have mild cognitive problems. However, because personality issues had emerged as central to the results, the order in which we discussed assessment findings and meanings would be critical. Ranking the findings by level, as follows, allows me to present them in a way that clients can best hear, integrate, and use:

- Level One findings coincide with the client's self-view.
- Level Two results modify the client's self-perception, but are not likely to threaten it.
- Level Three represents findings so different from a person's usual way of thinking about herself that she may reject them out of hand. (Finn, 2007, pp. 8–10)

Issues of Jackie's extensive family trauma comprised levels one and two and needed to be addressed first. Only then might she hear the level-three information explaining the disparity between her assets (high verbal IQ, academic strengths, and aspects of executive functioning) and her cognitive problems.

Teaching Point

Because adults bring a long history to an assessment, they will likely have ingrained beliefs about themselves and the life story they have lived. Honoring and understanding Jackie's uniqueness helped me to select the best order for feedback/discussion of findings.

I met with Jackie three times to go over findings and integrate them with her life events, questions, and concerns: (1) For the *Presentation of Findings and Discussion*, I met with Jackie alone. While addressing all results to a certain extent, we dealt primarily with attachment issues and explored the metaphor of a roadmap in making life changes; (2) the *First Intervention* session included Jackie and her therapist. I spoke with the therapist in advance, sharing with her the findings I had discussed and processed with Jackie. We then collaborated on the further meaning of results and agreed to use a therapeutic story as intervention. The metaphorical story reflected Jackie's interests and background and could open a discussion about changing her life story; (3) for the *Second Intervention* session, Jackie and I met to discuss career issues, with the Strong Interest Inventory (Harmon, Hansen, Borgen, & Hammer, 1985) as intervention; once more, we used the roadmap as a metaphor for change.

Presentation of Findings and Discussion: Attachment and Intelligence

Jackie and I met about one month after completing the assessment. She sought an overview to quickly allay anxiety, as do many clients when faced with a long discussion session. After I gave her a summary of results, we went through the findings, test by test, discussing her reactions to the findings and their meanings. I asked if she perceived any errors, if she felt that I or the testing process had wrongly depicted her, her life, or her performance. What new ideas might she have? What did she find true, clear, helpful, or confusing? How did she make sense of the data? Did she feel some results were based on her being tired or having a bad day? I looked for specific reactions and questions. This intervention individualized the findings and encouraged her to think and process and to feel valued for her ideas and opinions.

After looking at the data, we moved to the questions posed before the assessment began. I asked her to answer those questions with me—with the emphasis on *with*. I oriented this discussion around the psychological findings before attempting to talk about her cognitive issues or intelligence. Her questions about intimacy and sabotaging relationships provided context for discussing the multiple measures that indicated abuse. The AAP picture stimulus showing the child in the corner formed the foundation of our discussion. I showed her that card, and others indicating abuse, and then read aloud her responses to these cards. We discussed how and why these issues might continue to affect her life and relationships. She seemed very surprised that the family-of-origin and attachment issues had emerged so clearly and powerfully in her assessment and that they could still be affecting her. We talked about how people can be unaware of the roadmap they use in living out their life story and how an old story can be changed to a new and evolving one. We discussed the impact of her mother's bipolar disorder on her mother, the family, and Jackie. Though Jackie showed no signs of bipolar disorder, we discussed genetic risk factors for this medical condition and the need for reevaluation should symptoms arise.

We were mutually respectful of each others' ideas and perceptions and wove shared and different views into a meaningful discussion of assessment findings. Depression contributed to her thoughts of personal failure, hopelessness, and worthlessness, so I was challenged to balance corrective statements about her strengths with what I saw as a realistic view of her problems. Perhaps the major task of the assessment became changing her belief in the childhood story of her own "badness" and her mother's "goodness." Through this story, Jackie had attempted to protect her mother, and herself, from the awful truth about her mother's abusive parenting. To spare herself the grief of knowing, Jackie had carefully created self-hatred while she was very young. I hoped the evaluation would help her to find her way out of it and would provide her and her therapist with more direction. She seemed disoriented by the notion that her story was outdated, no longer necessary, and certainly not accurate. Changing such a powerful self-story *can* be disorienting. But she also began to show signs of guarded hope in subtle, quasi-optimistic comments about developing more intimate and longer-lasting relationships.

Teaching Point

When a client such as Jackie has unresolved attachment issues, an insensitive approach to sharing data can upend her life story and negatively affect her fragile sense of self. I individualized the method of sharing data to speak to her current situation but also to provide a bridge into a healthier one.

I could see that Jackie had started to recognize intelligence as only one of the factors that might influence her struggles with work and school. With that beginning, we moved on to talk about her concern that she was "stupid." We discussed different kinds of intelligence, memory, the ability to concentrate and learn, and areas that seemed to block her from doing as well as she wished. Neuropsychological testing had revealed her verbal IQ of 130 and other strengths; however, it also uncovered mild cognitive challenges and problems with attention, though these difficulties could be addressed by referral to appropriate professionals. I also mentioned ways of working with her unique neuropsychological makeup. Suggestions included choosing a career that used the strengths of her own neurodiversity and getting help with problems, if need be.

The Therapeutic Letter: Data Plus Metaphor

Research indicates that receiving both written and verbal feedback on assessment findings strengthens and reinforces a client's understanding and acceptance of the data. This acceptance enhances the positive outcome of collaborative/therapeutic assessment (Lance & Krishnamurthy, 2003). Before the discussion of findings with Jackie, I drafted a report addressing her questions and the data. Afterward, I incorporated her perspective, finalized my interpretations and recommendations, and mailed it to her. It was not a traditional report, but a personal letter using words and images I felt would connect with her. I did not include complete data in the letter, but instead, attached that information as an addendum.

For the most part, the letter conveyed information in a straightforward, though sensitive, style, but I also made judicious use of metaphor. From a neuropsychological perspective, metaphor can be an important means of understanding and assimilating information. Each hemisphere of the brain, while always working interactively with the rest of the brain, has a different style of processing information. The left hemisphere is partially devoted to logical operations and creating language. The right side uses imagistic aspects of metaphor and symbolism that can facilitate rapid and effective information processing. Metaphor integrates ". . . the ikonic mode of the right hemisphere and the linguistic mode of the left" (Cox & Theilgaard, 1987, p. xxvii) and can, therefore, be an important vehicle for therapeutic communication. Early in Jackie's letter, I said, "I think of an assessment letter as a kind of 'roadmap.' Choose the neuropsychological destination that most interests you, and then use parts of this map to find routes to that destination." Toward the end of the letter, I revisited the metaphor. "I have clarified potential destinations and routes in your neuropsychological roadmap based on your questions and assessment findings. As coauthor in the creation of the map, I hope you will continue to refine it."

Jackie had seemed to gain some insight from the Discussion of Findings session, and I believed the letter would add more understanding. However, I felt more could be done. I phoned her to arrange the appointment with her therapist and me, in which we would use the therapeutic story as intervention. Jackie said she had received the letter but was afraid to read it and didn't know why. I asked if she would like to come into the office and read it *with* me. She said no, that she would read the letter alone before our meeting. But, in the two weeks before we met, she did not read it. She was still frightened. This response was not strange, when you consider that the assessment findings and letter threw into disarray the story Jackie had enacted since she was very young. Psychotherapy has been called "a process of telling and retelling of stories" (Dwivedi & Gardner, 1997, p. 33). Giving up her old story would be very difficult, emotionally arduous, and a process, not an event.

Teaching Point

When discussing findings with a suicidal adult who has unresolved attachment issues, I remain flexible and positively responsive. If the client commits to an action such as reading a report but does not follow through, he or she may fear my reaction. I avoid words or actions that indicate "failure" to the client or, as in Jackie's case, may suggest the frightening maternal figure.

The Therapeutic Story: An Allegory of Jackie's Life

In collaborative/therapeutic neuropsychological assessment, metaphorical stories provide a significant tool. They can translate findings, convey mental health and/or cognitive messages, and encourage growth. Traditionally, metaphor was viewed as an unessential figure of speech, not seen as a part of everyday language. In that traditional usage, a word or phrase ordinarily used to describe one thing was directly applied to another only for special effect (Kövecses, 2002, pp. vii–viii).

Cognitive-linguistic work of the past three decades, however, has emphasized metaphor's place in thought, action, and everyday language, as well as its role in helping people better understand certain concepts. "Metaphors as linguistic expressions are possible precisely because there are metaphors in a person's conceptual system" (Lakoff & Johnson, 1980, pp. 3–6). In using metaphor, we engage the entire human communications system, not merely the language process.

While also writing stories for children, my coauthor (Allyn) and I focus mainly on adults and teens. A story-loving child lives inside most people, and as more than one adult has said, "Who wouldn't want their own story?" Story provides an accessible form of communication and, perhaps, explains the use of allegory in many cultures. In cultural usage, allegorical stories teach or explain ideas, giving people, things, and happenings hidden or symbolic meanings.

Three sets of skills create a story with impact: (1) choose two or three critical mental health and/or cognitive messages to embed in the story (more can overwhelm the reader); (2) select significant metaphors/metaphorical concepts from the person's life, interests, and/or imagery from testing; and (3) frame the story and messages in the precise words that will carry meaning to the individual receiving them. In our collaborative writing partnership, I select the messages and flag any assessment imagery that might be useful. Allyn finds additional detail in a personal-interests questionnaire filled out by the client, and then we discuss those in the context of story ideas. Once we have defined a general approach and specific message components, she weaves fact and metaphor into a creative allegory of the person's life.

Jackie had written on the personal-interests questionnaire, "I really love the theatre!" so we set her story in a theatre, with the main action occurring on the stage. A young woman, representing Jackie at her present age (30), enters an empty theatre with house lights dimmed.

> The young woman moves quickly down the center aisle and slips into a seat a few rows back from the stage. On stage is a two-character tableau, softly-lit and frozen in place: a girl of about eight sits drawing at one end of a long, wooden kitchen table; at the other end, the girl's grandmother bends over the

table, in the process of kneading dough. As the young woman sits, stage lights brighten and the scene comes to life.

Dialogue gives form to 8-year-old Jackie, who blamed herself for her mother's abuse:

Grandmother:	You're quiet today. Did something bad happen at school?
Girl:	Nothing bad happened at school—but I'm a bad person.
Grandmother:	What are you talking about? You're a sweet, kind, smart child!
Girl:	I'm stupid and bad. I make people angry at me. I should be ashamed of myself.

The astonished grandmother silently looks to the young woman in the audience, asking for help. The young woman joins them on stage and gives her 8-year-old self the good counsel and support she needed as a child, but never got.

Young Woman:	You feel you're bad because some people get angry with you. And you feel afraid, because you never know when something will make them angry again.
Girl:	Yes. But, if I could not be bad, then my mother wouldn't get angry. She gets so mad—it has to be because I do bad things.
Young Woman:	Your mother has a medical condition—one that causes her to be unpredictable. So she gets mad. You've done nothing wrong, and you are not bad.

The young woman suggests ways the girl can take care of herself and seek support from her father and grandmother. The story ends with the young woman awaking. She remembers all that occurred and resolves to act on the ideas expressed in her dream (Allyn & Engelman, 2007).

The First Intervention: Assessment Findings in Story Form

Messages embedded in Jackie's story addressed her self-concept, as intertwined with the abuse experiences we had discussed in the presentation of findings session. These messages included that (a) she was not stupid, but actually smart; (b) her mother's abuse did not mean Jackie was bad; and (c) she can take action now to change the story she's lived in all her life. Jackie, her therapist, and I met in the therapist's office for the story intervention. Before reading the story, I revisited certain topics from the discussion of findings session: (a) the subtle executive dysfunctions she showed on testing were real but could be addressed; (b) low self-esteem, self-loathing, anxiety, and depression worsened her mild cognitive problems; and (c) family-of-origin and abuse issues contributed to her mood problems and ensuing cognitive worsening.

"To successfully employ [therapeutic assessment] approaches to assessment, the clinician must set aside some of his or her traditional training and instead focus on being more playful and imaginative" (Handler, 2007, p. 58). With that in mind, I suggested we read the story aloud, since it was structured mainly in dialogue. Jackie read the role of the young woman, and her therapist spoke the words of the grandmother. I read narration at the beginning and end as well as the role of the little girl. Jackie remained enthusiastic throughout, becoming involved in the story and the interactions among the characters. Afterward, however, she quickly retreated, again becoming remote and self-protected; I could see that she was not fully processing the story's messages. Creative shifts occur moment-to-moment in an assessment, during testing, interview, phone calls, discussion, and intervention sessions. These shifts stem from nuances as well as from obvious nonverbal and verbal client responses. Jackie's retreat was nonverbal but also not subtle. Because the message of changing her story seemed critical to absorbing and acting on the others, I chose to revisit that idea using a personal experience. I mentioned how my own story had changed and how I found my way into the new story with the help of music.

Self-disclosure and ethical decision making in psychotherapy and assessment are complex. According to Lowman, Jourard, and Jourard (1994), "The therapist's use of self-disclosure demystifies both the therapist and the client. It allows more of the client's essence to come out and allows the interaction to become more of a dialogue" (online summary, par. 4) and "Humanistic psychology is defined in part by an effort of self disclosure that creates conscious awareness by helping ourselves and others come to an understanding of what is going on inside and possibly the forces that cause that" (online summary, par. 5). At this difficult juncture in Jackie's intervention, I chose to self-disclose:

Assessor: Jackie, as you consider how you might change your life story, please know that I understand. I've faced my own version of that scary situation. It's hard to know what to say to yourself, about yourself, if you're not saying the usual, negative things.

Jackie: I know! And it does scare me. It's almost like I don't *have* a self if I'm not hating me, and not having a self is even scarier than hating myself. What did *you* do?

Assessor: After I consciously stopped saying negative things, there was a void for awhile. Finally, I decided to fill the void and my mind with beautiful music. I focused only on the music and the joy it brought me. Eventually, I was able to replace negative thinking with more positive thoughts and with a sense of who I *really* am, not the old outdated story I told myself for so long.

Jackie: I've got to do something to break out of where I am before I can even think about "changing my story," as you put it. Maybe I could try music, too.

Assessor: *(with a smile)* I used Puccini. You can use whatever works for you to stop your negative thoughts—other music, art, reading, exercise, or something else.

Jackie: I love Puccini!

After this session, Jackie read the letter that had previously frightened her and began working with it in therapy sessions.

The Second Intervention: Career Decisions

Tentatively, Jackie began to embrace the idea that her cognitive and psychological difficulties could be dealt with and that change was possible. Because her career had been a major area of perceived failure, we set another appointment to discuss vocational planning. I framed our discussion around a thorough exploration of the Strong Interest Inventory (Harmon et al., 1985), integrated with other pertinent assessment findings. We had touched on these results in the initial discussion of findings session, though not at length, because personality and cognitive issues took precedence at that point. At this later meeting, we talked about Jackie's intelligence and passions and brainstormed about future career options. She felt despondent at being 30 years old and not "anything" yet. As had happened often in her life, she felt like a failure, this time because she was still casting around for a career to settle into. I told her that it was common for people her age to consider and reconsider career goals. I also said that vocations evolve during a lifetime, to fit ever-changing growth and desires, and that she was now in a perfect position to move forward with thoughtful career planning. My reframe of her negative self-view to one of normality decreased her statements of self-loathing. She expressed relief that others her age might not be totally settled on careers. I then offered to find her a vocational counselor. She readily accepted and engaged actively in the ensuing discussion.

CONCLUSION

Impact on the Client

Jackie and her therapist now meet three times a week instead of one. Jackie has earnestly discussed self-loathing and eliminating negative self-talk. She began to fill the void with positive self-talk and to embrace the possibility of a transformed, healthy self. In many assessment cases, I may hear little from a client once the assessment process has been completed. In Jackie's case, however, I have had ongoing contact. She requested, with her therapist's approval, that I undertake her therapy sessions when the therapist is out of town. Jackie said she felt helped by the assessment and would like to work more with me on assessment issues; she also said that the idea of working with me made her feel safe about her therapist going away. For two years now, I have met with her for a few sessions a year, most recently working further with career issues. She has worked successfully at the same job for three years and recently applied to graduate school. She is currently in a relationship that brings her joy. While she is tentative and fearful of long-term commitment, her therapist supports her as she moves forward with mini-steps toward healthy intimacy. She is no longer clinically depressed.

Impact on the Writer and Assessor: Collaboration and Self-Disclosure

Writer (Allyn): After writing this or any of our stories, I feel amazed by the extent to which collaboration can occur with one degree of separation. I never meet the clients for whom we write these allegories; and yet, through trust and collaboration with the assessor, a story evolves that can speak to the person. The other significant collaborator, of course, *is* the client. The more thoroughly he or she discloses with the assessor during the entire evaluation, the more detail becomes available. Coupled with the findings, these details infuse the story with the person's external and internal qualities. When the pieces come together, a story emerges that speaks to a client on one or more levels. In the earliest days of our stories, we may have expected them to be a zero-sum option—either helping 100% or a "failure." However, over time, they have evolved as one ingredient in the collaborative/therapeutic mix—an important one but seldom standing alone.

Assessor (Engelman): I felt conflicted about sharing personal information with Jackie, but I had travelled some of the same roads she was now on and felt my story might give insight and offer support. Deciding to self-disclose was a thoughtful, careful choice and one that worked out well, in that it has seemed helpful for Jackie. I became more comfortable with judicious self-disclosure in assessment. I appreciate the complexity of this assessment and that we were dealing not only with personality issues but also cognitive ones. I worked carefully to order the findings, so they could be received with as much openness as possible. Being able to discern which issues were levels one, two, and three made a huge difference in supporting Jackie overall. Finally, I feel that I can't remind myself too often that assessment measures are tools, not findings, and that life events are a primary avenue toward meaning in collaborative/therapeutic assessments.

No one intervention can be singled out as the source of Jackie's growth. The personal story about music and the reframe about career seemed to jump-start her understanding; however, they stood on the shoulders of the earlier collaborative/therapeutic endeavors. The entire assessment process, from interview onward, through testing, discussions, and interventions, including the therapeutic letter and story, laid the groundwork for her awakenings and for her transformation.

REFERENCES

Allyn, J. B., & Engelman, D. H. (2007). A story for "Jackie." Unpublished therapeutic story.

Blume, H. (1998, Sept. 30). Neurodiversity. The Atlantic. Retrieved from www .theatlantic.com/magazine/archive/1998/09/neurodiversity/5909/

Brown, L. H., & Unger, M. A. (1992). Sentence Completion Series. Lutz, FL: Psychological Assessment Resources.

Bruhn, A. R. (1989). The Early Memories Procedure. Bethesda, MD: Arnold R. Bruhn.

Butcher, J. N., Dahlstrom, W. G., Graham, J. R., Tellegen, A., & Kaemmer, B. (1989). Minnesota Multiphasic Personality Inventory-2 (MMPI-2): Manual for administration and scoring. Minneapolis: University of Minnesota Press.

Courtois, C. A., Ford, J. D., van der Kolk, B. A., & Herman, J. L. (2009). Treating complex traumatic stress disorders: An evidence-based guide. New York, NY: Guilford Press.

Cox, M., & Theilgaard, A. (1987). Mutative metaphors in psychotherapy: The aeolian mode. London, England: Tavistock Publications.

Dell, P. F., & O'Neil, J. (Eds.). (2009). Dissociation and the dissociative disorders: DSM-V and beyond. New York, NY: Routledge.

Dwivedi, K. N., & Gardner, D. (1997). Theoretical perspectives and clinical approaches. In K. N. Dwivedi (Ed.), The therapeutic use of stories (pp. 19–41). London, England: Routledge.

Exner, J. E., & Erdberg, S. P. (2005). The Rorschach, advanced interpretation. Hoboken, NJ: Wiley.

Finn, S. E. (2007). In our clients' shoes: Theory and techniques of therapeutic assessment. Mahwah, NJ: Erlbaum.

Finn, S. E. (in press). Use of the adult attachment projective picture system (AAP) in the middle of a long-term psychotherapy. Journal of Personality Assessment.

Fischer, C. T. (2000). Collaborative, individualized assessment. Journal of Personality Assessment, 74, 2–14.

George, C., & West, M. (in press). The Adult Attachment Projective Picture System. New York, NY: Guilford Press.

Handler, L. (2007). The use of therapeutic assessment with children and adolescents. In S. R. Smith & L. Handler (Eds.), *The clinical assessment of children and adolescents: A practitioner's handbook* (pp. 53–72). New York, NY: Psychology Press.

Harmon, L. W., Hansen, J., Borgen, F., & Hammer, A. (1985). *Strong Interest Inventory: Applications and technical guide.* Stanford, CA: Stanford University Press.

Holtzheimer, P. E. III, & Mayberg, H. S. (2008). Neuropsychiatric aspects of mood disorders. In S. C. Yudofsky & R. E. Hales (Eds.), *The American Psychiatric Publishing textbook of neuropsychiatry and behavioral neurosciences* (pp. 1003–1024). Washington, DC: American Psychiatric Publishing.

Kamphuis, J. H., Kugeares, S. L., & Finn, S. E. (2000). Rorschach correlates of sexual abuse: Trauma content and aggression indexes. *Journal of Personality Assessment, 75*(2), 212–224.

Kövecses, Z. (2002). *Metaphor: A practical introduction.* New York, NY: Oxford University Press.

Koziol, L. F., & Budding, D. E. (2009). *Subcortical structures and cognition: Implications for neuropsychological assessment.* New York, NY: Springer Science.

Lakoff, G., & Johnson, M. (1980). *Metaphors we live by.* Chicago, IL: University of Chicago Press.

Lance, B. R., & Krishnamurthy, R. (2003, March). *A comparison of three modes of MMPI-2 test feedback.* Paper presented at the annual meeting of the Society for Personality Assessment, San Francisco, CA.

Langenecker, S. A., Lee, H. J., & Bieliauskas, L. A. (2009). Neuropsychology of depression and related mood disorders. In I. Grant & K. M. Adams (Eds.), *Neuropsychological assessment of neuropsychiatric and neuromedical disorders* (3rd ed., pp. 523–559). New York, NY: Oxford University Press.

Lowman, M., Jourard, A., & Jourard, M. (1994). *Sidney M. Jourard, selected writings.* Marina Del Rey: Round Right Press. Summary of central ideas, prepared by Sonoma State University Psychology 307 students groups (Fall 2000). Retrieved from www.sonoma/edu/users/d/daniels/jourardsummary.html

Morey, L. C. (1991). *Personality Assessment Inventory professional manual.* Lutz, FL: Psychological Assessment Resources.

Psychological Corporation (The). (1999). *Wechsler Abbreviated Scale of Intelligence manual.* San Antonio, TX: Author.

Stein, D. J., & Rauch, S. L. (2008). Neuropsychiatric aspects of anxiety disorders. In S. C. Yudofsky & R. E. Hales (Eds.), *The American Psychiatric Publishing textbook of neuropsychiatry and behavioral neurosciences* (pp. 1025–1045). Washington, DC: American Psychiatric Publishing.

Teicher, M. H., Andersen, S. L., Navalta, C. P., Tomoda, A., Polcari, A., & Kim, D. (2008). Neuropsychiatric disorders of childhood and adolescence. In S. C. Yudofsky & R. E. Hales (Eds.), *The American Psychiatric Publishing textbook of neuropsychiatry and behavioral neurosciences* (pp. 1045–1113). Washington, DC: American Psychiatric Publishing.

CHAPTER

5

—⟫⋅⟨—

Collaboration Throughout the Assessment: A Young Man in Transition

Constance T. Fischer

Many psychologists prefer to complete their gathering of test data before discussing their impressions with the client. In contrast, I usually collaborate with the client *throughout* the assessment sessions, both of us revising and adding to our earlier understandings as we consider data from additional tests. We also continuously develop and revise our earlier ideas about alternative concrete ways in which the client could take up previously problematic situations. For me this joint discussion of impressions from early tests provides a framework for understanding later test data. This approach keeps both of us closely in touch with the client's actual life and encourages the client to participate actively. The process is itself therapeutic, aside from the development of concrete suggestions. Clients feel genuinely respected and progressively understood. They experience themselves as agents, and they are eager to try out in life what they have learned. When clients find early on that they are not being classified and explained, but that both persons are working together to understand, clients participate actively. This approach is described in my book, *Individualizing Psychological Assessment* (1985/1994; a second edition is in press). For an article, see, for example, Fischer, 2000.

JIM MANKINS

I had mentioned to a friend that I was hoping to receive an assessment referral of a person who would be willing for the assessment to be filmed and for segments to be shown in psychology graduate courses and professional workshops. My friend called shortly afterward to say that a coworker was eager to participate if I could schedule sessions soon, because he had to report to Officers' Candidate School (OCS) in 10 days. [OCS is a rigorous training program through which enlisted persons can become officers.] My friend mentioned that he anticipated that the assessment would work well for both Jim and me. He saw Jim as very bright and motivated, as usually fun to be around, but also as complex and private and as apparently driven (i.e., sometimes observed to be angry and impulsive). Jim had mentioned several times to him of late that he had issues on his mind that he wished he could address before showing up for OCS. [For awhile my subtitle was "I'm ready for OCS, right?," still a meaningful theme].

That same day I received an e-mail message from Jim identifying himself as the person with an interest in the assessment. I responded saying that I was pleased, and that I thought we could complete the assessment in two 3-hour sessions [my typical format is three sessions]. I asked him to please send me a list of the concerns he hoped we could address, and to please (at a particular address) arrange to take the Minnesota Multiphasic Personality Inventory–2 (MMPI-2; Butcher, Dahlstrom, Graham, Tellegen, & Kaemmer, 1989) and the Sixteen Personality Factor Test (16 PF; Catell, 1949/1984) and to mail the answer sheets to me. He did so readily, and he also took the initiative to send me a list of personal background items, including his Myers-Briggs (Myers & McCaulley, 1985) personality type (ENTJ). I e-mailed him my genuine thanks. The list included his age (29), that he was proud of having earned a college degree while serving several enlistments in two military branches (beginning the first at age 17), one after the other, that his parents were alcoholic, and that his father wasn't on the scene much but that he recalled as a boy watching his father angrily flip the kitchen table over.

Jim's e-mailed "questions I would like to explore" included: "Why do I have a lack of emotional attachment to others? Being guarded? Why do I tire of girlfriends both sexually and socio/emotionally? Why do I often feel trapped? I wonder why I often have low daily levels of affect (this is lessening now that officer school is approaching). I would like to know why I am insecure in giving orders to others. I have explored this and have come up with a list of when I think it is okay and when it is not, like you had asked."

FIRST SESSION

I had reviewed Jim's e-mailed material, his MMPI-2 profile, and I had taken notes from the Myers-Briggs type indicator about his self-reported personality type. I jotted down notes about my hunches and ideas that I wanted to explore. I had at hand Bender-Gestalt cards (American Orthopsychiatric Association & Bender, 1938), the Rorschach cards (Rorschach, 1923/1994), and the Thematic Apperception Test cards (TAT; Murray, 1937). I wound up administering only the Rorschach in this meeting and the TAT during the second meeting.

My presession notes from the 16 PF: "presented himself as bold, venturesome, thick-skinned, objective, utilitarian, unsentimental, self-assured, unworried, relaxed, patient. From one scale, his reasoning seemed to be abstract, flexible, persevering. Global factors: extraverted, sociable, independent, persuasive, willful." I later felt that those were indeed valid characteristics, but that of course he was much more complex—for better and worse. As it happened, I found it unnecessary to discuss his 16 PF profile, because we seemed to have acknowledged the same features that he shared with me in our conversation.

We Meet

Jim arrived 5 minutes early, dressed neatly in jeans and a T-shirt. I recognized a habitual military bearing in his slender, muscular body, buzz haircut, and ramrod straight but comfortable posture. We shook hands in the private reception area, and I thanked him for agreeing to my planned educational use of our work. I reviewed the consent form with him and explained that later he could specify any segments that he would not want to be shared with others. I said that from what I had reviewed so far, I thought that he would find our work to be well worthwhile. I explained that today we would review his goals, share our impressions of his

Myers-Briggs personality type, and discuss his MMPI-2 profile. I said that I was counting on him to correct any of my characterizations that struck him as being off-target. I said that we would conclude our first (3-hour) session with the Rorschach, which I would score and study between sessions.

☞ Teaching Point

Telling the client that you anticipate working collaboratively, even when not referring explicitly to "collaborative," encourages fuller participation. Sincere "thank yous" help clients to know that they are indeed partners in the assessment. Previewing the session's format helps clients to feel oriented and on board.

We entered my office, where I had moved two swivel chairs to face each other at about a 100-degree angle about three and a half feet apart, to accommodate the camera. I provided both of us with a lap board placed across the arms of our chairs, pen, and paper. I commented that I was relieved to have heard that Jim was a whiz with all things electronic, and that if necessary he likely could help me with the filming.

I quickly became aware of my frumpy and overweight appearance in contrast with Jim's straight posture, with both feet planted solidly. As I found myself straightening up and then intentionally adopting his posture for a moment, two recognitions occurred: (1) he, too, at some level was likely seeing me as in my late 60s—perhaps both grandmotherly and professional (nonthreatening?); (2) in my mirroring posture I experienced myself as being at "parade rest"—sturdily planted, ready to come to attention, but bodily somewhat relaxed. That sense turned out to be a lasting impression of Jim.

☞ Teaching Point

The descriptions in the preceding paragraph are the kind that I include in written reports to third parties, so that readers can form a visual image through which to picture later descriptions of comportment. Such descriptions also help readers to become aware of my perspectives and involvement through which my impressions were formed. Readers who are already familiar with the client then can readily compare these perspectives and impressions with their own.

We reviewed Jim's e-mailed list of items that he hoped we could explore and then discussed his self-reported Myers-Briggs type.

Discussion of Jim's Myers-Briggs ENTJ

CF: You told me that you are an ENTJ. (JM: Uh-huh.) How about telling me what that means to you . . . what your understanding of that is.

JM: Umm, well, I hear it's a very good military type. [We both laugh.] I think it was the executive or the administrator or something like that. So, the person is very organized, not specifically detail-oriented, more to do with the big picture than specific details (CF: Uh-huh.) I know when I saw the explanation it made a lot of sense.

CF: [nodding] You recognized yourself there?

JM: Yeah, yeah. Oh, and disregard for people's internal feelings and stuff like that. The bigger picture for me is the physical outcome rather than the internal emotional state.

CF: Yeah, I don't understand that aspect about you yet, but I bet that it's part of the difficulties with women that you were wondering about. Let's see, as is said of ENTJs, you take a comprehensive approach to organizational issues—good leader. You like acquiring knowledge and being well-informed; that's good. You enjoy reasoning things through and enjoy having intellectual conversations. That's positive, especially in that you also can be a natural leader—decisive. Apparently, once you have the information, you go ahead.

JM: Yeah. Sounds spot on.

CF: (after other discussion) That's all good stuff that will work for you all over the place.

JM: Especially with my career choice, right?

CF: Right; exactly—in the military or other management situations, it's quite positive. BUT here are some possible negatives. You quick decision-makers! [joint chuckling] While seeing what can be done, you can fail to notice other people's situations and concerns, as you said. (JM: Yeah.) Because you're being more intellectual about it, and if the person isn't speaking up (JM: Their side of the story, yeah . . .), you miss it. And I can imagine that that can happen in relationships with women.

JM: Yeah. That's funny. It's almost like right now you are narrating my last relationship.

Jim then described how he in effect ignored signals from a girlfriend and wound up angrily literally throwing his girlfriend's clothing and belongings out of his apartment, and never speaking to her again.

✍ Teaching Point

Workshop participants who have watched film clips of this assessment have commented with surprise that Jim and I readily entered into an interpersonal relationship, variously notable for its spontaneous smiles, intent listening, somber reflecting, mutual chuckles, companionable silences, and both of us remarking on connections. In their first year of graduate school in our Duquesne University program, students develop their own interpersonal ways of conducting collaborative intakes. My own style has been described to me as down-to-earth, direct, interpersonal, and as encouraging curiosity, initiative, and openness.

Comments From the MMPI-2

I took notes from Jim's MMPI-2 clinical profile and special scales, from a computer program; unfortunately, the record was accidentally erased by a later user. Having planned to print out the complete record, including the answer sheet, I "efficiently" destroyed Jim's hand-answered sheet.

My handwritten notes follow.

Clinical scales: Hypomania = 88; Social Introversion = 38; Depression = 34. Special scales: Cynicism = 51; Amorality = 81; Social Discomfort = 32; Antisocial Practices = 62; from the Content scales: Authority Problems = 63.

I began my comments to Jim by mentioning that—no surprise to us—his MMPI-2 profile indicated family problems. Jim raised his eyebrows in amazement, and nodded. He asked the not infrequent and only half-joking question, "Did it show that I'm crazy?" I reassured him that it did not at all. I did say that I imagined, from the history that he had sent me, along with several MMPI-2 scores, that some of the successful ways he found to cope with his parents no longer worked for him in his adult world. I mentioned in particular that I imagined that telling himself in effect back then that feelings didn't matter [from his "Antisocial Practices" and "Amorality" scores], and his leaping to action [Ma and Si] in order to avoid finding himself emotionally affected probably were no longer working for him. He looked somber, and nodded slightly. Later we spoke of his father's having in effect modeled angry outbursts through his "table-flipping." We also conjectured about the similarity between his father's outbursts and Jim's "letting off steam" by purposely going out to drive at 100 miles per hour.

Jim Engages the Rorschach

Jim picked up each card eagerly, and quickly spoke his responses (eight to fifteen seconds to first response). He was relaxed but efficient. He often turned the cards, but most responses were to the upright card. He was helpful during the Inquiry and nondefensive. By the time we reached card X, Jim was fully enjoying his encounters with the cards and turned this one into a sort of storytelling occasion, which was useful to us but made scoring difficult.

✍ Teaching Point

Often clients use the last Rorschach card to include what they believe they have not yet represented about their life. I think that Jim did that.

Here is the text of Jim's Card X responses:
Response 25. "I see a woman wearing a cloak. She looks quiet, soft-spoken. Robe is mainly blue, with a purple trim about midway up. I picture her being intellectual. It looks like she has 2 bird-like guardians. She's very important, but doesn't realize it. I see a lot of other creatures attempting to interact with her. It looks like a gathering of sorts." [From Inquiry: The woman is a small, unusual detail (Dd99) in D14; "Blue is assumed, but the small line indicates the other color" (a rare color projection, one of 3 in Jim's Rorschach).]

The guardians are D8: "Eyeballs are outlined, facing each other; protrusions coming off top of head. (CF: "Protrusions?") Beak. Ruffled, bumpy, like it would be feathers. . . . She's small because she's in the background."

"The bird guardians look very mean; they take their job too personal. I feel like this woman has a lot of influence on everyone. I picture her sitting in a very tall, tall chair—obnoxiously so, every bit of 20 feet high. But it doesn't separate her from anyone. I think she's very thankful for the bird guardians, but she wishes they would relax sometimes."

[Responses 26 and 27 are various pairs of creatures.]

Response 28—card inverted: "I also see her opposite. No one's paying attention to him. But he has a large influence from behind everyone, very Machiavellian. There's energy pulsing from him. He's not innately bad, but his actions can be seen as such. He's actually helping people more than they realize. The woman knows of him, and they meet secretly, but their relationship could never be made public. [*Inquiry:*] Same picture, everyone facing the girl. The guy (D5) is standing here. The darkness coming from the hands represents mystical power."

We discussed this particular card at length in our second session [see below].

Throughout the administration, I was surprised by the mounting number of inanimate movement responses (and even more so at the final count in his Structural Summary, 12). When we completed the Inquiry, I mentioned that I already knew from partial scoring as we went along that he appeared to be under much more stress than I had imagined, even though he had mentioned it several times. He agreed that he habitually hid his stress, often even from himself. I also conveyed to Jim that attending to the texture, as he often had, has been highly correlated with a longing for affection. He looked a bit startled, but he mused and nodded in clear assent. Finally, from his many complex blends (which turned out to be 20 of 28 responses), I mentioned that I would guess that he often was attuned to multiple facets of a situation, simultaneously being affected in many ways [surprised nods from Jim], and that on occasion both he and others were not aware of all that was going on for him [affirmative nod].

Teaching Point

First, I typically ask at the end of the Inquiry if the client would be interested in a few observations even before I have fully scored the Rorschach. Inevitably the answer is affirmative. The client appreciates the early hunches, sometimes providing me with the contexts in which they do and do not hold. The client's feedback helps me to dispense with some possible interpretations, and it sometimes expands what I had considered. My later reading of the Structural Summary is much better informed. Second, in Jim's case I assumed that our mutually respectful sense of each other, and Jim's sense of being safe with me, probably led to a freer, looser Rorschach than might otherwise have happened, but of course it clearly reflected his ways of moving through new, open-ended tasks under similar circumstances.

At the close of our first meeting, I asked Jim to bring to our next meeting a list of what he had learned so far. I said that I thought that he would add to it after we discussed his Rorschach and he had developed stories for some cards with scenes of people [TAT]. We would use these stories as an opportunity for Jim to notice his inclinations and to practice imagining interpersonal possibilities, especially ones of closeness and affection.

SECOND SESSION

Three days later, Jim again arrived a bit early, and we eagerly continued our work, which lasted for 3 hours.

Review of Rorschach

I commented that the complexity of his life was evident in his responses, and that I saw a readiness to enjoy engaging other people more freely. I mentioned his having seen "two people pulling away; or maybe mid-dance, holding hands and spinning around." I mentioned that the "two people playing pattycake" also looked like their knees were "rubbed like blood coming out." Still, he had said "Pattycake is like a promise to each other, like a handshake. A sense of hope in this picture. Progress." We agreed that he was now more hopeful of cooperative relationships, although he was aware that relationships sometimes include being hurt.

I commented on his many images denoting authority, rank, and recognition; I joked with Jim that soon he could wear his rank on his shoulders in shiny metal [one response referred to decorations being "very ornate; highly reflective and polished"; he also had reported a "very ornate warrior's helmet"]. He grinned in recognition of his anticipations of finally being an officer.

When I mentioned his introducing color where there was none, he readily acknowledged that he wanted more pleasantness in his life than was in fact there. He agreed that he worked at avoiding feeling sad or depressed. I said that I was pleased for him that he was so ready for positive, affective engagement with life and people, and that he was ready despite still being attuned to danger and the darker side of life. [He had spoken of a dangerous valley, a dead tree that nonetheless had a "brilliant offshoot teeming with life," "a mushroom cloud—nuclear fallout," followed by "an almost evil face in the cloud."]

Teaching Point

I offer my understandings both to check a client's level of agreement or disagreement and to help the client to reflect somewhat differently on his or her present or emerging stances. Of course, sometimes the client helps me to see that I have misinterpreted or have overestimated the person's level of awareness or near awareness.

I then returned to Jim's last response to Card X, and said, "I'd like for us to talk about your last, long account of the card: 'I see a woman wearing a cloak. She looks quiet, soft-spoken. Robe is mainly blue with purple trim halfway up. I picture her being intellectual. It looks like she has two birdlike guardians. She's very important, but doesn't realize it.' I'm thinking that woman is you." We laughed in joint recognition that we were in touch with Jim's concerns about being a leader.

JM: I know that I fell in love with *The Prince* years ago. [Jim was referring to a 16th-century book by Niccolò Machiavelli, written in hopes of his becoming an advisor to the Florentine Medici. He advocated practical rather than moral governance, and he has been seen as sometimes cunning, deceptive, and worse.] And I know there's been lots of times where I've been seen as the bad guy. But almost every single time, the people who have labeled me as the bad person have come up to me at some point later in their lives and thanked me for the influence that I had on their lives. [I nod in appreciation of such occasions.]

[Later] CF: Tell me more about what was going on in your ending to the Rorschach.

JM: Umm, well, with her being seen as so intellectual and everyone looking towards her. . . . I'm referring to her, but we could say this is part me too. . . . She has to be as modest as possible and be intellectual. And she's seen in this positive light. Now that figures to get the job done. They sometimes have to have a dark Machiavellian side that can be perceived as bad. But that person that seems bad is the same person who is the intellectual figurehead; there's a discord there and people have a hard time associating the two. You can't always let people know you're playing both roles.

[Later] CF: I'm not sure who the mean bird guardians are.

JM: [laughs] They may be my own defense style, maybe.

CF: Yeah, we do have to have our defenses to take care of ourselves. But you're wishing they would relax a little?

JM: Yeah, they take their job too seriously maybe.

[Still later] CF: I think that part of how you don't get into as affectionate a relationship or as intimate and committed a relationship as you would want is that you often have backed away from real people and thought of them as abstract people. In your Rorschach, there were some real people, but a lot of them were fantasy people, and even fantasy animals. [JM: Yeah.] So I would guess that you often relate to people in terms of roles—What's my role? What's his/her role? [JM: Umm. Instead of a person.] I imagine that that's been part of the appeal of the military for you: clear expectations and roles. But you know, I've found you to be very personable, easy to talk with, even though we do have sort of roles in this assessment situation. We've been talking and communicating, and learning. [JM: Going back, I see that I have been comfortable giving orders as long as my position is clearly spelled out.] Right. Then you're not risking yourself. But you know, life is much fuller when we also can tolerate ambiguity. And you tolerated ambiguity with these inkblots just fine. [JM: Yeah!!]

Following our developing the above and other understandings, Jim and I went back to how his rages had occurred, and talked about the ways that he personally already has available for sidestepping them. We tried out several phrases that Jim could recall when finding himself feeling threatened, thereby finding avenues to bypass becoming angry.

▗ Teaching Point

Working collaboratively with our clients enhances possibilities that they will be comfortable enough to make discoveries as we go along, or at least to find themselves sharing what they did not know so clearly before.

The TAT: An Opportunity for Jim to Notice His Inclinations and to Imagine Interpersonal Possibilities

Our collaborative assessment had already been therapeutic as Jim and I worked together to understand his situations, how he had taken them up, and what his alternatives might be. When I introduced Jim to the TAT task, I said that I thought the cards would provide him with opportunities to encounter his inclinations and to scan for alternative possibilities, including his sense of himself, his relationships with women, and being positively affectively attuned. The following are his five stories (the numerals are for the card numbers):

TAT 1. [The card shows a seated boy, with elbows on a table and his head resting between his hands. A violin is on the table in front of him.] This young man thinks he ate too much chocolate. His stomach hurts. He realizes that he has to practice the violin, but he doesn't feel like it because his stomach hurts. He'll get around to playing it. He'll have to wait a bit, but he'll get it done. Nobody will yell at him—he has to tell himself. [CF: How did the young man manage to get around to playing?] His reason for getting better is not apparent. Just always be prepared if the need ever arises.

TAT 14. [The card shows the silhouette of man in a dark room; he usually is seen as looking out the window.] A guy looking out on a starry night. A thought came to him in the middle of the night when he was sleeping. It inspired him so much he wanted to think about it—beautiful night sky. I hear a symphony in the background, like a movie—it's going to work; it's going to be all right. A big orchestra kicks in. Someone else was in his bed—wasn't sleeping alone. He made sure not to rouse them when he got up. [Jim puts the card down.] [CF: What will happen?] He might be inspired to write—definitely a process before action. He'll write something down. I see him waking up tomorrow and feeling invigorated. Just a big smile when his spouse asks him about his waking up (earlier).

Following our later discussion, Jim added to his story, saying that the man would enjoy sharing with his wife what a fantastic experience he had had.

TAT 15B. [A young boy sits in on the doorsill of what appears to be a cabin, face in his hands, barefooted.] I picture this little guy all alone. I don't know how he got there. He doesn't seem worried. He has a determined look—he's rugged. He has a lot of years on him for his being as young as he is. I picture his feet being very calloused. Maybe he's just taking a break before he goes on again. [CF: What will happen?] As always—he'll just pick up his pack and keeps going. Like a Marine. He knows that as long as he keeps moving he'll be all right. He's kind of hungry though. [CF: What stories might other people tell?] He may get in trouble. His Mom's in there making breakfast—but maybe not, from the look on his face. Maybe he fell, and hurt his knee, and is recovering. Maybe he's waiting for people to come home.

TAT 4. [A young man and woman, standing, facing each other; but he seems to be trying to leave. Most people see strife between them.] He's a Dr. Jekyll/Mr. Hyde guy. Sinister. I don't trust him. Hmm, I think she just confessed her love to him. And he's turning away. She's trying to stop him, to really get the message across. Maybe she told him she's pregnant. He's running away. She can't believe he's running away. I can't get past the look on his face. There's definite love interest there. It could also be an engagement party. The photographer caught them at an awkward moment.

Jim's later comments: He treats his significant others well, until he abruptly ends the relationship. Being in the military, he has gotten used to having to break ties. Transferring to a new branch, which he's doing via OCS, would allow him to have a family and a career. That branch is much more family-friendly than the other armed forces. He's been living out of a suitcase for 5 years. Once he is an officer, and the dust has settled, then he'll have more opportunities for long-term relationships. I gathered that he had not shared with others this interest in having a family.

TAT 10. [This card shows the heads and shoulders of an older man and woman, very close, he looking downward toward her.] I picture this as a very loving, caring couple. They've been together for many years. They're having a small dance on their 40th anniversary. Just enjoying each other. They have busy lives—this is a moment of solitude when they are together. It feels like the background noise quiets down when they're together. I don't see them thinking so much here as feeling complete. He's in a dark tux; she is in an evening gown. Maybe they're reflecting on their lives. Maybe they have grandkids. They feel whole and complete—just being with each other. This makes me think of my grandparents on my mother's side; they had their 50th anniversary a couple of years back. They bicker and fight, but also have moments together. I witnessed that. (CF: Hmmm?) Yes, I can imagine growing older together. . . . Erikson's generativity stage. [Jim was referring to the positive side of Erik Erikson's seventh stage of development, in which one is less self-concerned and more concerned with guiding the next generation.]

Jim recognized his sensitivities in his stories—they were indeed his stories, and then his hopes.

Teaching Point

Here we see that assessment can be of one's readiness for movement as well as of one's present situation. Jim took into account our earlier discussions as well as my having spoken of opportunities to scan for alternative possibilities. We both took his stories as showing us that Jim was acknowledging his attunement to stress and to strained relationships, while also being able to imagine an enduring loving relationship.

Jim's Summary of What We Learned Over the Two Days

As I had requested, Jim had in mind a list of take-home themes and points, to which he added during the second meeting.

Teaching Point

Asking the client to bring in a list of what we have learned so far encourages the client to use his or her own language and to attest to ownership of the ideas. The client's list also allows me to see what he or she has taken from our explorations. Unlike Jim's mental list, clients' lists are almost always written.

Jim's list:

- Reflect on how I feel (vs. acting right away, especially harshly).
- Think about how the situation is affecting me: Do I feel put down or restricted? [which we had discussed as the beginning of becoming angry—and which can be bypassed]
- I realize now that I'm ready for affection.
- I have to share my feelings with others if affection is going to happen. Don't be afraid.
- Nice to talk about the Myers-Briggs' good part of my code. But I have to be aware of the reciprocal side too.
- Relationships are not business operations.
- Try to see how other people might be viewing a situation; I might be seeing it differently.
- At times of stress I'm really alone—most vulnerable. I put up my guard—like the angry guardians [Rorschach].
- I'm a bit manic now, but a crash does not have to be severe.
- My combination of lack of respect for established law and spontaneity can be a recipe for disaster.
- Importance of reflection vs. immediate action.
- Be creative; but as an officer maintain order, respect for law.
- My relationship with my mother has affected me—also positively.

Now it was my turn to nod, in appreciation of Jim's thoughtful integration of the implications of our work.

Teaching Points

(1) I did not attempt to address each of Jim's questions, instead leaving some implications implicit. Jim's own formulation of his take-home points would serve him better than a list I might compose. With some clients, I ask them as we go to please describe what we seem to have just learned. (2) Of course there are many other areas that we explored and that we might have explored. My choices were those that I saw as pertinent to Jim's presented concerns. My comments to him were intended to meet and to extend his readiness to continue his progress. Our time constraints were a limitation but facilitated our development of cohesive themes without addressing every concern separately.

Closing

When I asked him, Jim said that there were no segments of the filmed sessions that he wanted me to delete from workshops or classes. He immediately provided his pseudonym when I asked for one, but only smiled when I cocked my head questioningly. As we stood up, Jim asked if I would like him to help move the office furniture back to its original arrangement (prior to accommodating filming requirements). I readily accepted. Then as we stood in my doorway to the hall, Jim grinned and said, "I *am* ready for OCS. And for more!" We shook hands heartily, then hugged (me on tiptoes), and he walked briskly but lightly to the elevators, without looking back.

Comments

Yes, Jim was a bright client, eager at this exciting but stressful transition time to maximize gains from the assessment opportunity. Although I always accommodate my approach to the particular person, all self-referred (and many referred) clients participate in a similar responsive, dialogical manner.

Outcomes

Jim had given his coworker permission to discuss his assessment. The coworker reported that after our first session Jim had enthusiastically thanked him for arranging the assessment. He said that our discussions were amazingly relevant and on target, and that he was continuing to reflect. He had anticipated a test-focused meeting and had found that instead we focused meaningfully on his life. He affirmed the coworker's earlier characterization of me as "interpersonal" and as having a sense of humor even while being an expert. Jim described me as both "open" and "sturdy," and implied that these characteristics led to his being more open than he had anticipated.

On his way out of Pittsburgh, Jim told the coworker that our closing session had affirmed his list of what he was taking with him from the assessment, and although he was still somewhat anxious as well as eager about starting OCS, he was now confident in his decision and in his readiness. Jim implied, but did not discuss, that he had learned much of personal importance. Once at OCS, Jim e-mailed to the coworker that his years in the military were paying off, that he was more advanced than most of the other candidates, and that one of the officers had asked him for help in the self-defense segment of training. Although the coworker was not aware of our work in regard to giving orders, Jim mentioned to him that he was having no trouble in giving orders. His last report was that he was graduating as one of the very top candidates in his class.

I sent an e-mail message to Jim, who was by then several months out of OCS, and now a commissioned officer. I congratulated him, and I asked if he would comment on how our meetings had worked out for him, for suggestions about the process, for anything he was still working on, how OCS had gone (and that I had heard very positive reports second-hand from our mutual friend). I also asked if he would like a copy of his summary of what we had learned. After receiving no response to my message nor to a repeat effort, I e-mailed our mutual friend to see if he had an additional e-mail address for Jim, and whether he had heard from Jim since OCS. The friend, too, had sent unanswered messages, and reported that Jim seemed not to have contacted any of his Pittsburgh associates.

I realized that despite Jim's having appropriated much of our work, his having cut off contact seemed to be another instance of his breaking relationships without warning. I found myself experiencing a familiar wish that I knew more about a former client's current well-being. After reflection, I concluded that I did not think I would conduct the assessment differently, unless somehow I had known to ask Jim if he would reply to a follow-up inquiry. I now recalled that Jim had mentioned that he regarded each of his enlistments as a closed chapter; I supposed that his graduation from OCS for him indicated that he could close his Pittsburgh chapter. I imagined him eagerly undertaking his new life as an officer.

⌦ Teaching Point

Our collaborative and therapeutic assessment efforts do not completely resolve issues. Insights and in-session practice of alternative ways of taking up events require, as Freud said, "working through" in life. As in psychotherapy, many insights and gains give way to old habits, but often are accessed again later. To help with the working through, collaborative assessors often arrange in advance for another session a month or more later. I had hoped that my checking in via e-mail would serve that purpose.

I chose this assessment for this chapter to illustrate collaborating therapeutically throughout the assessment, but also to illustrate that sometimes, collaborative assessments are not as fully satisfactory as we had wished.

REFERENCES

American Orthopsychiatric Association & Bender, L. (1938/1990). *Visual motor gestalt test*. New York, NY: American Orthopsychiatric Association.

Butcher, J. N., Dahlstrom, W. G., Graham, J. R., Tellegen, A. T., & Kaemmer, B. (1989). *Minnesota Multiphasic Personality Inventory–2*. Minneapolis: University of Minnesota Press.

Catell, R. (1949/1984). *Sixteen Personality Factor Questionnaire*. Chicago, IL: IPAT.

Fischer, C. T. (1985/1994). *Individualizing psychological assessment*. New York, NY: Routledge.

Fischer, C. T. (2000). Collaborative, individualized assessment. *Journal of Personality Assessment, 74,* 2–14.

Murray, H. (1937). *Thematic Apperception Test*. Cambridge, MA: Harvard University Press.

Myers, I. B., & McCaulley, M. H. (1985). *Manual: A guide to the development and use of the Myers-Briggs Type Indicator*. Palo Alto, CA: Consulting Psychologists Press.

Rorschach, H. (1923/1994). *Plates*. Berne, Switzerland: Verlag Hans Huber Hogrefe.

Therapeutic Assessment for a Treatment in Crisis Following Multiple Suicide Attempts

J. Christopher Fowler

As new data emerge regarding the efficacy and utility of therapeutic assessment (TA), the natural inclination is to expand the technology into different treatment settings and to utilize the model in increasingly complex treatment cases under various assessment modalities (Ackerman, Hilsenroth, Baity, & Blagys, 2000; Hilsenroth, Peters, & Ackerman, 2004; Smith & Handler, 2009; Tharinger, Finn, Wilkinson, & Schaber, 2007; Tharinger et al., 2009). Research has demonstrated that the TA approach leads to significant improvement in patient symptoms and increasing self-esteem (Finn & Tonsager, 1992; Newman & Greenway, 1997), and that TA and feedback are related to increased quality of the therapeutic alliance following an initial evaluation (Ackerman et al., 2000; Hilsenroth et al., 2004). Extensive TA case studies of psychotherapy consultations to treatments at an impasse (Finn, 2003; Peters, Handler, White, & Winkel, 2008) suggest that TA can be particularly helpful in opening a space for the patient and therapist to gain a greater understanding of the underlying causes of the therapeutic rupture.

The ideal outcome for therapeutic assessment is to have patients leave an assessment with new experiences while gaining new information about their psychology that ultimately helps them make changes in their lives (Finn & Tonsager, 1997). When approaching a consultation using the TA model with patients diagnosed with severe character pathology, psychotic symptoms, and multiple treatment-resistant disorders, the goals and aspirations of the consultation are necessarily tempered by the reality of the situation.

Nevertheless, I have found that the therapeutic model of assessment offers a sensitive, respectful approach to the patient as an active, invested member of the assessment process. Engaging the patient as an active investigator in understanding the nature of the difficulties respects the patient's intelligence, personal authority, and curiosity. The tone and techniques used in TA are well suited to a treatment in crisis, because the patient–therapist pair is frequently caught in a power struggle in which the space for understanding and reflection have collapsed. TA invites an opening of the space, through the introduction of a third party who uses a psychological test battery to create an opening into a conversation that, to date, has been too difficult to engage. The case presented as follows is one in which TA was used with moderate success to help Anne and Dr. X gain greater understanding of a therapeutic impasse associated with a near-lethal suicide attempt in the month prior to the consultation.

THERAPIST'S REQUEST FOR CONSULTATION

I received a distress call from a colleague (Dr. X) who feared that her 19-year-old hospitalized patient (Anne) was ultimately, though not imminently, going to commit suicide if something didn't shift in the treatment. Faced with the choice of terminating the treatment, or continuing with chronic crisis management of brief yet ineffective acute hospitalizations, Dr. X requested a consultation. I agreed on the condition that Dr. X and Anne could first agree to bringing in a consultant, and that I meet with Dr. X before starting the testing with Anne.

During my meeting with Dr. X, what impressed me most was her level of dedication to Anne, as well as her deep anxieties about Anne's suicidality. Dr. X told me that Anne had made six near-lethal suicide attempts in the span of two years, experienced waxing and waning command auditory hallucinations to kill herself, had a history of severe polysubstance abuse, and had a pattern of engaging in masochistic relationships with drug dealers.

Anne's childhood was marked by severe childhood neglect when her parents divorced in a protracted and acrimonious fashion that left Anne feeling caught in the middle, yet totally invisible. Finding no safe haven in either home, Anne turned to a peer group described as "the lost boys." Massive drug abuse and victimization by the drug dealers who supplied the group caused her to fall into a deeper depression, experience dissociative symptoms, and deepen her pathological attachment to people who used her for narcissistic gratification.

By the time Dr. X began working with her, Anne was suffering from command auditory hallucinations, periodic dissociation, and had made five suicide attempts, all of which required medium-length hospitalizations. Dr. X had been working with Anne for approximately four months, during which time she found Anne's communication style puzzling and provocative. Dr. X was deeply troubled by Anne's high risk for future suicide, and she worked to bring about stabilization in Anne's mood, concentration, and thought disorder. Dr. X also sought to develop an alliance in which she and Anne could develop a coherent narrative of Anne's life.

Just as Anne began responding positively to the antipsychotic medications and seemed to be developing a sense of trust, she made a near-lethal suicide attempt without warning. What troubled Dr. X more was the way in which she learned of the suicide attempt: Anne came to her session, sat down, and recounted the gruesome details of her suicide attempt without emotion. Horrified and thrown off-balance, Dr. X searched for precipitating events, but no triggers emerged and Anne seemed indifferent to the cause. Deeply shaken by the experience, Dr. X sought consultation from several senior therapists, all of whom considered Anne at high risk because she seemed unreachable. One suggested psychological testing as a possible avenue to gaining greater understanding of the mystery surrounding Anne's suicide attempts.

When I asked Dr. X if there were other questions or observations from her sessions, she spoke of an uneasy feeling that Anne had been torturing her with gruesome traumatic experiences throughout their four months of treatment. The latest graphic description of Anne's suicide attempt left Dr. X feeling as though she were being drawn into a sadomasochistic struggle without apparent therapeutic benefit. Dr. X experienced Anne's speech as assaultive, rather than communicative, and Anne often spoke of her past abuse with a wry smile that Dr. X experienced as menacing rather than as searching for help.

FIRST SESSION WITH ANNE

When we met in the lobby, I was struck by Anne's aloof, almost autistic, greeting. As I approached to say hello, she turned away and mumbled something incomprehensible. I invited her to join me in my office, and with that she bolted from the chair and walked down the hall several paces ahead of me. I awkwardly interrupted her march by letting her know my office was in the other direction. She whisked past me, and as I quickened my pace to catch up, it dawned on me that she might need to create considerable distance between us. Therefore, I slowed my pace and waited until she came to the end of the hall. I stopped at my office door, and when she turned around 20 paces away, I invited her into my office. She rushed into the room and sat down.

I began by explaining that Dr. X requested psychological testing in order to help understand more about what was getting in the way of their therapy, and that Dr. X had been particularly interested in better understanding Anne's suffering and suicidality. For an instant, Anne flashed a smile, then turned away and began staring at my books. I asked Anne what she would like to learn from the psychological testing and emphasized that this was an opportunity for her questions and her obser-vations as well. After an uncomfortable pause, she exclaimed, "I want to know how smart I am." I said it certainly seemed possible that we could get an estimate of her overall intellect, but I wondered why this was of particular interest. Anne feared that she might not be living up to her potential and explained that she had struggled with high school despite solid SAT scores. I asked if she had a theory about this discrepancy in her intellectual capacities and school performance. Pondering the question, she said she couldn't concentrate with so many people around and had trouble deciphering the teacher's words. She then exclaimed, "I like books! I just finished *Ulysses*." Sensing her excitement and engagement, I asked her about her take on Leopold Bloom. After a 10-minute recitation of the parallels between *Ulysses* and *The Odyssey*, her preference for stream-of-consciousness narrative forms, and Anton Chekhov, I gained immense respect for her range of functioning.

When I asked if she had other questions for the testing she hesitated, a faint smile crossed her face, then she promptly said no. I pondered that smile for a moment, then asked if there was something that she hoped Dr. X might learn from the testing. The smile broadened: "Yes, I want my therapist to know everything. I want her to read my mind. I hope the testing can teach her how to read my mind." I returned a smile, adding that this was one of the more interesting consultation requests I'd heard, and that I would give it some thought. I let her know that it seemed unlikely that the psychological testing would reveal everything in her mind, and it could not teach her therapist how to read her mind. Yet, I did have some hope that her engagement in the testing might help all three of us learn more about the nature of her struggles. She was openly displeased with this answer but agreed to continue with the testing.

COMPORTMENT DURING TESTING SESSIONS

Anne's approach to the testing was peppered with idiosyncratic responses, often followed by that same furtive smile, suggesting to me that she took particular pleasure in holding her own counsel. At moments I felt as though I was the dumb witness to an inside joke, unable to discern the rules or riddles that structured these moments of mirth. After administering individual tests, I inquired about her smiles and wondered if she had particular reactions to each test. A routine developed in which she stated that the test was interesting, then eagerly inquired, "Will Dr. X see these tests?" I answered in turn, "Yes, especially if you would like her to."

When we finished the battery of tests, I was left with the impression that Anne possessed a range of strengths and vulnerabilities including an impressive stamina to withstand five hours of psychological testing in one day. As she briskly exited my office, I was left with the impression that she had successfully kept me at a distance, yet had deeply engaged in the Rorschach, allowing possible access to some of her difficulties.

FORMAL FINDINGS

The testing battery consisted of the Wechsler Adult Intelligence Scale–III (WAIS-III; Wechsler, 1997), the Thematic Apperception Test (TAT; Murray, 1943), human figure drawings, and the Rorschach inkblot test (Exner, 2003). Anne showed a considerable range of intellectual functioning in her performance on the WAIS-III. While her composite IQ scores were in the average range, intrasubtest scatter was particularly notable for tasks involving retention and understanding of social conventions (Comprehension = 7), whereas abstract reasoning capacities were far superior (Similarities = 13). A similar pattern of difficulty comprehending social convention and social causality was observed in the performance subtests with a relatively elevated Picture Completion score (PC = 12), whereas a task that draws more heavily on understanding cause and effect in social relationships was considerably lower (Picture Arrangement = 8). Most striking was the number of idiosyncratic tangents Anne introduced. For example, when asked to explain the proverb, One swallow does not make a summer, Anne responded correctly, then added "It's like, get them while they're weak; attack them when they're weak and only a few, rather than waiting until they are many and strong."

Themes of fatalistic betrayal, violence, murder, and attacking vulnerabilities of the "other" played a prominent role in Anne's TAT narratives. In response to Card 13MF of the TAT (portraying a clothed man facing away from a half-nude woman lying in bed), she responded, "He was her husband and he found out she had a lover so he raped and killed her and he felt bad about it, but he still didn't want anyone to know it was him and so he blamed it on the lover." These forays into narrative discourse generally revealed a hostile and malevolent world, suggesting that Anne expected that others would react with murderous rage toward any rupture in the relationship. While her TAT, human figure drawings, and WAIS-III profiles were relatively free of blatant psychotic intrusion, her Rorschach protocol revealed difficulties with affect regulation, poor self-esteem, heightened narcissistic vulnerability, and severe thought disorder.

Her Rorschach Structural Summary indicated that Anne's general style of coping with problems and conflicts was to react rather impulsively and was driven primarily by poorly integrated and modulated emotional expression ($EB = 4:9.5$; $FC:CF + C = 1:7$). This, coupled with serious cognitive disruption and perceptual distortion, certainly raised the question of an ongoing psychotic process, despite adequate medication adherence and remission of auditory hallucinations. The fact that Anne's profile had elevated scores for the Perceptual Thinking Index ($PTI = 4$), Schizophrenia Index ($SCHIZ = 5$), Ego Impairment Index ($EII = 2.1$), and Suicide Constellation ($SCON = 7$), all in the context of a valid Rorschach record ($Lambda = .17$), suggested she had global difficulties in managing her internal life. The relatively high number of reflection responses ($Fr + rf = 3$), responses with aggressive content ($AgC = 5$), and a $WSUM6$ dominated by *Contamination* and *ALOG* scores strongly suggested a psychotic spectrum disorder. The protocol also revealed Anne's heightened concern over bodily integration and a damaged sense of self-esteem, in the context of a narcissistic style, used to bolster her crumbling self-experiences.

When I began integrating the Structural Summary into a psychoanalytic, phenomenological sequence analysis, the quality and texture of Anne's internal world and the nature of her thought disturbance came into stark relief. Anne produced a 21-response Rorschach protocol with some of the most blatantly malevolent and confusing imagery I have witnessed. Primary process aggression, boundary disturbance, and overwhelmingly malevolent objects were the rule rather than the exception. Where human movement was absent, the cold, grey steel of razor-sharp sexual devices, guns, and martial arts weaponry were in its place. As she invited me into this arena of her mind, her demeanor was relaxed, chipper, and without discernible anxiety. Take, for example, her sequence of responses to Card II:

Anne: Two witches and they are dancing around a pot.
           Inquiry:
Dr. Fowler: What makes it look like two witches?

Table 6.1 Anne's Structural Summary

Location Features		Determinants		Contents		Approach	
		Blends	**Single**	H	= 3	I : WS.WS.D.D	
Zf	= 14	Fr.Ma.FMa	M = 4	(H)	= 1	II : W	
ZSum	= 54.5	Ma.CF.ma.C'F	FM = 5	Hd	= 3	III : W.D	
ZEst	= 45.5	Fr.Ma.ma.CF	m = 3	(Hd)	= 0	IV : W	
		FMa.FT.FD	FC = 1	Hx	= 0	V : W	
W	= 11	Fr.FMa	CF = 3	A	= 5	VI : W.D.W	
D	= 8	FMp.FY	C = 4	(A)	= 2	VII : W	
W + D	= 19	FMa.CF	Cn = 0	Ad	= 1	VIII : W	
Dd	= 2		FC' = 3	(Ad)	= 1	IX : W.D.DdS	
S	= 3		C'F = 1	An	= 0	X : D.D.D.Dd	
			C' = 0	Art	= 0		
DQ			FT = 1	Ay	= 1	**Special Scores**	
+	= 8		TF = 0	Bl	= 5		Lv1 Lv2
o	= 13		T = 0	Bt	= 1	DV = 0	0 × 1 0 × 2
v/+	= 0		FV = 0	Cg	= 1	INC = 0	0 × 2 0 × 4
v	= 0		VF = 0	Cl	= 1	DR = 1	1 × 3 0 × 6
			V = 0	Ex	= 0	FAB = 1	1 × 4 0 × 7
			FY = 2	Fd	= 0	ALOG = 1	1 × 5
			YF = 2	Fi	= 0	CON = 1	1 × 7
Form Quality			Y = 0	Ge	= 0	**Raw Sum6** = 4	
			Fr	= 3	Hh	= 3	**Wgtd Sum6** = 19	
FQx	MQual	W+D	rF	= 0	Ls	= 0	
+ = 0	= 0	= 0	FD	= 1	Na	= 2	AB = 0 GHR = 1
o = 5	= 1	= 5	F	= 3	Sc	= 4	AG = 1 PHR = 6
u = 8	= 1	= 7			Sx	= 1	COP = 1 MOR = 2
− = 8	= 2	= 7			Xy	= 0	CP = 0 PER = 5
none = 0	= 0	= 0			Id	= 0	PSV = 0
			(2) = 2				

RATIOS, PERCENTAGES, AND DERIVATIONS

R = 21		L = .17	FC:CF+C = 1:7	COP = 1	AG = 1
			Pure C = 4	GHR:PHR = 1:6	
EB = 4:9.5	EA = 13.5	EBPer = NA	SmC':WSmC = 4:9.5	a:p = 10:2	
eb = 8:9	es = 17	D = −1	Afr = .62	Food = 0	
	Adj es = 12	Adj D = 0	S = 3	SumT = 1	
			Blends/R = 9:21	Human Cont = 7	
FM = 5	SumC' = 4	SumT = 1	CP = 0	PureH = 3	
m = 2	SumV = 0	SumY = 4		PER = 5	
				Isol Indx = 0.33	
			XA% = 62	Zf = 14	3r+(2)/R = .52
			WDA% = 63	W:D:Dd = 11:8:2	Fr+rF = 3
		Sum6 = 4	X−% = 38	W:M = 11:4	SumV = 0
a:p = 10:2	Lv2 = 0	S− = 0	Zd = +9.0	FD = 0.1
Ma:Mp = 4:0	WSum6 = 19	P = 2	PSV = 0	An+Xy = 0:21
2AB+Art + Ay = 1:21	M− = 2	X+% = 24	DQ+ = 8	MOR = 2
MOR = 2	Mnone = 0	Xu% = 38	DQv = 0	H:(H)+Hd+(Hd) = 3:4

PTI = 4	DEPI = 3	CDI = 2	S-CON = 7	HVI = 5	OBS = 0

Anne: This part is a pot—kinda morbid but it looks like blood (rapid-fire speech), witches with hoods on, hands pressed together. Looks like they're doing some kind of ritual. The black makes it look like blood but with red around it reminds me of blood and the shape of the red part looks like a pot, but it has black in it.

Dr. Fowler: What specifically makes it look like witches?

Anne: Ritualistic . . . it looks like their heads exploded.

My visceral reaction to the disjunction between Anne's malevolent, distorted imagery, and her ease with the image led me to a disturbing exclamation, "Oy Vey!," a rare pessimistic conclusion given my Catholic upbringing. "Oy Vey" conveyed my sinking hope for Anne, as well as my sense of her as foreign and unknowable. I felt like Lewis Carroll's Alice, sliding down the rabbit hole; the more I inquired into Anne's percepts, the more unmoored, thrown off-balance, and darkly convinced I became that the prognosis for Anne was entirely bleak. This reaction deepened to a near conviction when I handed her Card III. With genuine excitement, she exclaimed:

Anne: Wow, I remember this one. . . . This looks like a guy shooting himself in the head while looking in the mirror.
    Inquiry:

Dr. Fowler: Guy shooting himself in the head while looking in a mirror?

Anne: Yeah, looking in the mirror—Maybe he didn't shoot himself but got shot cause this looks blown out and looks like blood. It's a guy cause guys shoot themselves, right? Isn't that the statistics? That's what my mom told me.

Dr. Fowler: What makes it look like blood?

Anne: The red splattered around everywhere, like splashed.

Dr. Fowler: Mirror?

Anne: It's the same on both sides.

In her last response to Card III, Anne turned the card upside down and perceived an archway in a graveyard. During the inquiry she insisted that it looked like a graveyard because of the blood, the anatomy of a ribcage, and the shadowy nature of the blot. Further inquiry revealed a clear Contamination response in which both anatomy/blood morphed with a shadowy, dark image of a graveyard archway. Again my heart sank as I pondered her response.

Long after Anne left my office, I returned to her data in an effort to decipher any hint of a complex conflict or inner desire. I stumbled upon a curious element that escaped my attention on previous readings: The witches were pressing hands together! Here, in the midst of heads exploding, a witches' cauldron of black blood and red blood, confusion and bedlam, were two intact figures involved in a kinesthetic act of mutual recognition of the other's autonomy; that is, before she added that their heads were exploding. Thus, embedded in primary process aggression (the blood splashed everywhere), intense devaluation (the witches), strained logic (witches because of the ritualistic and a transparency response in the cauldron of red and black blood), and her disturbing ego-syntonic approach to the image was a percept of cooperative movement, and the highest level of object relating in Urist's Mutuality of Autonomy Scale (Urist, 1977), again, before the image was spoiled by the exploding heads.

This mass of confusion and primary process imagery concealed recognition of Anne's attention to the dimension of human contact. With this glimpse of an interest in human contact, I then returned to consider the other potential significance behind the repetitive imagery of cold, grey steel weapons. While the images conveyed her vigilance and expectation of outer persecution, their appearance on Card IV and VI of the Rorschach also led me to consider that she was guarding against the possibility of experiencing the achromatic color cards as textured. This was confirmed on Card VI when she perseverated on two metal weapons, then followed these with the percept of a stingray, which was largely determined by the texture of the smooth, mottled skin. This particular use of texture as using the differential shading to construct cold, flat surfaces was described by Paul Lerner (1991) as a repudiation of emotional needs due to a low expectation that such needs would be met.

Given this opening, I allowed myself to imagine that Anne might be attempting to adapt to the disorganizing and exciting experience of longing by making defensive use of hypervigilance, and that the expectation of malevolent treatment from others helped her refute her longing for contact. This set of tentative hypotheses helped me gain a more complex understanding of a woman who initially seemed chronically psychotic and grossly traumatized by her life experiences. Based on these interpretations, I wrote the following paragraph:

> While the percept on Card II reveals a great deal about her struggles and failure in containing affect, one can easily get lost in the affective storms and miss what she is conflicted by; namely, that the witches are touching hands. Throughout the Rorschach she embeds human contact in chaotic and highly malevolent images that easily distract herself and the other from a more basic struggle around dependency. An important feature of her growing wish for human contact is the way in which she disguises this longing.

I returned to Anne's response to Card III. Taking a moment to quiet my "Oy Vey" counter-transference response, I lingered on the percept of a man shooting himself in the head while staring into a mirror. For a moment, I imagined what it would be like to have Anne's imagination— to perceive a suicide execution in the same moment of staring into a mirror. What was the man (Anne's avatar) looking for while squeezing the trigger? This errant thought led me to consider the possibility that Anne was looking for some indication of an emotional register or recognition on the face in the mirror. I linked this to my "dis-ease" at being invited into a primitive form of narcissistic semiotic engagement in which Anne pressed me as the observer into experiencing deeply unpleasant emotional states. I wondered if she engaged in a similar process with Dr. X when she gleefully retold particularly gruesome scenes from her life. I combed my recent memory to see if Anne had glanced up at me while providing test responses. I recalled several furtive glances my way, especially when we were discussing what she wanted Dr. X to know. This meshed with my counter-transference reaction of feeling like an unwilling, unwitting, and mildly traumatized witness to Anne's gleeful romp through ghastly, gruesome, and thought-disordered imagery. Suddenly, I had a deep sympathy for both Anne and her therapist and what they both were enduring in the psychotherapy.

Turning to her next response, that of a graveyard—part archway, part human remains—revealed profound thought disorder, and made me also hypothesize that without the empathic reflection from another to join with and recognize her painful experience, she became far more disorganized, collapsing into a fragmented state. Thus, I began to consider her efforts to shock Dr. X (and me during the psychological testing) as a potentially adaptive effort to coerce an empathic response from another person. Perhaps Anne was attempting to evoke in her therapist—and by extension me as examiner—to experience the dreadful and messy emotions that she could not fully express. Based on my visceral recoil during the testing, I thought that Anne's efforts to have the other experience her painful life was likely a constantly failing attempt at a mirroring experience, thus leading her to further fragmentation and disorganization.

Based on this analysis of the data, I determined that my primary task in providing feedback to Dr. X would be to share these latter impressions, along with the formal findings. My feedback to Anne would be more complicated, requiring a flexible, spontaneous responsiveness to the ebb and flow of our feedback session.

FEEDBACK TO DR. X

After reading the psychological test report, Dr. X agreed to meet to discuss questions and comments that emerged. Dr. X's dedication to Anne shone through as she listened intently to my impressions of Anne's psychological organization. Dr. X was troubled by the intensity of Anne's cognitive distortions and severity of her thought disorder, despite the rapid improvement in overt command auditory hallucinations. On further reflection, Dr. X considered the possibility that Anne's "dissociative" lapses might be collapses into disorganization rather than symptoms of PTSD. I could not confirm that formulation; however, I noted that Anne showed no signs of avoidance or anxiety when she became deeply preoccupied with malevolent images. To the contrary, Anne seemed pleased with her productions, whereas I became increasingly disturbed. I shared my visceral reaction to Anne's responses and read the sequence of responses to Cards II and III of the Rorschach. Dr. X sympathized with me, sharing her sense of repulsion at many of the stories Anne had shared.

We then discussed the possibility that Anne's communications of graphic and gory memories likely served multiple purposes. First, they might communicate factual events that were too traumatic for her to tolerate. Second, it was possible that Anne was searching for an emotional resonance in Dr. X by creating the feelings of repulsion and disgust that Anne felt about her thoughts and feelings. And third, I shared with Dr. X my impression that, due to Anne's severe distrust of humans, she very well may have had to find ways of getting dependency needs met through indirect channels, such as having the therapist becoming so alarmed by her state that the therapist was moved to react with intense feelings and with alarm.

Dr. X sat quietly pondering these possibilities and then added that she had felt more tortured and subjected to graphic assault. She wondered if the same data could be approached from a more direct line of analysis of Anne's hostility. I commended Dr. X for this sensitive analysis, noting that it is common for victims to identify with an aggressor, taking on qualities of a malevolent abuser, and to treat others as one has been treated. I wondered if Dr. X had ever found herself identifying with Anne's earlier experiences of being witness to the maelstrom of her parent's divorce and her reckless adventures as a teen. I then told Dr. X that, while it was very possible that Anne was acting out hostility in an unconscious fashion during the sessions, one shred of evidence suggested that Anne was simultaneously trying to get closer to Dr. X. Though Anne's methods were deeply disturbing, dangerous, and destructive, it seemed to me that many of her efforts were trying to hide her longing for Dr. X in the midst of this chaos. I returned to the image of the two witches dancing around the cauldron holding hands, and invited Dr. X to imagine what it might be like for Anne to create such an image and how that image might portray a certain highly symbolized prototypic way of engaging with Dr. X.

Dr. X caught the edge of this empathy exercise and began recounting moments when Anne "danced around" topics in a kind of hide-and-seek game, drawing Dr. X into searching for her, only to slip away again— a game that puzzled and irritated Dr. X. This led to a discussion of how

Dr. X might introduce Anne to her longings for nurturance and the possibility that such premature introductions could lead to a recoiling and retreat. As Dr. X prepared to leave my office, I was aware that the intensity of Anne's recent suicide attempt and the powerful emotions stirred in the pair might be far too powerful to overcome with interpretations from a testing battery. Nonetheless, I wished Dr. X well and asked her permission to follow up in six months to see how the treatment was unfolding. She agreed, thanked me, and walked out of the office.

FEEDBACK SESSION WITH ANNE

Anne's first question to me was, "So how smart am I?" I was caught off guard because Anne and I had yet to enter my office. The public nature of her question, and her challenging tone, threw off my rhythm, leaving me feeling awkward and unsure of how to respond. I invited her into my office, and before she sat down, I said, "You're smarter than you know, you're certainly smarter than you think you are, and I would go so far as to say you're smarter than the intelligence testing suggests." Anne was visibly pleased with this response. Her next question was more pointed, "So did the intelligence test say I am stupid?" I told her the testing suggested her intellectual functioning was in the average range; however, she had a keen grasp of abstract reasoning and reading comprehension. "For example, you told me about *Ulysses*, and I know that it is no light reading. I also learned that classroom learning, where most secondary education takes place, does not play to your strengths because you can become overwhelmed by the presence of other people, and your thinking can sometimes become a bit clouded when someone's speaking directly to you. I think that's why you probably prefer books and learning on your own to that of direct one-to-one or classroom instruction."

Anne pondered this for a moment, seemed pleased, and then suddenly changed the topic. "So what else does the testing show? And did Dr. X see the test results?" I told Anne that, in addition to her being very smart, the testing revealed that she was vigilant and wary of people. Bringing the data into the here-and-now interaction, I imagined that Anne might be suspicious of my findings, and I was impressed that she agreed to show up for our meeting. I encouraged her to challenge my hypotheses, present disconfirming evidence, and let me know when I got it wrong: "After all, these are hypotheses, not hard facts. When you let me know I got something wrong, then I learn more from you and can revise my impressions." Anne agreed to this arrangement and asked for more feedback.

I told her that I thought that this vigilant approach could, at times, be quite adaptive. For example, I noticed that she scanned the entire ink-blots looking for a great deal of detail in the stimulus and wondered if she thought of herself as someone who takes in the big picture and tries to read and scan her environment quickly. She agreed, saying, "Where I'm from if you don't see what's going on, bad things can happen. I learned that when I was a kid, that you had to know who the good people were and who the bad people were." And then she added, with a lilt in her voice, "But it's not always easy to pick those people out." I agreed with Anne—none of us are perfect at picking out helpful people from those that may be more dangerous. I added that perhaps this way of living helped her at times, but it might interfere with her trusting Dr. X. I told her it was not necessary for Anne to pretend to trust Dr. X, but rather to risk talking to Dr. X about feelings of mistrust when they arose. She agreed.

She asked what else I told Dr. X. I wondered aloud if Anne was look-ing for something specific. With that she smiled and said, "I was trying to send messages to Dr. X through the stories." I asked, "So you hoped Dr. X got your messages through your stories?" Anne suddenly withdrew. Sensing her vulnerability in that moment, I backed off. "Well, I'm sure we can ask her to read the stories again, but I wonder if you'd be inter-ested in hearing what I have learned about your efforts to send Dr. X coded messages?" A nod confirmed this wish. "I believe you are work-ing hard to communicate feelings inside, and you hope that Dr. X may feel the same kind of pain and messy feelings that you feel." Anne was shocked: "How did you know? Can you read my mind?" I told her that I couldn't read her mind; rather, she was extremely engaged in the testing and that several of her responses helped me understand that she was des-perately trying to make a connection with Dr. X, despite fears of long-ings and of being hurt. She nodded. I continued: "I have a hunch that you put your body in harm's way as another means of evoking caring and protection from Dr. X. I hope you will consider speaking more directly about feelings, rather than damaging your body, because if you die there will be no chance to get the care and nurturing you want from Dr. X." Anne corrected me on this point. She told me that she was not trying to kill herself in order to get support from her therapist but thought that she was putting her body in harm's way in order to piss off her therapist. I wondered why she'd be motivated to upset and anger her therapist, and she added, "It's what I do with my boyfriends. When they get mad, at least I know that they care. I don't trust the words. They say they love me, but that could mean anything. But when they get angry because I've done something stupid, then I know that they care." I thanked Anne for this correction and told her that I thought this was a most important revelation. Anne agreed to my request to share this correction with Dr. X, and as our feedback session was nearing an end, I asked if she had other questions or comments. Anne added, "This was weird, but kinda fun too. Can you give my stories to Dr. X?" I agreed to her request, then suggested she and Dr. X consider reading the stories together, and perhaps Anne could give Dr. X some clues about embedded messages.

As I walked Anne to the door, I considered the possibility of pointing out to Anne that she, in fact, was trying to seek love and nurturance from another, but decided it was more important that Anne leave with a formulation that belonged to her. As the door closed, I worried about the likely repetition of Anne's covert operations due to her disavowed needs and longing and deep distrust of people. I hoped that she had taken in a few ideas and that in time she and her doctor would have a chance to decipher the chaotic internal experiences, thereby decreasing the risk of future suicide attempts.

FOLLOW-UP

Seven months later I learned several important facts. While the therapy deepened after the testing consultation when the pair decoded Anne's stories together, an interruption in the treatment derailed their progress. Following Dr. X's summer vacation, Anne was initially withdrawn, then returned to the pattern of self-destructive behaviors, making a suicide attempt by overdosing on medication prescribed by Dr. X. Facing repeated enactments and therapeutic impasse, Dr. X sought consultation from a senior analyst, who confirmed that Anne's overdose and battles were diversions from loving feelings. He suggested that they take up the issue of Anne's reluctance to communicate loving feelings and ended the consultation. Bolstered by a second opinion from a senior consultant, and witnessing the process in real time, Dr. X placed greater emphasis on the therapist–patient relationship and interpreted Anne's self-attack as a fear and avoidance of intimacy.

Following weeks of in-session rupture and repairs, the tide began to turn as Anne responded to the interventions. For example, instead of hoarding medications and then overdosing, Anne worked to convince her therapist to allow her beloved cat to be present during sessions. Dr. X saw this as a positive sign of Anne's attempts to bring the softer sides of her longing and desire for nurturance into the treatment, while simultaneously keeping up an argument with her therapist. Dr. X remarked that she was pleased with the shift from near-fatal overdoses and self-mutilation to a productive engagement in the sessions.

When undertaking a therapeutic assessment with a patient who is suffering from complex treatment-resistant disorders, the ambitions of the consultant must be tempered by the realities that the therapeutic impacts of the assessment may be slow and uneven. Anne and Dr. X struggled for many months following my consultation and required further consultation after another suicide attempt. The fact that Anne was able to complete a lengthy treatment, gain considerable ego strength, and break the cycle of suicidal and self-destructive behaviors is more of a testament to the long and arduous engagement between Anne and her therapist. At best, my consultation and that of another senior analyst could be viewed as necessary, but certainly not sufficient, interventions to break a therapeutic impasse. Rather, Anne and her therapist had to survive multiple rupture and repair cycles, suffer the anxieties of potential death, and gradually develop a more direct language for Anne's needs and desires, as well as her hostile feelings and distrust.

The therapeutic assessment model used in this consultation helped to focus Dr. X's initially vague questions and, more importantly, allowed

Anne to join in a collaborative assessment of her difficulties. Upon further reflection, I was left with the impression that for Anne the most important aspect of the psychological testing was an opportunity to shape the referral questions and ultimately to have the last word in the feedback session. Her final expression of the underlying desire and motivation for her provocatively destructive behavior ultimately allowed her to claim responsibility for her actions and gave the pair an opening to explore this dynamic.

REFERENCES

Ackerman, S. J., Hilsenroth, M. J., Baity, M. R., & Blagys, M. D. (2000). Interaction of therapeutic process and alliance during psychological assessment. *Journal of Personality Assessment, 75*(1), 82–109.

Exner, J. (2003). *The Rorschach: A comprehensive system* (4th ed.). Hoboken, NJ: Wiley.

Finn, S. E. (2003). Therapeutic assessment of a man with 'ADD.' *Journal of Personality Assessment, 80*(2), 115–129.

Finn, S. E., & Tonsager, M. E. (1992). Therapeutic effects of providing MMPI–2 test feedback to college students awaiting therapy. *Psychological Assessment, 4*, 278–287.

Hilsenroth, M. J., Peters, E. J., & Ackerman, S. J. (2004). The development of therapeutic alliance during psychological assessment: Patient and therapist perspectives across treatment. *Journal of Personality Assessment, 83*(3), 332–344.

Lerner, P. M. (1991). *Psychoanalytic theory and the Rorschach*. London, England: Analytic Press.

Murray, H. A. (1943). *Thematic Apperception Test manual*. Cambridge, MA: Harvard University Press.

Newman, M. L., & Greenway, P. (1997). Therapeutic effects of providing MMPI-2 test feedback to clients at a university counseling service: A collaborative approach. *Psychological Assessment, 9*(2), 122–131.

Peters, E. J., Handler, L., White, K. G., & Winkel, J. D. (2008). 'Am I going crazy, doc?': A self psychology approach to therapeutic assessment. *Journal of Personality Assessment, 90*(5), 421–434.

Smith, J. D., & Handler, L. (2009). 'Why do I get in trouble so much?': A family therapeutic assessment case study. *Journal of Personality Assessment 91*(3), 197–210.

Tharinger, D. J., Finn, S. E., Wilkinson, A. D., & Schaber, P. M. (2007). Therapeutic assessment with a child as a family intervention: A clinical and research case study. *Psychology in the Schools, 44*(3), 293–309.

Tharinger, D. J., Finn, S. E., Gentry, L., Hamilton, A., Fowler, J., Matson, M., Krumholz, L., & Walkowiak, J. (2009). Therapeutic assessment with children: A pilot study of treatment acceptability and outcomes. *Journal of Personality Assessment, 91*(3), 238–244.

Urist, J. (1977). The Rorschach Test and the assessment of object relations. *Journal of Personality Assessment, 41*(1), 3–9.

Wechsler, D. (1997). *Wechsler Adult Intelligence Scale–Third Edition (WAIS-III) manual.* New York, NY: The Psychological Corporation.

Using Therapeutic Assessment to Explore Emotional Constriction: A Creative Professional in Crisis

JAN H. KAMPHUIS AND HILDE DE SAEGER

CONTEXT OF REFERRAL

Arnold was a 37-year-old self-referred client, who sought help because of persistent work-related problems and pervasive, general unhappiness. One of his colleagues he had confided in had become quite concerned about him and had urged him to seek professional help in the academic clinic "to sort things out."

COLLABORATIVE GENERATION OF QUESTIONS AND THEIR PERSONAL CONTEXT

In generating and contextualizing the assessment questions, the following information was collected: Arnold was living with his wife and two young children and worked as a "creative" in commercial web design. Although he had found his work a source of satisfaction in the early years, he had increasingly lost pleasure in it, and now it felt like one great negative pressure to him. This led up to his first question: whether commercial web design was truly his field and whether he was cut out to be an entrepreneur.

In pursuing the context of this question, Arnold reported that he had discovered his artistic talents at the age of 16 and thought he might later do something with that gift. As it turned out, he became a web designer for a software firm, designing commercial sites. He was quite good at it and enjoyed considerable esteem from his colleagues for the quality of his work. Increasingly, however, he had been suffering under the pressure to be creative and the unrelenting time constraints imposed upon him. Moreover, he felt his work (and that of his peers) had often become superficial and based on "tricks and easy gimmicks." He had sensed he was losing the fun part of his job.

Lately, things had gotten so bad that Arnold felt suffocated at the office and had strong urges to escape. He denied panic attacks but confessed to spending sometimes close to an hour in the men's room to avoid questions from colleagues, meetings, or business assignments. Two weeks earlier, he felt no longer able to tolerate the anxiety he experienced while being at work, and he had called in sick. His colleagues were also a circle of friends, and his problems initially met with a lot of understanding. However, as weeks went by, the business started to suffer from his absence, and he was pushed to apply for health benefits from the social services of the Belgian welfare system.

Arnold had sought help to sort out his doubts about his life two years earlier. To get more in touch and "congruent" with his feelings, he had participated in an equine-assisted therapy workshop. While he reported some benefit from this experience, he felt it did not "stick," and he had been unable to translate his learning to his current life. He had therefore sought some additional input from a theologian who provided (nonreligious) "philosophical sessions," which he characterized as helpful, but both he and his counselor felt these sessions were no substitute for true therapy. His wife as well as a colleague had pushed him to seek more specialized help, as he was increasingly suffering from difficulty with concentration and noticeable apathetic and dark moods.

Arnold described his mood as generally tense and miserable during the past two months, but he would sometimes brighten during weekends or trips. A major frustration for Arnold was that he simply could not find or access any real passions inside himself, which made him feel "lazy" and "lifeless" at the same time. He suspected that these observations were related to the frustrations expressed by his wife, who had repeatedly told him "it drove her crazy he would just not stand up for his point of view" and would always stay so "reasonable and uninvolved." It was at this point that I[1] welcomed his questions regarding the origins of his lack of vitality, his doubts about personal laziness, and his difficulty finding and sticking to his position on issues.

As part of his own soul searching into the origins of his longstanding lack of passions and zest, Arnold was "pretty sure" that his intense, conflicted relationship with his father had something to do with it. He quickly related his father's childhood history, noting it was significant "to put things in perspective." When Arnold was 11 years old, his father suffered the sudden loss of *his* father. From that time onward, Arnold's father had been the primary caretaker of his siblings. From Arnold's perspective, this experience had marked and shaped his father's personality. He described him as very self-sufficient, wise, and with rather a strict sense of what was right and wrong, however always based on very rational arguments that nobody seemed able to counter. Even as an adolescent, Arnold had always considered his father's opinions to be well taken—"never nonsense"— but had also felt constricted by the ever-present rationality. Arnold had found it "not easy" to get angry with his father, as his analyses were utterly "reasonable, rational, sensible," and "worst of all, one always has the sense they were all meant well." Moreover, underneath his father's apparent self-sufficiency, Arnold had always sensed quite a bit of fragility; his father was never "light." In fact, while growing up, he had been reluctant to burden his father. Looking back, Arnold went through his "unusual" adolescence, "without major issues or upheavals" due to this reluctance, but he felt he had missed out on experimenting, on having "a moratorium" on [his] identity. As an adult, encouraged by his wife, Arnold had increasingly felt resentful of his father's hyper-rational and overbearing style, and he had a strong desire to tell his father how much space he took up and how little he left for others. "Did I become apathetic due to his overbearing

---

[1]"I" refers to the first author.

presence?" Arnold wondered. He had some anger toward his mother, who had let this all happen. She was described as nervous, distressed, and prone to feelings of guilt.

Our initial meeting thus yielded the following questions:

1. Is advertising truly my field? Am I cut out to be an entrepreneur?
2. How can I learn to get over my difficulties with concentration?
3. Am I lazy?
4. How can I develop or dig up passion in myself? How is it that I feel so little vitality right now?
5. How is it that I have such difficulty identifying what my position is about issues? How come I don't know what is real and what to defend?

⌐📝 Teaching Point

Note that this type of clinical interview does not (necessarily) address the standard content of comprehensive psychiatric intakes, including developmental milestones, sexual functioning, family-of-origin disciplinary practices, etc. All of these issues may be pertinent to understanding the client's questions and will then be asked and recorded, but more likely they are not and then foregone. In other words, the observation deck (Finn, 1996) of the interview is set by the client's questions—and ultimately by the client.

Another thing to note is that an informal "factor analysis" of the questions posed by the client can be fertile soil for hypotheses of what might be driving the client's core issues. For example, in this particular case, the difficulties with concentration and the phrasing of the questions "am I lazy?" may hint at depression, whereas the other questions suggest that the client has difficulties accessing his emotions and motivational resources.

IMPRESSIONS AND HYPOTHESES

Several observations elicited my curiosity about Arnold's way of handling his emotions and the effect this might have on himself and people close to him. Perhaps most notable in that regard was the notebook

Arnold carried with him to the sessions. It contained quotes of things that seemed important to him and included, among other things, notable comments from the theologian. Likewise, when I made a comment that Arnold deemed noteworthy, it was added to this little book, in careful, artistic handwriting. From the start, I had mixed feelings about this book, but it took me some time to articulate for myself what troubled me about it. On the one hand, I recognized the commitment to gaining insights from the sessions, as well as how ephemeral such insights can be, especially when cognitive processing is hampered by depressive and anxious affect. And, of course, it was gratifying to "get a score" in his notebook. On the other hand, it seemed that the notebook kept distance between Arnold and his immediate experience, as well as between him and me. Even when relating the potentially dire financial situation threatening his family, Arnold did not seem particularly emotional or aroused to me. The notebook became a symbol of what made it difficult to coexperience the emotional aspect of his current predicament, to get to know him, and to feel empathy in the moment. I wondered if the notebook expressed a more general, habitual way of keeping his emotions at bay, to himself and others.

STANDARDIZED TESTING

To assess a broad array of personality and psychopathology characteristics in a standardized fashion, we opted for the Minnesota Multiphasic Personality Inventory–Revised (MMPI-2; Butcher, Dahlstrom, Graham, Tellegen, & Kaemmer, 1989). To gain additional insight at the level of emotion regulation, self- and object relations, and internal resources and stresses, we administered the Rorschach Inkblot Method (RIM; Exner, 1995). Insights from the RIM were expected to yield incremental value in elucidating aspects of the question about his lack of vitality and passion (i.e., question 4) and about his difficulty finding and sticking to his perspective on issues (i.e., question 5). Finally, to test the hypothesis that his difficulties with concentration and his self-perceived "laziness" (i.e., questions 2 and 3) might be related to depressive and/or specific work-related stress symptomatology, we administered the Beck Depression Inventory (BDI; Beck, Ward, Mendelson, Mock, & Erbauch, 1961) and the Utrechtse Burnout Schaal ([The Utrecht Burnout Scale/Maslach Burnout Inventory]; Schaufeli & van Dierendonck, 2000), respectively. Of note, the first author specifically introduced these tests as "other ways to communicate about yourself and how you are doing, so that we can best answer your questions." Such introduction provides another opportunity to underscore the individualized and collaborative nature of the psychological assessment.

MMPI-2

Teaching Point

A first point worth noting is the VRIN elevation (T = 81). This score indicates that Arnold showed inconsistent responses to items that have very similar content. In fact, when conducting empirical research on groups, the recommended cut-point is a T-score of 80, which Arnold exceeds by one. Interestingly, the elevation jives well with a spontaneous comment Arnold made upon completing the MMPI-2. He noted that there were many questions where he wasn't sure what to put, for example, regarding whether "he enjoyed parties or not." It depended for him, he said, on when the party took place and if it was work-related or not, and he decided to just go with his first impulse and hoped that was okay. I was concerned about him exceeding the cut-point, but his readily interpretable profile and enthusiastic collaboration strongly argued against invalidity.

See Table 7.1. On the substantive scales, Arnold produced an MMPI-2 profile with multiple (i.e., five) Clinical Scale elevations. Going by the (MMPI-2) book (e.g., Graham, 2006), one should explore the various two- and three-point code types that may be constructed with these elevations and seek consistent, overlapping descriptions. Using the Harris Lingoes and content (component) scales, one might subsequently seek to fine-tune the interpretation. However, this profile is more meaningfully interpreted when relying on the Reconstructed Clinical Scales (RCs; Tellegen et al., 2003; Finn & Kamphuis, 2006).

Table 7.1   Arnold's MMPI-2 Clinical Scales

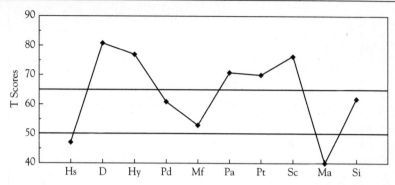

Note: Hs = Hypochondriasis, D = Depression, Hy = Hysteria, Pd = Psychopathic Deviate, Mf = Masculinity-Femininity, Pa = Paranoia, Pt = Psychasthenia, Sc = Schizophrenia, Ma = Mania, Si = Social Introversion. Excerpted from the MMPI-2® *(Minnesota Multiphasic Personality Inventory®-2) Manual for Administration, Scoring and Interpretation, Revised Edition.* Copyright © 2001 by the Regents of the University of Minnesota. All rights reserved. Used by permission of the University of Minnesota Press. "MMPI" and "Minnesota Multiphasic Personality Inventory" are registered trademarks owned by the Regents of the University of Minnesota.

See Table 7.2. As it turns out, many of the Clinical Scale elevations may be explained by the elevated Demoralization score (RCd = 81; see also Finn & Kamphuis, 2007, for a similar profile). Elevation on RCd involves generalized unhappiness associated with depression and anxiety, and provides a good global estimate of a person's current level of emotional functioning and distress. Of the remaining RC scores, the near elevated RC2 (Low Positive Emotions) and the elevated RC3 (Cynicism) were notable. Arnold's score on RC2 (Low Positive Emotions) fell into the top 10% of the normative sample. People with similar scores report few positive, interesting, or pleasurable experiences in their lives and tend to lead withdrawn, isolated lives. Lack of energy and difficulty making decisions are common. The elevated score on RC3, Cynicism, was a bit puzzling. RC3 concerns non-self-referential cynicism and conveys such attitudes as "other people are out only for themselves" and people tend to abuse others "if they can get away with it." Perhaps this elevation was due to Arnold's recently acquired cynical attitude toward his work.

Table 7.2   Arnold's Restructured Clinical Scales

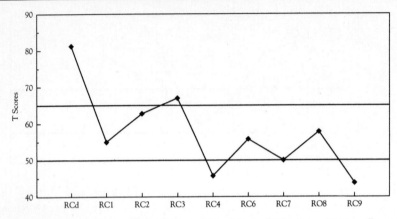

Note: RCd = Demoralization, RC1 = Somatic Complaints, RC2 = Low Positive Emotions, RC3 = Cynicism, RC4 = Antisocial Behavior, RC6 = Ideas of Persecution, RC7 = Dysfunctional Negative Emotions, RC8 = Aberrant Experiences, RC9 = Hypomanic Activation. Excerpted from the MMPI-2® *(Minnesota Multiphasic Personality Inventory®-2) Restructured Clinical (RC) Scales: Development, Validation, and Interpretation.* Copyright © 2003 by the Regents of the University of Minnesota. All rights reserved. Used by permission of the University of Minnesota Press. "MMPI" and "Minnesota Multiphasic Personality Inventory" are registered trademarks owned by the Regents of the University of Minnesota.

Rorschach Inkblot Method (RIM)

See Table 7.3. According to the Comprehensive System scores, Arnold could be categorized as super-extratensive $(EB = 2: 8.0)$, i.e., dependent on the external world for gratification and prone toward emotional discharge. Super-extratensive persons have an inflexible style of problem solving that is characterized by seeking outside input. Currently, there appeared to be many negative forces that worked against positive adjustment $(es = 19)$, and it was fair to say that Arnold was emotionally overwhelmed. In fact, in view of the elevated *S-CON*, he was at risk for self-destructive behaviors. The abundant shading responses suggested more about the nature of the negative forces. Specifically, Arnold's scores suggested the presence of distress and unpleasant emotional states, particularly associated with painful introspection $(V = 4)$ and anxiety $(Y = 4)$. Moreover, the elevated *DEPI* indicated significant depression.

Also notable in Arnold's scores was a strong tendency to withdraw from emotional stimuli $(Afr = .39)$. People with these scores tend not

Table 7.3 Arnold's Structural Summary

Location Features		Determinants		Contents		Approach	
		Blends	**Single**	H = 2		I : WS.W.D.WS	
Zf	= 25	CF.YF	M = 1	(H) = 4		II : WS.D.W.Dd.WS	
ZSum	= 93.5	m.C'	FM = 3	Hd = 1		III : WS.D.DdS.D	
ZEst	= 84.5	FT.FY	m = 3	(Hd) = 3		IV : W.WS.W.W	
		FM.FC	FC = 0	Hx = 4		V : W.D.W.D.Dd	
W	= 17	FV.M	CF = 5	A = 9		VI : Dd.D.D.W	
D	= 14		C = 1	(A) = 1		VII : D.Dd	
W + D	= 31		Cn = 0	Ad = 4		VIII : W.D.DS	
Dd	= 8		FC' = 1	(Ad) = 0		IX : DdS.D.D	
S	= 11		C'F = 0	An = 2		X : W.W.DdS.D.DdS	
			C' = 0	Art = 5			
DQ			FT = 0	Ay = 1		**Special Scores**	
+	= 9		TF = 0	Bl = 2			Lv1 Lv2
o	= 29		T = 0	Bt = 0		DV =	1 × 1 0 × 2
v/+	= 0		FV = 3	Cg = 0		INC =	0 × 2 0 × 4
v	= 1		VF = 0	Cl = 0		DR =	0 × 3 0 × 6
			V = 0	Ex = 1		AB =	3 × 4 0 × 7
			FY = 2	Fd = 1		ALOG =	1 × 5
			YF = 0	Fi = 0		CON =	0 × 7
			Y = 0	Ge = 1		**Raw Sum6**	= 5
Form Quality			Fr = 0	Hh = 3		**Wgtd Sum6**	= 18
FQx	MQual	W+D	rF = 0	Ls = 1			
+ = 0	= 0	= 0	FD = 0	Na = 2		AB = 1	GHR = 7
o = 14	= 0	= 13	F = 15	Sc = 3		AG = 1	PHR = 6
u = 15	= 1	= 11		Sx = 1		COP = 3	MOR = 5
− = 9	= 1	= 6		Xy = 0		CP = 0	PER = 0
none = 1	= 0	= 1	(2) = 9	Id = 1			PSV = 0

RATIOS, PERCENTAGES, AND DERIVATIONS

R = 39		L = 0.63	FC:CF+C = 1:7	COP = 3		AG = 1
			Pure C = 1	GHR:PHR = 7:6		
EB = 2:8.0	EA = 10.0	EBPer = 4.0	SmC':WSmC = 2:8.0	a:p = 9:1		
eb = 8:11	es = 19	D = −3	Afr = 0.39	Food = 1		
	Adj es = 13	Adj D = −1	S = 11	SumT = 1		
			Blends/R = 5:39	Human Cont = 10		
FM = 4	SumC' = 2	SumT = 1	CP = 0	PureH = 2		
m = 4	SumV = 4	SumY = 4		PER = 0		
				Isol Indx = 0.15		

			XA% = 0.74	Zf = 25	3r+(2)/R	= 0.23
			WDA% = 0.77	W:D:Dd = 17:14:8	Fr+rF	= 0
		Sum6 = 5	X−% = 0.23	W:M = 17:2	SumV	= 4
a:p	= 9:1	Lv2 = 0	S− = 7	Zd = +9.0	FD	= 0
Ma:Mp	= 1:1	WSum6 = 18	P = 6	PSV = 0	An+Xy	= 2
2AB+Art + Ay	= 8	M− = 1	X+% = 0.36	DQ+ = 9	MOR	= 5
MOR	= 5	Mnone = 0	Xu% = 0.38	DQv = 1	H:(H)+Hd+(Hd)	= 2:8

PTI = 1	DEPI = 6	CDI = 3	S-CON = 9	HVI = No	OBS = NO

to engage when they are emotional, which can be experienced as quite frustrating by their intimates. Thus, his scores suggested that while he was an emotionally responsive person, he kept these experiences private and found ways to quickly disengage from them. Specifically, Arnold made heavy use of intellectualization to escape from unpleasant, overwhelming emotions $(2AB + (Art + Ay) = 8)$.

Arnold appeared to hold a low estimate of his self-worth and tended to perceive others as more able, attractive, talented, and worthwhile $(3R + (2)/R = .23)$. Perhaps as a result, it appeared he preferred not to reflect too much on himself $(FD = 0)$. The high score on MOR provided strong evidence for his negative self-image and subjective depression; he was likely to have a sense of himself as damaged or defective and to hold pessimistic views of the outside world.

In the domain of interpersonal perception, two scores warranted attention. First, it was likely that when growing up, Arnold did not receive the attention, attunement, and recognition he needed $(Fd = 1)$. In his current social world, he felt uncomfortable and different from others. Although he was able to function in a matrix of cooperative relationships $(COP = 1)$, he probably did not identify with his social sur-round $(H: (H) + Hd + (Hd) = 2: 8)$.

In general, Arnold's reality testing and judgment were adequate and adaptive $(XA\% = .74)$, although some unusual perceptions were likely to occur. However, when he was angry or oppositional, the scores suggested that his thinking could derail and that his judgment might falter $(S- = 7)$.

This interpretation almost exclusively relies on the perceptual interpreta-tion of the RIM scores. However, some of Arnold's responses were particularly rich when examined from a content, associational point of view. For example, on Card IV, he saw "a view on the back of a dragon; a large, muscular back; it's a sad idea, a pathetic dragon," and to Card V, he associated "sort of a dark angel; shoulder here, the black makes it a dark angel," both strikingly consis-tent with his description of how he had experienced his father. Both his "sign-in" response, "this is a devil, a demon," and his "sign-out" response, "It looks like you are looking from above into a hole in the ground and two characters have something that they are throwing into that hole, with bad intentions," may speak to how he experienced himself and what was done to him. Overall, many morbid images characterized this RIM protocol.

Maslach Burnout Inventory (MBI, Dutch Translation)

Arnold was asked to complete the MBI to get a sense of his attitude toward his current job. The MBI consists of 15 items that are rated on a 7-point scale (0 = "Never applicable to me"; 6 = "Always/Daily applicable to me"). These items form three subscales: (a) "Exhaustion" (five items), which measures psychological/mental fatigue and the sense of feeling "burned out" or "finished" due to efforts at work; (b) "Distance" (four items) concerns a distant, cynical, and low commitment attitude toward one's job; and (c) "Competence" (six items) refers to the perception that one is capable of doing the work, is self-efficacious, and that one makes a valuable contribution to the organization and achieves valuable outcomes. Arnold's Distance scores were commensurate with those of workers with burnout complaints, and he endorsed items like "I am no longer as enthusiastic about my work as I used to be" and "I have grown more cynical about the effects of my work." Likewise, he endorsed most items indicative of mental exhaustion, including "I feel mentally totally exhausted by my work" and "A full day of work is a major burden for me."

Beck Depression Inventory (BDI)

The BDI was administered to assess the level and nature of depressive symptoms over the past week (Beck et al., 1961). The BDI has been established as the most widely used tool for assessing the level of depressive symptoms. It comprises 21 items and has strong psychometric properties (Beck, Steer, & Garbin, 1988). BDI scores can range from 0 to 63. Arnold scored 22, commensurate with a mild to moderate level of depression. Specifically, he heavily endorsed statements that involved self-reproach and guilt, as well as loss of interest and satisfaction.

REFLECTIONS AND HYPOTHESES

The MMPI-2, BDI, and RIM all suggested a level of depressive symptomatology that warrants clinical attention—in fact, of greater severity than I had picked up on during the interview. Certainly such a level of depressive symptoms speaks to Arnold's questions about his difficulty concentrating, and likely also to his sense of lacking vitality and lust for life. The RIM identified another essential dimension to help address Arnold's questions: his characteristic way of experiencing and regulating emotions. Although he was clearly capable of and perhaps even constitutionally prone to experiencing strong emotions, Arnold had adopted a tendency to avoid emotions and to refrain from sharing them interpersonally (which I had also noticed in how he related his current difficulties). Perhaps it was easier for him to communicate how demoralized and depressed he was on a test that required no social interaction (i.e., the MMPI-2), than to do so during the interview and the RIM, both of which required social interaction. I hypothesized that Arnold had learned that emotions were not safe for him, perhaps because, as suggested by the RIM and his personal account, he had not been supported in recognizing, containing, and regulating his emotions during childhood. Intellectualization had become a more trusted route.

In planning for the assessment feedback session, I expected that Arnold would recognize the manifestations of depression and demoralization and would be receptive to their seriousness if I showed the corresponding elevations in his MMPI-2 profile. In the language of TA, I expected this to be Level 1 information (i.e., familiar information, consistent with the client's current self-concept) for the client, or perhaps Level 2 (i.e., information that will nuance and reframe the client's self-concept) because of the severity (Finn, 1996). I surmised that the assessment information regarding his habitual emotional style and its possible origins would constitute Level 3 information (i.e., findings that are highly discrepant and/or less likely to be assimilated). This inspired the aim of the Assessment Intervention Session: to invite his habitual style of handling emotions *in vivo*, in order to share observations and have the opportunity to try out alternative adaptations.

THE ASSESSMENT INTERVENTION SESSION: IDIOGRAPHIC USE OF ASSESSMENT INSTRUMENTS

I shared with Arnold what the test findings indicated about the degree of his current demoralization and depression. He was a bit rattled by this feedback initially, but he expressed some relief about my urging that taking care of this problem should receive priority over anything else. It was, he said, "as if he got permission to take it seriously." I also told him that I thought these findings by themselves could probably account for some of the assessment questions he had posed (concentration, lack of vigor, etc.), but that there seemed to be more to his question about "lack of vitality" and "difficulty taking a stand"; if only because these difficulties probably preceded his current mood state. I suggested we would take a closer look at how he handled emotions and asked him if he was willing to try an experiment with me that entailed telling stories to picture story cards. Arnold, true to form, thought that was "very interesting." My aim with the AIS was to have Arnold actually experience the covariation between his feelings and experiencing passion, zest, and even strongly held personal opinions.

My hypothesis was based on the results of the standardized testing (esp. MMPI-2 and RIM) in the context of his personal account of growing up with an overbearing, hyper-rational father who could not be confronted because of perceived fragility. I opted for the Thematic Apperception Test (TAT; Murray, 1943), for its flexibility in possible instructions and the ambiguous but emotion-eliciting stimulus materials. I selected Card I (the boy with the violin), which commonly elicits themes of frustration, autonomy, and achievement. The theme of this card also seemed relevant to his difficulty taking a stand and defending it, and the difficulty expressing his (bottled-up) anger effectively, as suggested by the RIM. I expected he would notice but not express the boy's frustration and would submit to playing the violin. He related:

TAT I.1

A: I see a boy who has to play the violin. He is dreading it; he has to study, his father and mother told him to. He cannot find any enthusiasm for it, is staring at the stupid thing; what is fun about it, what? His parents told him it is not fun to learn it, but it will be fun to have mastered it.

JHK: How does the story continue?

A: Difficult . . . I don't know . . . Ultimately, he learns to play it, and is finally set free.

JHK: How does the boy feel?

A: Very unhappy; he can't make himself do it. Deep frustration.

I was struck by the parallel to how Arnold might experience his job situation, and it may have been productive to have shared this impression with him, but instead I stuck to my plan of getting him to emote, in order to gain access to his vitality and anger. I proceeded:

JHK: You came up with a story in which the child submits to the demands of the parents and ends up feeling very unhappy and frustrated. You know, sometimes people come up with very different stories, for example, in which the child expresses how it feels and that he doesn't want to play. Can you imagine coming up with a more assertive story, in which the boy ends up with less frustration?

A: That would be quite hard.

JHK: Are you willing to give it a try?

A: Okay then [takes a long time looking at the picture].

TAT I.2

A: He places the violin in such a way near the door that when the parent will enter the door, it will get crushed. He will not confront them, but will make it look like an accident.

JHK: What strikes you about this story?

A: I don't know . . . I guess he got what he wanted. . .

JHK: I'll tell you what struck me. Do you remember what I asked you, with this story?

A: Not exactly.

JHK: I suggested you try on a more assertive story for this situation. Do you think you did?

A: No.

JHK: Do you find it hard, to make an assertive story?

A: [nods]

JHK: What makes it hard?

A: I don't know. I am reminded of my own children. My son will tell me, "I don't want to go to the swimming lessons, I don't want to," and he in fact refuses. Secretly I am quite pleased with that; at least I don't pass it on. But I don't know how to do that.

JHK: Shall we try it one more time? Are you okay with that?

A: Yes, okay.

TAT I.3

A: [. . .] He picks up the violin and intends to embrace a very different style of music than hoped for by his parents.

JHK: (after a long silence) It's hard, isn't it . . . What happened in this story? You find creative ways, kind of passive or not-so-passive resistance, but you don't really express what you want. Let's try one more time to see what happens when you do.

TAT I.4

A: "I don't want to!" he says, and he slams the thing on the edge of the table. [Maximal confrontation!]

JHK: Wow. How did that feel to you?

A: It's not what I want. This is not good, not where I want to go.

JHK: It looks to me that when you start to feel some of the anger you need to assert yourself, a LOT of anger comes out . . . and in rather a violent way. No wonder you are concerned about getting to that point. . . . So . . . , I guess we don't want this much anger. Let's practice one last time making an assertive story.

TAT 18BM (man with coat)

A: Hmm . . . , given the way the picture is made, that's difficult. This is a man who is sent away, and who has resisted this for a long time but at a certain moment, he sees that resistance is futile. People are putting on his coat at the door. He accepts that it is pointless, you can see from everything that he does not want to.

JHK: (gives nonverbal cue to remind Arnold of the instruction)

A: . . . People are pushing him out. When he feels their hands, he says "get off of me, get your dirty hands off me," and he turns around to face the persons who are pushing him, and . . . I am not sure what he is doing. . . . This is very hard to come up with. It feels forced.

JHK: What did you feel when making up this story?

A: I don't know, I am not sure . . .

JHK: I am pushing you a little here: let's explore this some more, did you feel anything in your body?

A: Hmm, yes, I still feel it in my stomach, like it's contracting. . . . There is shame connected to it, it's embarrassing . . .

JHK: You seem very present to me, right now.

A: I am, it's quite uncomfortable, but I am definitely here.

JHK: More than before?

A: Definitely more than before, I feel very alive, but it is not all that comfortable.

✎ Teaching Point

In retrospect, I wish I had asked Arnold to make "1—not at all to 10—extremely" ratings of the degree of vitality he experienced immediately after telling each story. I think that would have provided both of us with additional convincing evidence of the association between experiencing (uncomfortable) emotions and feeling alive and vital. Nevertheless, we believe that this excerpt may exemplify how a successful Assessment Intervention Session may provide clients (and assessors) with experiences that bring test findings to life. Such experiences likely carry much more momentum for change than unilaterally presented insights that are easy to intellectualize.

SUMMARY/DISCUSSION SESSION

I decided to first present some of the major themes the testing revealed, before going into the specific questions posed by Arnold. One might also dive straight into the Q&A, but I thought it would work best with Arnold to set the stage by introducing the main ingredients first. My concern was that I might at some point during the session find myself in an intellectual discussion about how the MMPI-2 and RIM "work," and so I put some thought into how I would handle those moments.[2] After some small talk and orienting him to our

---

[2]Alternatively, as suggested to me during supervision, I might have let this happen and then have used the observation as an opportunity to notice this dynamic in vivo (e.g., "I notice that we are talking about the intricacies of the tests, and that we are losing some of the emotional intensity. Do you agree? What might that be about?").

respective roles (Me—expert on the tests, Arnold—expert on his life), I explained to Arnold:

"Before specifically going into your questions, I would like to share some of the main themes I believe our work has revealed." To preempt intellectual discussion, I continued:

> I will not go into how each test indicates what it does, as interesting as that is. Should you afterwards feel you want more information on that aspect of the assessment, we can schedule for that, but we have a lot of ground to cover, and I suggest we give that priority right now. Is that okay with you?

The following are selected and expanded excerpts from my planning for the feedback session. I started out with what we had already shared prior to the Assessment Intervention Session, which I knew to be Level 2 information for him:

> *Your bucket is spilling over.* Arnold, you are currently experiencing an overwhelming amount of negative emotions, including powerlessness and frustration. You ruminate a lot about your current predicament, which in part explains why it is so hard for you to put your mind to anything else. You are feeling despondent and are pessimistic about the future. The testing suggests strongly that you are overburdened by your current responsibilities and are unable to meet these right now, at home and at work. In sum, you are experiencing a lot of depressive feelings, and this requires serious attention: You acutely need additional support.

In response, Arnold indicated he had not quite recognized how serious these symptoms were, but he did feel the testing had been accurate.

Dangerous Emotions

> While growing up, you missed out on the necessary emotional attention and attunement. This has had an effect on how you see yourself, but even more on how you habitually handle emotions. Emotions are not a safe domain for you, as you could not count on support when overwhelmed. We develop and grow the

capacity to contain emotions by drawing on our caretakers when our "cup is spilling over." [Here I presented the metaphor of *cup and saucer*, developed by Finn (2003), to illustrate how parents help contain emotions for their children, and how this leads to internalization and internal resources for handling emotions]. When caretakers, for one reason or another, do not perceive and/or do not help you contain intense emotions, the capacity to handle emotions does not grow, and a child learns to fear and avoid emotional arousal because it is overwhelming to him.

It was quite clear to see how the cup and saucer metaphor really "took" for Arnold. I noticed how he seemed much more present than usual, almost perked up. He took no notes this time, but it looked like he was excited to scan his autobiographical memory for how this might make sense of his experiences. "I think you have something there," he said, looking me straight in the eye.

Central Dilemma

This brings me to what I see as your central dilemma of change: Keeping a distance from emotions has its pay-off—you can keep painful feelings at bay and prevent getting overwhelmed. But it also comes at a cost: It blocks permanent emotional processing and perhaps even more important to your questions, it goes at the expense of zest for life, vitality, and passion. You now long for this passion and zest, but you are quite understandably afraid to enter this emotional world by yourself.

A: "I don't know how get to my emotions," he said, "but I suppose you would recommend me seeking help for that? Do you know anyone who could help me with that?"

WRITTEN FEEDBACK FOR ARNOLD

The written feedback for Arnold included specific answers to his questions, much like the feedback outline presented previously, but was modified to accommodate Arnold's reactions to the feedback. As during the feedback session, I put in effort to connect test findings to shared experiences and to use a direct style, as I thought this would work best for Arnold.

How can I learn to get over my difficulties with concentration?

Arnold, you are currently experiencing so much distress and worry that there is no additional cognitive capacity for you to spare. More specifically, the testing suggests you are feeling helpless and unhappy, and you have strong doubts whether things will at all get any better. In addition, you currently lack activities that give you a sense of joy and fulfillment, lack energy, and experience great difficulty in making decisions. Together these complaints make for significant depression. Difficulty concentrating is part and parcel of depression; when your depression lifts, which is something I recommend you give priority to right now, it seems quite likely your ability to concentrate will restore itself too.

Am I lazy?

I did not find any evidence of "laziness" in the testing. On the contrary, the way you approached the inkblot tests suggested quite a bit of effort, like you were not looking for the "easy solutions." What then? First, the words you choose—"lazy"—suggest a tendency towards self-blame. Moreover, the tests show that you now have little energy and generally prefer to leave novel initiatives to others. Again, these findings may be accentuated by the depression you are going through: You may experience yourself and your ambitions quite a bit differently when you lose the "gray overcoat."

How is it that I have such difficulty identifying what my position is about issues? How come I don't know what is real and what to defend?

The testing suggests that emotions can be quite overwhelming for you. Moreover, both the tests and your life story suggest that you have been quite alone with your emotions when growing up. You were not shown how to safely experience your emotions, nor were you shown how to regulate them. You now prefer to keep emotions at a distance; you keep feelings to yourself, and by yourself, you don't allow too much to come in. It seems safer to "intellectualize feelings"—remember our discussion of the notebook—that is, to verbalize them, and in that way control and keep them at arm's length. Other people can sometimes sense this when being with you—I did, and I noticed the difference when you do access your emotions in the moment.

Of note: Emotions are our "prime movers"; they are essential for taking and keeping a stand. Something "feels" right, worthy of defending. Then there is something more specific: You harbor a lot of hidden anger. I think you learned at an early age to stifle that emotion in yourself. You could not afford anger, perhaps especially not in the presence of the "big, sad dragon." However, anger is a primary emotion to signal to yourself and others that limits have been reached, personal boundaries that should not be crossed, and that it is time to take a stand. Both your test scores and our vivid picture story task experience suggest that you find it difficult to be assertive (i.e., to ask for help, to refuse favors, etc.). Moreover, as we have seen, when you now DO get angry, there are strong indications that you find it difficult to modulate it and to maintain level-headed thinking. It may feel like the emotion takes over and that can be quite frightening.

How can I develop or dig up passion in myself? How is it that I feel so little vitality right now?

Arnold, our work together has yielded two factors that each by themselves can block the experience of passion and vitality: (1) significant depressive complaints and intrusive worrying, and (2) a marked tendency to avoid and withdraw from emotions. Avoiding emotions results in your being cut off from your passions and from your vigor. Indeed, what you are experiencing now is a lack of positive feelings, together with a general sense of unhappiness, doom, and self-reproach. To reclaim the positive, motivating feeling states, you first need to take the depression seriously. That is, you need to seek professional help of a more intensive, professional psychotherapeutic nature, I believe. At first, my recommendation is that these sessions should focus on ameliorating the depression, and later on they should be more emotions focused. This emotion work can help you reclaim your vitality by helping you recognize, experience, and ultimately modulate your momentary feelings; attention for these feelings is what you missed out on earlier in your life, and this has undermined your sense of what is "real" to you. This work will also help you dig up your passions, as you called them. I like that wording, and it reminded me of your final RIM response: "It looks like you are looking from above into a hole in the ground and two characters have something that they are throwing into that hole, with bad intentions."

Arnold, it has been a privilege to work with you. You invested yourself, and you have trusted me enough to show yourself during our meetings and in the testing. Our work has vividly shown to me how essential it is to feel our emotions in order to have or reclaim a sense of direction and motivation.

FOLLOW-UP

We decided to schedule a follow-up meeting in three months[3] to assess whether the treatment recommendations were working for him and to learn about new insights that might have come to him during that time period. About halfway during that time interval, I received the following, highly gratifying note from Arnold:

Dear Jan,
I wanted to let you know that I am starting to feel much better over the past couple of weeks. The sessions with Dominique help me and the meds are working. I feel I have chosen the right path. Next week we go on a holiday and I look forward to that. If all goes well, I expect the "Feeling good" book from David Burns you recommended will have arrived, and I will stick it inside my suitcase. As agreed, I will contact you in about two months. I still owe you song lyrics, and here they are [excerpt from a Dutch song]:

A butterfly cannot pull a load
And a carthorse cannot float

---

[3]Unfortunately, this session had not yet transpired when this manuscript was due.

It's about what you choose to see
It's about how you choose to be

PERSONAL IMPACT

For me, this case underscored the central importance of case conceptualization, and how crucial it often is to not attempt doing this by oneself, but to consult others when stuck (or even when not). It is in that context that I want to acknowledge the very valuable contributions both from Stephen Finn and the Viersprong assessment team in helping me plan the assessment intervention and feedback session. It is my personal conviction that without a clear case conceptualization—which TA forces you to do more than regular assessment because of the highly personalized questions to be addressed—you cannot expect the feedback to be helpful, as you have not codeveloped a personal narrative that better fits the client's life and presenting problems. I also think that (a) the intense collaborative effort at generating such a case conceptualization, (b) the feedback session during which assessor and client aim to articulate a more fitting narrative regarding the assessment questions, and (c) the intimate nature of this collaboration help explain why I simply do not forget my TA clients. More than in regular information-gathering assessment (Finn & Tonsager, 1997), one has indeed entered "into the client's shoes" (Finn, 2007), and this tends to deliver experiences to both assessor and client that stick.

In addition, together with Arnold I discovered vividly how disempowering it is to be disconnected from one's emotions. Emotions are our action tendencies, and when disconnected from them, we feel out of control of our lives and of our destinies. On a more personal level, I noticed how much more alive, real, and frankly likable Arnold felt to me when he did connect to his emotions.

REFERENCES

Beck, A. T., Steer, R. A., & Garbin, M. G. (1988). Psychometric properties of the Beck Depression Inventory: Twenty-five years of evaluation. *Clinical Psychology Review, 8,* 77–100.

Beck, A. T., Ward, C. H., Mendelson, M., Mock, J. E., & Erbaugh, J. K. (1961). An inventory for measuring depression. *Archives of General Psychiatry, 41*, 561–571.

Butcher, J. N., Dahlstrom, W. G., Graham, J. R., Tellegen, A., & Kaemmer, B. (1989). *Minnesota Multiphasic Personality Inventory-2 (MMPI-2): Manual for administration and scoring*. Minneapolis: University of Minnesota Press.

Exner, J. E., Jr. (1995). *A Rorschach workbook for the comprehensive system* (4th ed.). Asheville, NC: Rorschach Workshops.

Finn, S. E. (1996). *A manual for using the MMPI-2 as a therapeutic intervention*. Minneapolis: University of Minnesota Press.

Finn, S. E. (2003). Therapeutic Assessment of a man with "ADD." *Journal of Personality Assessment, 80*, 115–129.

Finn, S. E. (2007). *In our clients' shoes: Theory and techniques of therapeutic assessment*. Mahwah, NJ: Lawrence Erlbaum Associates.

Finn, S. E., & Kamphuis, J. H. (2006). The MMPI-2 RC Scales and restraints to innovation, or "What have they done to my song?" *Journal of Personality Assessment 87*, 202–210.

Finn, S. E., & Tonsager, M. E. (1997). Information-gathering and therapeutic models of assessment: Complementary paradigms. *Psychological Assessment, 9*, 374–385.

Graham, J. R. (2006). *MMPI-2: Assessing personality and psychopathology* (4th ed.). New York, NY: Oxford University Press.

Murray, H. A. (1943). *Thematic Apperception Test manual*. Cambridge, MA: Harvard University Press.

Schaufeli W., & van Dierendonck, D. (2000). UBOS, *Utrechtse Burnout Schaal [The Utrecht Burnout Scale/Maslach Burnout Inventory] Manual*. Lisse, The Netherlands: Swets & Zeitlinger B.V.

Tellegen, A., Ben-Porath, Y. S., McNulty, J. L., Arbisi, P. A., Graham, J. R., & Kaemmer, B. (2003). *MMPI-2 Restructured Clinical (RC) Scales: Development, validation, and interpretation*. Minneapolis: University of Minnesota Press.

Tellegen, A., & Ben-Porath, Y. S. (2008). *Minnesota Multiphasic Personality Inventory-2 (MMPI-2-RF): Technical manual*. Minneapolis: University of Minnesota Press.

⟞⟩◆⟨⟝

Therapeutic Assessment Involving Multiple Life Issues: Coming to Terms With Problems of Health, Culture, and Learning

HALE MARTIN AND ERIN JACKLIN

The value of Collaborative/Therapeutic Assessment lies largely in building bridges. The first bridge is into the client's life. This bridge is built out of the client's concerns, history, test data, and relationship with the assessor. The second important bridge is then coconstructed by the assessor and the client to reach new understandings and pos-sibilities in the client's life. It is constructed from test data but also by the assessor–client relationship, experiences during the assessment, and interactions with others involved with the client. We present here a Therapeutic Assessment case that offered substantial challenges to and ultimately an illustration of the bridge-building process central to the Therapeutic Assessment approach (TA; Finn, 1996, 2007).

The most obvious challenge approaching the assessment was the fact that the client had a long history of unsuccessful interventions to address the problems in his life. He had dropped out of high school, been impervious to drug rehabilitation, and had not been helped by the outpatient or inpatient services he had received. He seemed unreachable and also to have limited capacity for insight.

The client had a rare genetic disorder that had substantially affected the trajectory of his life. The resulting physical characteristics had contributed to the development of his coping style and defensives. His unique circumstances were out of the mainstream and would require sensitive attunement to the specific influences in his life in order to reach meaningful understandings that would facilitate change. For example, he often had been viewed as someone to excuse from accountability. An effective intervention would need to focus on his experience and not what others might project onto those with similar disabilities.

The client grew up in a family that emigrated from a Middle Eastern country when he was a small boy. Mixed cultural influences can create contradictions and confusion for children who grow up in two worlds. TA offers a sensitive and flexible phenomenological lens to understand the nuances of multiple cultural influences on development. For example, our client's parents were at a disadvantage in advocating for their son in a school system with which they were not familiar. A family intervention session highlighted the important role family dynamics played in our client's difficulties and in his ultimate movement to a healthier adjustment in life. Careful consideration would be necessary to avoid under- or over-pathologizing our client.

The client had a troubled learning history, which suggested limited ability, significant learning disabilities, or some unique characteristics that hindered success in school. His learning differences likely stemmed, in part, from the genetic disorder. Test data indicated limited ability but did not capture his surprising effectiveness in certain aspects of his life. Again, an approach that was effective in integrating both nomothetic and idiographic data would be important in arriving at useful understandings. These aspects of the case and the increased complexity from their interactions highlight the challenges in building bridges into our client's life experience and then on to new possibilities for his life. This case will illustrate the usefulness of the TA approach in addressing these challenges.

Another bridge was necessary in that this assessment was conducted by a graduate student under supervision. The supervisor, Hale, is a professor who teaches and supervises assessment in a doctoral clinical psychology program. At the time of this assessment, Erin, the supervisee, was in the fourth year of her doctoral training. Erin and Hale had developed a good working relationship with each other. Nevertheless, a supervisory relationship requires good communication to arrive at mutual understandings—effectively building bridges between each other in order to construct meaningful bridges for the client. We will highlight some aspects of this collaboration.

LAYING THE FOUNDATION

Pouya, a 27-year-old male, initially contacted Hale after a referral from a local clinic for a learning disability assessment. He hoped to qualify for extended time or other accommodations on the General Educational Development (GED) test, an equivalent of a high school diploma. He agreed to work with a graduate student under supervision, at a reduced fee for the assessment. Erin agreed to take the case and contacted Pouya by phone to arrange the first meeting.

In the initial interview, Erin worked with Pouya to develop the central questions to be addressed by the assessment. Pouya jumped at the opportunity to codirect the assessment. It quickly became clear that he was interested in more than a learning disability evaluation. Erin took his barrage of questions seriously and discussed with him a potential shift in the initial plan for the assessment in order to accommodate his expanded range of questions. Pouya heartily agreed. Erin and Pouya eventually whittled his many questions down to five that seemed to capture his major concerns about his life:

1. Do I have a learning disability and, if so, what can I do about it?
2. Am I depressed?
3. Why do I become frustrated around authority and stop listening to them?
4. Why haven't I been in a serious relationship, and why am I so scared and self-conscious about myself?
5. What can I do to have somebody beside me in my life in a healthy, 50/50 relationship?

It was clear from these questions that Pouya was open to help and that he and Erin had started constructing a sturdy bridge of communication in their first meeting. They began what would be an ongoing discussion of the context and history surrounding these questions. In the following sessions, Pouya brought in pages of handwritten notes filled with ideas about the questions, further history he wanted to discuss, and thoughts about issues that arose.

Through these conversations and notes, Erin learned that along with his three older siblings, Pouya had been raised by his well-educated and financially stable parents. His parents had hoped Pouya could get better medical care in the United States for his rare genetic disorder. The disorder can be manifested in a variety of characteristics, such as short stature, learning problems, and social difficulties, but its presentation varies widely among individuals afflicted with it. Pouya stated that his diagnosis was never fully explained to him, but he had long felt his parents did not expect as much of him as of his older siblings because of the disorder.

Pouya also shared that he had a history of low academic functioning, culminating in his dropping out of high school in the 10th grade. In addition, he struggled for years with mental health issues, primarily depression and substance abuse. He reported he had been in multiple treatment settings, with little or no improvement. In his teenage years, Pouya's parents placed him in a drug rehabilitation center, where he looked for ways to get high on whatever substances were available. He was later briefly hospitalized on an adolescent inpatient psychiatric unit until he turned 18 and "aged out" of the program. He had also participated in outpatient psychotherapy as a teen and young adult, but he did not find this useful. When Erin asked Pouya what, if anything, was different in this mental health setting, he replied that this was the first time he was seeking help, rather than being forced into treatment. He also noted a similarity between the assessment and when he finally stopped abusing substances in that he had chosen to get sober.

Pouya also described intractable problems in creating and maintaining friendships and romantic relationships as well as an overly close and conflicted relationship with his parents. When the assessment began, Pouya was speaking to his parents three to four times a day on the phone. On the one hand, his Middle Eastern upbringing valued close-ness with family, but on the other hand, Pouya regularly fought with his parents. He readily admitted to behaving in a manner he called "manip-ulative" in that he would try to get his parents to give him things or to do what he wanted by "acting like a five-year-old." In addition to his problems with his parents, Pouya identified a history of recurrent prob-lems with people in authority, dating back at least to high school, and described himself as very defiant at times.

Erin relayed to Hale that she found Pouya likable. She also noted how accommodating he was and how easily he had connected to her. He seemed much younger than his 27 years, and she felt drawn to take care of him by his youthful presentation and physical appearance. She was also aware, however, of feeling "put off" by him at times.

Erin discussed with Hale her observation that Pouya could be vulner-able and ask for help but that he also demonstrated poor insight into the motivation of those around him who could help him and the way in which his actions affected others. At times, Pouya seemed to believe others could and should be able to read his mind and were purposely choosing to thwart him by not acquiescing to his wishes. One strik-ing example involved Pouya desperately needing and wanting help with schoolwork. However, instead of asking directly, he would tell his teachers and counselors, "I am just going to drop out," and eventually he did drop out. When telling this story, Pouya expressed anger that his teachers and counselors had not intervened. He shared his strong belief at the time that dropping out was the clearest way to show them how desperately he needed help. Despite this apparent lack of insight into how his behaviors were perceived, Pouya demurely acknowledged, "I knew I was acting wrong," but he couldn't figure out what else to do.

We started to see what his relationship with his parents was like and how it could be difficult to build a relationship with him. We wondered how his history of failures in mental health settings, his difficulties with authority figures, and his tendency to engage in manipulation would play out in this relationship with Erin.

🖐 Teaching Point

By actively collaborating with the client, the client offers a wealth of information that otherwise might be unnoticed or even withheld. In fact, in stark contrast to his reports of his behavior in previous mental health settings, Pouya worked hard to give as much information as possible, which likely increased his confidence that the results were accurate. The bridge into the client's world is made stronger when there is a strong sense of collaboration.

The Dilemma of Change

Erin also perceived that Pouya was struggling with ambivalence. For example, he expressed a desire to change how he manipulated others, but he described in great detail, with hints of pride in his voice, how he got others to do what he wanted. He admitted he was unsure if he was really willing to abandon this behavior. In a world where Pouya felt largely ineffective, here was something he was really good at, and it helped him get his needs met. It would take some work to help him see the unintended consequences of his manipulation and the ways in which this behavior was probably making it harder for him to truly get his needs met since it kept him from building the lasting, meaningful friendships and relationships he so desperately desired.

The Testing Plan

During the following sessions, Erin completed many tests with Pouya, including the Wechsler Adult Intelligence Scale, fourth edition (WAIS-IV; Wechsler, 2008), Woodcock-Johnson Tests of Achievement–III (WJA-III; Woodcock, McGrew, & Mather, 2001), the Rorschach Inkblot Method (Rorschach, 1943; Exner, 2003), and the Minnesota Multiphasic Personality Inventory–2 (MMPI-2; Butcher, Dahlstrom, Graham, Tellegen, & Kaemmer, 1989). These tests were administered in standardized fashion and provided important data to ground the assessment in empirical findings and to inform and guide the sessions and conclusions that followed. Furthermore, we remained responsive and flexible to the flow of the work. In fact, several adjustments to the plan were made, including adding the Stanford-Binet Intelligence Scales, fifth edition (SB-5; Roid, 2003).

UNPLANNED AVENUES

Cognitive Testing

The learning disability question was a key component of the assessment. The results of the WAIS-IV showed cognitive functioning in the Low Average range, but with substantial variability among subtests and index scores. For example, within the Verbal Comprehension Index, Pouya's scores on Vocabulary (scaled score = 5) and Information (scaled score = 6) (both of which can reflect academic experience as well as cultural influences) were significantly lower than his score on Similarities (scaled score = 9), which is a verbal reasoning test. Also, his Working Memory Index score (standard score = 97), which reflects verbal memory and facility, was significantly higher than his other index scores (standard scores on the Verbal Comprehension Index = 81, Perceptual Reasoning Index = 81, and Processing Speed Index = 79). The WJA-III scores reflected academic achievement only slightly below what would be expected given the WAIS-IV results, but with notable strength in oral language skills (standard score = 95). Overall, the data from the WAIS-IV and the WJA-III did not fully explain the thoughtful and articulate person who was in the room with Erin. Therefore, we decided to add the SB-5 (Roid, 2003) to try to round out our understanding of Pouya's intellectual abilities.

Table 8.1   Results of Cognitive Testing

Wechsler Adult Intelligence Scale–IV			
Index	Standard Score	Percentile	Confidence Interval (95%)
Verbal Comprehension	81	10th	76–87
Perceptual Reasoning	81	10th	76–88
Working Memory	97	42nd	90–104
Processing Speed	79	8th	73–89

(continued)

Table 8.1   (Continued)

Stanford-Binet Intelligence Scales, fifth edition

IQ Score	Standard Score	Percentile	Confidence Interval (95%)
Fluid Reasoning	82	12	76–92
Knowledge	80	9	74–90
Quantitative Reasoning	94	34	86–102
Visual-Spatial Processing	74	4	68–84
Working Memory	94	34	87–103
Nonverbal IQ	79	8	74–86
Verbal IQ	87	19	82–94
Full Scale IQ	82	12	78–86

Note: VRIN = Variable Response Inconsistency scale; TRIN = True-Response Inconsistency scale; F = Infrequency; Fb = Back F; Fp = Infrequency Psychopathology; L = Lie; K = Defensiveness; S = Superlative Self-Presentation; Hs = Scale 1, Hypochondriasis; D = Scale 2, Depression; Hy = Scale 3, Hysteria; Pd = Scale 4, Psychopathic Deviate; Mf = Scale 5, Masculinity-Femininity; Pa = Scale 6, Paranoia; Pt = Scale 7, Psychasthenia; Sc = Scale 8, Schizophrenia; Ma = Scale 9, Hypomania; Si = Scale 0, Social Introversion. Excerpted from the MMPI®-2 (Minnesota Multiphasic Personality Inventory®-2) Manual for Administration, Scoring, and Interpretation, Revised Edition. Copyright © 2001 by the Regents of the University of Minnesota. All rights reserved. Used by permission of the University of Minnesota Press. "MMPI" and "Minnesota Multiphasic Personality Inventory" are trademarks owned by the Regents of the University of Minnesota.

The SB-5 offers the advantage of testing similar cognitive abilities in both verbal and nonverbal domains. Pouya's highest index scores on the SB-5 came in Working Memory (standard score = 94) and Quantitative Reasoning (standard score = 94), while his lowest index score was on Visual Spatial Processing (standard score = 74). The overall pattern of scores indicated that Pouya performed best when tasks were verbally mediated, and he struggled with tasks that were nonverbal in nature. Even in areas of challenge for Pouya, such as visual-spatial processing, he performed better when the task was presented verbally than when the task was primarily nonverbal. By looking at both sets of data, we felt confident that Pouya's deficits in performance were, in part, due to his difficulty with nonverbally mediated material.

With this insight, we understood that Pouya's low average scores on measures of overall intellectual abilities were probably underestimates of his innate intelligence because of three factors: (1) his history of inconsistent education and lack of exposure to academics beyond 10th grade, (2) his relative weakness in nonverbal cognitive abilities, and (3) perhaps some influences from cultural differences.

Understanding Grows

In general, the test results indicated that, though Pouya was experiencing depression, it was more complicated than just that. On the MMPI-2, which largely reflects the way in which one sees oneself and presents to others, Pouya came across as very distressed, and he reported serious problems in nearly every area covered by the test.

However, despite some painful images, the Rorschach, which reflects deeper, fundamental aspects of oneself that are sometimes out of one's awareness, suggested less distress and greater capacity to handle adversity compared with the MMPI-2 data. The Rorschach results showed some areas of difficulty stemming in part from underlying developmental deficits but also sufficient resources to meet the stresses in his life. We were particularly encouraged by indications of a capacity to accurately reflect on himself and the situations in which he finds himself as well as an interpersonal focus.

The contrast between the MMPI-2 and Rorschach results, coupled with Pouya's history of presenting himself in a way that pulls for help from others, led us to see the elevated MMPI-2 profile as a cry for help indicative of his intense desire to have his pain seen and acknowledged. His MMPI-2 profile provided another example of Pouya's pattern of coming across to others as worse off than he really is. The data suggested that Pouya had come to believe what he said about himself; he was not aware of some of his strengths and was likely capable of more than he gave himself credit for.

Furthermore, the MMPI-2 findings suggested that Pouya felt as though others were not on his side, and he even worried that people were out to get him. These feelings affected not only how Pouya interacted with others but also his expectations about people. He expected that others would disappoint him, if not take advantage of him. At the same time, the food response on the Rorschach (an unreachable fish in the ice) suggested that Pouya had intense dependency needs. His difficult bind was in needing meaningful connections with others, but at

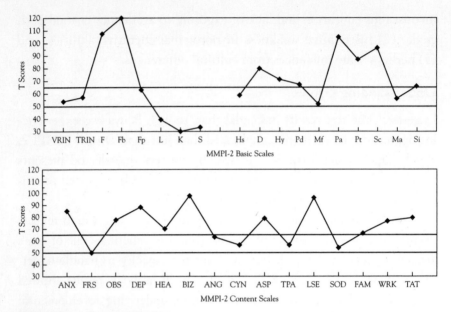

Figure 8.1   MMPI-2 Results

Note: VRIN = Variable Response Inconsistency scale; TRIN = True-Response Inconsistency scale; F = Infrequency; Fb = Back F; Fp = Infrequency Psychopathology; L = Lie; K = Defensiveness; S = Superlative Self-Presentation; Hs = Scale 1, Hypochondriasis; D = Scale 2, Depression; Hy = Scale 3, Hysteria; Pd = Scale 4, Psychopathic Deviate; Mf = Scale 5, Masculinity-Femininity; Pa = Scale 6, Paranoia; Pt = Scale 7, Psychasthenia; Sc = Scale 8, Schizophrenia; Ma = Scale 9, Hypomania; Si = Scale 0, Social Introversion. Excerpted from the *MMPI®-2 (Minnesota Multiphasic Personality Inventory®-2) Manual for Administration, Scoring, and Interpretation, Revised Edition.* Copyright © 2001 by the Regents of the University of Minnesota. All rights reserved. Used by permission of the University of Minnesota Press. "MMPI" and "Minnesota Multiphasic Personality Inventory" are trademarks owned by the Regents of the University of Minnesota.

Note: ANX = Anxiety; FRS = Fears; OBS = Obsessiveness; DEP = Depression; Health = Health Concerns; BIZ = Bizarre Mentation; ANG = Anger; CYN = Cynicism; ASP + Antisocial Practices; TPA = Type A Personality; LSE = Low Self Esteem; SOD = Social Discomfort; FAM = Family Problems; WRK = Negative Work Indicators; TRT = Negative Treatment Indicators. Excerpted from the *MMPI®-2 (Minnesota Multiphasic Personality Inventory®-2) Manual for Administration, Scoring, and Interpretation, Revised Edition.* Copyright © 2001 by the Regents of the University of Minnesota. All rights reserved. Used by permission of the University of Minnesota Press. "MMPI" and "Minnesota Multiphasic Personality Inventory" are trademarks owned by the Regents of the University of Minnesota.

the same time not trusting others enough to be meaningfully connected. Thus, Pouya had learned to get his dependency needs met by manipulating others by acting less capable than he was. He described this in the Rorschach extended inquiry (Handler, 1999a, 2008) as "putting on a costume," and he was relatively aware of his tendency to present himself as incapable in an attempt to elicit help from others. However, there appeared to be some basis in reality for Pouya's beliefs about others not being on his side. Being an immigrant, being smaller than others, and having distinctive facial features had left him vulnerable to being treated poorly by his peers as a child. These beliefs were also distorted by his somewhat problematic judgment and reality testing as seen on the Rorschach.

Rorschach Extended Inquiry (Handler, 1999a, 2008)

The flexibility of TA, along with a trusting supervisory relationship in which Erin felt supported, allowed her to be creative in testing sessions. This reached a high note after the Rorschach administration. The extended inquiry that Pouya and Erin completed after the formal test administration helped Erin continue to build bridges with Pouya as they worked toward potential answers to his questions.

On the Rorschach, several percepts were particularly meaningful to Pouya and were highlighted in discussion after the procedure was complete. For example, on Card II Pouya had responded "a heart down here that's kind of been splattered . . . maybe they are hearts that are coming together." In the extended inquiry, Pouya explained that he saw this as "love and happiness," saying, "I wish I had that." When Erin asked about being splattered, Pouya explained that "The hearts connected with such a force that they went 'splat,' but stayed connected because of their love for each other . . . love can be hard, yet gratifying at the same time, the rough times are the splatter, but your heart still keeps shape because of all the love . . . love is painful and unending." On Card VI Pouya had seen "Something that has been cut open. You just can see the insides of it, I don't know what the outside looks like—I'd say it's some kind of animal, it's been skinned." In the extended inquiry he elaborated, saying, "it might be me that's cut open . . . cut me open and take everything away. . . . I'm vulnerable, yet also stuck in the dark. Everyone else sees, but I'm in the dark." On Card VIII Pouya reported, "two bears . . . climbing a mountain that's made out of ice, and on the second layer there's two fish, one on each side that are inside the ice." In the extended inquiry Pouya described this image as being about survival for him, explaining that he wants to be powerful and strong like a bear, but that he sees himself as not surviving. "I'm not getting the fish in the ice, I'm just struggling every day just to get by."

These images captured Pouya's experience of love, vulnerability, and survival. By discussing what they meant to him, the testing results hit home and poignantly highlighted for Pouya his painful experience. Not only did he see himself more clearly, but the extended inquiry also allowed him to experience a powerful communication of his inner state to another person. He felt seen, understood, and accepted.

Teaching Point

An extended inquiry can substantially deepen the understanding of the client that is starting to emerge from the testing data and provides rich images to use in communicating with the client. The combination of nomothetic and idiographic information gathered through both a standardized measure and an extended inquiry add to the bridges of understanding and may point the assessor and client toward new ways of being.

Family Intervention Session

Another area in which we shifted our original assessment plan was in the decision to have a family session, which is typically not done for adults. Pouya raised the possibility of this meeting himself. Although his parents lived out of state, they had a visit planned for near the end of our testing. Pouya asked that Erin help explain to them some of our recently coconstructed understandings about him and his patterns of behavior. Specifically, he wanted to convey to them his tendency to behave in manipulative ways and his difficulties with authority figures. These patterns seemed to play out in his intense and conflicted relationship with his parents, so it seemed like meeting as a family might offer some opportunities for in vivo exploration of the family patterns and perhaps provide an opportunity to begin transforming them. We were aware that Pouya was pulling on Erin to take care of him, but we thought this opportunity was worthwhile. Given that family dynamics were a big part of Pouya's life, we hoped a family meeting would move the family story about Pouya to something more conducive to his continued growth.

In the family session, Erin focused primarily on facilitating a conversation between Pouya and his parents, so she let Pouya take the lead in terms of content. The ensuing conversation helped him address some longstanding resentments toward his parents and bring up his manipulative behaviors. With some help, Pouya also discussed possible changes in his behavior. The session ended in laying ground rules for future communication between Pouya and his parents and thus shifting the patterns that were frustrating to them all.

A secondary effect of the family session is that it helped Erin build an understanding with Pouya about how his behaviors were perceived by others. It also showed him how he tended to misinterpret others' behaviors by relying on too little information from which to draw accurate conclusions. An example that struck Pouya deeply was in discussion of his resentment that his father had not intervened when, as a boy, Pouya often lied about very important matters. Pouya was sure his father knew the truth but did not hold him accountable like he did others because Pouya was not worth the bother. His father was surprised that Pouya had lied and had all along believed Pouya's lies. They discussed this misunderstanding in the session and both came to a more accurate account of the event. Finally, meeting his parents and observing Pouya interact with them helped Erin understand him even better than before and provided material for further work.

These unplanned avenues contributed to the bridges of understanding being built to Pouya and his life. They also deepened the relationship between Pouya and Erin. These experiences, along with the standardized test data and his life story, formed a sturdy basis for answers to Pouya's questions. Perhaps more importantly, these unplanned avenues introduced new ways of being for Pouya. This was especially true of the family session, in which Pouya broke new ground with his parents.

Teaching Point

The TA approach is flexible and open to the unique circumstances and needs of each client, which allows assessors to work effectively and enhance the leverage to effect change. The session with Pouya and his parents engaged his family system and addressed important issues that had been barriers to change. This family meeting built new bridges of understanding between Pouya and his parents.

BRIDGES INTO NEW WAYS OF BEING

Assessment Intervention Session

Because problems in relationships were central to Pouya's questions, we decided to use the Thematic Apperception Test (TAT; Murray, 1943) for the assessment intervention session (Finn, 2007). We hoped the TAT would elicit responses from Pouya that illustrated his characteristic patterns in and expectations of relationships and would therefore allow an opportunity before the summary/discussion session to explore these problematic patterns and investigate where there was room for shifts. Overall, the intervention session felt like an important turning point in the work with Pouya. He and Erin had frank discussions of how his assumptions about relationships, which were beautifully illustrated in his stories, got in the way of reaching his goals of building strong friendships and romantic relationships and avoiding manipulation. We thought Pouya's openness to Erin's suggestions was in part due to the process-oriented focus of the intervention session. Erin held a nonjudgmental stance, which allowed Pouya to drop his defenses and be more accurate in his own judgments. Through a gentle, reflective approach, Erin was able to largely disarm Pouya's tendencies to become defensive when challenged, which allowed his insight to grow.

Erin initially administered TAT cards in the standard manner, but near the end, she discussed with Pouya the themes she was noticing among his stories. These themes centered on loss, death, and being left by loved ones. Erin noticed the characters with whom Pouya often seemed to identify generally failed to express wants or needs in the relationship and appeared helpless to influence what was happening. Erin went back through the stories with Pouya, asking if these observations rang true to him as well. Pouya understood that he often fell into the same pattern in relationships in his own life. Erin then asked Pouya to try to "rewind" one or two of the stories he had told, and play around with how the characters express their wants and needs to each other. Initially Pouya struggled with this task, but he was able to retell several stories in a way that did not eliminate all painful outcomes, that had the characters talk more openly about their feelings, and that allowed the characters to have conflict *and* be emotionally close.

After Pouya retold the stories with more balance, he and Erin explored the themes in his stories of "loss, death, not being connected, and not being able to communicate clearly." Erin introduced the idea that this way of viewing ambiguous situations was perhaps Pouya's "automatic pilot" way of viewing relationships. They then discussed ways he could notice and disrupt this pattern. As Erin had encouraged Pouya's attempts to try something different in his stories, she also encouraged him to try new ways of being in his daily life.

Pouya and Erin went on to discuss further that being able to imagine things going differently (as they had just practiced) is a prerequisite for actually behaving in a different way. They also considered a recent example when he left an angry message for a friend who had been out of contact with him for a few weeks, saying, "Thanks a lot for ignoring me, I guess I know what kind of friend you are!" Erin helped Pouya rewind the interaction, imagine different scenarios, and choose from among them how he would like to respond. They explored how he had assumed that his friend was angry at him and ignoring him purposefully to hurt his feelings. Pouya had not considered that there could be other potential reasons for his friend's behavior. Once Pouya rewound the tape and turned off his automatic pilot, other ways to understand the situation emerged. He came up with several alternative ways he could have behaved, and he chose one he thought could have been more effective. Instead of jumping to the conclusion that his friend was angry at him and intentionally ignoring him, Pouya decided he could have expressed his feelings and checked out the situation by saying, "We haven't talked in a while, and I am wondering how things are going for you. I miss talking to you, and I hope that even if there is something upsetting you, you will give me a call, and we can discuss it."

We thought this exercise was a huge step for Pouya. He was able to nondefensively see his initial behavior toward his friend was based on very little information and was likely to create a conflict between them, even if there wasn't one there to begin with. He admitted that there might be some ways in which this behavior works for him, because it lets him be "right" and makes his friend into the bad guy. While satisfying in part, this is not in line with his bigger goal of building relationships with others. Viewing his friend as a "bad person" who mistreated him is more comfortable than risking that he may have done something to upset his friend, may be partly to blame for them losing contact, and may need to talk about this and take responsibility in order to repair the relationship.

Erin was very heartened by this intervention session and felt she had made a major step toward bridging the gap between Pouya's initial reactions and the behaviors we were hoping to help him set as goals in the summary/discussion session. Erin was also pleased to see how willing Pouya was to examine his own motivation and behaviors in this session and felt that she and Pouya had built a bridge of trust between them that would be vital to the success of the summary/discussion session and to his future growth.

Though Erin expected this session to be about bringing Pouya's understanding of himself closer to our understanding of him based upon the test results and our conversations, she noted that her understanding was also transformed. Erin saw much more flexibility in Pouya than was suggested by the test results and more emotional and intellectual ability to shift than she had expected. Even now, long after her work with Pouya ended, this session continues to be a touchstone for her about how important it is to hold conceptualizations of clients loosely and remain prepared to be surprised by what people are capable of understanding and changing. She recognized the power of the scaffolding coconstructed with a client through a trusting relationship and gentle, collaborative curiosity.

✍ Teaching Point

The assessment intervention session uses the momentum generated through insight and relationship to provide the client with a powerful experience—a bridge to new ways of being. With Erin's help, Pouya created new solutions to old problems, and he tried on these new solutions in ways directly related to his recent life. Thus, the feelings associated with new behaviors were alive and made it an experience rather than just another thought.

Summary/Discussion Session

The assessment intervention served as a good stepping stone to the summary/discussion session, which felt collaborative and wrapped up the ongoing conversation over the last eight sessions. Together Erin and Pouya went over each of his initial questions and discussed both his and her ideas about potential answers and how the test results fit or did not fit. Because Pouya had made so much movement toward understanding himself more accurately, there were few areas of insight to explore with him. Pouya's ideas about the potential answers to his questions were, for the most part, informed by previous conversations and thus were in line with the information Erin wanted to share with him.

However, Erin felt there were yet a few areas of relationship building to explore with him. She was confident their relationship and the previous processing of the test experiences, especially the intervention session, would allow Pouya to hear new, more deeply embedded information that perhaps he would not have heard and understood in the traditional approach to assessment. In particular, the conversation about the extent of his manipulation skills—which Erin thought would be painful for him—went smoothly. We attributed this, in part, to the empathy Erin had developed for Pouya and how he had long ago ended up stuck in this dysfunctional pattern of behavior for understandable reasons. Furthermore, Erin and Pouya were able to begin to address ways in which his tendency to manipulate others had come up in their work together. This was quite a step for Pouya.

Teaching Point

The collaborative work ultimately culminates in therapeutic progress that allows the client to move to new ground over sturdy bridges that can now be traveled. Pouya may still need some help from time to time, but he knows both intellectually and intuitively a new and healthy way in life.

Letter to Pouya

As is the custom in TA, Erin crafted a personal letter to Pouya to summarize the results of the assessment and to serve as a reminder of his areas of growth. This letter is the final bridge between client and assessor, and it preserves the personal truths established through the assessment process for future cloudy moments. Erin put on paper what had emerged from the summary/discussion session in answer to Pouya's original questions.

In response to Pouya's questions about relationship problems, Erin wrote:

> One aspect that likely did not happen ideally when you were growing up was developing the capacity for an appropriate adversarial relationship. This capacity develops gradually, usually in relationship with parents at first. It involves defining yourself in new ways that are at odds with powerful people in your life. How they respond to your challenge determines how you learn to be adversarial, an important capacity in life. I suspect that it was difficult to be effectively adversarial with your parents because you were protected so much by your mother, and couldn't get a rise out of your father no matter how outlandish your behavior.
>
> At times, you can come across to others as less capable emotionally than you really are, and they often respond by taking care of you. It appears that you developed this skill in part because of your strong feelings as a child that you were somehow different from others and that people had to be brought to your side in life. Manipulation was a creative solution for you at the time, and helped you to feel that others were "on your side." However, every time you act as if you aren't able to do something in order to get help, you chip away at your self-confidence and start to believe that you are incapable of doing things for yourself. . . .
>
> Learning to appropriately assert yourself and ask directly for what you need from others will allow you to create a more flexible and effective approach to others. Learning to do this will help you manage conflict without reverting to manipulation. It may also allow you to feel more comfortable being close to others. Furthermore, feeling increasingly confident that you can hold your own in the event of any conflict, may allow you to better express negative emotions in relationships than you currently do.

Erin wrote the following as part of the answer to Pouya's question, "What can I do to have somebody beside me in my life in a healthy, 50/50 relationship?":

> Another important aspect of developing trusting relationships is working on your 'trust meter.' Right now, you tend to trust people too quickly and then reject them completely the first time they break your trust or hurt your feelings. By building up trust slowly with someone, you are going to be better able to decide if they are trustworthy, and you will limit how easily you are hurt. One way to develop a better 'trust meter' is to ask trusted people for help deciding how much to trust someone. You can work on this with a therapist or with another trusted person. For example, you could bring up a story of an interaction with someone, and then collaborate in deciding how much to trust that person. You can also work with your therapist to express to the other what hurt or disappointed you and explore how to repair the relationship.

Teaching Point

The assessment findings are finely tailored to the client in words and images that the client can relate to and understand because the client has created or at least cocreated them. This understanding, along with the experience of the assessment, allow the answers to seem true and applicable to the client—and to thus foster therapeutic change in the client's life.

The Value of Supervision (Handler, 1999b)

Supervision of the assessment worked well; Erin and Hale maintained a good flow of communication between them and collaborated effectively. We had regular in-depth discussions of the work Erin was doing with Pouya. Erin reported what had happened and discussed her thoughts and reactions. Hale listened a lot, asked questions, and at times offered suggestions in an effort to share his experience and knowledge to aid the assessment. He also supported and encouraged Erin in a way, she later reported, that allowed her to take risks. She felt comfortable knowing that Hale had confidence in her abilities and that she had backup when she needed it. She also reported that the supervision kept her focused on the salient aspects of the work.

Erin felt one of the important aspects of the supervision for her was help in keeping a "good handle" on her reactions to Pouya. Erin experienced firsthand Pouya's ability to evoke caretaking reactions in those engaged with him. Early in the assessment, we understood Pouya's tendency to quickly give his power to another person and then develop resentment that ultimately undermined the relationship. By not taking the power from him, despite her urge at times to do so, Erin modeled a new balance for Pouya in the relationship. She became quite good at catching and resisting being manipulated. This balance was a subtle but important aspect of the assessment. Her success in this ultimately increased Pouya's confidence in his ability to have a "50/50 relationship." The collaboration at the heart of TA was well-suited to help Pouya take appropriate responsibility for himself.

Teaching Point

The collaborative model that works well with clients also works in supervision. Being understood, supported, and respected results in a win for everyone: client, supervisee, and supervisor. It builds bridges to new understandings and competence for all involved.

Summary

And so ended the assessment of Pouya. Follow-up contact suggests he was well-served by the work. His questions had been answered, and new avenues for living had been effectively opened for him, not just through knowledge gained but also through experience. By the end of the assessment, he had embarked on building his own bridge—a healthy connection with his parents. He had also learned and tried out healthy options with other relationships, including with Erin. His self-confidence and self-esteem had increased, and he felt hopeful that he could have things he longed for—like a healthy 50/50 relationship.

REFERENCES

Butcher, J. N., Dahlstrom, W. G., Graham, J. R., Tellegen, A., & Kaemmer, B. (1989). *Minnesota Multiphasic Personality Inventory–2*. Minneapolis: University of Minnesota Press.

Exner, J. E. (2003). *The Rorschach: A comprehensive system, Volume 1: Basic foundations and principles of interpretation* (4th ed.). Hoboken, NJ: Wiley.

Finn, S. E. (1996). *Manual for using the MMPI-2 as a therapeutic intervention*. Minneapolis: University of Minnesota Press.

Finn, S. E. (2007). *In our client's shoes: Theory and techniques of Therapeutic Assessment*. Mahwah, NJ: Erlbaum.

Handler, L. (1999a). Assessment of playfulness: Herman Rorschach meets D. W. Winnicott. *Journal of Personality Assessment, 72*, 208–217.

Handler, L. (1999b). Supervision in therapeutic and collaborative assessment. In A. Hess, K. Hess, & T. Hess, *Psychotherapy supervision* (pp. 200–222). Hoboken, NJ: Wiley.

Handler, L. (2008). A Rorschach journey with Bruno Klopfer: Clinical application and teaching. *Journal of Personality Assessment, 90*, 528–535.

Murray, H. A. (1943). *Thematic Apperception Test manual*. Cambridge, MA: Harvard University Press.

Roid, G. H. (2003). *Stanford-Binet Intelligence Scales* (5th ed.). Itasca, IL: Riverside.

Rorschach, H. (1943). *Psychodiagnostik* (5th ed., P. Lemkau & B. Kroonenberg, Trans.). Berne, Switzerland: Hans Huber. (Original work published in 1921).

Wechsler, D. (2008). *Wechsler Adult Intelligence Scale* (4th ed.). San Antonio, TX: Psychological Corporation.

Woodcock, R. W., McGrew, K. S., & Mather, N. (2001). *Woodcock-Johnson III Tests of Achievement*. Itasca, IL: Riverside.

CHAPTER

9

Collaborative Assessment for Psychotherapy: Witnessing a Woman's Reawakening

Patrick J. McElfresh

The Swiss psychiatrist Carl Gustav Jung (1875–1961) was one of the first pioneers in assessment to suggest that a comprehensive exploration of a client's world during the initial stages of psychotherapy could be invaluable for long-term treatment. I am not talking here of Jung's popular word association experiments, but rather his approach to a client's initial dream. Jung (1916, 1934) suggested that the initial or "herald" dream provided valuable information about a client's current concerns, struggles, and hopes. Such dreams often revealed prescient information about how the person's therapy would take shape, how he or she experienced the therapist, and what central issues would require attention. Jung (1934) provided striking examples in which events that transpired much later in a person's psychotherapy were reflected in a client's initial dream. Indeed, at the conclusion of psychotherapy, a subsequent rereading of a person's initial dream was often revealed to be chillingly oracular.

Jung's approach to a client's initial therapy dream resonates with my experience of conducting Collaborative Assessments at the beginning of psychotherapy. I have found that assessments conducted in a collaborative and therapeutic manner can reveal meaningful information about a person's concerns, his or her strengths, and even entrenched and poorly understood issues that are likely to resurface during the course of psychotherapy. I have been impressed by the extent to which my clients remember and utilize intake assessment findings even months after they occurred. It has been fulfilling to witness how quickly Collaborative Assessments facilitate a genuine therapeutic alliance and illuminate relationship dynamics within the therapy. Finn (1994) has found similar successes with his therapeutic use of assessment with his and other referred therapy clients.

In this chapter, I will present my assessment and psychotherapy work with a woman whom I will call Anna. This case will illustrate the key features of an intake Collaborative Assessment (Fischer, 1985/1994, 2000) conducted within the framework of psychotherapy. I will highlight how our assessment findings informed case formulation, identified what would be recurrent themes in the treatment, and enhanced our therapeutic relationship. Additionally, I hope the case presentation conveys that assessments conducted collaboratively and therapeutically can indeed be life changing for clients.

ANNA'S ASSESSMENT AND PSYCHOTHERAPY

Context of the Referral

Anna was in her late forties when she referred herself for psychotherapy due to ongoing struggles with depression, poor self-esteem, and a lack of motivation or direction in life. She was afraid that she was "slipping" into a deeper depression and was concerned that medications for depression and anxiety were no longer helping her. She described a "constant, unrelenting suffering." Anna said that she was having relationship problems with her husband, but she was vague and guarded when asked to give specific examples of this problem.

Anna attributed her difficulties primarily to losing her job two years before our assessment. She was a manager for a thriving small business for nearly 20 years before it closed due to an economic downturn. She talked with pride about having worked her way into a management position "with only a high school diploma" and spoke of the job loss as a "huge blow" to her identity. Anna was in the midst of finishing an associate's degree in a health-related field, but she was conflicted about obtaining employment with her new degree. She felt that any new position in her chosen discipline would be a demotion. Yet, Anna also reported feeling unworthy of applying for positions, saying that her background was "not worth anything." Anna said that she had been struggling unsuccessfully for nearly four months to write a resume for job applications.

Anna's mother died when she was only 11 years old. She said that she took it upon herself to care for her father and siblings following her mother's passing. Despite being the oldest sibling, she was the last to move out of the family home and to marry, and she was the only sibling who had not earned a college degree. When I asked her, Anna denied resenting her family and blamed herself for her failures in love and work. Being protective of her family and being self-effacing pervaded our initial meeting. I noted that although Anna easily shared painful details about her past, she did so with little affect. In this regard, she tended to discuss these experiences in a matter-of-fact manner, arms crossed, and with little vocal intonation.

At the conclusion of our initial meeting, Anna agreed to take part in assessment sessions to help clarify issues for psychotherapy. I told her that the sessions would involve the completion of a few assessment instruments and ongoing discussion. I noted that we would work together to form impressions of her current difficulties, strengths, and concerns. I encouraged Anna to think of questions she would like to address through our assessment work, and she agreed to fill out a Sentence Completion form prior to our next appointment.

Teaching Point

Having the client provide questions prior to the exploration of the client's concerns and use of assessment instruments helps focus discussions. Additionally, specific and concrete questions facilitate the descriptive and contextual approaches implicit in Collaborative Assessment.

The Intake Collaborative Assessment

Anna arrived for our first assessment session appearing more distressed than she had been during our intake appointment. She said that she was nervous about "getting tested" and was concerned about what the process would uncover. She added that she had been unable to identify questions for our session. I reassured her that the purpose of the assessment was not a psychological x-ray aimed at pointing out diagnoses or character flaws. I explained that our focus rather was to understand what it was like to live in her world. I reiterated that she was a coassessor—that she was responsible for providing examples from her experiences to help us make sense of assessment findings—but that I would help her with any aspects of the assessment she felt unsure of, including identifying questions.

Anna appeared immediately more relaxed by my reassurances as she sat back in her chair and smiled, and we focused our attention toward questions for the assessment and the administration of the Personality Assessment Inventory (PAI; Morey, 2003) and the Rorschach (Exner, 2003). I again encouraged Anna to think of a couple of questions that she had about herself. She reported that she continued to "draw a blank." After a few minutes, she stated, "The only thing that I can think of is 'Why am I so depressed?'" Questions such as these are not uncommon in psychological assessment. However, they are often impossible to answer.

Teaching Point

Global why questions presuppose cause, and hence, such queries typically place immense pressure on the assessment process, and particularly the assessor, to produce the golden answer that discloses once and for all why the client is the way she or he is.

Psychological assessment instruments are not designed to address causality, but instead aim to assist clients by providing clarity to questions/problems, helping them to catch glimpses of how they typically engage themselves, others, and their worlds, and presenting possible alternatives to problematic approaches. Hence, my standard practice is to ask clients to refocus why questions as what, when, where, and how questions. These question formats present the possibility for more focused, descriptive, and contextual work.

With my help, Anna developed two questions to help guide our assessment work:

1. What happens that prevents me from feeling comfortable and confident? Is it something that I do to myself?
2. In what situations or scenarios am I most likely to have the hardest time coping?

Following the first formal assessment session, I scored and interpreted the PAI and Rorschach and prepared some notes integrating test findings and information from our discussions. When Anna returned for a second assessment session, I asked if she had any reactions or questions from our previous session. Anna said that she felt very uncomfortable during the administration of the assessment instruments, and she reported that her experience with the Rorschach would likely "stay with her for a long time." This comment seemed initially to speak to her discomfort with the Rorschach administration; however, little did either of us know how telling this comment would be for her psychotherapy. Anna then asked, "Well, how depressed am I?"

I informed Anna that she did appear to be feeling markedly depressed and uneasy. Her assessment findings, presented in Table 9.1, suggested that she tended to ruminate, felt inadequate and powerless, and had a very poor opinion of herself. These findings were consistent with Anna's existing view of herself, and she nodded in agreement as I shared these

Table 9.1   Anna's Indicators of Depression and Situational Stress

PAI: DEP (82) – ANX (73) code	Rorschach: DEPI = 5
AnxC = 80	SumV = 1
DepC = 80	WsumC':WsumC = 2:2.5
DepA = 72	D = 0
STR = 68	es = 7

impressions. Her assessment data also validated her report that her distress was related to intense situational stress. Anna immediately noted that her job loss and frequent arguments with her husband were likely reflected in this finding.

We next directed our focus toward her first assessment question regarding not feeling comfortable or confident. Anna said that she asked the question because she rarely experienced moments in which she felt confident and at ease with who she was. She suggested that lacking confidence had been a problem for her as long as she could remember and that her self-esteem had dramatically worsened since losing her job. She related the poor self-esteem to the fact that she really didn't like who she had become since losing her job and to feeling "eternally judgmental" of herself.

I shared the findings presented in Table 9.2 with Anna, and she immediately reported recognizing herself. In an attempt to more fully understand Anna's self-critical approach, we revisited her first Rorschach response and had the following exchange:

Patrick: So this judgmental, critical view of yourself seems to occur in a variety of places. Let's return briefly to your first Rorschach response (Card I). You said, "The first thing that comes to mind is a bat, which . . . I don't like bats. There's no reason for it. I don't know why. I know they're harmless, but I just don't like them. Why am I seeing a bat? They're so ugly. I'm screwing up already, aren't I?"

Anna: (smiles) I told you that I hated that test.

Patrick: Let's sit with this response for a moment, because it seems to reflect what we're talking about. The first response on the

Table 9.2   Anna's Indicators of Negative and Critical Self-Perception

PAI: DEP – ANX code	Rorschach: Mor = 1
DepC = 80	An = 2
AnxC = 80	Response style

Sentence Completion:

1. It's hard for me to admit *that I'm a good person.*
5. My earliest childhood memory is *being told that I was obese.*
6. What I needed but didn't get from my mother was *feeling of approval.*
12. My body *is fat.*

Rorschach is typically referred to as the "sign-in" response. It's thought that people tend to be careful about how they present themselves on this first item. In this little snippet, where you are maybe being careful about what you show me, there is a lot of self-criticism and doubt.

Anna: Yeah. Well, that's me . . . I'll give you a quick "for instance." I was on an internship for my program this past spring, and a doctor asked me to complete a complicated task. I spent the whole day bullying myself in my mind and hadn't finished it. I eventually went up to the doctor and said that I wasn't going to get it done. He very kindly asked me to sit down and said, "Why not? You know what you're doing." He asked me what I should do, and when I answered, it was right on. The doctor told me that he noticed this tendency in me to second-guess myself too much and said that I was too hard on myself. It really hit home for me. I'm so hard on myself that I keep myself stuck.

Patrick: So, being very critical of yourself prevents you from doing what you are capable of doing and maybe from things that you would like to do. Can you think of instances when you are not self-critical?

Anna: You know what? This is sad, but I can't. When your mother was constantly criticizing you, you realize what she's saying must be true.

Patrick: So you see this approach touching your history a bit, too?

Anna: Forget that. I'm responsible for me. I'm not here to blame anyone.

Patrick: I hear you, Anna. However, I think that we have stumbled upon important stuff here that seems to cause you a lot of pain and suffering.

As Anna and I continued to explore instances of her self-critical approach, we discovered possible answers to her second assessment question, "In what situations or scenarios am I most likely to have the hardest time coping?" She was remarkably self-critical across various contexts, and in fact, she could not identify any instances of feeling nonjudgmental. She said her passivity in relationships arose from feeling inadequate and criticized (as reflected in her Rorschach Human active to passive movement ratio: $Ma:Mp = 0:2$). She suggested that her tendency to constantly focus on her negative view of self prevented her from seeing the big picture in situations (Rorschach Organizational Activity score: $Zd = -4$, which is often interpreted as signifying a person who is easily distracted by small details). She wondered if she had grown so accustomed to her negative self-evaluation that it resulted in predetermined outcomes. Anna discussed a recent family event that she believed illustrated her observations, which provided an opportunity for insight.

Anna: I only attended because I thought it would make my father happy. I just knew going in that people would ask me about work and see me as a failure, and I would end up leaving early. That's what happened.

Patrick: So this is what you mean by predetermined outcome?

Anna: Yeah, but I'm realizing now as we sit here, that no one actually said anything critical to me. They were more concerned with having fun. I avoided everyone until people stopped making the effort to talk to me, then I left. I'm starting to see that I manage to do things that keep me feeling the way that I do. I don't think I like that.

Patrick: Knowing this now, maybe you can do something different.

Anna: Easier said than done. I don't stick with difficult things for long these days. You should know that now.

Anna's revealing observations and insights shed light on a major theme (i.e., paralyzing self-criticism) that would be a central focus in psychotherapy. Her somewhat testy reaction provided me with useful guidance about her tolerance for emotional material and alerted me to be attentive to her struggles with difficult personal insights, as she may be tempted to terminate therapy. Her assessment questions had helped to focus our goals for psychotherapy, to understand how she participated in problematic and recurring life approaches, and to catch a glimpse of what our relationship in therapy might entail. However, Anna and I discovered that the most compelling theme, which would set the tone for the whole of her psychotherapy, developed not from an assessment question but from an unexpected revelation from the Rorschach administration.

✍ Teaching Point

Although assessment questions help focus collaboration, unexpected findings can often arise that can be valuable for clients' understanding of presenting issues. When such instances occur, it is important to take the opportunity to explore lived-world examples related to these findings.

In the initial session, Anna struggled to complete a scorable Rorschach record and became visibly shaken during the initial administration of the cards. She rejected cards VI, VIII, IX, and X and thus provided only seven responses. Her responses were notably self-effacing, contained few resourceful percepts (e.g., human movement-M, and color-C), and were marked by several dysphoric variables (e.g., shading responses-Y, responses with morbid content-MOR). I was familiar with Exner's (1988) commentary on brief and "barren" Rorschach protocols and was concerned that, from a normative standpoint, her record would not be interpretable. I recalled articles written by Brickman and Lerner (1992), Fischer (1994), and Finn (2007b), which suggested that brief and atypical Rorschach protocols could be useful for understanding assessment participants' dynamics.

✍ Teaching Point

It can be productive to discuss the Rorschach response process and the content in percepts with participants who produce brief protocols.

I initiated the following dialogue.

Patrick: Anna, [the Rorschach] seemed quite difficult for you.
Anna: You could say that. That was one of the hardest things I've ever done.
Patrick: What was that like for you?

Anna: I don't know . . . frustrating. I just couldn't see anything.

Patrick: Sometimes when people provide few responses, it suggests that
          they are being careful about revealing themselves. Was
          that your experience?

Anna: No. I've actually felt very comfortable with you . . . I don't
          know.

Patrick: It seemed to me that you did tend to hold yourself back. You
          also questioned or rationalized much of what you did share.

Anna: I really don't believe that I was keeping things from you. In fact,
          I actually wish that that was the case. (Paused, looked down at
          the table) I'm pretty worried that I couldn't see anything.

As Anna and I talked further, it did appear that she was not being defensive during the administration and was uncomfortably surprised at her inability to provide percepts. Following guidelines recommended by Exner (1988), I asked her to look again through every card in order and to share any additional percepts so that we would have a scorable record to discuss. Anna became more upset during the second administration and began crying by Card V. I asked, on two occasions, if she would like to end the administration, but she wished to continue. Eventually and with great effort, Anna was able to produce 15 total responses and utilized every card.

Before the second assessment session, I scored Anna's Rorschach (see Table 9.3) and prepared interpretive questions. I was surprised to find that the major variable that would suggest defensiveness (Lambda = .69) was within normal limits. Additionally, Anna's record suggested limited creative and imaginative resources (human movement-M = 2), and she appeared to avoid emotionally valenced stimuli but was nevertheless affected by them (ratio of form-based color to less form-based color FC:CF + FC = 1:2, Affective ratio-Afr = .50). It appeared that she was struggling to find the resources to make sense of her world, especially when situations were emotionally laden. Her Rorschach responses stood in stark contrast to her appearance in our meetings as an intelligent and witty person. I looked forward to exploring this contradiction with her.

As mentioned earlier, Anna reported at the beginning of our second session that she had been unable to stop thinking about her "stressful Rorschach debacle." She also reported noticing difficulties with her ability

Table 9.3   Anna's Rorschach Structural Summary

Location Features	Determinants	Contents	Approach
	Blends	H = 1,0	I : WS
Zf = 9	**Single**	(H) = 0,0	II : D.D
ZSum = 23.5	2:15	Hd = 2,0	III : D
ZEst = 27.5	Mp.mpo	(Hd) = 0,0	IV : W
	Ma.CF.Yfu	Hx = 0,0	V : W.W
W = 5	M = 2	A = 7,0	VI : Dd
D = 8	FM = 1	(A) = 0,0	VII : D.D
W + D = 13	m = 2	Ad = 1,0	VIII : D.Dd
Dd = 2	FC = 1	(Ad) = 0,0	IX : DS
S = 2	CF = 2	An = 2,0	X : W.D
	C = 0	Art = 0,0	
	Cn = 0	Ay = 0,0	**Special Scores**
DQ	FC' = 2	Bl = 0,0	**Lv1 Lv2**
+ = 3	C'F = 0	Bt = 0,0	DV = 0 × 1 0 × 2
o = 12	C' = 0	Cg = 0,0	INC = 1 × 2 0 × 4
v/+ = 0	FT = 0	Cl = 0,0	DR = 4 × 3 0 × 6
v = 0	TF = 0	Ex = 0,0	FAB = 0 × 4 0 × 7
	T = 0	Fd = 0,0	ALOG = 0 × 5
	FV = 0	Fi = 0,0	CON = 0 × 7
	VF = 1	Ge = 0,0	**Raw Sum6 = 5**
	V = 0	Hh = 2,0	**Wgtd Sum6 = 14**
Form Quality	FY = 0	Ls = 1,0	
	YF = 1	Na = 1,0	AB = 0 GHR = 2
FQx MQual W+D	Y = 0	Sc = 0,0	AG = 0 PHR = 1
+ = 0 = 0 = 0	Fr = 0	Sx = 0,0	COP = 0 MOR = 1
o = 8 = 2 = 8	rF = 0	Xy = 0,0	CP = 0 PER = 2
u = 3 = 0 = 3	FD = 0	Id = 0,0	PSV = 1
− = 4 = 0 = 2	F = 6		
none = 0 = 0 = 0	(2) = 6		

RATIOS, PERCENTAGES, AND DERIVATIONS

R = 15	L = 0.67	FC:CF+C = 1:2	COP = 0	AG = 0
		Pure C = 0	GHR:PHR = 2:1	
EB = 2:2.5	EA = 4.5 EBPer = NA	SmC':WSmC = 2:2.5	a:p = 2:3	
eb = 3:4	es = 7 D = 0	Afr = 0.50	Food = 0	
	Adj es = 6 Adj D = 0	S = 2	SumT = 0	
		Blends/R = 2/15	Human Cont = 3	
FM = 1 SumC' = 2 SumT = 0		CP = 0	Pure H = 1	
m = 2 SumV = 1 SumY = 1			PER = 2	
			Isol Indx = .20	

		XA% = .73	Zf = 9	3r+(2)/R = .40			
		WDA% = .85	W:D:Dd = 5:2:8	Fr+rF = 0			
	Sum6 = 5	X−% = .27	W:M = 5.2	SumV = 1			
a:p = 2:3	Lv2 = 0	S− = .25	Zd = −4.0	FD = 0			
Ma:Mp = 0:2	WSum6 = 14	P = 7	PSV = 1	An+Xy = 2			
2AB+Art + Ay = 0:15	M− = 0	X+% = .53	DQ+ = 3	MOR = 1			
MOR = 1	Mnone = 0	Xu% = .20	DQv = 0	H:(H)+Hd+(Hd) = 1:2			

PTI = 1	DEPI = 5*	CDI = 3	S-CON = 7	HVI = No	OBS = No

From Exner (2003). *The Rorschach: a comprehensive system* (Vol. I). Hoboken, NJ: Wiley.

to use her imagination in day-to-day situations. As she and I discussed her Rorschach findings, Anna became more visibly upset and tears began streaming down her cheeks. The following exchange occurred:

Patrick: I can see how difficult this discussion is for you. What are you feeling?

Anna: I am still in absolute shock at how poorly I did on that test. I'm a reasonably smart person. The fact that I wasn't able to come up with even simple pictures or whatever suggested that I'm really not well.

Patrick: That is interesting. I experienced a similar sense of confusion when I reflected on your Rorschach. I have experienced you as witty and perceptive and wondered how it was that you were unable to see more.

Anna: You know what? This is no news to me. (Anna became tearful and her voice softened.) As part of my old job, I used to be able to travel quite a bit. I went to New England's shore, often, in the autumn. It was so peaceful. Anyway, in the past, I used to be able to visualize myself on that beach. No matter how stressed I felt I could always, you know, "take myself there." I haven't since I lost my job. I knew that I lost myself, but I didn't realize how bad.

Patrick: So that beach was your calm place. Can you picture it now?

Anna: (Tearfully) No. (Paused and became more tearful) No. I can't even see something in an inkblot! Where am I? Who am I? It's like I'm dead inside, or at least asleep somewhere. The thing that really gets me, as we've discovered doing these tests, is that it seems to be partially my own doing. I've always had that sense, but to have it verified here really sucks. I'm lost. I feel like I'm just . . . here. Not living. Maybe this is more than depression. Maybe I need help to wake up.

Patrick: So the Rorschach experience, as hard as it was for you, helped you to recognize yourself. You also realize that there is a part of you that you aren't in touch with right now, but that is still there.

Anna: Yes.

Patrick: I can't help but think of your final Rorschach response. The final response on a Rorschach record is popularly referred to as the "sign-off" response, and it's typically thought to signify a kind of "if you didn't see me, here I really am" expression. Your sign-off response reflects what we're talking about here. It was [Card 10], "Leaves on a tree. Not the whole, but the separate parts . . . the color and darker shading. It's just hanging there, basically dead, and just waiting to fall to the ground." What do you make of this response?

Anna: Here I really am.

Anna's assessment sessions were revealing for both of us. She discovered that she had lost touch with herself, had grown accustomed to being self-punitive and highly critical of the self that she did know, and perhaps recognized that therapy would require her to face challenges beyond depressive symptoms. I learned that therapy with Anna would likely be quite challenging, but that she was resilient and brave. After summarizing these experiences together, Anna and I took what we learned with us into our psychotherapy sessions. Notice that both content and process observations from Anna's Rorschach assessment were discussed in the attempt to clarify an important process with which she was struggling. This discussion not only illuminated the degree of her distress but also identified a point of potential intervention.

Teaching Point

This selection demonstrates that attention to lived experience helps to deepen understanding of themes that emerge during assessments.

Recollections of Assessment Findings During Psychotherapy

Anna's initial therapy sessions were slow-going, but over time she began to discuss her family relationships, her ongoing resentment at making constant sacrifices in her marriage, and her self-imposed roadblocks to finding meaningful employment. Our therapeutic alliance seemed solid, but Anna found it difficult to explore topics with any depth. She seemed to grasp interpretations and connections made in therapy on a cognitive level, but she rarely allowed herself to be emotionally evoked. Anna often remarked about her Rorschach assessment throughout the first 6 months of therapy. She reported that she no longer "felt depressed," and she became increasingly less self-critical over time.

Despite her successes, Anna twice expressed the desire to terminate psychotherapy. Her first suggestion for termination occurred in the fourth month of therapy during a time that she began to more clearly realize how critical her mother was toward her and how she (Anna) prevented herself from pursuing her own life goals for the purposes of taking care of her siblings and father. She noted that she remembered similar themes from her intake Sentence Completion, which she said suggested to her that it was important to focus on how her family history related to her current situation. Anna recalled that she had avoided discussing her role in her family during our assessment sessions and remembered attributing critical traits to her mother on the Sentence Completion (see Table 9.2). Consequently, she decided to remain in therapy.

By month six, Anna had begun to experience and express anger about her longstanding tendency to repress her own desires in order to meet everyone else's needs. Her anger was more regularly directed toward her husband. Outside of sessions, he criticized her for "seeing a shrink." Anna reported feeling guilty about being in therapy, began to criticize herself more regularly, and stated that she felt "torn between two men." She again expressed the desire to leave therapy. I reassured Anna that her reaction was to be expected. She had been talking about sacrificing the few things that gave her pleasure, and she was being faced with the decision to give up therapy, which was for her and her alone. I also suggested that she appeared to be developing feelings for me and that she was unsure how to handle them. The following exchange then occurred:

Patrick: I understand that things are beginning to get more difficult in here, but it seems as if you are on the precipice of something very important. To leave now, I believe, would be premature.

Anna: You know, all of the things that you mentioned are probably true. I even think that I might have started to dream again. . . . I think, I can't remember any of them if they are happening. At the same time, I'm doing well enough. I'm afraid that things are going to get worse again.

Patrick: They may. However, I believe that you could handle it. You refused to give up during one of our earliest sessions when you struggled with the Rorschach, and it resulted in important discoveries. What if similarly important discoveries await you now?

Anna agreed to remain in psychotherapy and reported that she would reassess the situation in one month. Neither one of us was prepared for what followed.

Anna's Reawakening

Anna appeared elated when she arrived for our next session. She excitedly exclaimed that she had a dream and remembered it. She recounted the dream as follows:

> I'm in an old house, and apparently I've been assigned the task of taking record of a recently deceased person's belongings. I think that the person was elderly and an important figure in my life. As I'm going through his or her things, I begin to notice many things that I want . . . some of the things are new, but others I recognize from my past. I can have them, but am reminded that I first have to go through an accountant that is helping me with the person's belongings. I think his name was Patrick J. Fulkerson.

Anna's dream suggested to her that she was perhaps recovering her ability to reconnect with herself. We discussed the potential connections between her ability to experience pleasure and her history with her deceased mother, who had been critical of her. I reflected the striking similarity between my name and the name of the accountant in the dream. Anna understood this feature to indicate the importance that therapy played in reconnecting to her desires and the ability to experience pleasure.

Anna continued to dream for several months to follow. In the three months following her initial dream, she applied for positions in her new field and quickly secured full-time employment. Anna demonstrated more affect in sessions and reported that her relationship with her husband had improved. At the end of the eighth month of therapy, Anna entered the session with a troubled look, and it appeared as if she had been crying. Struggling to catch her breath, she said that she had encountered her first difficult day in some time. While at work, she stood by a window and closed her eyes. To her amazement, she fantasized that it was autumn and that she was sitting on her favorite New England beach listening to the waves. Anna began sobbing as she looked toward me and exclaimed, "I'm awake! I'm back! I'm back!" I struggled to maintain my composure while witnessing this important moment.

Anna and I saw each other for only three more months. I asked her about the crucial moments that seemed to most benefit her:

Patrick: What about therapy was most helpful to you?
  Anna: Lots of things. Gaining an understanding of my role in my distress, understanding how my background has influenced me, my relationship with you . . .
Patrick: Do any particular sessions stand out to you as being the most important?
  Anna: You'll never believe this, but I would say the first few sessions we had together when we talked about my test results. Those sessions were hard, and I would be fine if I lived the rest of my life without having to do another Rorschach. But there was something about the way you worked with me that allowed me to see myself acting and doing things that were really . . . revealing, unnerving. I just knew that I could trust you and that you were working hard to see me for who I am. Believe it or not, it was the Rorschach that let me know that I was safe with you, and that experience kept me coming back when I thought about dropping out. I don't think that we would have accomplished what we did in here without those initial sessions. And I feel like I can easily trace where I started and where I am now. This was remarkable.

This was one of the most rewarding moments that I have experienced as a clinician. I was delighted and awed to hear that Collaborative Assessment had made such a difference for her. My experience has shown me that descriptions such as Anna's are common following Collaborative Assessments. Clients often report that they feel "listened to" and respected. This case highlights that genuine therapeutic outcomes can be achieved and that they can facilitate subsequent psychotherapy.

☞ Teaching Point

Psychological assessment is most likely to be therapeutic when assessors (1) collaborate with clients, (2) maintain transparency when discussing test findings, (3) ground their findings in clients' lived-world examples, and (4) present themselves genuinely with respect to the client's ability to serve as expert on his or her life.

SUMMARY AND CONCLUSION

My assessment work with Anna highlights several features of Collaborative Assessment that work to facilitate the therapeutic process. The following paragraphs highlight a few final teaching points from Anna's assessment. First, *Collaborative Assessment encourages and facilitates therapeutic alliance and often provides opportunities for developing rapport, trust, and empathy* (Fischer, 1985/1994). Anna validated these claims and suggested that our assessment work encouraged her faith and trust in me during the assessment and in subsequent psychotherapy. Recent research conducted on intake Collaborative Assessments has demonstrated enhanced therapeutic alliance months into psychotherapy (Hilsenroth, Peters, & Ackerman, 2004).

Second, *because Collaborative Assessment is necessarily a shared endeavor between assessor and client, it encourages participation.* Collaborative Assessment participants are asked to actively explore their assessment questions with assessors and thereby are encouraged to develop curiosity about their psychological lives. These features are likely to be helpful for exploration in psychotherapy and additionally result in improved therapy retention rates (Ackerman, Hilsenroth, Baity, & Blagys, 2000).

Third, *Collaborative Assessment practices aim to provide an accessible and understandable glimpse of a person's approach to the world that is based in real-life experiences.* Hence, assessors and clients are able to avoid the use of complex psychological constructs. This practice affords assessor and client the ability to develop a shared language that is unique to the person's circumstances and assessment situation. The development of mutually understood terms for discussing psychological phenomena has long been identified as a nonspecific factor in effective therapies (Frank, 1961).

Fourth, although specific questions are explored in Collaborative Assessments, findings do not have predetermined outcomes. Insights developed during intake assessments truly emerge out of careful exploration. Findings that are unexpected but validated by personal experience are more often the rule than the exception. Such findings require assessors and clients to revise impressions. Collaborative Assessment can be instructive for therapy in that it models an openness to the unknown. This finding leads to my final teaching point: *Collaborative Assessment conducted prior to psychotherapy can aid the therapy and enhances therapeutic alliance.*

These observations are only a few indications of how Collaborative Assessment can facilitate psychotherapy, and they point toward the directions in which such assessment practices can potentially provide demonstrable benefits. However, it is up to assessment psychologists to make similar efforts in clinical practice. Finn (2007b) issued the following challenge encouraging practitioners to move beyond limiting assessment practices:

> How many assessors do you know who never give assessment feedback to clients, or who mail them a long, boiler-plate report full of technical jargon and other meaningless phrases? How much effort are we putting into developing better validity scales—important to be sure—but instead of researching what things one can do at the beginning of an assessment so that clients want to reveal all they can to a psychologist? And how can we as a profession sit by quietly and continue to let shoddy psychological assessment practices take place that are dehumanizing and even damaging

to clients? As I can best tell—this is possible only if we ourselves don't fully appreciate the true power and potential of psychological assessment. (pp. 20–21)

My work with Anna taught me about the potential of Collaborative Assessment. Her case is a powerful example of how psychological assessment can contribute to a person's psychotherapy in an observably meaningful way and can enable people to change their lives.

REFERENCES

Ackerman, S. J., Hilsenroth, M. J., Baity, M. R., & Blagys, M. D. (2000). Interaction of therapeutic process and alliance during psychological assessment. *Journal of Personality Assessment, 75*(1), 82–109.

Brickman, A. S., & Lerner, H. D. (1992). Barren Rorschachs: A conceptual approach. *Journal of Personality Assessment, 59*(1), 176–184.

Exner, J. E. (1988). Problems with brief Rorschach protocols. *Journal of Personality Assessment, 52*(4), 640–647.

Exner, J. E. (2003). *The Rorschach: A comprehensive system: Basic foundations and principles of interpretation* (Vol. I). Hoboken, NJ: Wiley.

Finn, S. E. (1994). Testing one's own clients mid-therapy with the Rorschach. Paper presented at the annual meeting of the Society of Personality Assessment, April 15, 1994, Chicago, Illinois.

Finn, S. E. (2007a). Appreciating the power and potential of psychological assessment. In *In our clients' shoes: Theory and techniques of Therapeutic Assessment.* Hillsdale, NJ: Erlbaum.

Finn, S. E. (2007b). Giving feedback to clients about "defensive" test protocols. In *In our clients' shoes: Theory and techniques of Therapeutic Assessment.* Hillsdale, NJ: Erlbaum.

Fischer, C. T. (1985/1994). *Individualizing psychological assessment.* Hillsdale, NJ: Erlbaum.

Fischer, C. T. (1994). Rorschach scoring questions as access to dynamics. *Journal of Personality Assessment, 62*(3), 515–524.

Fischer, C. T. (2000). Collaborative, individualized assessment. *Journal of Personality Assessment, 74*(1), 2–14.

Frank, J. D. (1961). *Persuasion and healing.* Baltimore, MD: Johns Hopkins University Press.

Hilsenroth, M. J., Peters, E. J., & Ackerman, S. J. (2004). The development of therapeutic alliance during psychological assessment: Patient and therapist perspectives across treatment. *Journal of Personality Assessment, 83*(3), 332–344.

Jung, C. G. (1916). General aspects of dream psychology. In R. F. C. Hull (Ed.), *CW, Vol. 8: The structure and dynamics of the psyche.* New York, NY: Bollingen.

Jung, C. G. (1934). The practical use of dream analysis. In R. F. C. Hull (Ed.), *CW, Vol. 16: The practice of psychotherapy.* New York, NY: Bollingen.

Morey, L. C. (2003). *Essentials of PAI assessment.* Hoboken, NJ: Wiley.

10

Therapeutic Assessment of Severe Abuse: A Woman Living With Her Past

CAROL GROVES OVERTON

A referring psychiatrist told me that after participating in a Therapeutic/Collaborative Assessment, her patients display heightened self-esteem, renewed hope, and new motivation. They come to therapy with issues they want to discuss. It was for these reasons that she (the psychiatrist) made the referral presented in this paper of a patient she had been seeing for three years. The patient was shared with another, much older psychiatrist, who had been working supportively with the patient for 12 years. When they both made the referral, they were both frustrated, because they saw no progress in their work with the patient.

CLIENT'S BACKGROUND

The client, Julie, was a 35-year-old woman who looked and spoke as though she were about 17 years old. I had to consciously keep in my mind that it was a 35-year-old woman who sat across from me. She presented with a childhood history of continuous and sadistic sexual, physical, and emotional abuse at the hands of both parents. When Julie was five years old, her parents gave her up for adoption rather than face charges. She remembers her mother exclaiming, "Yea! I'm finally getting rid of you!" Julie spent less than one year in a foster home, where she felt safe, but she was then adopted by wealthy parents, at age six. She told the following about arriving at her new, adoptive home:

> My mom said I was dirty and she had to wash me and start over with nothing kept from the past. She was going to get rid of anything I came with and she wanted to change my name, but then she didn't. She made me grow my hair out to make me look like her. I was afraid of my mom and when she washed me I felt afraid and couldn't say anything. I feared being drowned. I felt so low because she said I was dirty. I felt ashamed of being dirty.

What ensued were years of battling between the two of them, with Julie thinking that her adoptive mother was trying to make Julie into a copy of her, which was different from how Julie wanted to be. Her mother was "into frills," but Julie was "into sports," and she had a difficult time with anything feminine. In high school, Julie injured her leg, leading to a series of operations, ending all sports participation, and leaving her with a permanent, slight limp. She said that she had been at her best when playing sports; somehow, it cleared her mind and made her feel better. She said it used to be her outlet.

Shortly after her injury, Julie descended into depression and began having dreams and intrusive thoughts of her earlier abuse. Although Julie was very distrustful of others, she did manage to establish a sense of comfort and trust in her relationship with a psychologist whom she saw for two years. When he moved across the country, Julie's depression intensified, and she began a series of psychiatric hospitalizations that spanned more than a decade.

When I met Julie, she was living by herself in an apartment, with her adoptive parents paying all her expenses. She carried diagnoses of Major Depression, Dysthymic Disorder, Avoidant Personality Disorder, and Dissociative Identity Disorder. She was very lonely but very socially avoidant. She had gotten a part-time clerical job but otherwise spent all her time alone, in her apartment. She was sure her "stupidity" would cause her to lose her job, and she lived every day in fear of being fired. In addition, she continued to be preoccupied by thoughts of her previous abuse and flooded by feelings of vulnerability and of impending victimization.

The younger psychiatrist's efforts to delve into the traumatic material with Julie had been met first with Julie's strong resistance and then with her flat refusal. When Julie came to see me, her question was, "How can I get past the abuse?" She wrote the following: "The vicious circle I am in even now is going over and over in my head the first six years' events and I get nightmares remembering what happened to me and I can't put it behind me. It keeps coming back to me in dreams and nightmares. And it rules my life and what I think about (snakes and sex)."

In addition, Julie was concerned about being controlled by her mother. An older sister, also adopted, told her, "You always do what she wants, and you don't have to." Julie's response was, "But if I don't, what if I screw up?" She was plagued with low self-esteem, in part, because her biological mother had convinced her she was "an imbecile." She still believed it.

PREVIOUS ASSESSMENT

During one of her hospitalizations, 12 years earlier, Julie had been given a full battery of psychological tests, including the WAIS-R (Wechsler, 1981), Rorschach (1921; Exner, 2003), Thematic Apperception Test (TAT; Murray, 1943), MMPI-2 (Butcher, Dahlstrom, Graham, Tellegen, & Kaemmer, 1989), and the Bender-Gestalt (Bender, 1938). The psychologist summarized, in part:

> Julie is a young woman of average intelligence who appears to suffer from a long-standing and deeply ingrained characterological depression which has been exacerbated by recent stresses, to the extent that a major depression is now very much in evidence. The patient's outlook is so morbid and gloomy that her perceptions become biased by virtue of the depressive filter through which she views the world. . . . Julie approaches others with an attitude of widespread apprehension and mistrust, feeling exceedingly vulnerable in what she perceives as a dangerous and

malevolent environment where victimization is imminent. Her painful anticipation of harm . . . has become crystallized into an avoidant personality pattern, the magnitude of which is quite severe.

The psychologist diagnosed a Major Depression, superimposed upon an Avoidant Personality Disorder, and suggested that, with the remission of the Major Depression, a Dysthymic Disorder would be expected to persist.

CURRENT THERAPEUTIC ASSESSMENT

Julie's earlier assessment had occurred at a time when results were not shared with the client. Consequently, she was never told she had scored within the average range of intelligence. Furthermore, because of her severe depression, I agreed with the previous psychologist that her results probably represented an underestimate of her actual functioning. I included the WAIS-R in the battery of tests I administered, with the hope that I could utilize the results to compare her performance with the WAIS-R taken in the past. I also wanted to convince Julie she was not "stupid," as she believed. I also included the Rorschach, TAT, Early Memories Test (Bruhn, 1992), MMPI-2, and The Psychotherapy File (Ryle, 1990).

The Psychotherapy File is a little-known but exceedingly useful self-assessment instrument developed by Ryle (1990). It consists of a listing of what he describes as Traps, Dilemmas, and Snags—behavioral patterns that do not achieve what a person wants but are difficult to change. I utilize the Traps and Dilemmas; I have rewritten them in the first person and have added additional Traps. Traps are vicious circles, such that however a person tries, things get worse instead of better. The following is an example:

Feeling under-confident about myself and anxious not to upset others, I worry that others will find me boring or stupid, so I don't look at people or respond to friendliness. People then see me as unfriendly, so I become more isolated from which

I am convinced I am boring or stupid—and become more under-confident.

With regard to Dilemmas, Ryle says persons often act as they do, even when they are not completely happy with it, because the only other ways they can imagine seem as bad or even worse. These false choices can be described as Dilemmas, or either/or options. People often don't realize that they see the world like this, but they act as if these were the only possible choices. The following are examples:

Either I keep feelings bottled up, or I risk being rejected, hurting others or making a mess.

If I get what I want, I feel childish and guilty; if I don't get what I want, I feel angry and depressed.

The clients read through the listing, indicating what does not apply to them, what applies, and what applies strongly. After they finish and understand what the various patterns are about, I encourage them to add additional patterns that they think apply to them.

For the purposes of the present chapter, I will focus on our work with the WAIS-R, Rorschach, and, to a lesser extent, The Psychotherapy File.

THE WAIS-R AS A THERAPEUTIC INTERVENTION

Teaching Point

Finn (1996) suggests beginning feedback sessions with something about which the client is aware, or perhaps just barely aware. He states, "Begin with findings the client will accept and gradually move to the findings that challenge the client's self-concept" (p. 64). Following his guidelines, I began with those aspects of Julie's positive WAIS-R results that were incongruent with her view of herself but easier for her to accept, and reserved for last Julie's participation in the tug-of-war with her mother.

During the earlier administration of the WAIS-R, Julie achieved a Verbal IQ of 99, a Performance IQ of 102, and a Full Scale IQ of 101, all falling within the Average Range. On the current administration, she obtained a Verbal IQ of 106, a Performance IQ of 117, and a Full Scale IQ of 112. Her Full Scale IQ was now in the High Average Range.

I told Julie that this was the same test as the one she had taken 12 years ago, and that we could compare our results with those earlier results. I showed her a chart, summarizing this comparison. I told Julie the current results indicated she had Above Average intelligence, but in 1988, she was functioning in the Average range. I said that the psychologist back then thought the test results underestimated her intelligence, because Julie was so depressed at that time.

Carol: Do you notice any difference in your thinking when you are depressed?

Julie: It's very difficult to think then, and sometimes I can't think at all.

We agreed that the current results—that she had above average intelligence—were more accurate.

Carol: Who do you think can measure intelligence better, the other psychologist and myself, working with the actual intelligence test, or your biological mother?

This question seemed to stun her—she just laughed and shook her head.

I moved on to my next chart. I told Julie that this chart gave us a more detailed summary of our current results. Using a separate chart I showed her the names of the WAIS-R subtests, and I explained what they were. I explained that the far right column indicated range of intelligence, and the far left column showed what percentage of the population obtains scores in each range: I told her that 16% of the population obtain scores in the above average range, 68% obtain scores in the average range, and 16% obtain scores in the below average range. With a little more explanation, Julie was able to figure out and tell me that six of her scores were as high as scores obtained by most people, and four of her scores were higher than scores obtained by 84% of the population.

Next, I explained what each subtest meant, and we discussed how she did on each, with me emphasizing how well she did on Similarities and what that meant. When we finished, I brought up some of the self-disparaging remarks she had made about her intelligence earlier.

Carol: What do you think about your remarks now?
Julie: (Laughing) I'd say they were stupid—but that would be wrong! . . . I guess I just automatically think the worst about myself. (Crying, but smiling) This is the best thing anybody's ever told me.

This intervention certainly did not solve Julie's self-esteem problems, but it helped and gave her a basis for starting to look at herself differently.

THE RORSCHACH AS A THERAPEUTIC INTERVENTION

Julie's Rorschach was like that of many trauma victims (Table 10.1). She had a high *Lambda* (1.38), combined with frequent breakthroughs of material obviously related to her earlier abuse. The following are some of her responses:

Card II: These could be eyes or a face, or something, me! . . . Of course this is all bloody stuff, like from my head. (*Inq*: eyes, face, my mouth, but there's still blood . . . like this stuff here, coming out of my head . . . She [biological mother] made them pull the rug out and stood over me, laughing at me.)

Card III: This definitely looks like blood. (*Inq*: Looks like a drop of blood, been smeared [*wmll smeared?*] because the way it usually runs down your face, trickle down, it's thicker and it looks like somebody just went like that [*puts thumb on blot*].

Card VII: Looks like two women, face-to-face, this kind of looks like a knife blade, and it's in the woman's head. If you made this into a body, she doesn't have any legs unless they're all squished up.

Card X (reversed): These could be two eyes, mouth, kind of scary looking, mean probably. (*Inq*: With purple and red, looks like bruises on the face [*wmll scary?*]. The way the eyes are shaped, and with the eyebrows. My dad used to make me scared; he has big, bushy eyebrows.)

Table 10.1   Rorschach 1 Comprehensive System Structural Summary

Location Features	Determinants	Contents	Approach
	Blends	**Single**	H = 2	I : WS.WS.W

Location Features		Determinants	Contents		Approach
Zf = 10		**Blends** **Single**	H = 2		I : WS.WS.W
ZSum = 28.5		M = 3	(H) = 0		II : DdS:W
ZEst = 31.0		FM = 0	Hd = 4		III : D.D
		m = 0	(Hd) = 4		IV : W
W = 8		FC = 1	Hx = 1		V : W.W
D = 7		CF = 3	A = 6		VI : Dd.D
W + D = 15		C = 0	(A) = 0		VII : W
Dd = 4		Cn = 0	Ad = 0		VIII : D.Dd
S = 3		FC' = 0	(Ad) = 0		IX : D
		C'F = 0	An = 2		X : Dd.D.D
		C' = 0	Art = 0		
DQ		FT = 0	Ay = 0		**Special Scores**
+ = 4		TF = 0	Bl = 3		Lv1 Lv2
o = 13		T = 0	Bt = 0		DV = 0 × 1 0 × 2
v/+ = 0		FV = 0	Cg = 0		INC = 0 × 2 0 × 4
v = 2		VF = 0	Cl = 0		DR = 2 × 3 0 × 6
		V = 0	Ex = 0		FAB = 0 × 4 2 × 7
		FY = 0	Fd = 0		ALOG = 0 × 5
		YF = 0	Fi = 0		CON = 0 × 7
Form Quality		Y = 0	Ge = 0		Raw Sum6 = 4
FQx MQual W+D		Fr = 0	Hh = 0		Wgtd Sum6 = 20
+ = 0 = 0 = 0		rF = 0	Ls = 0		
o = 9 = 1 = 9		FD = 1	Na = 0		AB = 0 GHR = 1
u = 3 = 1 = 1		F = 11	Sc = 1		AG = 1 PHR = 9
− = 7 = 1 = 5			Sx = 1		COP = 0 MOR = 7
none = 0 = 0 = 0			Xy = 0		CP = 0 PER = 0
		(2) = 5	Id = 1		PSV = 0

RATIOS, PERCENTAGES, AND DERIVATIONS

R = 19	L = 1.38	FC:CF+C = 1:3	COP = 0	AG = 1
		Pure C = 0	GHR:PHR = 1:9	
EB = 3:3.5	EA = 6.5 EBPer = NA	SmC':WSmC = 0:3.5	a:p = 0:3	
eb = 0:0	es = 0 D = +2	Afr = 0.46	Food = 0	
	Adj es = 0 Adj D = +2	S = 3	SumT = 0	
		Blends/R = 0:19	Human Cont = 10	
FM = 0 SumC' = 0 SumT = 0		CP = 0	Pure H = 2	
m = 0 SumV = 0 SumY = 0			PER = 0	
			Isol Indx = 0.00	

		XA% = 0.63	Zf = 10	3r+(2)/R	= 0.26
		WDA% = 0.67	W:D:Dd = 8:4:7	Fr+rF	= 0
	Sum6 = 4	X−% = 0.37	W:M = 8.3	SumV	= 0
a:p = 0:3	Lv2 = 2	S− = 1	Zd = −2.5	FD	= 1
Ma:Mp = 0:3	WSum6 = 20	P = 5	PSV = 0	An+Xy	= 2
2AB+Art + Ay = 0	M− = 1	X+% = 0.47	DQ+ = 4	MOR	= 7
MOR = 7	Mnone = 0	Xu% = 0.16	DQv = 2	H:(H)+Hd+(Hd)	= 2:8

PTI = 3	DEPI = 5	CDI = 2	S-CON = 4	HVI = No	OBS = NO

I scored Julie's Rorschach according to the Trauma Content Index (Armstrong & Loewenstein, 1990), a measure of traumatic intrusions into the Rorschach setting. A score of .3 or above suggests the likelihood of intrusions; Julie's score was .74. Her earlier Rorschach was the same.

Teaching Point

The Traumatic Content Index has been validated on patients with independently confirmed sexual abuse (Kamphuis, Kugeares, & Finn, 2000). Because there are other conditions (e.g., borderline personality disorder or psychosis) that may result in a positive TCI, neither the Rorschach itself nor the TCI should be taken as objective evidence of sexual abuse. A positive TCI suggests that further clinical inquiry is warranted.

In discussing her Rorschach with Julie, I told her that she seemed to have a wall in her mind, behind which she had placed all the painful memories and feelings from the past. But these memories kept on breaking through that wall. When they did, it felt as thought they were real, or could be happening today, and she would feel extreme anxiety, sometimes even panic. It became difficult to think clearly or critically. She could hardly function and had no interest in the real world. Her Rorschach reflected all of this happening.

I explained to Julie that the Rorschach usually reflects a person's personality, but not when they were experiencing so much interference. I suggested an experiment that involved her taking the Rorschach a second time. This time, she was to try to set aside the unwanted images from the past and concentrate on the inkblots in front of her—that is, concentrate on *what was there* on the card. What did the cards really look like? We were interested in two things about her second Rorschach. First, by her own effort, did she have the ability to set aside the disturbing thoughts and images that overwhelmed her personality during the first Rorschach? Second, if she could hold back this intrusive material, what would be the effect on her personality? Would we see that she could function much better? Julie agreed to the experiment.

Teaching Point

By giving the Rorschach a second time, with more focused instructions, we are interested in Julie's ability to focus on reality when she is asked to do so. When clients do well with these focused directions, compared to the traditional approach, they are typically reassured that they have the ability to experience the environment with clarity (Peters, Handler, White, & Winkel, 2008).

Immediately following this second administration, it was obvious that Julie did have the ability to ignore the influence of intrusive material and to focus on the blot itself. It was difficult, but she did it. In our next feedback session, we contrasted the interpretations from the first and second Rorschachs (Table 10.2). I asked Julie about any differences she experienced during the two Rorschachs.

Julie: I know I was working much harder on the second Rorschach.
Carol: I agree. I think that during the second Rorschach you put your-
        self into a "working" state of mind, but during the first, you were
        in a "passive" state of mind. In a working state of mind, you
        were able to exert control over your thinking; in a passive state
        of mind, you went along with whatever popped into your head.

What follows are Rorschach changes that Julie and I discussed.

On Rorschach 1 Julie's *Lambda* was 1.38 and both *D* and *Adjusted D* were +2, but *es* was 0. On Rorschach 2 (Table 10.2), *Lambda* was 0.88, both *D* and *Adjusted D* were 0, and *es* was 5. Julie had tried to keep her traumatic memories behind a wall in her mind, but it really didn't work—the memories did break though—as seen on Rorschach 1. Her first Rorschach indicated that what she did succeed at doing was to lose touch with the rest of her feelings. Her focus on keeping out her traumatic memories kept her from becoming involved with the world outside herself. So she noticed little about the outside world and remained detached and uninvolved. When Julie put herself into a working state of mind, however, she changed her focus to the world outside herself. This

Table 10.2   Rorschach 2 Comprehensive System Structural Summary

Location Features		Determinants		Contents		Approach	
		Blends	**Single**	H	= 2	I : Dd.W	
Zf	= 11	FM.FC.FC'	M = 2	(H)	= 0	II : D	
ZSum	= 35.0	FM.CF.FC'	FM = 1	Hd	= 0	III : D	
ZEst	= 38.0		m = 0	(Hd)	= 0	IV : W.W	
			FC = 1	Hx	= 0	V : W	
W	= 6		CF = 0	A	= 9	VI : Dd.D.D	
D	= 7		C = 0	(A)	= 0	VII : D	
W + D	= 13		Cn = 0	Ad	= 0	VIII : WS.W	
Dd	= 2		FC' = 0	(Ad)	= 0	IX : D	
S	= 1		C'F = 0	An	= 1	X : D	
			C' = 0	Art	= 0		
DQ			FT = 0	Ay	= 0	**Special Scores**	
+	= 7		TF = 0	Bl	= 0		Lv1 Lv2
o	= 7		T = 0	Bt	= 1	DV =	0 × 1 0 × 2
v/+	= 1		FV = 0	Cg	= 0	INC =	0 × 2 0 × 4
v	= 0		VF = 0	Cl	= 0	DR =	0 × 3 0 × 6
			V = 0	Ex	= 0	FAB =	1 × 4 0 × 7
			FY = 0	Fd	= 0	ALOG =	0 × 5
			YF = 0	Fi	= 0	CON =	0 × 7
Form Quality			Y = 0	Ge	= 0	**Raw Sum6** = 1	
FQx	MQual	W+D	Fr = 2	Hh	= 1	**Wgtd Sum6** = 4	
+ = 0	= 0	= 0	rF = 0	Ls	= 3		
o = 13	= 2	= 12	FD = 0	Na	= 1	AB = 0	GHR = 3
u = 2	= 0	= 1	F = 7	Sc	= 1	AG = 0	PHR = 0
− = 0	= 0	= 0		Sx	= 0	COP = 2	MOR = 0
none = 0	= 0	= 0		Xy	= 0	CP = 0	PER = 0
			(2) = 5	Id	= 0		PSV = 0

RATIOS, PERCENTAGES, AND DERIVATIONS

R = 15	L = 0.88		FC:CF+C = 2:1	COP = 2	AG = 0
			Pure C = 0	GHR:PHR = 2:0	
EB = 2:2.0	EA = 4.0	EBPer = NA	SmC':WSmC = 2:2.0	a:p = 2:3	
eb = 3:2	es = 5	D = 0	Afr = 0.36	Food = 0	
	Adj es = 5	Adj D = 0	S = 1	SumT = 0	
			Blends/R = 2:15	Human Cont = 2	
FM = 3	Sum C' = 2	Sum T = 0	CP = 0	Pure H = 2	
m = 0	Sum V = 0	Sum Y = 0		PER = 0	
				Isol Indx = 0.40	

			XA% = 1.00	Zf = 12	3r+(2)/R	= 0.73
			WDA% = 1.00	W:D:Dd = 6:2:7	Fr+rF	= 2
		Sum6 = 1	X−% = 0.00	W:M = 6.2	SumV	= 0
a:p	= 3:2	Lv2 = 0	S− = 0	Zd = −3.0	FD	= 0
Ma:Mp	= 1:1	WSum6 = 4	P = 7	PSV = 0	An+Xy	= 1
2AB+Art + Ay	= 0	M− = 0	X+% = 0.87	DQ+ = 7	MOR	= 0
MOR	= 0	Mnone = 0	Xu% = 0.13	DQv = 0	H:(H)+Hd+(Hd)	= 2:0

PTI = 0	DEPI = 3	CDI = 3	S-CON = 4	HVI = No	OBS = NO

change in focus opened her to experience in the real world. It would seem that noticing and becoming involved in the real world outside herself might be a way to distract her from her internal focus.

Julie's Rorschach 1 contained no blends, four $DQ+$ responses, but two DQv responses. Her second Rorschach contained two complex blends of good form quality, seven $DQ+$, one $DQv/+$, and no DQv responses. When Julie's thinking and emotions were not dominated by intrusive memories, it looked as though her thinking, how she saw the world, and her emotional reactions all became more complex.

On Rorschach 1 Julie's $X-\%$ was 0.37, and $WSum6$ was 20. On Rorschach 2, $X+\%$ was 0.87, and $WSum6$ was 4. I told Julie that when she was in a passive state of mind, and dominated by her memories, she very often didn't see things the way they really were; instead she would distort things. She also didn't think very logically or clearly. When she was in a working state of mind, on Rorschach 2, she had the ability to see things very much as they really were, and her thinking was logical and clear.

On Rorschach 1 five of six minus responses involved human content, and the sixth minus was a mutant animal. She had two *Pure H*, four *Hd*, and four *(Hd)* responses. Four of six minus responses were coded MOR, and all Special Scores were to human content. Her second Rorschach contained no minus responses, two *Pure H* responses, and one Special Score (*FAB1*), and no MOR. I told Julie that it looked like her early abuse experiences had given her a very pessimistic view of other people. She was very guarded and suspicious of people's motives. These attitudes caused her to see threat and danger, when it wasn't there. I also said it seemed that she had trouble thinking logically and clearly when she was dealing with other people. When she concentrated on what was really going on in situations, however, she had the ability to see things clearly and to think clearly and logically. Rather than distorting her view of a person, she could see him or her the way most people did.

On Rorschach 1 *Ma:Mp* was 0:3. On Rorschach 2 *Ma:Mp* was 1:1. In Julie's passive state of mind, it seemed that she had gotten into looking to others to make her decisions for her and to solve her problems. However, if she got herself into a working state of mind, as she did on Rorschach 2, it became clear that she could think purposefully and deliberately about how best to deal with problems and challenging situations. This finding related to a sore spot for Julie. She believed that she was totally controlled by her mother. However, these results opened up the possibility that Julie was contributing to the situation. We identified this as an issue to work on in therapy.

On Rorschach 1 MOR was 7, An + Xy was 2, and H: (H) + Hd + (Hd) was 2:8. On Rorschach 2 MOR was 0, An + Xy was 1, and H: (H) + Hd + (Hd) was 2:0. Julie's very real, negative early experiences had led her to distort how she thought about and valued herself in her current life. She thought of herself as damaged and vulnerable. When Julie concentrated on what was outside of herself, on what was out in the world, she lost her preoccupation with distorted ideas about herself.

On Rorschach 1 FC:CF + C was 1:3, and the content included three blood responses and one of purple and red bruises. The two CF responses were minus form quality. On Rorschach 2 FC:CF + C was 2:1, and content included a "red butterfly," "rose petals," and "a snow-covered mountain over the center of the earth, which is red and orange and hot" (her FAB1). There were no minus color responses. Julie was having difficulty controlling intense emotional responses, which tended to occur when she experienced a breakthrough of memories and images into her conscious experience, and when she distorted things and saw threat that was not there. When Julie concentrated on the world around her, and worked to see things as they are, her emotions were quite normal (modulated and appropriate).

On Rorschach 1 H: (H) + Hd + (Hd) was 2:8, COP was 1, AG was 1, GHR:PHR was 1:9, and M and FM with pairs included one AG interaction. On Rorschach 2 H: (H) + Hd + (Hd) was 2:0, COP was 2, AG was 0, GHR:PHR was 3:0, and M and FM with pairs included two positive interactions ("dogs nuzzling," "girls dancing together"). Julie was guarded and mistrusting of people. She was not very comfortable in interpersonal situations, and she did not expect things to go positively. However, Julie could work to keep herself from assuming that people were like her early abusers. When she did this, she could look at people for who they really were, and decide that interacting with some people would be okay, in fact, even positive and fun.

Julie was thrilled with the changes we saw on her second Rorschach. Her experience gave her a taste of how difficult but how possible it was to set aside intrusive material from the past. It also gave her a taste of how well she could function if she did. She was primed to learn the skills that would enable her to do just that.

I also discussed Julie's first Rorschach with her in terms of the conceptual underpinning articulated by Rorschach (1921) and later elaborated by Schachtel (1966). Let me describe this theoretical perspective.

Rorschach (1921) said that the color, human movement, and form determinants were the representatives of three essential human capacities: (1) color as the capacity for emotional rapport; (2) movement as the capacity to turn inward and experience an inner life; and (3) form as the capacity for logic or disciplined thinking. He said further that the optimal goal of development would allow for the greatest growth possible for each of these capacities. At the same time, however, the growth of each should not suppress the development of the others. For example, the overdevelopment of form could arrest the development of introversive (movement) or extratensive (color) features and sacrifice the ability to experience. Thus, there is a tension among the three developing capacities, such that they somehow oppose each other. Figure 10.1 represents a basic personality template illustrating the capacities and the tensions among them.

I would suggest that the FC:CF + C ratio represents an individual's resolution between the capacities of color and form (including the logical relations between forms). Following from Rorschach's notion that color was the capacity for emotional rapport, I previously (Overton, 2000) suggested that the FC:CF + C ratio represented a range of affective modes of relating within one's interpersonal world, with each relational mode reflecting a characteristic emotional display, as delineated by the Comprehensive System. Does the ratio suggest that the intensity of emotion experienced with others overwhelms the reality testing of form and the logic of relationships perceived, making for chaotic interactions? Or does the resolution between form and color allow for appropriate and modulated emotional interactions with others? The Human Movement responses represent an individual's resolution between

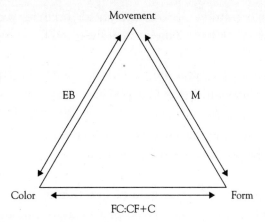

Figure 10.1   Basic personality template

the capacities of movement and form (including the logical relations between forms). Are conceptualizations realistic and logical, or does the movement capacity (the inner world) so overwhelm form such that ideas defy reality and logic? The EB *ratio* represents an individual's resolution between color and movement capacities. Is the focus of the personality the promotion of one's own ideas, or is the focus more toward forming emotional relationships with others? And, finally, each experience type, and thus personality, represents a synthesis of the resolution of all of these tensions.

In addition to the introversive-extratensive dimension (*EB*), Schachtel (1966) reminds us that Rorschach also proposed a dilation-coartation dimension, represented by the relation of form to movement plus color responses. The dilation-coartation dimension of the experience type describes the relation of one's emotional capacity for experience (represented by M and C) to one's conscious, critical, intellectual functions (represented by F). Schachtel (1966) said "the quality of this relationship can enhance or stifle the person's capacity for a full experience of reality" (p. 77). Of the coartative types (those whose form responses greatly predominated over their sum of M and C responses), Rorschach (1921) said

> . . . these types are distinguished primarily by logical discipline. In achieving this discipline, however, introversive and

extratensive features become atrophied; in other words, they sacrifice their ability to experience fully. (p. 92)

Rorschach's coartative types are those individuals who typically obtain High *Lambda* scores within the Comprehensive System.

From this dimensional perspective on Rorschach 1, Julie's M responses reflected the influence of her inner world on her conceptualizations, and thus on reality testing and logic:

> Card I: Scary mask, eyes, mouth, just thinking about Halloween, could be a witch. (*Inq*: Looks like a witch's hat, and the way the eyes are shaped, looks scary [*wmll scary?*], looks scary, like somebody's mad, mad-crazy or mad-angry, if she's mad-crazy, it would be her, the biological mother.)
>
> Card III: This is a person and this is a person, and this is a part of the heart ripped from one person, and part of a heart from another person . . . almost looks like the two people are at a stand-off. (*Inq*: Like facing off, *heart?*) This is heart shaped.
>
> Card VIII: Right here, looks kind of like sad eyes. (*Inq*: Just looks sad, somehow, maybe eyes half-closed or something.)

Form quality ranges from ordinary to minus, and each M response involves special scores. Her *FC:CF + C* ratio, 1:3, reflected the intense and unmodulated emotions she experienced during interpersonal encounters, most likely because she imposed templates of early abusers on others. Her *Afr* of .46 reflects her resulting social avoidance. The relationship between her M plus C responses and her F responses reflected an imbalance toward F, suggesting Julie had a greatly reduced ability to experience life fully. In Julie's case, this imbalance was not due to the greater development of form over movement and color capacities. Instead, in an attempt to escape her painful memories, Julie had walled off those memories, but in the process, she had closed down whatever personality resources she might have. By default, she was left with a "form" existence, involving little interest in and involvement with the world outside herself.

In discussing Julie's first Rorschach with her, I told her the Rorschach depicts personality as each person's unique organization of the capacities for self-creativity, for relationship seeking, and for disciplined thinking. All of a person's functioning—including how she related to her world— derives from this unique organization. I explained Figure 10.1 to her, and we discussed each of the three capacities. I defined the capacity for relationship seeking (color) as the extent to which a person desires and had the willingness to seek affective relationships with others. I said the capacity for self-creativity (movement) reflected how much a person was motivated to pursue and promote her own ideas—despite what others think. It reflected how freely she dipped into her imagination to come up with her own ideas and ways of solving problems, and how much she asserted herself in the world. I said the capacity for disciplined think-ing reflected how much a person's thinking was influenced by external sources of direction, for example, by her culture, her education, or by parental values and instruction. I told her that each of these sources of direction may have been internalized by the person, but they originated outside rather than being her own ideas. As well, I said, the capacity for disciplined thinking also reflected the ability to submit your thinking to tests of logic, rationality, and reality adherence.

I further explained that, for each person, these three capacities develop together in an interrelationship that determined how the per-son experiences his life. We expect *relatively* even development among the three capacities; we don't expect one capacity to develop to a great extent while the other two lag far behind. At the same time, the three capacities are never exactly even, as the slight imbalances among them make for differences among people. For example, some people pre-fer pursuing and promoting their own ideas, compared with spending time with others. For these individuals, the capacity for self-creativity would be somewhat more developed than the capacity for relationship seeking.

After reviewing Table 10.1, Julie and I turned to what her personal template looked like (Figure 10.2). What we saw was an imbalance that reflected a reduced space for living and experiencing. The template illus-trated that Julie had coped with her early abusive experiences by walling off parts of herself that had been influenced by those experiences, and thus reminded her of those experiences. When she did this, however, her capacities for self-creativity and for relationship seeking were also blocked. By default, what she was left with mostly was the capacity for disciplined thinking.

Julie: (pointing to the capacity for disciplined thinking) I think I'm stuck over here! All I do is what my mother says to do. Is self-creativity in me gone?—just not there anymore?

Carol: No, because if it were, and you had *only* disciplined thinking, then you would be much like a robot, like the Vulcan, Mr. Spock—purely logical and without a sense of humor at all.

I told Julie we could say that not all, but a good part of her capacities for self-creativity and for relationship seeking were being held hostage behind that wall in her mind. It felt too scary to go back there and reclaim those parts of herself. As a result, self-creativity became difficult, because tapping into those aspects of her mind that provided creative ideas and solutions to problems also risked tapping into painful memories, feelings, and relivable experiences behind the curtain. Instead, unable to utilize her own resources and initiative (self-creativity), she tended to follow and conform with what people in authority want and to depend on them for direction. She often had difficulty knowing what it was she wanted, and she was hesitant to assert

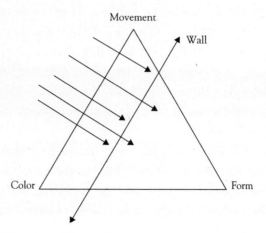

Figure 10.2   Julie's personality template

herself. Also, relationship seeking became difficult because she was afraid relationships would be as hurtful and painful as her early bad experiences. Thus, she was overly cautious and often avoidant in her relationships with others.

Julie's template also showed that her painful memories—the disturbing ideation and fearful feelings—often broke through the wall in her mind and flooded her awareness (these breakthroughs are represented by the arrows breaching the wall in Figure 10.2). When they did, it felt as though they were real or could happen today, and the anxiety she felt was debilitating. At these times, her "disciplined thinking" was overwhelmed, and it became difficult to think clearly. Her thinking could become illogical and unrealistic. The flooding occurred during the day, often when some event triggered a breakthrough, and at night, when this material intruded upon her dreams. When we reviewed Julie's MMPI-2 results, it became clear how distressed and worried she was about her thinking at these times.

To help Julie gain some control over these disturbing intrusions, I introduced several tools. These included the technique of Thought Stopping (McKay, Davis, & Fanning, 1997), a list of distraction techniques, the "clear thinking drill" (McKay, Fanning, & Paleg, 1994), and a checklist for recognizing when you're mixing up the present with the past (McKay et al., 1994). I also suggested, that once she did gain some control, she might take it as a long-term goal to work with her therapists to slowly dismantle that wall and integrate all aspects of herself. If she did so, she could expand her space for living and reclaim and develop her capacities for self-creativity and for relationship seeking.

Teaching Point

When the intensity of emotional experiences results in major distortions of reality, the clinician needs to assist the client, helping him or her to modulate the intense emotions by creating a holding environment that brings feelings of comfort and security.

MOVING PAST THE ABUSE

Julie's question was, "How do I get past the abuse?" We had seen that if she kept herself in a working rather than a passive state of mind, she was able to set aside intrusive thoughts, to set aside reactions based on those thoughts, and, instead, to focus her attention and intelligence on the world outside herself. Her efforts resulted in an expanded experience of herself, a greater utilization of her resources, and a much richer relationship with the world around her. Her thinking was more logical, and she saw things much more realistically. I told Julie she was in a working state of mind, as well, when she took the intelligence test. She had to focus on the questions I was asking, and she had to focus on the materials she was given to work with. It was in a working state of mind, then, that she was best able to utilize her above average intelligence. I suggested it was much more difficult to stay in a working state of mind during the Rorschach than the intelligence test, because the ambiguous shapes of the inkblots could easily provoke intrusion and experience of walled-off material. Because of this, taking the Rorschach was much more like dealing with the real world (full of people) than was the intelligence test. Her success on the Rorschach suggested she could do as well in the real world. In addition, Julie now had an array of techniques to help her control the intrusions.

The results of the assessment suggested, however, that Julie felt quite ambivalent about moving on and taking charge of her life. One of her TAT stories (Card 13G) reflected this ambivalence. Her story was about a girl who kept trying to find her way out of a maze. Every time she got close to getting out, something would happen so that she would find herself at the beginning again. I told Julie I thought what she was saying about herself through this story was:

> Part of me wants to find my way out and get on with my life, but it's scary to try, so part of me doesn't want to. When I come close, somehow *I* do something so that I have to start all over again.

What kept Julie from moving on? In our discussions, she said she was afraid that if she took charge of her life, she might screw up.

This fear kept her from trying, and it kept her in passive, dependent relationships with important adults in her life. We also talked about how eating too little, eating too much, and spending too much all serve, at least in part, as ways of self-sabotaging—who could trust Julie to be on her own?

Julie had gotten into a dependent relationship with her mother, in part because her mother seemed to have a controlling personality, and in part because Julie doubted her ability to take the initiative and was afraid to try. In her early memories, Julie repeatedly stated that she had no control over her life—because of her mother:

> The earliest memory of my mom is her dressing me in clothes she picked out and also making my hair look like her. People would then say to her—"Oh, she looks so much like you." I didn't get to pick out my own clothes until college. Again, I have no control over my life—it's more like my life is her life. I wanted to please her but the only way was to go along with her.

Another TAT story (to Card 1) told us more about Julie's control issue:

> A little boy who was sitting and staring at his violin, thinking why is my mother making me take lessons for this? Appears to be very pensive and concentrating very hard, but also looking a little bored. If he had a wish it would be that he could play the violin very well and it wasn't as difficult as it is.

I told Julie this picture provided an opportunity to tell a story about learning something new and about working at something challenging and finally achieving. I asked her to notice that her little boy did not interpret his situation as an opportunity for him to master something, but as an occasion for him to resist being controlled. He might appear to be concentrating, but actually he was bored, because he wasn't doing anything, except maybe daydreaming that things could be different than they are. And certainly his inactivity was frustrating his mother!

What Julie's story suggested about her was that without her realizing it, she converted opportunities to take charge into situations where she was being controlled or forced to do something. Julie said the following two dilemmas were true for her:

> If I must, then I won't. It is as if when faced with a task I must either gloomily submit or passively resist. (Other people's wishes feel too demanding, so I resist by constantly putting things off, avoiding them, etc.)
>
> If I must not, then I will. (Other people's rules feel too restricting, so I break rules and do things which are harmful to me.)

Julie wanted to change, to manage her own life, but when individual opportunities presented themselves, she became fearful that she would screw up. So she did nothing, she procrastinated, or she diverted herself with obsessive activities. Then her mother would step in and tell her she should do what she's been avoiding. Now, Julie felt controlled, and this would make her angry, so she would passively resist this control by not doing what her mother wanted. In this way, she got back at her controlling mother—and her tug-of-war with her mother diverted her from realizing what she was really doing, which was giving in to her fears of screwing up and *choosing* to do nothing. I told Julie, "The more you choose to do nothing, the more afraid you will become that if you tried, you would screw up." We coauthored the following vicious circle to describe the situation Julie had gotten herself into:

> Feeling fearful I will screw up, I don't do the things I could do to manage and improve my life. But then my mother steps in and tells me I have to do these things—in her way. It makes me angry to be controlled like this, so I passively resist doing these things, and my life stays the same. But the more I avoid managing my life, the more fearful I become that, if I tried, I would screw up. Feeling fearful I will screw up . . .

So, another very important way Julie could help herself to move on was to deal with her fear of trying. This was an issue she could explore and come to grips with during her therapy sessions.

This concluded my work with Julie. I was able to stay in contact with her older psychiatrist for two years after the assessment. He reported that Julie was successfully using her tools to control her abusive memories and that she had not had any further psychiatric hospitalizations.

Requests for copies of Julie's written report may be sent to the author at cgoverton@verizon.net.

REFERENCES

Armstrong, J., & Loewenstein, R. J. (1990). Characteristics of patients with multiple personality and dissociative disorders on psychological testing. *Journal of Nervous and Mental Disease, 178*, 448–456.

Bender, L. (1938). *A visual motor test and its clinical use. Research Monograph Number 3*. New York, NY: The American Orthopsychiatric Association.

Bruhn, A. (1992). The early memories procedure: 1. A projective test of autobiographical memory. *Journal of Personality Assessment, 58*, 1–25.

Butcher, J. N., Dahlstrom, W. G., Graham, J. R., Tellegen, A., & Kaemmer, B. (1989). *Minnesota Multiphasic Personality Inventory–2: Manual for administration and scoring*. Minneapolis: University of Minnesota Press.

Exner, J. (2003). *The Rorschach: A comprehensive system* (4th ed.) Hoboken, NJ: Wiley.

Finn, S. E. (1996). *Manual for using the MMPI-2 as a therapeutic intervention*. Minneapolis: University of Minnesota Press.

Kamphuis, J. H., Kugeares, S. L., & Finn, S. E. (2000). Rorschach correlates of sexual abuse: Trauma content and aggression indices. *Journal of Personality Assessment, 75*, 212–224.

McKay, M., Davis, M., & Fanning, P. (1997). *Thoughts and feelings: Taking control of your mood and your life*. Oakland, CA: New Harbinger.

McKay, M., Fanning, P., & Paleg, K. (1994). *Couple skills: Making your relationship work*. Oakland, CA: New Harbinger.

Murray, H. A. (1943). *Thematic Apperception Test manual*. Cambridge, MA: Harvard University Press.

Overton, C. G. (2000). A relational interpretation of the Rorschach color determinants. *Journal of Personality Assessment, 75*, 424–448.

Peters, E., Handler, L., White, K., & Winkel, J. (2008). "Am I going crazy doc?": A self psychological approach to Therapeutic Assessment. *Journal of Personality Assessment, 90*, 421–434.

Rorschach, H. R. (1921). *Psychodiagnostics*. Bern, Switzerland: Bircher.

Ryle, A. (1990). *Cognitive-analytic therapy: Active participation in change*. Chichester, England: John Wiley & Sons.

Schachtel, E. G. (1966). *Experiential foundations of Rorschach's test*. New York, NY: Basic Books.

Wechsler, D. (1981). *Wechsler Adult Intelligence Scale-Revised (Manual)*. New York, NY: The Psychological Corporation.

Assessments of Children, Adolescents, and Young Adults

11

Therapeutic Assessment of an Adolescent: An Adopted Teenager Comes to Feel Understood

MARITA FRACKOWIAK

A neuropsychologist colleague of mine called and asked me to collaborate. I can't do this alone, she said. "We need a comprehensive neuropsychological and emotional/personality assessment to help this family." I completed a psychological assessment that utilized attachment theory, and she conducted a full neuropsychological evaluation.

INITIAL SESSION

When I first met Mary, a 14-year-old client, and her mother, I felt sad. Mary was uncomfortable in my office, shut down, and impatient when her mother was talking. She rolled her eyes at her mother or interrupted, saying "Stop already" when her mother answered my questions. Any attempt on my part to engage Mary was met with a quick "I don't know" or silence. Several times she covered herself up with a blanket and made complaining or whining noises, indicating that she was ready to leave. Her mother,

Ms. Smith, a single woman in her 60s, looked tired, spent, and completely overwhelmed by her daughter's behavior. Each of her attempts to redirect or engage her daughter was met with even louder complaining, or Mary ignored her mother. Mary's mother grew increasingly frustrated as the session progressed, stating "See what I mean? She is like this all the time, but this is nothing compared to what happens at home."

Mary's mother struggled with posing assessment questions; she desperately wanted to tell me about how much the two of them argued and how disobedient Mary was. She talked about Mary's difficulties at school, both academically and behaviorally, and she wondered if the current school was a good fit and if Mary would benefit from being in a residential treatment center. As her mother provided examples of Mary's angry behavior, Mary grew more irritated. It was time to interrupt this dynamic, so I asked Mary's mom to wait in the waiting room while I met with Mary alone. I was curious to see what she would be like after her mother left the room, a standard practice in Therapeutic Assessment with teens.

When her mother left, Mary relaxed a bit. She looked around my office and picked out a game. She asked if we could play it, and I agreed. Mary was eager to set up the game and spontaneously told me about others she enjoys, naming Mancala as her absolute favorite. I wasn't familiar with the game; she showed great surprise when she learned that and took initiative in telling me about it. Her behaviors spoke louder than words to me. She smiled, giggled, and made mild self-deprecating comments when she missed a turn. She kept looking at me, carefully checking me out and communicating what felt to me like a deep longing for a connection. I looked back at her, and when our eyes met I smiled gently; she returned a quick smile and looked away. I found myself feeling very maternal toward Mary. Sensing her underlying fragility, I wanted to protect her, mirror her delight in the game, and treat her very gently.

Before Mary left that day, I mentioned to her that I would like to meet with her regularly to work on some psychological tests, to play, and to draw. She agreed. Routinely, I ask teens to think about their own assessment questions and invite them to share their goals for the assessment. With Mary, my goal at that point was to help her feel safe and comfortable.

As I often do in my assessments with adolescents, I began meeting regularly with Mary to complete various measures while I simultaneously met with her mother to gather Mary's developmental history, her mother's perspective, and to assess potential systemic dynamics contributing to Mary's current problems.

MARY'S STORY AS TOLD BY HER MOTHER

Ms. Smith had always wanted to adopt a child. She adopted Mary at age 6, from an Eastern European country, when she was in her 50s. At that time she was single, but involved in a long-term romantic relationship, owned a successful business, and was ready to become a mother. At the time of her adoption, Mary was living with her aunt and uncle. She had been removed from her biological mother's custody due to physical and sexual abuse by her mother and her mother's boyfriends. She bore scars on both of her upper arms, reportedly from glass and knife cuts, as well as cigarette burns. Mary was also legally blind in her left eye and had been legally deaf in her left ear prior to partial corrective surgery. According to Ms. Smith, when the adoption was in process, the adoption agency "dropped Mary off" at Ms. Smith's hotel for 10 days while they were finalizing the paperwork.

When Mary arrived in the United States, numerous very significant difficulties were evident, including fear of people, sexual inappropriateness with men, shoplifting, physical fighting with other children and adults (biting, kicking, scratching), fear of being alone, self-injury (e.g., hitting her head against the wall, pinching herself), hoarding food and other objects, and rocking back and forth. Ms. Smith reported that she did everything she could to show Mary love and care. She worked on helping Mary feel safe in the home and with other family members. She spoiled Mary with toys, clothes, vacations, and a comfortable room of her own. Throughout the years, Mary continued to have significant problems, but with time she also began to show signs of positive adjustment. She learned English within six months and started to play with other children. Within a couple of years, she stopped hoarding food, rocking herself, and hitting her head against the wall. She began to enjoy family life, grew closer to her grandmother, and started to enjoy school and pleasurable activities typical for children her age.

However, Mary continued to struggle socially when interacting with adults or peers, did not make or keep friends, and preferred to play with much younger children. Her interactions with peers were characterized by making quick, intense connections and then very abrupt endings when a friend said or did something to upset her. Mary also continued to be afraid when she was home alone, and she called her mother's or neighbor's phone repeatedly just to talk to someone. As she entered adolescence, some of her difficulties shifted into what her mother labeled behavioral problems and oppositional, angry behaviors. She struggled with completing chores and didn't respect her mother's wishes. In fact, Mary's "out-of-control" behaviors had become unmanageable and dangerous. Examples included attacking her mother while riding in the car with her, having screaming episodes and threatening self-harm, acting defiantly at school (e.g., laughing loudly during class, flashing her teacher, disrupting other students), breaking things, talking on the phone with strangers she met in a chat room, and hoarding things again (e.g., food, books).

Sadly, Mary's behaviors intensified and came to a climax when she was admitted to the adolescent unit at the local psychiatric hospital due to aggression toward her mother. Through the years, Mary had been seen in outpatient therapy by several local therapists and had been prescribed numerous psychotropic medications, with rather limited positive results. When I asked Ms. Smith to reflect on what might have contributed to Mary's breakdown and hospitalization, she stated she wasn't sure, but thought it might have been a combination of hormones, being a teenager, and not liking being told what to do. As a side comment, Ms. Smith added that it was unfortunate that things had been so hard for Mary lately, especially since "Kate" arrived. Kate was an exchange student from the same country where Mary was adopted, who had hopes of being adopted by Ms. Smith and staying in the United States. According to Ms. Smith's report, Kate was "great": smart, responsible, helpful around the house, and fun to be with. She tried to help Ms. Smith with parenting Mary, since she was a few years older, and she often redirected Mary or stepped in and commented on her "inappropriate behavior" toward her mother. Ms. Smith expressed a strong desire to adopt Kate and offer her a permanent home and the opportunity to attend college in the United States.

I was convinced Ms. Smith loved Mary and wanted what was best for her, but she did not know how complex Mary's emotional needs were and how she could accurately respond to them. Because of Mary's history of abandonment, her attachment insecurities had been terribly "triggered" by the arrival of another "daughter" into her household. Ms. Smith's personal history included an abusive early childhood, history of alcohol abuse (she had been clean and sober for many years at the time of the assessment), and long-term underlying depression. I began to appreciate all that she was dealing with. I saw a mother "at the end of her rope," desperate for help and overwhelmed by the demands of raising a child with multiple significant needs. I felt compassion for her, rather than just frustration about her parenting skills. But, I admit that I felt frustrated and sometimes judgmental, thinking: "How can this mother not realize what she's doing to her daughter?!" It was an ongoing challenge for me to balance my frustration and compassion. At times, just like Ms. Smith, I too felt overwhelmed.

MARY'S STORY

In my second meeting with Mary, I asked her to Draw-A-Person (DAP; Machover, 1949). She agreed, but asked not to be rushed, saying, "Everybody rushes me all the time." I promised to give her plenty of time to complete her drawing. The following conversation occurred:

Assessor: Can you tell me about the girl?

Mary: This would be me when I get older. I want to change my hair to purple. She is 15 years old. Her name is Lina.

Assessor: She looks pretty cool with her purple hair and bright clothes.

Mary: Yeah, but she is kind of mad right now.

Assessor: What made her mad?

Mary: Friends were not being nice to her, started calling her names and stuff, telling her that she is ugly. She is homeless, you know.

Assessor: How terrible for Lina, it must be hard for her.

Mary: Yeah, I get called names too, you know. It's really boring to live in my neighborhood; there are no kids there. I just sometimes get an urge to go to somebody's house and want to be with somebody and play.

Assessor: Sounds like you feel lonely?

Mary: I feel lonely, and I get really bored too. I get bored at school. I like to read, play games. I like to chat online with people. I get my feelings out on a web chat. I can make friends in the chat room and talk to them whenever I want. Did you know Kate got her visa extended for another month? She is going back after that.

Assessor: And how do you feel about that?

Mary: Happy. I will have attention from my mom. . . . She [Kate] is 17 and we didn't like each other at first. Now it's okay, but it's hard to get used to changes, you know.

This short exchange gave me a window into this 14-year-old girl and provided us with several themes that continued to evolve over the sessions that followed.

Mary felt terribly alone and different from her peers. She did not have any friends. The school she attended was very small and had a special needs focus. There were about five students per classroom, and it was located in a different city about 30 minutes away from where Mary lived. Many of her fellow students had developmental disabilities. Mary said she liked one of the girls from her school who was younger and also struggled academically. Mary described spending her afternoons at home while her mom worked long hours and sometimes even brought her work home with her. Mary stated that one way to spend more time with her mother was to work in her office as an assistant. For a brief period of time during the summer, Mary helped organize files at her mother's office, and she liked doing this. When asked about how she spent her time alone, Mary responded that talking to people in chat rooms was fun, but it got her in trouble with her mom because she gave out personal information to "some guy she met online." When I asked her to tell me about her arguments or fights with her mom, Mary said, "My mom and I are having a hard time," saying that their arguments got intense very quickly and they both ended up screaming at each other, slamming doors, and cussing. She added, "I don't think I have anger; I have sadness and confusion, but when my mom wants me to do something, I get mad."

Mary then told me that she didn't have any memories from her childhood. She vaguely remembered living with her aunt and uncle before coming to the United States. Since she spontaneously brought up the topic of memories, I decided to administer the Early Memories Procedure (EMP; Bruhn, 1992). The client is asked to write a brief narrative about five memories from childhood, answer structured questions about each memory, and then rate each one on clarity and pleasantness. I administered the EMP orally by reading the prompts and writing down her memories for her.

MARY'S EARLY MEMORIES

Mary's first early memory was at age six when she spent her first Christmas with her mom. She reported feeling happy. She told her second memory, at age seven, as follows:

> Kids asking about these [she pulled up her sleeve to show me numerous scars on both of her upper arms]. When I first got here from [country] I went to a daycare. They all wondered what happened. I said I got bit by a dog, but it was someone who cut me with a knife. [What is the clearest part of the memory?] Kids asking what happened. [What is the strongest feeling in the memory?] Confused. [If you could change the memory in any way, what would that be?] Kids not asking me, and it not being there, I guess.

Mary's next three early memories were about meeting teachers at school and feeling confused, meeting her adoptive grandmother and feeling excited, and meeting her mom's boyfriend and feeling nervous. For her sixth memory, Mary chose a recent memory:

> Spending time with my mom, me and her, boyfriend is gone. A couple of weeks ago I got to spend time with her and we went on a sightseeing tour. Tour bus stopped in different places and you went out and walked around. [What is the clearest part

of the memory?] Spending time alone together. [What is the strongest feeling in the memory?] Happy.

I told Mary that this short task helped me understand just how important it is to her to have alone, uninterrupted time with her mom, and how that helped her feel cared for and loved. I added that sometimes kids who were hurt by people in their life take longer to develop trust and connection to others, and that once they do, every time that connection gets threatened (e.g., when a person is not there or when she pays attention to other kids or people), the kids can feel terribly hurt, lonely, and even mad. Those feelings can be very strong because they can be a reminder of some of the old pain and hurt. I told her, "It's like the hurt all blends together and gets to be too much to bear. That's when a person can explode with feelings."

Mary listened to my explanation, and when I finished she summarized our discussion by saying, "Yeah, sometimes I get so mad because my mom is not paying attention. When she gets mad back and leaves to go to her bedroom, I get even madder. That's when I scream, and kick, and break things."

Mary's explanation made sense to me, but I could also understand how these same behaviors would be experienced by her mother. Mary had short-lived but very intense experiences of emotional flooding (i.e., meltdowns) when her needs were not met or when her abandonment wounds were reopened. Her ability to express herself was very limited, and thus she resorted to disruptive, obnoxious, and at times even dangerous behaviors that provoked her mother into withdrawal and self-protection, which further escalated Mary's behaviors. I felt sad for Mary, keeping in mind this child's severe trauma and abandonment history, and seeing her as a small, innocent child in a 14-year-old's body. In the subsequent three weekly sessions, I worked with Mary on completing self-report measures, the Adult Attachment Projective Picture System (George & West, 2001), and the Rorschach Inkblot Test (Exner, 2003).

FAMILY SESSION

After administering all of the measures, I invited both Mary and her mother for a family session, a standard procedure in Therapeutic Assessments with adolescents (Tharinger, Finn, Gentry, & Matson, in press). It helps to illustrate the systemic aspect of the child's difficulties, and most of the time the session is highly informative and can be transformative for some families. I selected a few of the Roberts Apperception Test (McArthur & Roberts, 1982) cards focused on both anger and sadness. One of my goals for the joint session was to see how Ms. Smith responded to Mary's painful affect and, if possible, to provide them with a positive experience of connecting around painful feeling rather than fighting or arguing. Mary's destructive and oppositional behaviors were probably a deep pool of painful feelings, which neither she nor her mom knew how to address.

We started together, and I asked both mother and daughter to come up with a story about what was happening in the picture and what the characters are thinking and feeling. The challenge is, I added, that you both have to agree on the story, so work together. Mary and her mom worked on three stories together, and the following themes emerged: (1) Ms. Smith did a nice job of engaging Mary and encouraging her to tell her story first; (2) it took Mary awhile to tell parts of the story, and Ms. Smith stayed patient with her; (3) Ms. Smith struggled with mirroring the feelings Mary introduced in the story, such as characters feeling frustrated, tired, angry, or confused, and she tended to ask Mary for an intellectual explanation rather than staying with the feelings; (4) Ms. Smith tended to put a "happy ending" on each story, while Mary insisted that the characters were feeling very sad and/or mad; and (5) as Ms. Smith failed to mirror Mary's or the character's affect, Mary became more disinterested in the task and started to fidget on the sofa, complain about the test being "boring," and ask when we would finish.

I then met with Ms. Smith alone for a brief discussion while Mary got some tea and waited in the waiting room. I asked Ms. Smith for her observations and comments. She stated she thought the activity went well, but she wished Mary had participated more and complained less, adding that this behavior was very typical of her. Ms. Smith also noticed that she liked to put a "happy ending" on each story, but she didn't have an explanation when I asked her what might have led her to do that. I used my time with Ms. Smith as an opportunity for some attachment- and attunement-focused parent coaching. First, I praised her efforts and ability to engage Mary; then I suggested that maybe we could "try an experiment" and finish the task in a different way when Mary came back. I told Ms. Smith that the testing results had helped me understand that sometimes Mary becomes flooded by her feelings, and in those moments she is likely to behave like a much younger child. I asked Ms. Smith to "stay longer with the feelings" Mary brought into the stories by (1) reflecting the feelings: "Oh, she is feeling sad"; (2) offering empathy: "That must be so hard for her to feel so alone"; and (3) joining with the feeling: "I can see why she feels angry about what her friend said; that was mean. I get angry too when someone says something mean to me." Ms. Smith was willing to try it out, but stated that she might forget some of the steps. I reassured her that I would be there to help, if needed. I explained that sometimes kids feel more settled and better understood when adults "stay with feelings" rather than trying to solve things for them or trying to make them feel better. At first, Ms. Smith didn't understand how this could work, but she was willing to try. Mary came back, and I asked this mother–daughter duo to look at three more cards and to tell stories.

What happened in the room then was almost difficult to believe. Ms. Smith diligently tried and did a beautiful job of using the three examples of responses that we had discussed. She seemed calm, focused, and present when interacting with Mary. Most importantly, she stayed with the feelings as I had coached her to do. Mary sat next to her, and by the time they were looking at the second card, Mary was sitting glued to her mother's side, comfortably folded alongside her mother's body, resting her head on her shoulder. She was focused, calm, and interested in the activity. The stories they told had some positive psychological elements, such as (1) range of feelings the characters experienced; (2) collaborative communication between characters or examples of connectedness and relationships; and (3) ability to make a repair and/or an apology.

We discussed how different from the first time the experience was for both Mary and Ms. Smith, and they agreed that they liked their interactions much better the second time around. I suggested we think about how this could fit with their everyday life, and our conversation focused on how they both have exploded at each other when they were tired, frustrated, or felt inconvenienced by the other. Ms. Smith admitted that when Mary has become oppositional, she has lost her patience very quickly and started yelling at Mary. Mary stated that it makes her mad when her mom comes to her room and tells her to do something. We used a metaphor of fire and how, when one gets mad (or catches on fire), the other one catches on fire very quickly, too. When they are both on fire, things go terribly wrong. I was glad to hear Ms. Smith say that she would work on staying calm, or "putting her fire out," before Mary catches on fire.

MIDASSESSMENT MEETING WITH MS. SMITH

Before meeting with Ms. Smith for a "discussion of results" session, I invited her again for an individual meeting to reconnect with her and to address individually what I had observed in the joint session with Mary. As the assessment progressed, I had been concerned about Ms. Smith's level of emotional functioning. Every time I saw her bring Mary to my office, she seemed extremely tired, overwhelmed, and spent. I expressed my empathy for her and my understanding of how hard it must be to manage all she managed in her everyday life. As I said this, Ms. Smith looked at me with tears and responded, "You have no idea how bad I wanted to have a drink just a couple of days ago during one of Mary's episodes. I am at the end of my rope." I knew that this strong, independent woman had reached her limit in many ways, and knew that to utilize the assessment findings and help Mary, she needed to feel taken care of and understood. I prepared for the "discussion of results" session by balancing the needs of mother and daughter; I felt connected to both of them, and I hoped that both would continue to receive ongoing support and care.

SUMMARY/DISCUSSION SESSION

I met with my neuropsychologist colleague to make sense of our independent test results. We quickly realized that we were looking at the same picture and were able to create one cohesive narrative about what might be happening with Mary. We found ourselves collaborating on ideas and recommendations that would address Mary's numerous needs. To explain the neuropsychological tests results, my colleague met with Ms. Smith for a short feedback session, while it was agreed that I would meet with her for a long discussion session, during which I would explain all of the results by helping her understand how they affected Mary.

CREATING A COHERENT NARRATIVE

Neuropsychological Test Results

On the neuropsychological evaluation, Mary demonstrated relative strengths in aspects of working memory, verbal fluency, word recognition in reading, and spelling. Sadly, she also demonstrated numerous significant difficulties related to Attention Deficit Hyperactivity Disorder (ADHD), Mathematical Learning Disability, Developmental Coordination Disorder (dysgraphia), and Nonverbal Learning Disability (NVLD). In addition, the evaluation indicated diffuse organic brain dysfunction with increased lateralization to the right hemisphere. Mary showed significant difficulties with integration of visual-spatial details, integration of abstract designs, and problems with conceptual problem solving and social problem solving. Last, her overall cognitive functioning as assessed by the Wechsler Intelligence Scale for Children-Fourth Edition (WISC-IV; Wechsler, 2003) fell in the Borderline range of functioning, with a Full Scale IQ of 79 (8th percentile), Verbal Comprehension Index score of 85 (16th percentile), Perceptual Reasoning Index score of 77 (6th percentile), Working Memory Index score of 97 (42nd percentile), and Processing Speed Index score of 78 (7th percentile). Our hypothesis was that the early physical abuse, particularly hits to the head on the left side, resulted in not only Mary's hearing loss in her left ear, but also trauma to the brain and hence numerous cognitive deficiencies. In other words, Mary had very real deficits her mother was not aware of that affected her functioning in numerous ways.

Personality/Emotional Test Results:
Emotionally Overwhelmed Family System

When I met with Ms. Smith for the summary/discussion session, the first thing I focused on was how overwhelmed and exhausted she must be.

I appreciated her by sincerely reflecting that I didn't know if I would have been able to do all that she had done. She started to cry. I knew from all of our discussions that Ms. Smith had begun to shift in the direction of seeing Mary as a deeply hurt child rather than a willful, defiant teenager. My goal for the session was to help Ms. Smith integrate both of these views and have a deeper and more complex understanding of Mary's internal world and psychological functioning.

Significant, Long-Term Depression and Poor Self-Esteem

I started my discussion by focusing on Mary's depressive feelings. This was something that Ms. Smith already knew, what Finn (1996) described as Level 1 information. I explained that the test results, especially the Rorschach and BASC-2 (Rorschach Depression Index: $DEPI = 5$, BASC-2 self-rating: Depression, 93rd percentile; parent rating: Depression, 99th percentile; Reynolds & Kamphaus, 2002) suggested that Mary had been functioning with symptoms of an underlying, long-term dysthymia, which affected most areas of her life and predisposed her to be unmotivated, moody, or pessimistic (*Coping Deficit Index* $= 4$; $D = -1$; $Adj D = -1$). More recently she had also experienced more intense symptoms consistent with major depression, including feeling helpless, irritable, and easily provoked, sad and lonely much of the time, crying, and feeling hopeless about the future. I also showed Ms. Smith Mary's self-rating, at the 99th percentile on the Sense of Inadequacy scale of the BASC-2, which was consistent with her Rorschach results, indicating that she struggled with poor self-esteem and with feeling damaged, insecure, or not good enough (*Morbid* $= 2$, Egocentricity Index: $3r+(2)/R = 0.13$).

I suggested that on a deeper level Mary didn't feel loveable or worthy and had not yet internalized a view of herself as a good human being. Ms. Smith agreed, and we had a discussion of what might happen to Mary when she felt badly about herself. I hypothesized that Mary, like other teens and children with very low self-esteem, behaves in ways that push others away, which leads her to feel rejected and ultimately "confirms" her view of herself as bad and unworthy. As I shared this hypothesis with her mother, I saw a sense of relief. She said that it made her feel hopeful to know this about Mary. Ms. Smith had been interpreting

Mary's behaviors solely as oppositional, cruel, and willful, and she had felt hopeless about things ever getting better.

Concrete and Distorted Thinking and Emotional Dysregulation

My assessment findings indicated that Mary's thinking was quite concrete and inflexible (Rorschach *Perseverations* = 1). I suggested to Ms. Smith that Mary seemed to interpret the world and other people in rather idiosyncratic, dichotomous ways (e.g., she is either a friend or an enemy; this is good or bad) without considering the complexities of human interactions. She often used one piece of information to form her opinion about a person or an event, and she made decisions based on insufficient evidence. Ms. Smith agreed and shared an example of when Mary permanently broke off her relationship with a friend because of one thing the friend said to her. I explained that Mary also showed some evidence of distorted thinking (*WSum6* = 28; X–% = 0.47) about herself and her environment, which even more negatively impacted her judgment, decision making, and ability to relate to other people (*Good Human Responses: Poor Human Responses* = 0:4; *Cooperative Movement* = 0; *Pure Human* = 1). Mary struggled when asked to integrate multiple sources of information. She could also get "stuck" in her thoughts regardless of evidence suggesting that her ideas were not accurate.

Last, Mary's thinking became significantly worse when she was in an emotionally flooded state, making the high-stress situations even more difficult to cope with (Emotional Control: FC/CF+C = 0/3; *Pure* C = 2). This finding, I stressed to her mother, was very important to consider when interpreting some of Mary's behaviors or responses. What in many situations might look like oppositional or stubborn behavior on the surface could actually be a product of Mary's concrete thinking process rather than her behavioral acting out. Following my explanation, Ms. Smith and I talked about examples of Mary's flooding and becoming stuck in her thinking. Ms. Smith said she was grateful to know this information and felt relief, once again, to know that it wasn't Mary being willful, but instead, the way her brain works. I suggested that in those moments of conflict, instead of reasoning with Mary, it might be better to hold her and help her calm down. On several occasions, after the discussion session,

Ms. Smith referenced this information as "one of the most important things I learned about Mary and the best advice I have gotten."

Disorganized Attachment

Finally, Ms. Smith and I began talking about Mary's emotional attachment. I explained that Mary's attachment pattern as assessed by the Adult Attachment Projective Picture System (AAP; George & West, 2001), was "Insecure-Disorganized, alternate Dismissing," a form of insecure attachment that is associated with various forms of severe emotional disturbance (Lyons-Ruth & Jacobvitz, 1999). Anything that triggered feelings of abandonment, betrayal, grief, and so on (e.g., the arrival of the foreign exchange student, being alone when her mother was at work) had the potential to "set Mary off" and to provoke hurt, anger, and emotional decompensation. When children with disorganized attachment are under stress, their actions and responses to caregivers are often a mix of behaviors, including avoidance and resistance to closeness, as well as increased neediness and clingy behaviors. They often show what researchers call approach-avoidance (Main & Solomon, 1990). Ms. Smith was very interested in this information and provided examples of Mary's behavior; she stated that having the "attachment frame" helped her understand Mary better and that she could understand Mary being insecurely attached considering her early history.

I added that a person with dismissing attachment often appears not to value relationships or to care deeply about others. This is a defensive strategy that Mary maintained to deal with the pain of her early attachment disruptions and trauma. This is a way she protected herself from the underlying grief and depression, and the fear that she would be rejected or hurt in close relationships. I shared with Ms. Smith that adoptees often feel that it is too dangerous to love and be loved authentically, because they can't trust that they won't be abandoned again (Axness, 1998). She said to me, "I worried that she just didn't love me, but now I understand why she would want me one minute and push me away the next minute."

I recommended individual therapy to help Ms. Smith cope with her own strong feelings and reactions and to get parenting support. I also recommended individual and peer group therapy for Mary. Ms. Smith readily agreed to both. At the end, we addressed the question of "Should Mary go to a residential treatment center?" I felt pulled in several directions: the trauma of being sent away that would be recreated for Mary, her multiple neuropsychological and emotional needs, and the reality of her mother's complete exhaustion and limited parenting skills. I asked if Ms. Smith would be willing to start first with an intense outpatient program (which would include supports for both her and Mary) and to see what happened. I left the possibility of residential treatment open should things get significantly worse or should Mary become dangerous to herself or others.

Summary/Discussion Session With Mary

After my meeting with her mother, I met with Mary to go over the main assessment findings, and as we talked we created a collage with pictures and words. Mary divided a page into two sections: "Good skills!!!" and "Please, help needed!" and placed various key words such as "attention and focusing," "expressing feelings with words," "using art to feel calm," and so on while we talked. Both of us looked for pictures in magazines to represent the key concepts to decorate Mary's page. This is not a typical TA method of conducting a discussion session with a teen, but it seemed appropriate for Mary due to her cognitive limitations and her interest in drawing and art. Mary agreed to see an individual therapist, and both Mary and her mom expressed interest in continued work with me, focusing on their relationship and communication.

I met with them for several more weeks to help them create a more structured, calm environment in their home. We worked on behavioral rewards, reestablishing a routine, organizing things in the home to help Mary make sense of her environment, and emotional expression. Simultaneously, Mary worked (and continues to do so) with an individual therapist, who also meets regularly for parent coaching sessions with Ms. Smith. I haven't seen Mary or Ms. Smith in several months, but I regularly see the therapist involved and hear brief updates. Their lives continue to be difficult, but the two are managing their interactions much better. I understand that although Mary and her Mom continue to have various conflicts, the question of sending Mary to a residential treatment center has been dropped, and this mother–daughter duo are trying their best to figure out a way to interact and live with each other.

☜ Teaching Points

1. In assessments involving an adopted individual, it is important to gather a detailed, chronological story of the adoption. Without this, the assessor could miss significant sources of unresolved grief and loss in either the adoptive parents and/or the child.
2. Understanding adoption as "the primal wound" or an early attachment trauma (Axness, 1998; Verrier, 1993) might be an important aspect of an assessment with adopted children and teens.
3. It may be important to conduct both a psychological and neuropsychological assessment in complex trauma cases. Helping clients integrate the findings and make sense of test results by translating them into "everyday" life situations can provide understanding, relief, and deeper empathy, and can help establish more reasonable expectations for family members.
4. Adolescents with cognitive difficulties might prefer to create an art project or be given a story instead of engaging in a discussion session.
5. The importance of simultaneously developing a relationship with the parent(s) as well as the teen serves as a platform for change in Therapeutic Assessment with adolescents. Working with Ms. Smith alone or working with Mary alone would not have produced the shift required for this family. The process of Therapeutic Assessment with teens is a delicate balance of supporting and challenging all members of the family (Tharinger et al., in press).

REFERENCES

Axness, M. W. (1998). *What is written on the heart: Primal issues in adoption.* Adoption Insight, Volume 1. Reseda, CA: Author.

Bruhn, A. (1992). The early memories procedure: A projective test of autobiographical memory, Part 1. *Journal of Personality Assessment, 58*(1), 1–15.

Exner, J. E. (2003). *The Rorschach: A comprehensive system, Vol. 1: Basic foundations* (3rd ed.). New York: Wiley.

Finn, S. E. (1996). *A manual for using the MMPI-2 as a therapeutic intervention.* Minneapolis: University of Minnesota Press.

George, C., & West, M. (2001). The development and preliminary validation of a new measure of adult attachment: The Adult Attachment Projective. *Attachment and Human Development, 3,* 55–86.

Lyons-Ruth, K., & Jacobvitz, D. (1999). Attachment disorganization: Unresolved loss, relational violence, and lapses in behavioral and attentional strategies. In J. Cassidy & P. R. Shaver (Eds.), *Handbook of attachment: Theory, research and clinical applications* (pp. 520–554). New York, NY: Guilford Press.

Machover, K. (1949). *Personality projection in the drawing of a human figure.* Springfield, IL: Charles Thomas.

Main, M., & Solomon, J. (1990). Procedures for identifying infants as disorganized/disoriented during the Ainsworth Strange Situation. In M. T. Greenberg, D. Cicchetti, & E. M. Cummings (Eds.), *Attachment in the preschool years: Theory, research, and intervention* (pp. 121–160). Chicago, IL: The University of Chicago Press.

McArthur, D., & Roberts, G. (1982). *Roberts Apperception Test for Children manual.* Los Angeles, CA: Western Psychological Services.

Reynolds, C. R., & Kamphaus, R. W. (2002). *The clinician's guide to the Behavior Assessment System for Children (BASC).* New York, NY: Guilford Press.

Tharinger, D. J., Finn, S. E., Gentry, L., & Matson, M. (in press). Therapeutic Assessment with adolescents and their parents: A comprehensive model. In D. Sakllofske & V. Schwean (Eds.), *Oxford Press handbook of psychological assessment of children and adolescents.* New York, NY: Oxford University Press.

Verrier, N. (1993). *The primal wound: Understanding the adopted child.* Baltimore, MD: Gateway.

Wechsler, D. (2003). *The Wechsler Intelligence Scale for Children* (4th ed.). San Antonio, TX: The Psychological Corporation.

Collaborative Storytelling With Children: An Unruly Six-Year-Old Boy

LEONARD HANDLER

I thank Herbert Potash, Guy Edlis, Barbara Handler, Howard Pollio, Justin Smith, Lotte Weinstein, and the second-year graduate class at the University of Tennessee for their helpful suggestions. They have significantly improved the manuscript.

COLLABORATIVE STORYTELLING

I believe stories have the power to produce dynamic changes in children, adolescents, and adults. This belief is supported by therapists who have written about psychoanalytic psychology (e.g., Bettelheim, 1976; Bucci, 1995; Gardner, 1993; Luborsky & Crits-Christoph, 1990; Spence, 1982; Winnicott, 1971) and those who have written about narrative therapy (e.g., Barker, 1985; Lieblich, McAdams, & Josselson, 2004; McLeod, 1997; Mills & Crowley, 1986; Smith & Nylund, 1997; White & Epston, 1990). Adherents of both disciplines would probably agree that childhood narratives, which are fraught with pain, anger, and/or sadness, become the negative narratives of the adult self—unless there is intervention to alter the narratives. This can be done through the healing stories told by the collaborative assessor or through helping parents change the negative narrative(s) of their child. Of course, the greatest therapeutic change occurs when both approaches are combined (Finn, 2007; Smith & Handler, 2009; Smith, Handler, & Nash, 2010; Smith, Nicholas, Handler, & Nash, 2011; Smith, Wolf, Handler, & Nash, 2009; Tharinger, Finn, Wilkinson, & Schaber, 2007). The case of Billy, to be presented later in this chapter, illustrates the effectiveness of such a combined collaborative approach, for both the child and the parents.

Before discussing Billy, I would like to describe my journey in the development of collaborative assessment with children and adolescents, using storytelling. Early in 1981, I became dissatisfied with my traditional play therapy approach in treating children. Progress was painfully slow in many cases, and it seemed that there was much chaff but little wheat in each session. A similar observation was made by Altman, Briggs, Frankel, Gensler, and Pantone (2002): "Frequently child therapists who opt for an open-ended play approach . . . find themselves either engaged in or observing some activity that feels as if it lacks any emotional import" (p. 200).

Traditionally trained play therapists have been taught to carefully avoid directing or shaping the activities of the child in the process of therapy. The therapist's role is restricted to the observation and description of the child's play (Axline, 1947/1989). I found this approach to be overly confining; often the child would play alone. I wanted to find another way, but I was unclear as to how and where I might find it. I tried using drawings as a therapeutic technique rather than just as assessment tools. I asked children to draw and tell a story about each drawing. I hoped the stories would be laden with important thematic content, but they often lacked dynamic material. I knew that the approach I wanted was going to be more interactive, emphasizing the relationship between the child and me. Many years later, Altman et al. (2002) expressed what I had in mind:

> Interpersonal [Relational] therapists . . . believe that in order
> to become significant to the child [the therapist] must be seen
> in a way that activates the child's preexisting, intense, and

sometimes problematic hopes and fears. For therapeutic change to occur, one must be able to conceive that something new and unexpected could occur in the interaction with the therapist that could upset the child's expectations and lead to change in [his or] her internal object representations. (p. 11)

I remember the day things changed. I found myself face to face with Alice, a frightened five-year-old girl whose mother brought her for therapy because she was anxious and unhappy (Handler & Hilsenroth, 1994). She stood just inside my office door, silent and frozen. Alice's mother had been hospitalized for a physical problem for about a year, when the child was two or three years old. She felt guilty about her absence and attempted to compensate by being ever-present and indulgent. So there I was, with Alice, wondering what to do next. I decided to ask her if she would like to draw, and she nodded "Yes." I then asked her to "draw a make-believe animal, one that no one has ever seen or heard of before" (Handler, 2007, p. 60). The instructions I gave Alice were asking her, indirectly, to engage in fantasy in her play-drawing (Handler, 1999). She surprised me by literally attacking the paper with her pencil, scribbling rapidly all over it. She placed a small dot in one of the loops formed by her scribbling. I then asked her to tell me a story about the make-believe animal. She pointed to the dot and said, "This little fishie is stuck inside the momma fishie, and she can't breathe and she's drowning." Alice was telling me how she was experiencing her mother's attempts to reconnect with her (Handler, 2007, p. 60).

I told Alice a story that contained a therapeutic message in response to her call for help. "This little baby fishie [pointing to the dot] is stuck inside the momma fishie and she can't breathe; she's dying. But along comes a big helper fishie and he makes an opening in the momma fishie and the baby swims out and she's free!" (Handler, 2007, p. 60). Alice was now very animated and smiled broadly; she asked if I could tell her the story again, and so I did. She left my office in quite the opposite way from which she entered it. I shared the stories with her mother, and she began to modify her approach. I felt my story had been effective for Alice because of her dramatic reaction and her request for a repetition of my story.

During the next session, the now active, spontaneous, and chipper little girl made another scribbled drawing, but this time she left an opening in one of the loops. In Alice's story, the baby fishie repeatedly swam inside the momma fishie, nursed, and swam out, freely, emphasizing the normal separation and individuation process described by Mahler (1975). It was proof to me that the child had heard and appreciated my message. Soon after my experience with Alice, I began to use the game with several other child clients. One such client, Billy, illustrates the use of the fantasy animal drawing game throughout assessment and treatment.

BILLY'S STORY

I chose to present the case of Billy in this chapter because much of our therapy was conducted with fantasy animal drawings and stories and because most of the stories told were developed from our collaboration. Billy, a small, pale, dark-haired, six-year-old boy, appeared immature for his age, but it was soon obvious that he was functioning intellectually at a superior level. He spoke in complete, complex sentences and demonstrated excellent knowledge about how the world worked, physically and mechanically. Billy's mother, an art teacher at a nearby small college, and his father, a physician, had recently moved their family from Oregon to Tennessee. They had one other child, a girl, who was two years younger than Billy.

Billy's mother spoke to him as if she were talking to an adult. She was puzzled about why he would not comply with her loosely focused directions. For example, she would tell Billy it was time to go to bed, but the message was posed more as a question: "Isn't it a good time to go to bed?" Billy ignored her. She would then repeat herself, now in a louder voice, and Billy would answer, "No, it's NOT time to go to bed." Soon she became agitated and began screaming at him. Billy would then put his hands over his ears and would rock back and forth, often screaming as his mother had, in a shrill, piercing tone. Finally, Billy's mother or father might spank him and he would begin to cry, sometimes for long periods. His mother also described Billy as "suspicious." She also said he had frequent temper tantrums and refused to do his school work.

It was clear to me that there was a significant lack of healthy mirroring (defined here as the importance of children's needs to "have their achievements affirmed, in a timely manner" and for the child to experience "prideful satisfaction" from these accomplishments [Silverstein, 1999, pp. 51–52]) for Billy in his present home situation. Instead of praise, encouragement, and other positive feedback, there was anger and punishment in his interactions with family members and school personnel. Instead of healthy grandiosity, which typically melts away when the child is faced with reality in his or her environment, Billy's extreme grandiosity and entitlement were probably being used as a defense against emotions aroused from his negative environment.

Although I recognized that Billy was cleverly controlling and resistant, it was also obvious that he needed to have some firm but benign directions and limits. However, I was concerned with the primitiveness of his reactions and wondered whether he was moving into an autistic type of adjustment. He was socially inappropriate, both at home and at school. For example, if another child had something he wanted, he would grab it from him or her. If the child resisted, Billy would hit him or her. He also threatened a girl in his class with a pair of scissors, and the school authorities came very close to expelling him. I noted that most of his aggressive behavior did not seem to be driven by anger, but rather by a desire to be dominant and by an immaturity that is typical of a two- to three-year-old child: "I want it so it's mine; I'll take it."

Billy's mother had also been raised with few boundaries or limits. Therefore, after I started to see Billy, his mother and I began to work on parenting skills, specifically devising ways to approach the boy to provide effective boundaries and limits, and finding opportunities for positive, supportive interactions. After several weeks, Billy's mother reported that he was becoming more compliant. She also asked if I could help her husband learn to parent, as she was learning to do. I met with him several times to work on parenting skills. He, too, was raised with few boundaries or limits and had no idea about how to effectively raise a child.

Billy was eager to direct our therapy sessions and tried to make me comply with his wishes in a variety of clever ways. For example, he refused, in a polite and gentle manner, to do what I wanted him to do, and insisted on *his* suggested activities. Ordinarily, I let the child choose the activity, but I felt this approach would be counterproductive for Billy. Allowing him to structure the activity was quite similar to what went on at home. In our first session, when I refused, politely, to act on his suggestion for an activity, he withdrew to a large armchair and curled up in it, sucking his fingers. He was mute and withdrawn for most of the session; I wondered if I had done the right thing. Certainly this was not productive, I thought; I needed to find a better way. In the last 10 minutes of the session, Billy began to communicate with me again, in an active and animated fashion, but (as I pointed out to him) we did not get to do what he wanted, *nor* what I wanted.

At the beginning of the next session, I requested that Billy draw a make-believe animal, one that no one had ever seen or heard of before. He worked willingly and furiously on the drawing, taking a very long time to add details. He described it as "a Three-Headed Animal" (see Figure 12.1). I asked Billy to make up a story about it. Here is the (edited) story he told:

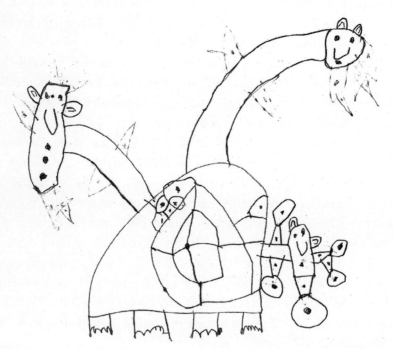

Note the erased spines on the top right and left.

Figure 12.1   Three-Headed Animal

Billy: Once upon a time, a long, long time ago, there lived a Three-Headed Animal . . . A Lion came. The Lion was scared of the animal. (He smiled smugly.) Then the Three-Headed Animal said, "Why are you scared of me?" "Because you have spines!" I think that might be the end.

Dr. H: (reluctantly) Well, I don't know.

Billy: "Well (He began rocking back and forth, obviously anxious, and addressed the Lion), you don't have to be afraid of me; I won't hurt you."

Dr. H: And the Lion said, "Well, you look like you have a bad, bad, bad temper. You might hurt me with your spines, or try and eat me," said the Lion.

Billy: "But these spines are *only* to protect *me* from bad animals."

At this point I recognized that Billy was symbolically expressing his vulnerability and his defense against it, as he did at home with his parents. Given a choice, Billy's approach was to take control. He angrily rejected my accusation about the use of his spines and told me he felt falsely accused of intending harm. Instead, he explained, he was merely protecting himself from perceived harm at the hands of dangerous animals, which probably meant his parents and other authoritative adults. I also recognized that the Three-Headed Animal (who probably represented Billy) was in charge, rather than the Lion (who probably represented me), reflecting Billy's attempts to "manage" dangerous adults. I decided to reverse the situation, to provide a powerful yet benign and helpful picture of adults.

Dr. H: So the Lion said [firmly, but gently], "You know, I am the King of the Jungle. Everyone listens to me and does what I ask because I am the king of the whole jungle. I make the rules and you need to obey them and we can be friends. You will *not* need all those spines to protect you, because I will protect you. That's what a king does."

Billy: But he didn't hear the Lion so well, so I'm drawing ears, but that wasn't part of *my* story.

Dr. H: So the Lion said, "I hope you heard what I said."

Billy: Well, I kind of heard it, but now I have ears, so I can hear you better.

I was delighted to see that Billy was cooperative and willing to listen to my message, which described the protective function of parents. He surprised me by his willingness to do what I asked, with no resistance, but given Billy's frequent resistance described by his parents, and his reaction to me in the first session, I felt his newfound acceptance was obtained too easily.

Dr. H: "Yes," said the Lion, "I am very, very, very good at protecting everyone in the jungle, *especially* three-headed animals, so you can put away your spines and let *me* do the job. I will teach you how to do it, and then it will be your turn, when you've grown up."

At this point I added another traditional parental function to emphasize the support and preparation a child needs to become a competent adult. I felt it was important to let Billy know that there was a special place of authority for him in the future, and that I was dedicated to seeing him grow up and become mature. But in his next response, Billy was saying that his protective stance was an inborn trait rather than an acquired one, and therefore could not be modified.

Billy: Well, I was born with these spines, so I can't take them off and put them away.

Dr. H: "Well," said the Lion, "How about making covers for the spines so they won't poke anybody, so you can still have them?"

Billy: If you put covers on them they'll fall off, so we can't do that.

Dr. H: "Well, what can we do?" said the Lion.

Billy: The only thing we can do is make a machine that takes them off very easily.

Dr. H: "Well," said the Lion, "I know a doctor who has just such a machine, and he can take them off and he can give them to you to keep, just in case you ever need them again."

Billy: Well, you never know when there might be a bad animal sneaking up, so I will always need to keep them on. *I don't want to take them off!*

After all that bargaining, Billy "shut the door" and emphatically ended our negotiations. I decided to see just how far he would go in his refusal, and I wondered if he did the same thing with his parents. I later learned from Billy's mother that he did so.

Dr. H: "Well," said the Lion, "You better come up with some idea because they can't stick out the way they are."

Now here comes another surprise. Given the responsibility of solving the problem of removing his protective defenses (the spines), Billy's response was to take a chance and comply, which he did, happily. Rather than become resentful, he seemed to feel pleased that a firm boundary was established, indicating to me that firmness and support would work well at home and at school, in helping Billy be more cooperative.

Billy: Well, the spots on them are guns, and if the guns start to shoot, the spikes will fall off easier and easier. Your turn now.
Dr. H: Let's help you shoot the guns at a safe target, and then the spines will fall off.
Billy: OK, let's do your idea (He began to laugh). Let's do that. (He began to sing and started to make walking movements with his fingers). They find a safe target now. Now I shoot my guns. And ready—set—GO! (He began to make exploding sounds and erase the spines. Notice the mostly erased spines in the drawing and the ears drawn on the heads).
Dr. H: So the Lion says, "Three-headed animal, as you grow up you will become King of the Jungle when I am finished being king. You will be next and I will save all these spines for you, so when you are all grown up you can have them, just in case you need them."

Billy's mother reported that when he came home, after the session, he drew rainbows and hearts all weekend. She also reported that since the last therapy session he had been more loving and cooperative at home. I shared Billy's story with her, and we discussed the issue of control between them in more detail. I pointed out his initial resistance in the story and his compliance when he felt supported. We also discussed his feelings of vulnerability and his need to defend himself from harm at home and school. Billy's mother was initially saddened that he felt so vulnerable in the family setting; she was determined to repair the problem.

Not every session early in Billy's treatment was so productive. For example, only several months after we began, Billy drew a Circle Animal, which had many circles, from which came many small confetti-like pieces of paper. The Lion (LH) said it was littering the jungle, so all the holes had to be sealed up. Billy insisted on having one open hole, but the Lion King said "no"; he told the Circle Animal he could either comply or leave the Jungle. Billy then drew a suitcase and told the Lion King he was leaving. As the Circle Animal left, he made a loud noise. The Lion King told the Circle Animal that the jungle was a quiet place, whereupon the Circle Animal drew a horn and played loud music. Then the Lion King sent out a skunk to "stink" the Circle Animal out of the jungle, but the Circle Animal drew a shower to wash away the smell. Just before the session was over, the Lion King sent in 20 skunks, and the Circle Animal informed the Lion King that he was mad!

Several months later, Billy drew a Mouth on Tummy Animal (see Figure 12.2). There was less collaboration on this story, compared with the others. This story was more like mutual storytelling, probably because we both had important information to share with each other.

Dr. H: Once upon a time, a long, long time ago . . .
Billy: There lived a make-believe animal. He liked to eat frogs for lunch, supper, and breakfast. He met a Lion. He was scared of the Lion. When he was scared, these little things came out on the bottom of his mouth. The Lion scared him so much, the little things came all over his mouth, and then the Lion ate him. The end.
Dr. H: Now it's my turn to tell a story. Once upon a time there was a Mouth on Tummy Animal. He was always hungry for more, more, more. He wanted to eat everything, not just frogs.

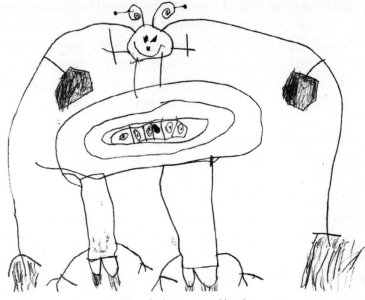

Note the long arms and hands.

Figure 12.2   Mouth on Tummy Animal

But there wasn't enough food around to feed him. The other animals were eating all the food and there wasn't enough for Mouth on Tummy Animal. He was getting very, very, very hungry and he was also getting very, very, very angry. "Where's my food?" he shouted. So along came the Lion; he was afraid of the Lion. So the Lion said, "Why are you afraid of me?" "Because you are the King of the Jungle and you growl," Mouth on Tummy Animal said. "Well," said the Lion, "I may growl, but I'm not mean. I know you're hungry and I've come to help you." So the Lion showed the Mouth on Tummy Animal how to get food and very, very, very soon they became friendly and the Lion always helped the Mouth on Tummy Animal get along and find plenty of good food. The Mouth on Tummy Animal grew big and strong, and when he got older, he even helped the Lion.

Billy: (Drew arms and hands on the Mouth on Tummy Animal and interrupted.) Now he could pick up his food so none of the birds had to help him pick up his food and put it in his mouth, but when he didn't have hands, he couldn't do it. He grew muscles—the kind of muscles only Mouth on Tummy Animals can have, a little stronger than people's muscles, but not much. Like Lion muscles. He then drew a boundary line and explained, "Let me tell you what that is. When anything goes through it, it'll break—pretend break, not really break. It helps him stay safe. Nothing can get through it, except for itself."

Despite his acceptance of the Lion in the first story, and the Lion's emphasis on nurturance, Billy was still afraid of the benevolent but authoritative King of the Jungle. However, the story content seemed to reflect Billy's partial acceptance of the Lion's supportive message and his identification with the Lion. For example, he drew hands on the Mouth on Tummy Animal to allow the animal to feed itself, and it grew in strength, comparing its muscles to those of the Lion. Nevertheless, he ended the story with his emphasis on a boundary line of sorts ("Nothing can get through it, except for itself" and "It helps him stay safe"), probably indicating his wariness and mistrust of adults.

Several more months into therapy, Billy drew a Light Animal. He told a story that seemed to be setting up a contest to test his ability to control our relationship. He said that when the Light Animal was asked a question, small lights "would glow at night, in the dark." Then Billy (smiling mischievously) said the Lion King told the Light Animal he didn't need the lights, whereupon Billy challenged the Lion King: "Yes, I do need them!" In response, I had the Lion King insist that the Light Animal take the lights off, and replace them with an ample night-light, because the Light Animal might need the nightlight to feel safe. However, I emphasized that the Lion King would not allow having both lights simultaneously. The Light Animal expressed satisfaction with the Lion King's decision, and the Lion King praised the Light Animal: "That is very, very, very good. We like to see animals who are afraid of the dark have one nightlight on so they can feel very, very, very safe."

The Light Animal mentioned that he had decorations on his body, to which the Lion King responded, "When you grow up those decorations will become a very, very fluffy mane, like the one around my neck, and that will say that you are King of the Jungle." At this point, Billy drew a large mane in the neck area, and the Lion King said, "Light Animal, you've got to wait your turn before you can be King of the Jungle, so you'd better erase that." Billy then erased the mane. However, in the morning, Billy "found" that the Light Animal had grown another question light, despite knowing he was not allowed to do so. The Lion King responded, "Sadly, instead of getting ready to grow a mane in five or ten years, you grew a question light, so if you keep growing them, I'm sad to tell you that you will not be able to become King of the Jungle, when it's your turn."

Billy: "OK" said the Light Animal. It got late and the King of the Jungle said, "Time to go to bed" and all the animals went to bed [makes sleeping noises], and cock-a-doodle-doo, it's morning, and the Lion comes to take off the question light, but he *didn't* grow another one [this time].

Dr. H: Then the Lion said, "It's good you didn't grow another one this time. Now you will become King of the Jungle when it's your turn to become King of the Jungle."

Billy tested the Lion King's determination and found it was firm; he then complied with the Lion King's rules, going to bed when the Lion King said it was time to do so, and growing only one light.

Several more months into therapy, Billy's mother complained that he was still not complying consistently at home, and she labeled him "passive-aggressive" because he ignored her directions. She still shouted at him sometimes, and he had been screaming at her. Billy and I role-played that home situation. I was the mommy, and he was a two-year-old baby. We played out the scenario his mother described, except that I did not get angry. Instead, I was playful but firm, and he complied. We then agreed that Billy would draw another make-believe animal.

Billy: I'll name it a Lightning Animal (see Figure 12.3). Once upon a time, there was a Lightning Animal and it was the animal that made the lightning. The Lightning Animal thought he was so powerful, he could knock down anything or anybody. [Billy looked at me with a knowing smile and pointed to me to continue the story; I say no.] Do you know anything yet? [he was

Figure 12.3   Lightning Animal

asking me to pick up the story. He added scribbled lines to the drawing, saying ". . . And all this stuff is lightning, light . . . *ning!*"]

Dr. H: And the Lion said, "You don't need all that lightning."

Billy: Yes, I do. The reason why I need it is because it protects me . . . from animals that you can't destroy, that are very dangerous, so dangerous that you can't destroy them.

Dr. H: What makes those animals so strong and so dangerous?

Billy: The way they were born. Some animals are born so very strong and dangerous.

At this point, Billy's story probably illustrated the way in which he experienced his mother and father. I imagined how this little boy viewed himself in comparison to them; he was trying to survive what he experienced as their very powerful attacks. In his imagination, his parents were born at full power, and Billy had to engage them in any way he could. As you will soon see, he trusted me; the Lion had the responsibility of protecting him from the angry, powerful creatures that might annihilate him.

Dr. H: The Lion said, "I can tame *any* animal, no matter how strong or how dangerous. I have special ways to tame them and to make them safe, even very, very, very dangerous ones."

Billy: Oohhh? (Expressing surprise and interest) "Well," said the Lightning Animal, "I can get rid of my lightning and change my name. It will change to 'Let the Lion Do It' Animal."

Dr. H: "Well," said the Lion, "I can certainly do it. I also know how to make any animal safe."

Billy: It [the lightning] can't be gone by itself. "You have to use your powers," said the Lightning Animal to the King of the Jungle.

Dr. H: So the Lion called to the sun. "Sun, sun, shine on the Lightning Animal with all your power and make the lightning go away when I growl." And the Lion growled and the sun shone very, very, very brightly on the Lightning Animal, and it dried up all the lightning, and very, very soon the lightning disappeared. "I will be with you and near you, and I will keep you safe. I will not let any animal hurt you. I will make sure they will turn into *kind* animals."

Billy: (Singing) Now my name is 'Let the Lion Do it All.'

In this collaborative story, I was assuring Billy that he didn't need the defensive omnipotent stance he was using with his parents and other adults. I would never have offered such protection if I were not also working with both cooperative parents, helping them learn more adaptive parenting skills. At this point in the treatment, Billy was more trusting, and his efforts to be the dominant figure in his family and at school were somewhat diminished.

Somewhere in mid-therapy, Billy demonstrated that he was able to temper his grandiosity. He could admit that he wasn't all-knowing and all-powerful and sometimes needed assistance. For example, he drew a Lollipop Animal-Sucker Animal and wanted it to grow many suckers, so he could "share them with other animals." He wanted only one for himself.

Dr. H: So the Lion King said, "You are wonderful! You have made all the animals in the jungle happy today. You were not self-ish. You gave all your suckers away to the animals and you are a champ! I am the King of the Jungle, but you are learning fast, and when you grow up—if you can keep doing things like this—I will make *you* King of the Jungle, when you are fully grown. How do you feel about that?"

Billy: "Great, but *I can't really be king, because I don't really know the rules of the jungle,* and all I really do is to grow lollipops and share them, except for one. I keep just one of them and that makes me feel good, just one of them."

Dr. H: "Well," said the Lion King, of course you don't know what to do to be King of the Jungle, but I will teach you. Every week we will have lessons, so by the time you are grown, you will know just what to do. We can talk about what has to be done.

Here, Billy seemed to have tempered his grandiose approach and was willing to acknowledge that he was not all-knowing. In addition, he was now eager to share, where before he often demanded and took what he wanted, with little consideration for the feelings of others.

It was now nine or ten months into the therapy, and Billy had made more progress. However, his mother reported that he was not listening to his father, who got very angry with Billy. Billy played with a toy called Tubers and Zots. It consists of long and medium-size flexible polystyrene "tubers" of different colors, and various colored shapes that fit on the tubers, called "zots." I asked Billy to construct a make-believe animal and then make up a story about it. He constructed a large animal, which he called a Bigger Animal. The choice of the Bigger Animal was probably fueled by his recent negative interactions with his father.

Billy: Once upon a time, a long, long time ago, there was a Bigger Animal. He was bigger than any other animal. (Singing) If you know something, let me know. And the Lion said, "Why are you bigger than all the other animals?" "Well, I was born that way. Another reason," said the Bigger Animal, "is that I like being bigger than all the other animals in the jungle."

Dr. H: (with mock surprise) *You do?*

Billy: The Bigger Animal liked being that way. He told the truth; he really *did* like being that way. Then the Bigger Animal went to the door of the jungle and, and there was the Shower Animal, making noise. "Stop making noise and I'll let you come in," the Bigger Animal said.

Dr. H: And the Lion said, "Bigger Animal, you are very big, but you are *not* in charge of all the animals of the jungle. That's my job. Every animal is welcome here, as long as they behave themselves and they get along with everybody. Animals are certainly welcome here if they follow my rules and get along with everybody. If not, I must sadly, sadly, put you out."

Billy: The end.

Above and beyond Billy's defensive need for power and control, he was now more openly hungry for enthusiastic positive feedback in his collaboration with adult authority figures, which is illustrated in the next drawing and story, toward the end of therapy. Billy drew another Light Animal (see Figure 12.4), and we collaborated on the story:

Billy: Once upon a time, there was a Light Animal, and the Light Animal made lights and little light bulbs. And that's true! And

Note the medal Billy drew for himself saying "1st" with an attached ribbon.

Figure 12.4   Light Animal

at night the Light Animal could help the other animals in the jungle, to see. [Pointing to me] You're the Lion King.

Dr. H: The Lion King said, "Light Animal, you're wonderful! Thank you for being so helpful."

Billy: You're welcome. [Sings diddle, diddle, diddle 10 times]. The Light Animal was happy and he asked the other animals, "Can you guys go ask the Lion King if he likes me?"

Dr. H: The animals said, "Why don't you ask him yourself? Try and talk to him."

Billy: OK [He walks with his fingers to the Lion King]. Lion King, do you like me?

Dr. H: "Oh yes! Of course I do," the Lion King said, "because you are so good and friendly, and helpful to the other animals. I like animals who are not selfish and who help others."

Billy asked the Lion King if there was anything he needed him to do, and the Lion King suggested that he could pay special attention to the baby animals. Billy enthusiastically followed the Lion King's suggestion. Then the Lion King said:

Dr. H: "Light Animal, you are wonderful. I will award you a special medal."

Billy: YA YEE! Here's your medal! Here's your medal! Here's your medal! (Billy, very excited, adds a medal to his drawing. Then he sings a song, "Con-tin-ue the Part—y!")

DISCUSSION

Billy and I collaborated for over a year, playing the make-believe animal game often in our sessions. He introduced the Lion, the King of the Jungle in almost every story we coconstructed. His controlling approach soon gave way to one in which he assisted the Lion and eventually happily deferred to the Lion as the authority. He was no longer a behavior problem, at home or at school. In fact, he was given an "A" in behavior during the last two grading periods (about five months).

The collaborative use of stories with embedded therapeutic messages was useful in helping Billy both send and receive symbolic messages with me, allowing us to discover alternatives to problem emotions and behaviors. Billy often attempted to challenge some of the symbolic messages, but he eventually "heard" them, just as I "heard" his symbolic messages. We were eventually able to find a comfortable space that bound us together for positive growth and development. Our dialogues helped me create new solutions to Billy's behavioral problems, and they seemed to allow Billy to also do so. His parents did the same in their reframing of Billy's problem behaviors.

It is important to point out that the make-believe animal game can be used as an assessment tool and as a therapy tool. It can also be used as a tool to monitor improvement in therapy. In the case of Billy, I used the game for all three; I ruled out autism as Billy's problem and understood the contribution of family dynamics as one major problem. In addition, I used the game to symbolically discuss with Billy his fear of his parents and his need to be in charge. I used the results in each of the stories to track therapeutic progress.

I had four goals in my work with Billy and his family. The first was to help him deal with his externalizing and internalizing problems, which resulted in dysregulation at home and school. A second goal was to help Billy's parents understand the source of his problem behaviors and to help them be more empathically attuned to Billy's experience as a family member. The third goal was to "guide [his] parents in shifting their attitudes and interactions with their child in ways that will foster positive child and family development" (Tharinger, Finn, Gentry, Hamilton, et al., 2009, p. 238). A fourth goal was to help Billy's mother and father develop effective parenting skills, and to assist them in finding more appropriate means of communication and collaboration with Billy.

Billy's attitude toward authority figures changed drastically; his newfound ability to be friendly and empathic was clear from the content of his stories and from the way in which he dealt with me. My response to his attempts to control me and others was designed to help him control and contain his grandiosity, to cooperate and receive praise and admiration for his successes, and to help him trust adults. In most of my stories I provided reassurance, and the admiration of his achievement Billy sought so hungrily, the message that he would not be harmed by adults, and the message that he had the ability to become a competent adult (Kohut, 1971, 1977). I also emphasized that I would provide assistance for him to do so. This very same message was given to Billy by his parents. I shared with them the stories we coauthored and the meaning behind them on a regular basis. Billy's parents were eager and competent learners.

My responses to Billy's attempts to control me emphasized my recognition of his need for secure attachment and protection, which he attempted to cover with grandiosity and a desire for control, much like Max, the boy in the children's book *Where the Wild Things Are* (Sendak, 1963). Max was pictured wearing a golden crown, actively ruling the wild animals with his scepter. Like Max, Billy eventually gave up his precious position as king, to be at home and obtain nurturance from his mother. Billy began to recognize that adults were often benign and helpful to him, and that they had a great deal of interest in seeing him grow and prosper. He was therefore able to give up his use of an omnipotent and grandiose defense of power and control and to allow adults to help him with age-appropriate skills. He could now trust and rely upon adults, or as Billy said, "Let the Lion do it." His mood improved as well, and he became more playful. His initial fearfulness and suspicion of adults in authority gave way to a desire to collaborate, to be helpful, and to enjoy the positive interaction with others, especially adults in an authoritative position.

Billy's intense hunger for mirroring, including his desire for praise for his social and academic accomplishments, is most clearly indicated in his joyous response when the Lion King awarded a medal to the second Light Animal. The reader will recall the great excitement shown by the Light Animal—"YA YEE! Here's your medal! Here's your medal! Here's your medal," as he added the medal to the drawing. He actually broke out in song for his celebration.

Billy's parents initially took much of the responsibility for their son's resistant and acting-out behavior. They acknowledged their anger at him for making their lives more difficult, but they nevertheless initially blamed *him* for being "difficult" and for his bad behavior. Posttherapy, his parents understood Billy's fear of them and his need to protect himself from those whom he saw as very powerful and harmful adults. They acknowledged their past anger, describing it as a "cycle of anger in our family" and also admitted that they had been much too permissive and indulgent with Billy when he was younger. They acknowledged my role in helping them to more fully understand the systemic family problem, and they pointed out the importance of my role in supporting and reassuring them throughout the therapy process. They especially noted the importance to them of "being able to trust" and "being listened to" during our work together.

I received a letter from Billy's mother, which contained, in part, the following information:

> When we came to see you, Billy and our family needed help. Our parenting styles had been overly permissive and indulgent. We had great trouble getting Billy to mind the simplest requests. Putting on shoes and washing hands would often turn into great battles, with much yelling and anger. In school, he was regularly escorted out of the classroom for refusing to cooperate with his teachers. Billy has received A's in conduct the past two grading periods. To what do we attribute the changes? Thank-you, Dr. Handler.
>
> We have learned to control anger in our reactions to Billy, and emphasized the importance of routine, and setting clear limits. [He needed] structure at home and at school [and] expectations and rules that are consistent. He used to have screaming fits, but now there are few problems. My goal as a parent now is to be predictable and encourage and reinforce positive self reliance. I have learned parenting is not a battle of wills, where one is the authority and others are ruled with fear of punishment or threat. It is about respect, and teaching responsibility, encouragement, spending focused time making your child feel loved, establishing routines so that everyone knows what is expected, setting clear limits, and setting children up for success.

To illustrate Billy's improved mood over the course of therapy, I suggest that the reader note the difference between the awkward and worried expressions on the make-believe animals' faces in Figure 12.1 and the engaging, happy, smiling face of the Sunshine and Moonshine Animal

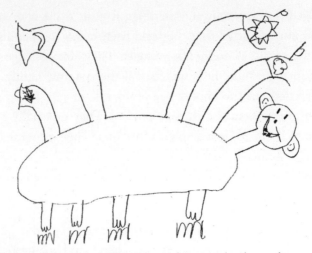

Note the smile of the sunshine and moonshine animal, indicating happiness.

Figure 12.5   Sunshine and Moonshine Animal

(see Figure 12.5), one of the last figures Billy drew. If Billy were here with me now as I write this last paragraph, he would be saying, "The End," so I'll say it for him, "The End!"

✍ Teaching Points

It is very important to highlight the factors that lead to success in collaborative storytelling. They are listed as follows:

1. Establish a playful, nonthreatening relationship that facilitates a spontaneous creative atmosphere between the child and the clinician.
2. In constructing a therapeutic story, the clinician should employ the process of externalization in which the characters symbolize members of the child's family or other key people in their lives. Externalization attributes the child's thoughts, feelings, and actions to the characters in the story, not directly to themselves. For example, Alice's fishie represented herself.
3. In telling a story, the child often symbolizes him or herself in the family context. Stories that recognize a child's painful issues should be responded to by developing symbolic messages of empathic understanding and, if possible, stories that offer solutions to the problem.

4. Evaluate family dynamics before storytelling, to help design a story for the child.

5. The clinician's story should emphasize the problem, symbolically, and present a solution that is healthy and positive for the child.

6. The clinician's story should support, encourage, and positively affirm the child if possible, and provide positive reassurance that the child will develop into a "successful" adult.

7. In crafting a therapeutic story, the clinician should keep an image of the child's or family's problem in his or her mind. This helps guide the clinician in crafting a therapeutic response to the child. Conceptualize collaborative constructions as if you are participating in a special conversation and in an imaginative and playful manner.

8. While the child's story may express multiple issues, focus on the issue that is overriding and use it to make up your story. Choose an issue that shouts out to you.

9. Periodically work with parents and other family members where appropriate, sharing the child's stories and their meaning concerning the child's problem(s). (See Tharinger, Finn, Austin, Gentry, et al., 2008.)

REFERENCES

Altman, N., Briggs, R., Frankel, J., Gensler, D., & Pantone, P. (2002). *Relational child psychotherapy*. New York, NY: Other Press.

Axline, V. (1947/1989). *Play therapy*. Boston, MA: Houghton Mifflin.

Barker, P. (1985). *Using metaphors in psychotherapy*. New York, NY: Brunner/ Mazel.

Bettelheim, B. (1976). *The uses of enchantment*. New York, NY: Knopf.

Bucci, W. (1995). The power of the narrative: A multiple code account. In J. Pennebaker (Ed.), *Emotion, disclosure and health* (pp. 93–104). Washington, DC: American Psychological Association.

Finn, S. (2007). *In our clients' shoes: Theory and techniques of Therapeutic Assessment*. New York, NY: Routledge.

Gardner, R. (1993). *Storytelling in psychotherapy with children*. Northvale, NJ: Jason Aronson.

Handler, L. (1999). The assessment of playfulness: Hermann Rorschach meets D.W. Winnicott. Invited Special Series, The Assessment of Psychological Health. *Journal of Personality Assessment, 72*, 208–217.

Handler, L. (2007). The use of therapeutic assessment with children and adolescents. In S. Smith & L. Handler (Eds.), *The clinical assessment of children and adolescents: A practitioner's handbook* (pp. 53–71). Mahwah, NJ: Lawrence Erlbaum Associates.

Handler, L., & Hilsenroth, M. (1994, April). The *use of a fantasy animal drawing and storytelling technique in assessment and psychotherapy*. Paper presented at the Annual Meeting, Society for Personality Assessment, Chicago, IL.

Kohut, H. (1971). *The analysis of the self*. New York, NY: International Universities Press.

Kohut, H. (1977). *The restoration of the self*. New York, NY: International Universities Press.

Lieblich, A., McAdams, D., & Josselson, R. (Eds.). (2004). *Healing plots: The narrative basis of psychotherapy*. Washington, DC: American Psychological Association.

Luborsky, L., & Crits-Christoph, P. (Eds.). (1990). *Understanding transference: The CCRT method*. New York, NY: Basic Books.

Mahler, M. (1975). *The psychological birth of the human infant*. New York, NY: Basic Books.

McLeod, J. (1997). *Narrative and psychotherapy*. London, England: Sage.

Mills, J., & Crowley, R. (1986). *Therapeutic metaphors for children and the child within*. New York, NY: Brunner/Mazel.

Sendak, M. (1963). *Where the wild things are*. New York, NY: Harper & Row.

Silverstein, M. (1999). *Self psychology and diagnostic assessment*. Mahwah, NJ: Lawrence Erlbaum Associates.

Smith, C., & Nylund, D. (Eds.). (1997). *Narrative therapies with children and adolescents*. New York, NY: Guilford Press.

Smith, J. D., & Handler, L. (2009). Why do I get in trouble so much?: A family Therapeutic Assessment case study. *Journal of Personality Assessment, 91*, 197–210.

Smith, J. D., Handler, L., & Nash, M. R. (2010). Therapeutic Assessment for preadolescent boys with oppositional defiant disorder: A replicated single-case time-series design. *Psychological Assessment, 22*, 539–602.

Smith, J. D., Nicholas, C., Handler, L., & Nash, M. R. (2011). Examining the clinical effectiveness of a family intervention session in Therapeutic Assessment: A single-case experiment. *Journal of Personality Assessment, 93*, 149–158.

Smith, J. D., Wolf, N. J., Handler, L., & Nash, M. R. (2009). Testing the effectiveness of family Therapeutic Assessment: A case study using a time-series design. *Journal of Personality Assessment, 91*, 518–536.

Spence, D. (1982). *Narrative truth and historical truth: Meaning and interpretation in psychoanalysis*. New York, NY: Norton.

Tharinger, D., Finn, S., Austin, C., Gentry, L., Bailey, K., Parton, V., & Fisher, M. E. (2008). Family sessions in psychological assessment with children: Goals, techniques, and clinical utility. *Journal of Personality Assessment, 90*, 547–558.

Tharinger, D., Finn, S., Gentry, L., Hamilton, A., Fowler, J., Matson, M., Krumholz, L., & Walkowiak, J. (2009). Therapeutic Assessment with children: A pilot study of treatment acceptability and outcome. *Journal of Personality Assessment, 91*, 238–244.

Tharinger, D., Finn, S., Wilkinson, A., & Schaber, P. (2007). Therapeutic Assessment with a child as a family intervention: A clinical and research case study. *Psychology in the Schools, 44*, 293–309.

White, M., & Epston, D. (1990). *Narrative means to therapeutic ends*. New York, NY: Norton.

Winnicott, D. (1971). *Therapeutic consultations in child psychiatry*. New York, NY: Basic Books.

13

Rorschach-Based Psychotherapy: Collaboration With a Suicidal Young Woman

NORIKO NAKAMURA

EAST MEETS WEST

The Rorschach, which originated in Switzerland and developed in the context of Western culture, was introduced to Japan as early as 1925. Psychologist Dr. Yuzaburo Uchida founded the Rorschach publication *Psychodiagnostik* in Japan, and he immediately started to research the methodology and gathered Rorschach data (Sorai & Ohnuki, 2008). Uchida's first paper, "Experimental and Psychological Studies on the Types of Character," came out in 1930. He sowed the seed of the Rorschach in Japan, and since then it has been developed such that it is now widely used.

The phrase "East meets West" implies an encounter with the unknown or unseen elements of a different culture. "East meets West" also expresses my standpoint as a Rorschach-based psychotherapist when dealing with clients; I try to make no assumptions about shared values or experiences, but rather use the Rorschach test collaboratively with a client to view or discover that client's personal culture and to form the basis for ongoing therapy (Nakamura & Nakamura, 1999a, 1999b).

This chapter presents one such collaboration involving a young woman, whom I call Mariko, who was obsessed with the idea of committing suicide. She was hospitalized so often and regularly that a reserved bed was kept for her in the local psychiatric hospital. However, during therapy with her, I found that the Rorschach could become a tool to understand her complex and rather chaotic personality mechanisms, allowing the client and myself, together, to look objectively at both the positive and the negative aspects of her psychological state. That process enabled both of us to reevaluate her strengths, which became the new foundation on which to build the outpatient therapy. Incorporating feedback sessions with the client during the course of therapy increased mutual understanding and enabled closer collaboration on the client's path to recovery. The record of her footprints shows how she moved forward from lost life to real life and also shows how collaborative assessment can be used to facilitate ongoing treatment. I will place special emphasis on her initial test results and the way in which they changed at the end of two years of therapy.

PRESENTING ISSUES

Mariko was referred to me from the psychiatrist in her region. While in high school, she had been diagnosed as suffering from borderline personality disorder. She had become seriously anxious, irritated, and unable to join her classmates. Gradually she missed school and started self-damaging behavior such as wrist cutting and overdosing, and also experiencing hyperpnea. Her suicide attempts had occurred on many occasions while she was in a dissociated state, and afterward she had no memory of them. The psychiatrist indicated that her loss of sense of self or self-feeling/existence seemed to be her most serious problem. He indicated that Mariko had had some individual psychotherapy, but it had not continued for long. At the time she was referred to me, Mariko was being medicated with antidepressants as well as major tranquilizers; in total she was taking 10 kinds of medication daily to prevent her habitual suicidal acting out.

CLIENT'S BACKGROUND

Mariko was a 21-year-old woman with a younger sister and younger brother. Her parents were under 50 years old and high school graduates. The father was a businessperson and the mother worked part time. Her parents described Mariko as having been a very clever, studious, and well-behaved girl since childhood.

However, important losses she experienced repeatedly from age 13 to 15 had a profound and negative effect on her life. Mariko's favorite singer after she entered junior high school committed suicide by hanging when Mariko was 13, resulting in her becoming very depressed. After that, she became the fan of another singer, whose songs followed the same theme as that of the previous singer—namely not wanting to grow up—but that singer died of a heart attack only a year after her previous loss. Then, just when she had lost all reason for living, she encountered a third singer, who in effect became a soul saver for her. However, tragically, he also committed suicide by overdosing one year after the death of the previous singer, when Mariko was 15.

The situation was made worse in that at the time she lost the third singer at age 15, she was also experiencing difficulties at school. Some delinquent boys were disrupting the class, a situation that made her unhappy. She fought with them, but no one backed her up, resulting in her becoming isolated from everyone in the class. In response, she devoted herself to study, but it made the situation with her classmates worse.

The singer Mariko lost at age 15 had been her only lifeline. After that third loss, Mariko started to suffer from finger tremors, vertigo, and palpitations, and she visited a psychiatrist for medication. She confessed that from that time she had a sense that being alive was wrong and that the right thing to do was to die and to go to the other world, where her favorite people were. Mariko began cutting her wrists and overdosing. Several times she was also found in potential suicide situations, standing on a bridge or having wandered off into the mountains, but she had no conscious memory of how she had gotten there.

She was given psychotherapy and psychiatric treatment for six years, from age 15 to 21, during which time she had numerous and frequent hospitalizations for suicide attempts and depression. In the year before she was referred to me, she had been hospitalized four times for periods ranging from three days to three months. As the result of a friendship developed with a nurse during the last hospitalization, Mariko decided to keep on living and seek help for her problems. With the backing and support of the referring psychiatrist and her parents, she moved alone to Tokyo and started a course of therapy with me.

ASSESSMENT

Tests Administered

Over the course of three years, I tested Mariko three times. The first assessment was when she was 21 years old, and I administered the Rorschach, the Profile of Mood States (POMS; Pollock, Cho, Reker, & Volavka, 1979), projective drawings (of a fruit tree, a house, a person, and a family), the Wechsler Adult Intelligence Scale-III (WAIS-III; Wechsler, 1997), and the Uchida-Kraepelin (U-K) test (Kashiwagi et al., 1985). I conducted an initial session (90 minutes long) followed by assessment interviews at my office in three consecutive sessions, each one week apart. The fifth meeting was a feedback session. Mariko was retested when she was 22 in my office by another psychologist (to avoid bias that might arise because I was her therapist), not including the WAIS-III and the Kraepelin. And finally, she was retested one year later at age 23, again by another psychologist, repeating all of the initial tests except for the U-K. Each retest was followed by a feedback session.

The first retest was requested by Mariko because she had been able to support herself alone as an outpatient on pharmacotherapy but without a single hospitalization, and she wanted to confirm how much she had changed. The WAIS-III and the U-K test were not administered during the retest because of the client's time and financial constraints. However, as therapy progressed and Mariko began to show improvement, she reported that her part-time work was being praised, and she expressed the desire to start working full-time. I then offered a second retest, including the WAIS-III, to check if she was capable of full-time employment.

Feedback

I typically hold a Rorschach feedback session, about 50 minutes long for individuals and 90 minutes for couples and families, and use the whole session time to share the data and discuss the results of the Rorschach test by looking at the Structural Summary cluster data together. I take the seven cluster boxes from the Structural Summary and make a copy, attach it to a clipboard, and show it to the client(s). I prepare the copy by marking the admirable and positive strengths of the results in green and the warning areas and noteworthy facts in yellow. As we go further, I add arrows to show the expected directions after therapy, or that the client's responses at the feedback session confirm the data, or that indicate changes from the previous assessment.

RESULTS OF MARIKO'S INITIAL ASSESSMENT

Rorschach

The adult nonpatient data collected from 240 Japanese (Nakamura, Fuchigami, & Tsugawa, 2007) indicate that only 2.5% of participants are positive (8 or more) on the *Suicide Constellation*. Mariko's *Suicide Constellation* of 8 (Table 13.1) confirmed that she was an urgent risk and revealed her chronic and serious psychological condition well. Moreover, her *DEPI* was 6, plus 8 of the 13 different conditions in *DEPI* were positive, and 5 of them were based on affective difficulties. A psychiatrist's medical support was essential in order for outpatient therapy to be successful.

She was *HVI* positive and put energy into protecting and guarding herself from the outside world. Nevertheless, $Zd = -7.5$ showed her carelessness and that she was an underincorporator. On the one hand, she was super alert and tried hard to avoid negative issues coming up, but on the other hand, she could never be successful using this strategy if she failed to process important information. Mariko's being in such chaos or panic might have been caused by this handicap in processing.

Despite all of these risks, the most important finding from the Rorschach was the positive side of her psychological functioning. She had resources to cope with day-to-day living, as shown in the *EA* of 22.5, and considerable openness to the complex world, as shown in the *Lambda*

Table 13.1 The Structural Summary From Mariko's First Assessment

Location Features

Zf	= 25
ZSum	= 77.0
ZEst	= 84.4
W	= 23
D	= 7
W + D	= 30
Dd	= 1
S	= 3

DQ

+	= 13
o	= 14
v/+	= 0
v	= 4

Form Quality

	FQx	MQual	W+D
+	= 0	= 0	= 0
o	= 17	= 9	= 17
u	= 7	= 3	= 7
−	= 6	= 1	= 5
none	= 1	= 0	= 1

Determinants

Blends	Single	
FC'.M	M	= 5
M.m	FM	= 1
CF.M.m	m	= 0
M.FY.FC.Fr	FC	= 1
M.CF	CF	= 2
FC'.FD	C	= 1
M.FD	Cn	= 0
FC'.M	FC'	= 0
M.Fr	C'F	= 1
CF.m	C'	= 0
FV.CF	FT	= 0
CF.YF.m	TF	= 0
	T	= 0
	FV	= 0
	VF	= 0
	V	= 0
	FY	= 0
	YF	= 0
	Y	= 0
	Fr	= 0
	rF	= 0
	FD	= 0
	F	= 8
	(2)	= 8

Contents

H	= 10
(H)	= 3
Hd	= 1
(Hd)	= 4
Hx	= 0
A	= 3
(A)	= 0
Ad	= 0
(Ad)	= 0
An	= 2
Art	= 2
Ay	= 0
Bl	= 2
Bt	= 2
Cg	= 0
Cl	= 1
Ex	= 1
Fd	= 0
Fi	= 1
Ge	= 0
Hh	= 3
Ls	= 1
Na	= 0
Sc	= 2
Sx	= 0
Xy	= 0
Id	= 6

Approach

I	W.WS.WS.WS
II	W.W.W
III	D.Dd.D.D
IV	W.W
V	W.W.W
VI	D.W.W
VII	W.W.W
VIII	W.W.W
IX	W.D.W
X	D.W.D

Special Scores

	Lv1	Lv2
DV = 1	1 × 1	0 × 2
INC = 1	1 × 2	0 × 4
DR = 6	6 × 3	0 × 6
FAB = 0	0 × 4	2 × 7
ALOG = 0	0 × 5	
CON = 0	0 × 7	
Raw Sum6 = 10		
Wgtd Sum6 = 35		

AB	= 0	GHR	= 10
AG	= 0	PHR	= 8
COP	= 0	MOR	= 5
CP	= 0	PER	= 1
		PSV	= 0

RATIOS, PERCENTAGES, AND DERIVATIONS

R = 31		L = 0.35	FC:CF+C	= 2:8	COP	= 0	AG = 0
			Pure C	= 1	GHR:PHR	= 10:8	
EB = 13:9.5	EA = 22.5	EBPer = 1.4	SmC':WSmC	= 4:9.5	a:p	= 5:13	
eb = 5:7	es = 12	D = +4	Afr	= .41	Food	= 0	
	Adj es = 8	Adj D = +5	S	= 3	SumT	= 0	
			Blends/R	= 12:31	Human Cont	= 18	
FM = 1	SumC' = 4	SumT = 0	CP	= 0	Pure H	= 0	
m = 4	SumV = 1	SumY = 2			PER	= 1	
					Isol Indx	= 0.16	

				XA%	= 0.77	Zf	= 25	3r+(2)/R	= .45
				WDA%	= 0.80	W:D:Dd	= 23:2:7	Fr+rF	= 2
		Sum6	= 10	X−%	= 0.19	W:M	= 23:13	SumV	= 1
a:p	= 5:13	Lv2	= 0	S−	= 0	Zd	= −7.5	FD	= 2
Ma:Mp	= 2:11	WSum6	= 35	P	= 9	PSV	= 0	An+Xy	= 2
2AB+Art + Ay	= 2	M−	= 1	X+%	= 0.55	DQ+	= 13	MOR	= 5
MOR	= 5	Mnone	= 0	Xu%	= 0.23	DQv	= 4	H:(H)+Hd+(Hd)	= 10:8

PTI = 1	DEPI = 6	CDI = 3	S-CON = 8	HVI = Yes	OBS = NO

score of 0.35. She was overconfident (*D* and *AdjD* both +4 and +5) and not easily beaten by stress. She seemed to be a hard worker, as shown in the Processing Information cluster (high *Zf* = 25, *W* = 23, and *DQ+* = 13), and her reality testing confirmed that she was able to function well in society (*XA%* = 0.77, *WDA%* = 0.80, *X+%* = 0.55, and *P* = 9).

All of these positive features underpinned her social life, masking the problem, but under the surface, her life was quite chaotic. Uncontrollable emotions (*CF* = 7, *C* = 1, *FC* = 2), painful feelings and confusion (*C'* = 4, *Vista* = 1, *Color-shading blends* = 3) were reined back by a reluctance to involve herself in emotional situations (*Afr* = 0.41). This seesaw dynamic was evident in her entire character. For example, in the Control section, *FM vs. greater stress* (*m* = 4) caused intolerable, uncomfortable feelings. The fact that she had only one *FM* revealed the root of her unrealistic self-understanding and disconnection from her own volition. Another example lay in her self-image: Two reflections clearly revealed her over-valued self-image, but she had a lower *Egocentricity Index* (0.45) for someone who had two reflections. One *Vista* and five MOR responses with two Anatomy responses revealed the damage underlying her super self-image.

Despite the positive side—namely the strength and adaptability in her psychological dynamics as shown on the Rorschach—Mariko ended up being the opposite of what she appeared to be on the surface. Her inner life was full of chaos, as shown in the special scores *FAB2* = 2 and *WSum6* = 35. Usually, special scores show a deviation in thinking, but in Mariko's case both two *FAB2* and six *DR* responses revealed her damaged emotions. Her two *FAB2s* precisely showed her confusion, and resulted in two color-shading blends (e.g., R7, Card II: "Headless people looking for their own heads." [*Inq.*] "It seems unreal and I am facing someone who is not me and because this is pale and the head is red, different from the body, so I'm looking at another me, looking in a mirror to confirm we each have no head."). All of her DR responses were evidence of her overwhelming unhappiness (e.g., R3, Card I: "It looks like a devil's carved seal" [*Inq.*] "It's the image of a devil in me. If I do something bad, my heart will be stamped with this kind of seal."). All of these special scores directly revealed the impact her emotional difficulties had on her ideation.

Unfortunately, Mariko buried all of this antagonistic, unhappy, seesaw dynamic in passivity (*a:p* = 5:13, *Ma:Mp* = 2:11), and she seldom faced reality, which made it difficult for others to understand her correctly. Moreover, her passivity had prevented her from knowing her self more fully. Mariko was unaware that she was psychologically overloaded. She did not understand who she really was. She knew she had two sides to herself, but she could not see the whole picture and was therefore unable to make use of her rich psychological resources because she had no control over herself. For example, she cut her wrists when she was asleep or found herself standing on a bridge and about to jump off it, without having any memory of going there.

POMS

The results of the Profile of Mood States (POMS; Pollock et al., 1979) revealed Mariko's chaotic emotional state. Three out of six different emotional experiences were in the danger zone, namely Confusion (84T), Tension-Anxiety (77T), and Depression (75T). Also Fatigue (68T) and Vigor (36T) were in the warning zone, adding to her emotional burden. Only Aggression-Hostility (52T) fell within the normal range.

WAIS-III

Mariko's Verbal IQ was 118 (subtests average 12.3), while her Performance IQ was significantly lower at 87 (subtests average 9.7) and reflected her perfectionism. She was slow-moving and double-checked all of her answers, resulting in lower than average scores. In contrast to her fairly well-developed verbal abilities, Mariko's Performance subtest scores showed a wide degree of scatter, from the highest, Picture Completion (14), to the lowest, Digit Symbol (5).

Drawings

I asked Mariko to create four drawings: a fruit tree, a person, a house, and a family. Among them, I will choose only "a fruit tree" and compare the original with the retest and second retest. At this first assessment (see Figure 13.2), Mariko drew a coco palm, but coco palms were not part of her usual living environment.

U-K Test

Mariko's energy to complete the task was within the normal range in that she completed 1,183 digits; at least 1,000 digits are needed for any

🖐 Teaching Point

The U-K test is a serial addition test, which requires an individual to perform calculations as fast and accurately as possible within 30 minutes. It is administered using preprinted paper containing 15 lines of random, single-digit, horizontally aligned numbers. For each minute of the test, subjects are instructed to begin a new line regardless of their position on the current line. Each line contains an excess of calculations such that the subjects are not able to finish any line for a particular minute before being prompted to move on to the start of the next minute by the assessor's prompting. This test is usually performed for two 15-minute cycles of work separated by a 5-minute rest. The resulting mental work curve (Figure 13.1) is useful in understanding how much an individual can put his or her energy into certain work. Although this test (based on Kraepelin's Arithmetic Test [1902] is old, it is nevertheless relevant and works well.

normal deskwork. Her working curve showed rather good concentration, stability, and efficacy of learning.

FEEDBACK

Before making a feedback appointment, I usually ask the clients who they want to have included at their feedback session, and Mariko requested that her mother be present. I do not have a fixed order for explaining the results, but I prefer to start from the visually easy, uncomplicated results and gradually move to the more complicated ones. For Mariko, I started with the POMS profile because it is simple and easy to understand, and it is a good entry exercise for the rest of the feedback session. The three of us sat together closely and looked at the same sheet of results.

POMS

I began by summarizing two points about the POMS findings for Mariko and her mother. First, I explained that these results represented unstable, changeable emotional experiences, and that they showed Mariko's emotional condition on the day of the assessment. Second, I pointed out the three different zones represented in various colors: red, yellow, and white areas representing danger, warning, and normal emotional conditions, respectively. I told Mariko and her mother that we usually expect to see the results fall in the white area. For a 21-year-old woman, not working or studying or under any apparent external stress, Mariko's profile was a great surprise both to me as well as to Mariko and her mother. Five out of six emotional experiences were in either the "danger" or "warning zone" areas of the profile. The results revealed that Mariko was suffering seriously from confusion, tension-anxiety, and depression. In addition, two other scores were in the warning zone: fatigue and vigor. These two, together, could result in a person losing energy. Mariko was actively interested in my explanation and looked content with these severe results, nodding quite often and providing an affirmative "yes, that's right" or "just as I thought" while I explained each result. She said she was happy to have her inner experience documented, because it had been difficult for her to explain her inner chaos to her prior therapists and counselors. She had been frustrated at not being able to explain her real difficulties. Her mother was also able to understand why Mariko had been hospitalized so often.

WAIS-III

Next, I moved on to the WAIS-III result. By looking at the result graphs together, we all understood that Mariko's higher VIQ of 118 was as expected. Mariko and her mother were glad to see that the highest score was on Comprehension and thought it represented her well. Mariko recalled that her brain didn't work as much as she wanted when she did Arithmetic and Letter-Number Sequencing. Actually, despite her efforts, she made careless mistakes and errors. Her mother explained to me how the lowest Coding score was confirmed by behavior from Mariko's daily life. Mariko and her mother competed to offer examples of how she was slow at school in completing drawings and sewing classes. It was quite revealing how Mariko could compete well when she could use her accurate focusing ability. On the contrary, she took longer to perform and moved very slowly when visual-motor coordination was needed. Mariko could not perform quickly; this was true for every action. For example, putting on her coat after she finished her therapy and leaving the room took three times longer than it did for most clients. We confirmed from this that we had to be careful not to put her in a situation with time pressure, especially when she chose a job.

U-K

I moved on to show Mariko and her mother the U-K curve (Figure 13.1). The reason for looking at Kraepelin next was again that this result is graphically demonstrated and easy to look at and understand. First, it encouraged her to see that her energy level was within the expected range (1,183 digits). Moreover, her working curve showed that she had worked well and that her performance was quite stable and followed the expected curve line.

Rorschach

The last results we looked at were those from the Rorschach. I introduced the seven cluster boxes as representatives of the human mind. I named and explained them in this order: Control, Emotions (=Affect),

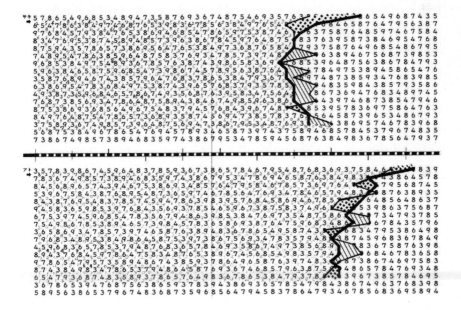

Figure 13.1 Mariko's U-K Test Graph

Note: The above figure shows Mariko's results. The thick black line is the postulated line, and the fine line indicates Mariko's actual results. In the first half of the test, Mariko did not achieve the postulated point from the start and for the first three minutes, but after that she responded in excess of the postulated line (shaded area), revealing that she is a hard worker. Also, her results do not vary widely from the postulated line, indicating that she can work consistently.

In the second half of the test, Mariko again did not achieve the postulated thick dark line at the beginning. Her two first- and second-half slow starts show how in a new and unfamiliar situation she is guarded, hesitant and nervous. Nevertheless, overall, Mariko's result line is within a healthy range of the postulated line, showing that she has sufficient energy (more than 1,000 responses) and can work consistently with concentration and willpower.

Interpersonal Skill, Self-Image, and Eye Function (=Cognitive Triad). I explained that Processing is how information gets from the outside into the mind; Mediation is the internal judgment of what information comes in, and Ideation labels the result of the judgment. I also used metaphors to aid understanding.

I began from the Control cluster explaining that it is like the cockpit of a plane that the person pilots. I explained how complicated Mariko's inner world was by going through the clusters, starting from the positive results. High EA (22.5) represented Mariko's inner resources, which we had already confirmed from the fact that her IQ was fine and from her having been well-behaved and studious when she was younger. On the negative side, I explained that the Zd of −7.5 indicated that Mariko was expending so much energy fruitlessly to gather information; it was like trying to collect water with a sieve or to inflate a punctured balloon.

At the Rorschach feedback session, both Mariko and her mother were very excited and pleased that the assessment had so accurately identified key points and had revealed Mariko's complex condition, whereas previously she had been unable to make herself understood by anyone. It helped Mariko to build herself up by recognizing her own resources and capabilities. She began to understand why she behaved the way she did, and this was the beginning of her recovering control over her life. Mariko and her mother quickly decided that Mariko should move to Tokyo and start a course of therapy with me.

CHANGES DURING ONGOING THERAPY

During therapy we periodically reviewed the seven-cluster data from the Rorschach again. When Mariko got a part-time job serving at a McDonald's fast-food restaurant, no matter how hard she tried, she could not keep up with the pace of the work required of her. She blamed herself and thought she was useless. By showing her the initial Rorschach data again (Zd = −7.5), I could explain that she would be better off to find a job that did not include time pressure. As a result, she found a job working part-time for a fashion store, which suited her well, and where she was respected for her sense of responsibility. The Rorschach results also helped Mariko understand that a full-time job would overload her, and she therefore chose to work only part-time.

I was able to show Mariko through the Rorschach results that she had a complex image. On the one hand, she had many good traits, such as the ability to be a good housekeeper, although she was unable to recognize this without feedback from others. She began to understand that she undervalued herself, and that this happened when she compared herself to others. For example, she grew up thinking that her sister was more attractive than she was and that her parents thought the same. However, on a visit home she recalled my comment that her comparison might have been too harsh, so she looked at some old family photograph albums. To her surprise, she found that *she* was the more attractive one.

FIRST RETEST

When Mariko was retested one year later, after 30 sessions of psychotherapy, some dramatic changes had taken place. Her self-image showed an improvement (MOR dropped from 5 to 3) and her *Vista* response had dropped to zero. Her Zd of -7.5 improved to -3.0, indicating better control over information.

During the collaborative feedback for the retest, Mariko was delighted to see the new findings as a change she recognized; one *Texture* response occurred, one *Food* response, and *Afr.* went up from 0.41 to 0.50, all showing that she recognized her need to be supported and to allow people to come closer to her. She explained she gradually could rely on others and enjoy sharing relationships.

At my suggestion Mariko tried various jobs, identifying the parts that were easy and those that were not, and she learned from those experiences. This worked surprisingly well. She reported to me that she had decided to return to her previous part-time job at McDonald's, but changed the working time to 5–8 a.m., when there were fewer people and it was not busy, so she could take time to do the work. Because of the very early hours, her salary was good and others thanked her for working "unsociable" hours. This clever decision illustrated that she was erasing what John Exner called the "Cinderella syndrome" passive style (Exner, 2005) as evidenced later by her first retest Ma:Mp ratio of 7:4 (compared with 2:11 in the original assessment). She became dramatically active, and that attitude was quite the opposite of the way she had been a year earlier.

It should be noted, however, that not only positive changes occurred, but also many conditions remained the same or even shifted in a negative way. The retest was requested by Mariko because she felt she had changed, but the results showed, for example, that FM stayed at 1, m increased from 4 to 5, and Lambda had become too low (from 0.35 to 0.17), which was the opposite direction from my expectation. This change may have been because Mariko was so passive and tried too hard to comply with the wishes of others, including myself. Also, her second POMS result hardly changed at all. In my mind, this indicated that Mariko wanted others to perceive her as being in bad shape.

After seeing these results, I started to recommend that Mariko eat out, rest more, go back to her parents' home frequently, despite the high transportation costs, and find new strategies to entertain herself. Also, because of her passivity, she had agreed to listen to many friends' woes for hours on the telephone, but I discouraged her from doing so until she had improved her own condition. See Table 13.2.

Table 13.2   Mariko's First Retest

RATIOS, PERCENTAGES, AND DERIVATIONS							
R = 27		L = 0.17		FC:CF+C = 0:9	COP = 1		AG = 4
				Pure C = 2	GHR:PHR = 10:5		
EB = 11:10.0	EA = 21.0	EBPer = N/A		SmC':WSmC = 4:10.0	a:p = 11:6		
eb = 6:6	es = 12	D = +3		Afr = 0.50	Food = 1		
	Adj es = 8	Adj D = +5		S = 2	SumT = 1		
				Blends:R = 12:27	Human Cont = 14		
FM = 1	SumC = 4	SumT = 1		CP = 0	Pure H = 10		
m = 5	SumV = 0	SumY = 1			PER = 2		
					Isol Indx = 0.07		
			XA% = 0.78	Zf = 23	3r+(2)/R		= 0.48
			WDA% = 0.81	W:D:Dd = 21:5:1	Fr+rF		= 2
		Sum6 = 5	X−% = 0.15	W:M = 21:11	SumV		= 0
a:p = 11:6		Lvl-2 = 1	S− = 0	Zd = −3.0	FD		= 3
Ma:Mp = 7:4		WSum6 = 19	P = 9	PSV = 0	An+Xy		= 3
2AB+Art + Ay = 4		M− = 0	X+% = 0.56	DQ+ = 12	MOR		= 3
MOR = 3		Mnone = 1	Xu% = 0.22	DQv = 3	H:(H)+Hd+(Hd)		= 10:4
PTI = 1	DEPI = 5		CDI = 1	S-CON = 6	HVI = No		OBS = No

SECOND RETEST

Rorschach

By the time of the second retest, Mariko was no longer on any medication. Her MOR responses dropped from 5 to 3, and all dramatic personal morbid references and references to death, demons, and the devil had disappeared. The new MOR responses were expressed in conservative, less urgent ways, such as "two people crying" (Card II). I considered these to be healthy responses and evidence of the power of the projective test to show that Mariko now had her feet on the ground and was not living in another world.

Mariko's Suicide Constellation had fallen from 8 to 3, and she was no longer positive on DEPI; she had clearly moved out of her depression and suicidal emergency. Neither of these indices is expected to change quickly, but Mariko's results reflected the benefits of 55 therapy sessions over a course of two years.

Another significant change was the Lambda score, which at the first retest had dropped to 0.17, but had now risen to 0.69. I surmised the reasons were because she had become less complicated (Blends 12 reduced to 5) and no longer overworked her thinking and emotions (EA dropped to 10.5). Her original D and Adj D scores of +4 and +5 respectively indicated her overconfidence in her abilities and inability to see her limits, but the new scores were 0 and +1, showing that she was now in touch with reality.

Mariko's initial test showed her to be HVI positive, but at the first retest she was not. However, this was not the good result it seemed, because it depended on her T score of 1, which was based on her having seen ". . . the trail of slime left by a snail." Therefore, although the second retest showed Mariko was again positive on HVI, I believe this showed she had returned to her own coping style.

Another significant Processing result was that the Zd of −7.5 from her initial test changed to +1.0. Additionally, Mariko's W:D:Dd scores had dramatically improved, showing that she could gather information better, was more settled, and could trust herself more. Connected to this was her self-image (2 Reflections dropped to 0). Exner (2005) stated that the Reflection score is stable and that age 13 or 14 is the time for a person to become "decentralized" and start thinking of others. In my therapy I took Mariko back to that time when she lost the first singer. The result was that she redeveloped her ability to trust in others, including myself as her therapist. She also changed her self-perception, from having to be unique to being a regular human being. She had reached a healthy balance between her perception of herself and others (*Egocentricity Index* = 0.37). See Table 13.3.

POMS

This test revealed her energy had increased and depression decreased, and all scores now fell within a normal range.

WAIS-III

Mariko's Performance IQ increased 25 points, although her slow reaction time remained. She could concentrate better and her visual-motor coordination improved.

Table 13.3 Mariko's Second Retest

RATIOS, PERCENTAGES, AND DERIVATIONS						
R = 27	L = 0.69		FC:CF+C	= 1:4	COP	= 0	AG = 1
			Pure C	= 2	GHR:PHR	= 6:3
EB = 5:5.5	EA = 10.5	EBPer = N/A	SmC':WSmC	= 2:5.5	a:p	= 4:6
eb = 5:5	es = 10	D = 0	Afr	= 0.50	Food	= 0
	Adj es = 7	Adj D = +1	S	= 2	SumT	= 0
			Blends:R	= 5:27	Human Cont	= 9
FM = 2	SumC = 2	SumT = 0	CP	= 0	Pure H	= 3
m = 3	SumV = 1	SumY = 2			PER	= 1
					Isol Indx	= 0.07

			XA%	= 0.70	Zf	= 13	3r+(2)/R	= 0.37
			WDA%	= 0.77	W:D:Dd	= 7:15:5	Fr+rF	= 0
		Sum6	= 2	X−%	= 0.22	W:M	= 7:5	SumV	= 1
a:p	= 4:6	Lvl-2	= 0	S−	= 0	Zd	= +1.0	FD	= 1
Ma:Mp	= 2:3	WSum6	= 8	P	= 4	PSV	= 0	An+Xy	= 3
2AB+ (Art + Ay) = 3		M−	= 1	X+%	= 0.52	DQ+	= 8	MOR	= 3
MOR	= 3	Mnone	= 0	Xu%	= 0.19	DQv	= 4	H:(H)+Hd+(Hd)	= 3:6

PTI = 0	DEPI = 4	CDI = 2	S-CON = 3	HVI = Yes	OBS = No

Drawings

Here I will compare all of the fruit tree drawings from her three tests (Figures 13.2 to 13.4). The first and second drawings were almost identical in size and shape, and they had no roots, although the type of tree differed. At the first retest, Mariko commented that her tree did not have roots, like herself, as she was working as temporary staff, sometimes having no work and not working when she felt ill. In the second retest, she drew a cherry tree, which she described as having a thick trunk with solid roots and lots of fruit, a healthy tree. This appeared to show that she had become stable and fruitful and her reference to the tree being healthy also connected with the Vigor score on her POMS test.

RESULTS OF CLIENT FEEDBACK QUESTIONNAIRES

After the second retest feedback session with Mariko and her mother, I asked them each to complete a questionnaire to get feedback from them

Figure 13.2   Mariko's First Drawing of "A Fruit Tree"

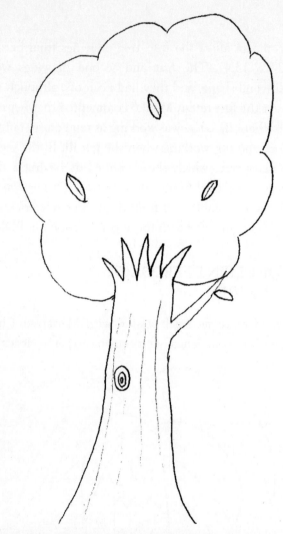

Figure 13.3   Mariko's Second Drawing of "A Fruit Tree"—First Retest

about the assessment. In response to the question, "How well did the assessment meet your expectations?" Mariko wrote: "Until I came here, I didn't know what I was hoping or thinking. That's why what was reported through the assessment became a clue for me. I completely trusted the assessment and heavily relied on it, and I was not disappointed." To the question "What would you tell a friend who was considering getting an assessment from me?" Mariko wrote: "This is not a place where you will be told what to do or what not to do. This is a place where you can organize your thoughts or reorganize your thoughts." Finally, she also wrote: "When I was in [her hometown], whatever I talked about to my counselor I felt was in vain and meaningless, whereas here I feel my opinion was accepted and respected, but I was given a new perspective and I felt every therapy session was worthwhile."

Mariko's mother wrote: "Everyday counseling by myself as a mother, which was more intuitive, and the scientific regular counseling by the therapist, together with all the support from related people as a kind of community counseling, altogether the three types brought her success. If any one of these had been missing, there would be no such Mariko as we see today." This statement was correct—that Mariko was multi-dimensionally supported by herself, her mother, her friends, and her therapist. The feedback sessions were important not only to understand Mariko herself but also to recognize that we were experts of three different kinds: Mariko as the expert on herself, her mother as an expert

Figure 13.4   Mariko's Third Drawing of "A Fruit Tree"—Second Retest

on Mariko's long-term care, and myself as a therapy expert. It was a rare experience that these three different experts from different backgrounds were able to share the same language or viewpoints that were gained from the feedback sessions.

CONCLUSION

I have shown how I gave feedback to Mariko on the results of her tests and used the results to structure a course of ongoing therapy. This experience was like standing together on an observation deck, as Finn (2007) has said, ensuring that we were both headed in the same direction for the course of therapy. The collaborative assessment was beneficial and effective, and it helped transform Mariko's life so that she was better able to cope with her emotions and function more successfully in society.

From my viewpoint as a therapist, I was somewhat surprised at the first retest scores, like the lowered Rorschach *Lambda* and the POMS Confusion still being in the danger zone, because Mariko had said that she felt she had improved. However, I knew this was a serious case in which I would not quickly see changes, so I did not expect a dramatic improvement at that point. Nevertheless, I felt challenged, and the results had the effect of making me want to fight harder in the second round of therapy. Then, when all of the results of the second retest showed a dramatic positive change, I felt extremely gratified.

In this case I believe Mariko and I worked well together, but this was because we both had her family's support, and at no point did her parents doubt my therapy. This affected the way I worked subsequently with other clients, and I have found that my therapy is most effective when I have such moral and practical support behind the client and myself to back us up.

Final Teaching Points

1. Testing prior to psychotherapy can provide a valuable roadmap for client and therapist to use during the therapy, and ongoing discussion of assessment results can aid clients in making sense of the events happening in their lives.

2. Retesting during psychotherapy can help client and therapist take stock of progress and identify areas that still need to be worked on. In order to compare scores from previous testing, it is better that another person, rather than the psychotherapist, conduct the repeat test administrations, as there is evidence that a prior therapeutic relationship can influence scores on such tests as the Rorschach (Exner, Armbruster, & Mittman, 1978).

3. Adolescents and young adults, especially those who are confused about who they are, can greatly benefit from a psychological assessment because it helps them with the crucial developmental step of identity development. The assessment does not circumvent this step by telling them "who they are"; instead, it provides them with information they can test in their daily lives to find out if it fits for them.

REFERENCES

Exner, J. E. (2005). *The Rorschach: A comprehensive assessment system* (Vol. 2, 3rd ed.). Hoboken, NJ: Wiley.

Exner, J. E. Jr., Armbruster, G., & Mittman, B. (1978). The Rorschach response process. *Journal of Personality Assessment, 42*, 27–38.

Finn, S. E. (2007). *In our clients' shoes: Theory and techniques of Therapeutic Assessment.* Mahwah, NJ: Erlbaum.

Kraepelin, E. (1902). *Dementia praecox.* New York, NY: Macmillan.

Kashiwagi, S., Yanai, H., Aoki, T., Tamai, H., Tanaka, Y., & Hokugoh, K. (1985). A factor analytic study of the items for the personality description based on the principle of the three traits theory for the work curve of addition of the Uchida-Kraepelin psychodiagnostic test. *Shinrigaku Kenkyu (The Japanese Journal of Psychology), 56*, 179–182.

Nakamura, N., & Nakamura, S. (1999a, July). *Further methodological considerations on the RFBS (Rorschach feedback session).* Presentation at the XVIth Congress of the International Society for the Rorschach and Projective Methods, Amsterdam, The Netherlands.

Nakamura, N., & Nakamura, S. (1999b). The method and therapeutic effectiveness of RFBS (*Rorschach Feedback Session*). *Japanese Journal of Psychotherapy, 25*(1), 31–38. (In Japanese.)

Nakamura, N., Fuchigami, Y., & Tsugawa. R. (2007). Rorschach Comprehensive System data for a sample of 240 adult nonpatients from Japan. *Journal of Personality Assessment, 89* (Suppl. 1), S97–S102.

Pollock, V., Cho, D. W., Reker, D., & Volavka, J. (1979). Profile of Mood States: The factors and their physiological correlates. *The Journal of Nervous and Mental Disease, 167*(10), 612–614.

Sorai, K., & Ohnuki, K. (2008). The development of the Rorschach in Japan. *Rorschachiana, 29*, 38–63.

Wechsler, D. (1997). *Wechsler Adult Intelligence Scale—Third Edition* (WAIS-III) (manual). New York, NY: The Psychological Corporation.

14

Collaborative Assessment of a Child in Foster Care: New Understanding of Bad Behavior

Caroline Purves

Books such as L. M. Montgomery's *Anne of Green Gables* (1908) allow us to imagine the life of an orphan child in foster care as a triumph of spunk over circumstances. An imaginative little girl who has lost her parents is taken in by an elderly brother and sister to help them run their farm. Although she was not the young boy they had requested from the orphanage, she nevertheless won their hearts and became the beloved focus of their lives.

Who were the foster children of that time, and of our time until the mid-50s? They were children who had lost their parents from death, due to illness or suicide, or who were unwanted when the stepparent abused

This chapter is dedicated to Constance Fischer, Stephen Finn, and Leonard Handler, who have done so much to refine and expand my thinking about collaborative assessment. Thanks also to Michael Schrecker and Matthew Madrone, the IT team at WestCoast Children's Clinic, for their help in preparing this manuscript.

them. For an example, see *A Hole in the World: An American Boyhood* by Richard Rhodes (1990). These children found their way to orphanages, which were often managed by religious groups. Informal fostering was more common than realized when, during World War II, women who had to go to work farmed their children out to neighbors. Many children in Europe were shipped to safer locations, such as children from London who were sent to the countryside, where they boarded with strangers, or others who were shipped across the ocean to Canada until the war ended.

Dislocation of children is a very old story. Is the foster care population of today in our urban areas different from these children of the past? Those who work in the field will give a resounding yes! Their typical first response is to describe the extreme and early level of trauma experienced by these children. In reasonably healthy families, children are protected from painful and frightening events by parents who can support them and contain their fears. The newborns and early infants of Winnicott's "good enough" parents have been protected from their own uncontained impulses and from the assaults of society, culture, and poverty by the ministrations of a caretaker who is able to manage their needs (Winnicott, 1975).

Children who end up in the present-day foster care system more often than not come from parents who are hopelessly inadequate. Not only are they unable to provide a safe caregiving environment to create some armor from a hostile world, but in many cases, these parents are themselves part of the hostile or indifferent world. Adding further insult to psychological injury, the babies are often born with drugs in their system because of the parents' substance abuse. Thus, there may be an initial physical fragility that must be addressed by careful nurturing. Sadly, this nurturing can be unavailable, either because the parental figures do not know what the special needs of the infant are or because they are not able to provide these special needs for the child. For a deeper understanding of the interface between culture, class, poverty, and race and the individual personality, see *The Analyst in the Inner City* by Neil Altman (2010). He also discusses the transmission of intergenerational trauma, which is relevant to the case being presented in this chapter.

THE CASE OF TANISHA

Referral

Tanisha, a 10-year-old African American girl, was referred for an assessment by her social worker, Ms. Lamb, because her therapist wanted help with understanding her "behavior problems." Indeed, Tanisha's behavior problems were myriad: stealing, fighting, rage, noncompliance with her foster parent, and inappropriate sexual acting-out. Ms. Lamb also wanted to know if Tanisha was struggling with an insecure or disorganized attachment style, which could interfere with successful bonding with her foster caregivers. Her therapist said that after three years of therapy, there was no significant change in Tanisha's behavior. He wondered if there could be an organic component to her problems.

Tanisha's background was a microcosm of the societal and familial problems described previously. She was a 10-year-old African American girl whose mother suffered from a seizure disorder of many years, exacerbated by illicit drug use. When she was five, Tanisha became involved with Child Protective Services because her mother was hospitalized during a series of brief seizures. There was no one available to care for her. The family had long been homeless; five prior referrals had been made to Child Protective Services charging neglect. Tanisha's mother was unable to follow through with her referral to a drug treatment program that would take her and her daughter; this lapse led to Tanisha's first placement in foster care.

Reading through the carefully detailed summary of Tanisha's life in foster care until the time we met for our first assessment visit was a painful experience. By then Tanisha was in her fourth placement, and this one seemed problematic. The pattern of her response to the placements quickly became evident. Initially, she joined with the family and seemed to do well. The social workers remarked on her promising adjustment; teachers remarked on her progress. However, this rosy picture began to change rather quickly into something quite different. Tanisha's cooperation and cheerful joining into the family morphed into opposition. She lied openly, and most difficult for the foster parents to manage, she exhibited sexualized behaviors toward other children. Although a couple of the families hung in for quite a while, eventually hands were thrown up in helplessness and despair (or anger!), and Tanisha was sent on her way.

Complications stemming from her biological parents added to the distress and confusion. In her first placement, Tanisha kept in touch with her parents, particularly her mother, even though the visits were erratic and the parents were still homeless. When Tanisha was seven, she was told that her mother had been found dead, possibly from a drug overdose. Shortly after, a maternal aunt offered to take Tanisha into her home. During this period, her biological father materialized, creating confusion and havoc for Tanisha, filling her head with promises of reunification and instructing her to lie about being abused in the foster home. Tanisha's lying and stealing increased with accusations of abuse, hurled now at her father, who refused to see his daughter anymore. He reportedly said to the social worker, "When she's 18 I will see her. Then Children's Protective Services will be out of the picture." Tanisha was kept with her maternal aunt for almost three years, until the aunt felt she could no longer manage Tanisha's behavior, despite dedicated collateral work with the therapist.

Tanisha was removed and placed in her fourth foster home, which is where she was living at the time of our evaluation. With something of a chill up my spine, I read the final report, which noted how much Tanisha had "settled down" with the change of placement; how she was doing better in school, and how well she seemed to be fitting in with the lives of her "new family." This serenity had dissolved by the time of our first session, when a furious foster mom had administered several kinds of punishment to Tanisha for stealing Easter candy from Tanisha's foster sister's Easter basket. What was especially galling for the foster mother was that she had taken extra care to put lots of candy in Tanisha's basket. There was no obvious reason, she felt, for her to sneak candy from her sister. Tanisha's version was that the other children at school had their candy with them and hers was at home, so she had to let the class know she also had been given candy for Easter. In her account to me, she left out how she lied to her foster mother about the incident, but only revealed how she felt devastated by the punishment.

Assessment Sessions

Tanisha was so upset at the first meeting that she could not focus on any testing. Our immediate task was to address the conflict that was going on in the home. She had the fantasy that after I heard her side, I would be able to intervene with her foster mother and everything would be just fine. I said I would be glad to talk with both of them, but the outcome might not be something she would like. The assessment had already turned into a therapeutic encounter. We had the talk, and even though the outcome was indeed not what she had hoped for, hearing that the mom still liked her even though she was angry helped Tanisha to settle down and enter into "testing mode." She came up with her own questions:

"How can I change my behavior?" and "How can I remember what I am supposed to do?"

This Easter candy episode offered several hypotheses into understanding the inner life of this child. First, her impulsivity and inability to think first and act later was clear. She saw the basket, she wanted candy, and nothing close to a thought or consequence entered her mind. The difficulty in delaying gratification was obvious. Even though her own filled basket was at home, she nevertheless wanted some candy at that moment. Then, her distortion about what happened and the terrible sense that she would no longer exist for the foster mother suggested an undeveloped sense of object constancy. In other words, if the mother figure was not in her immediate sight, she no longer existed in the child's mind, nor she in the mother's mind. Furthermore, the actual facts of the incident were long lost; the story she created to defend herself took on the power of absolute truth. Only when she could accept that the foster mother could care for her despite being angry was she able to settle down.

The testing sessions consisted of many and varied instruments. Using both cognitive and projective (performance based) instruments, I asked a lot of Tanisha. She completed selected subtests of the Wechsler Intelligence Test for Children–III (WISC-III; Wechsler, 1991), Trail Making Test A and B (TMT; Reitan, 1958), Bender–Gestalt Test (Bender, 1938), various projective drawings, including the House-Tree-Person (Buck, 1966) and the Kinetic Family Drawing Test (Burns & Kaufman, 1970), the Rorschach inkblot test (Exner, 1993), and selected cards from the Thematic Apperception Test (TAT; Murray, 1943) and the Children's Apperception Test (CAT; Bellak & Bellak, 1998). Testing proceeded over two sessions, with the not-surprising need for frequent encouragement, support, and gentle insistence to bring her back to the task at hand. Her tendency was to chatter away about herself, giving her opinions about life, my hair, whatever seemed to come into her mind. There was a constant pull for her to have my attention. Despite her distractibility, ultimately she worked hard and produced useful and valid results.

Test Results

Tanisha's scores on the WISC-III placed her in the Low Average range of intellectual functioning, with Similarities and Block Design her highest scores (scaled scores of 12 and 10, respectively; mean of 10). On the other hand, Comprehension and Picture Arrangement, both measures that look at various kinds of interactions in the social world, were significantly lower than her average (scaled scores of 4 in each case), suggesting that both her understanding of the rules and common-sense approach to the mores of our society, and her perceptions of social interactions, were seriously distorted.

This distortion of perceptions was common in Tanisha's Rorschach responses, where her reality testing was severely impaired. It was not a question of bizarre percepts as much as her forcing her percepts into the contours of the blot, whether they fit or not. For example, on Card IX she saw "a backbone" in the center detail, but then extended it into the pink area, spoiling the fit. Her next response to the whole card was "a crab, including its butt," again in the pink area, which is a minus form. She had many science responses, either of unusual or minus form quality, which seemed to be a defensive maneuver against more unsettling images, for example, "a person peeing on the toilet" on Card IV, or "a bird attacking an insect with teeny wings" on Card VI.

A dysphoric emotional tone was predominant in her projective stories (selected cards from a combination of the TAT and CAT), where all her stories began with sadness. In fact, on the second card she said, "These are all about sadness." It was as if the sad mood became pervasive almost to the point of perseveration. Sometimes she pasted on a happy ending, one that seemed to come out of nowhere, but she was not always able to do so successfully. For example, to the picture of a lion sitting in a chair, smoking his pipe, she ended the story with, "He suddenly felt sad about something but he didn't know what . . . he didn't do nothing wrong. He's got that worried face on." This mirrored her feelings about the Easter basket and her bewilderment about the punishment.

Many of Tanisha's sad stories ended with a magical happiness that was brought about by an adult figure or just the next day bringing about a happy feeling. To the first TAT card, that of a boy sitting at a table looking at a violin, she told the following story: "A boy. He wants to play the violin, but he cannot learn. So he's sad and he felt bad about it. The violin is sitting on the table right now. He cannot do it so, oh well." I asked her to tell me more, what is going to happen? She finished with, "He's going to tell his violin teacher that he cannot play the violin and he needs help. Hopefully, the teacher will help him and he will learn best."

Sustaining painful feelings or having a thought-out solution to a problem were not in Tanisha's repertoire. Mood changes just seemed to happen. The attachment literature describes these shifts of mood and splitting of good and bad as typical of insecurely attached children. Given Tanisha's history of neglect from birth and changes of placements, an insecure attachment style would be expected. Splitting is the inability to hold both the good and the bad feelings about a person at the same time; the capacity to hold both is considered to be a positive developmental step in the young child. For a deeper understanding of attachment theory, see for example, *Attachment Theory, Child Maltreatment and Family Support* (Howe, Brandon, Hinings, & Scholfield, 1999) and *Healing Trauma: Attachment, Mind, Body, and Brain* (Siegel & Solomon, 2003).

This split between "good" and "bad" was seen in her drawings as well—her drawing of a tree, thought to be an unconscious representation of the self, was of a 100-year-old oak tree that was going to be "teared down," while the kinetic family (K-F-D) she drew was an idealized version of a happy family—a mom and dad and daughter with huge presents neatly tied in a bow for their child. The contrast between the aging, doomed tree and the only child in the classically happy family is painfully striking. One might extrapolate that this dichotomy mirrors what actually has happened in her various placements. Tanisha started with the fantasy that this family would be the one she imagines that wants her, but she ends up being "teared down" and rejected.

The Rorschach of 19 responses overall provided a rich record from a child who scores in the Low Average range on the Wechsler Intelligence Scale for Children (see Table 14.1 for the Structural Summary). There were many elements on the Structural Summary to think about. To start with, her high *Lambda* of 2.17 pointed to a worldview of simplistic absolutes with little openness to complexity. For Tanisha it was an all-or-nothing world. Furthermore, the *XA%* and the *WDA%* of 9 were significantly low. These measures told us that even when it was easy to find responses that fit the blot, she tended to distort them. In other words, even without a complex view of her environment, she was also distorting reality. What most people see easily was not so obvious to her, leaving her without a strong base from which to make her judgments.

In terms of her perceptions of others, Tanisha had two poor human content responses compared to one good human response (*GHR:PHR* = 1:2). Her three white space responses, along with the AG (aggression) response, pointed to a tendency to feel something of a loser, to be on the outside, while always being ready to fight back, the "chip on the shoulder" mentality. And the *FC:CF* ratio (*Form Color* vs. *Color Form*) of 1:2 showed that when she did fight back, it was more likely to be highly emotional rather than modulated. Thus, she jumped to conclusions based on faulty perceptions and a chip on her shoulder.

Tanisha's *W:M* ratio (the ratio of whole responses to that of human movement responses) of 16:1 was also noteworthy. The *W:M* ratio is called the "aspiration ratio" and ideally should be 2:1. This was a somewhat unusual combination, suggesting a person who perceived her world, however distorted, in simplified black-and-white terms; who was oppositional and feeling alienated; and who tried extremely hard to create meaning with few resources to draw upon. Furthermore, her *Coping Deficit Index* (*CDI*) was positive, indicating that she had a hard time dealing with stress, that she often felt helpless in the face of what seemed to most children to be ordinary demands. The Rorschach Structural Summary gave powerful insight into the demands Tanisha experienced from both the outer and the inner world and her limited capacity to cope adequately with them.

What jumped out at me in particular was the complete absence of pairs. The norms tell us that the average number of pairs for a 10-year-old is nine (Exner, 1993). Because of the symmetry of the blots, pairs are

Table 14.1   Tanisha's Structural Summary

Location Features		Determinants		Contents	
		Blends	**Single**	H = 1	
Zf = 16		CF.m	M = 0	(H) = 0	
ZSum = 55		M.m	FM = 1	Hd = 1	
ZEst = 52.3		Cf.m	m = 0	(Hd) = 0	
			FC = 1	Hx = 0	
W = 16			CF = 0	A = 5	
D = 2			C = 0	(A) = 0	
W + D = 18			Cn = 0	Ad = 3	
Dd = 1			FC' = 0	(Ad) = 1	
S = 3			C'F = 0	An = 2	
			C' = 0	Art = 1	
DQ			FT = 0	Ay = 0	**Special Scores**
+ = 4			TF = 0	Bl = 1	Lv1 Lv2
o = 14			T = 0	Bt = 0	DV = 0 0 × 1 0 × 2
v/+ = 0			FV = 0	Cg = 0	INC = 0 0 × 2 0 × 4
v = 1			VF = 0	Cl = 0	DR = 0 0 × 3 0 × 6
			V = 0	Ex = 1	FAB = 0 0 × 4 0 × 7
			FY = 0	Fd = 0	ALOG = 0 0 × 5
			YF = 0	Fi = 0	CON = 0 0 × 7
Form Quality			Y = 0	Ge = 0	Raw Sum6 = 0
FQx MQual W+D			Fr = 0	Hh = 0	Wgtd Sum6 = 0
+ = 0 = 0 = 0			rF = 0	Ls = 0	
o = 5 = 1 = 5			FD = 1	Na = 1	AB = 0 GHR = 1
u = 8 = 1 = 7			F = 13	Sc = 5	AG = 1 PHR = 2
− = 8 = 2 = 7				Sx = 0	COP = 0 MOR = 0
none = 0 = 0 = 0				Xy = 0	CP = 0 PER = 0
			(2) = 0	Id = 1	PSV = 0

RATIOS, PERCENTAGES, AND DERIVATIONS

R = 19	L = 2.17	FC:CF+C = 1:2	COP = 0 AG = 1
		Pure C = 0	GHR:PHR = 1:2
EB = 1:2.5 EA = 3.5 EBPer = N/A		SmC':WSmC = 0:2.5	a:p = 2:3
eb = 4:0 es = 4 D = 0		Afr = 0.46	Food = 0
Adj es = 2 Adj D = 0		S = 3	SumT = 0
		Blends/R = 3:19	Human Cont = 2
FM = 1 SumC' = 0 SumT = 0		CP = 0	PureH = 1
m = 3 SumV = 0 SumY = 0			PER = 0
			Isol Indx = 0:11

		XA% = 0.63	Zf = 16	3r+(2)/R = 0.00
		WDA% = 0.61	W:D:Dd = 16:2:1	Fr+rF = 0
	Sum6 = 0	X−% = 0.37	W:M = 11:4	SumV = 0
a:p = 2:3	Lv2 = 0	S− = 0	Zd = +2.5	FD = 1
Ma:Mp = 0:1	WSum6 = 0	P = 3	PSV = 0	An+Xy = 2
2AB+Art + Ay = 1	M− = 0	X+% = 0.42	DQ+ = 4	MOR = 0
MOR = 0	Mnone = 0	Xu% = 0.21	DQv = 1	H:(H)+Hd+(Hd) = 1:1

| PTI = 2 | DEPI = 4 | CDI = 4 | S-CON = N/A | HVI = NO | OBS = NO |

easy to find. Tanisha had none. Her *Egocentricity Index* was zero! Here is a child who was demanding constant attention, whose drawings of a tree and a girl took up a lot of space, yet whose sense of self was fragile, limited, and unconsolidated. She was a child who, as an infant, had not experienced the loving gaze of a maternal figure and could not give to others a sense that they existed for her. She took up a lot of space in her environment, yet severe attachment difficulties and a poorly developed sense of self did not allow for internal development. Both her capacity to relate comfortably with other people and her ability to look at her world in a reasonably objective and realistic way were severely compromised.

Writing a Feedback Story for Tanisha

The challenge of this assessment was to find a way to present the findings to Tanisha so that she would be (a) not overwhelmed, (b) able to understand herself better, and (c) able to find some hope. Furthermore, just as challenging was the task of helping the adults in her life find some understanding of the underlying dynamics that were driving Tanisha's difficult and exasperating behaviors. Even though not many hours were available because of the funding source, I wanted to make the presentation of the findings as rich and useful for all concerned as the time would allow—to challenge myself to make this assessment a truly collaborative experience for Tanisha and her caregivers.

Creating a feedback story for children demands a light touch with a depth of underlying seriousness. The difficult issues that the child faces must be addressed so that the experience resonates with her real life. Conversely, information about too many conflict areas cannot easily be absorbed, just as too much information offered to adults for their feedback cannot easily be absorbed. As I struggled with a welter of information, I tried to imagine what would be most helpful for Tanisha. She would respond best, it seemed to me, to something practical but that also touched her inner experience. It struck me that the lack of pairs was the clue. It was such a striking finding, and in tandem with some of the other measures, suggested a way to think about Tanisha's inner life. This absence of pairs, along with the other measures that captured the distortions of reality [*Perceptual Thinking Index (PTI)* of 2, low scores on

Picture Arrangement and Comprehension, and the paucity of resources to cope with the demands of her life ($W:M = 16:1$)], pointed my thinking as to how easily she could become overwhelmed with anything that to her mind suggested that she was being overlooked or slighted.

After much thought and much discussion with colleagues, I came up with the following story:

A DUCKLING NAMED MATILDA

A Story for Tanisha

CHAPTER 1: WE MEET MATILDA DUCK

Matilda Duck was called Tilly by most of the other birds and animals who knew her. She lived with her family near a lake and went to a school that was half by the water and half in the sandy cove. This was very convenient because some of the students liked to paddle in the lake at lunch recess and some of them preferred to roam around in the grass and sand. Tilly liked both parts of her school, and she liked her class too, where she worked hard at her lessons.

Tilly wasn't quite a baby duckling, as she had grown out of her soft, fuzzy down and was slowly growing her sleek smooth feathers. But she was still young, so there was a mixture of soft and sleek, some pale yellow and some moving into shiny brown. The funny thing was that there was a mixture inside her that most other people didn't know about. Inside she was both a baby duckling and a duck who was growing up to be a big duck. These different parts of Tilly could pop out at different times. Sometimes she sounded very grown duck-like and other times like a little duckling. Naturally this was puzzling to her teachers and parents. Sometimes even Tilly wasn't quite sure which part of her would pop out, and she would be just as puzzled. But she was a smart duck and worked very hard to try to sort things out.

CHAPTER 2: TROUBLE IN THE SCHOOLYARD

It was lunch recess. Tilly and her friend, Jemima, were playing and quacking away to each other a mile a minute (as they say in the duck world), and up came Keesha, who was an old friend of Jemima's. "Quack, hi, hi, Jemima," said Keesha, and gently rubbed her beak against Jemima's wing. In a flash, Tilly felt herself—well, she didn't know what it was she felt, but she just knew that she had to do something to stop whatever it was or, strange as it seems, she thought she would disappear. So, instead of saying, "hi, hi" to Jemima, she gave a loud squawk and brought her webbed foot down hard on Jemima's webbed foot.

The feathers flew, the air was filled with loud quacks and angry squawks. Ms. Turkey, who was on yard duty for that week, ran over as fast as she could (which wasn't very fast because she was a rather large turkey!). "Stop that this instant, you ducklings, gobble, gobble, gobble! Come with me, Miss Matilda Duckling. We're going to the office right now."

"Not fair," wailed Tilly. "*She* butted in. It's not my fault!" she quacked in an angry voice. But Ms. Turkey didn't listen to what Tilly had to say. ("As usual," Tilly thought to herself. But she was crying a little and didn't have enough breath to say it out loud.)

The principal, Mrs. Grey Goose, gave a big sigh when she saw Tilly. "Oh, Matilda," she said (Principal Goose believed in using her students' formal names). "What shall we do with you? This is the fourth time this month."

"No, Mrs. Grey," Tilly corrected her, "it's only the third time— and it wasn't my fault. It's just not fair."

"Humph," said Principal Grey Goose. She wasn't used to being corrected by students. Nor did she like it when Tilly answered back. (Actually Tilly had noticed that most grown-up ducks and other birds didn't like it when she answered back, but she often felt so mad that she just couldn't stop herself.) "You know, Matilda, I don't think you are happy when you get into fights with the other ducks, or when you answer back to the big ducks. It's time we figured out how to understand you better. I am going to tell your Mama Duck to make an appointment with Dr. Tortuga. Dr. Tortuga has been around for many, many years. I think you will find her very interesting."

"Yikes, yikes, quack, quack!" yelped Tilly. Inside her head she was thinking, "I'm not sure about this. But I do feel not-so-happy, and I'm a brave and strong young duckling. I bet I can handle any old Dr. Tortuga."

CHAPTER 3: THE VISIT TO DR. TORTUGA

Tilly and her mother swam across the lake to Dr. Tortuga's office. They waddled through a grassy tunnel until they came to a large room under some trees. Dr. Tortuga *was* old. She was a huge tortoise with a thick shell. She looked at Tilly through tiny gold-rimmed glasses. When Mama Duck explained why they were there, that they wanted to understand Tilly better, and help her be a happier young duckling, Dr. Tortuga nodded. "Yes," she said very slowly, "I think I can help you. Now, young Tilly, let's get to work. Are you game?"

Tilly wasn't quite sure what that meant, but she said yes anyway, to show just how brave she was. And, goodness gracious, what a lot of different things Dr. Tortuga gave her to do. She answered questions, sort of like school, but not really. She looked at funny pictures, she told stories, she did drawings, she told the doctor all about school. Then, when they were all finished, Dr. Tortuga looked at her for several minutes through the tiny gold-rimmed glasses. "Yes," she said very slowly, "I know what's the problem. You are suffering from a severe case of Invisibilitis."

"Invisibil, invisibil, what? Quack, quack!" yelped Tilly. "I can't even say it. What does it mean?"

"It means," said the old doctor, "that you have a fear of being invisible. That deep down inside you there is a terrible worry that you could disappear, that people wouldn't be able to see you."

"Oh my, quack, quack, quack." For a moment Tilly was at a loss for words. She just could not think of what to say. Her thoughts were tumbling around in her head, so that she almost felt dizzy. Finally, she calmed down. "Is it serious? Will I die from this?"

"Yes, Tilly, it is serious, but, no, you won't die. In fact, this condition is one that can be remedied." Tilly wished the doctor wouldn't use such big words, but she thought she understood. "There is a very kind brown owl that will help you become visible."

"Oh, I know this Mr. Owl, I already visit him. You mean he can help me with this serious invisi, invisi, whatever you call it."

"Indeed, yes, and so can your Mama Duck and your teachers. We will all work together so you can become the very special duck that everyone will recognize. And you will find, Tilly, that after a while, without you even knowing it, you will have more fun with your friends and become a happier duckling."

Tilly felt a tiny flutter insider of her heart. She wasn't quite sure what it was, but she thought maybe it was some of her sad feelings floating away and her good feelings getting just a bit stronger.

The end. (and the beginning of the change that Matilda hoped for)

Presenting the Feedback Story to Tanisha and Interested Adults

Now that I had a story for Tanisha, the question was how best to present it. Typically, when performing an assessment for the Department of Human Services, a written report is sent to the referring social worker, who then decides who receives copies and, if one is so inclined, who and how to give the results. Fortunately, Ms. Lamb and I had worked together in the past, which had given her the experience of a collaborative model. This model, apart from the direct help to the immediate caretakers and the child, offers a different relationship with the "system" social workers. Although they usually know the child in care better than anyone else, judges and lawyers often give more credence to a psychological report than to the workers' opinions. Including them in the assessment in a more collegial way not only benefits the psychologist, but creates a working relationship that extends to the child and family.

There were at least three possibilities of how to arrange the presentation of the findings: (1) to meet with Tanisha first in the presence of her foster mother; (2) to discuss the findings first with the entire team without Tanisha; or (3) to meet first alone with Tanisha. After talking with Ms. Lamb, the social worker, and Tanisha's therapist, who were the two people who had known her the longest, we decided on a team meeting. The team consisted of the people most directly connected with her, followed by a session alone with Tanisha. The aim of this meeting was to help the team realize a more nuanced and layered personality, that there was more to Tanisha than just a bad girl. Yes, she was a girl with obnoxious and demanding behavior, one who tested the patience of the adults who had the authority to care for and direct her. But I hoped that by understanding aspects of Tanisha's personality they couldn't see directly, they would see beyond the "bad" girl to the desperately terrified inner parts of her, which were driving the behavior. More specifically, I wanted the foster mother, through more understanding of Tanisha's "unnecessary" behavior, to allow herself slightly more flexibility in her discipline. I also was hoping that the therapist, who was under tremendous pressure to "improve her," would worry less about correcting her behavior, and focus more on the inner loneliness and emptiness. In other words, the feedback session was aimed at developing empathy for Tanisha, empathy that would help her team become more creative in their responses to her.

The group of adults in Tanisha's life turned out to be larger than I had anticipated. In addition to Ms. Lamb, the foster parent, and her therapist, the CASAR worker (child advocate for the court) was also present. My original intention was to begin the discussion with their questions and presentation of the findings. However, on the spur of the moment, I decided on a different opening gambit. I handed each one of them a copy of Matilda the Duck, Tanisha's story. After initial laughter and puzzlement, silence reigned as each one sat with the copy of the story. The foster mom laughed out loud at one point, saying, "That's Tanisha, for sure!" Nods of agreement, occasional chuckles, and thoughtful silence were the prevailing mood as they set the story down and began to talk about Tanisha. I offered them examples from her testing to help clarify the dynamics of Tanisha's interior life, which was fueling her impulsive and demanding behaviors. For starters I showed them the significantly low scores on her intelligence scales, the Comprehension and Picture Arrangement subtests, to illustrate her woefully poor grasp of the social environment. Her passivity in the face of demands, illustrated on the first Thematic Apperception Test card, was relevant: *A boy. He wants to play the violin, but he cannot learn. So he's sad, and he felt bad about it. The violin is sitting on the table right now. He cannot do it so, oh well.* The foster mother offered some examples that supported the findings.

The weakness of the self, her impulsivity and cognitive difficulties, along with her depression and anxiety, seemed to me elements that were more easily understood and accepted because of the metaphors in Matilda's story. Taking in the story somehow allowed objections and defensive responses to be bypassed, creating sympathy for Tanisha and a willingness to think about different ways of effectively responding to her.

Next on the agenda was to present the findings to Tanisha. A separate visit was arranged just for her. If she wanted, which she did as it turned out, she could invite her foster mother to sit with her as she and I talked about the assessment. When Tanisha came in for her feedback, she really didn't much care to hear about her strengths and weaknesses, or her results, even though she had posed questions herself initially. "How can I learn to change my behavior?" was her question. She seemed so quietly anxious that I decided to bypass the details of the assessment findings with her. Instead, just as I had done with the adult team, I handed her the story of Matilda the Duck. She decided to read it herself out loud, but she soon reached the end of her capacity for sustained reading (this was a chapter book, after all!). She asked me to read the rest of it to her. Once she settled into the story, she was fascinated. Some of it seemed just like her; she could see herself in the actions of Matilda. "It's got clues," she said with excitement. Dr. Tortuga, she thought, might have been me. Mr. Owl, she opined, was probably her therapist. Thrilled that she was going to have her own copy of the book, she gave me a big smile and a hug, as we said good-bye.

Outcomes

It would be heartening to be able to say that this experience, the collaborative assessment, turned Tanisha's life around. Also, the hope was that the experience would provide the caretakers with a new vision of her that would allow them to change their view of her as an unworkable bad child and to find more understanding and empathy for her. In a limited way, this was the outcome. There was a moment of shared support and empathy as the team struggled with ways of helping Tanisha, which continued for a while in her current placement. Sadly, with the level of depression, impulsivity, and hopelessness, along with poorly developed ego structures carried by Tanisha, change would be a lifelong project. Furthermore, the match between the child in foster care and the foster parent is the crucial element in the success of the placement.

In Tanisha's case, the collaborative assessment supported the foster mother's understanding for some time. Ultimately, her rather rigid expectations of children's behavior in the face of Tanisha's continued sexualized acting-out got the better of her genuine sympathy, and she was no longer willing to keep the child. Despite a less than ideal happy ending, the work of the assessment was not in vain—at least for a short while in Tanisha's life she was understood by her caretakers and felt her story gave her a direction for self-awareness and some control of her life.

Teaching Points

1. Collaborative assessment requires far more thought, creativity, and work than the standard assessments. One might wonder if the outcome is really worth all this time and effort in a foster care situation in which the outcome is weighted with so much difficulty. The argument can be made that the collaborative approach is all the more desirable in these less than ideal situations. Children in foster care can and do feel that they are really uncared for. Children in general yearn to be seen and understood as much as our adult clients. Fostered children, while they can present a defended self, long to be understood even more than most, as they so often feel invisible, as our young client clearly did. Taking the time to transmute the findings into an accessible form for them is a gift that holds meaning for them over time, one that they can return to whenever they are inclined. It is a means of taking the child's deepest anxieties and offering to help them in a tolerable format.

2. What is the value of the team involvement in the assessment of a child in the foster care system? While involving the various players in a foster child's life is time-consuming and often cumbersome, the benefits are worthwhile. Rarely does one person hold the child's history the way a parent does. Various individuals in their roles in the system, be they a current social worker, therapist, foster parent, or other involved person, usually know only pieces of the child's life experience. Thus, they tend to view the child's behavior through their particular lens. Having various adults together to talk about the assessment findings allows a more complex understanding of who this child is and why he or she might be behaving in the way he or she does. It also allows compassion for the role each one plays in the child's daily life and understanding of the demands each one experiences. In my experience, the social worker, who is usually the most involved in the difficult decisions for the child, is appreciative of and helped by the collaborative work.

REFERENCES

Altman, N. (2010). *The analyst in the inner city: Race, class, and culture through a psychoanalytic lens* (2nd ed.). New York, NY: Routledge.

Bellak, L., & Bellak, S. S. (1998). Children's Apperception Test. Larchmont, NY: C.P.S. Inc.

Bender, L. (1938). *Visual motor gestalt test and its clinical use.* New York, NY: American Orthopsychiatric Association.

Buck, J. (1966). *The House-Tree-Person technique,* revised manual. Los Angeles, CA: Western Psychological Services.

Burns, R., & Kaufman, S. (1970). *Family drawings (K-F-D): An introduction to understanding children through kinetic drawings.* New York, NY: Brunner/Mazel.

Exner, J. E., Jr. (1993). *The Rorschach: A comprehensive system, Vol. 1: Basic foundations* (3rd ed.). New York, NY: John Wiley & Sons, Inc.

Howe, D., Brandon, M., Hinings, D., & Scholfield, G. (1999). *Attachment theory, child maltreatment and family support.* Hillsdale, NJ: Erlbaum.

Montgomery, L. M. (1908). *Anne of Green Gables.* Toronto, Canada: Ryerson Press.

Murray, H. A. (1943). *Thematic Apperception Test manual.* Cambridge, MA: Harvard University Press.

Reitan, R. M. (1958). Validity of the Trail Making test as an indicator of organic brain damage. *Perceptual and Motor Skills*, 8, 271–276.

Rhodes, R. (1990). *A hole in the world: An American boyhood.* New York, NY: Simon & Schuster.

Siegel, D., & Solomon, M. (Eds.). (2003). *Healing trauma: Attachment, mind, body, and brain.* New York, NY: W. W. Norton.

Wechsler, D. (1991). *Wechsler Intelligence Scale for Children, third edition* (WISC-III): Manual. New York, NY: The Psychological Corp.

Winnicott, D. W. (1975). *Through paediatrics to psychoanalysis.* London, England: Hogarth Press.

⊷◆⊶

Therapeutic Assessment With a 10-Year-Old Boy and His Parents: The Pain Under the Disrespect

Deborah J. Tharinger, Melissa E. Fisher, and Bradley Gerber

We illustrate the comprehensive model of Therapeutic Assessment (TA) with children with the case of a 10-year-old boy, his mother, and his stepfather. The case was conducted as part of a larger project, the Therapeutic Assessment Project (TAP), which has been described elsewhere (Hamilton et al., 2009; Tharinger, Finn, Gentry, et al., 2009; Tharinger, Krumholz, Austin & Matson, in press). The TAP was designed to (a) study the efficacy of TA as an intervention (specifically the process, outcomes, and consumer satisfaction), (b) train graduate student assessors in using the TA model with children and adolescents, and (c) offer free comprehensive assessments to the community. The comprehensive model of TA with children typically consists of 8 to 10 weekly sessions that take place over a 2- to 3-month period. We have found that meeting weekly allows time between sessions for parents to process what they are learning, begin to shift their interpretations of their child's behavior, and construct a new story about their child and family. This schedule similarly allows the assessors time to absorb findings and plan thoroughly for each upcoming session.

Each TAP assessment is conducted at our university-based setting by a team of two advanced graduate students in a doctoral-level professional psychology program, supervised by licensed psychologists who are experienced in TA. In the TA model used in TAP, one assessment team member works primarily with the child and the other with the parent(s). The assessment team comes together for all joint meetings with the child and parents. The assessment team for the case presented here consisted of the second author, Melissa Fisher, and the third author, Brad Gerber, both doctoral students. The case was supervised by Deborah Tharinger, the first author, professor and licensed psychologist. Melissa worked with the boy as he completed the testing, as well as with the parents in joint sessions. Brad worked primarily with the parents, including sitting with them as they observed and discussed their child's testing sessions. For the research portion of TAP, the child and parents completed pre- and postassessment research measures, as well as brief interviews after each session of TA. Informed consent and assent was obtained, including permission to include their case study in a published book. Names and demographic information were changed to protect their identity.

In this case study, we highlight and illustrate 13 *Teaching Points* across the multiple components of the comprehensive TA model. First, we address (1) gathering assessment questions, (2) working with the parents as they observe and process their child's testing sessions, and (3) testing the child. Following, we comment on the centrality of the relational experiences and then describe and illustrate (4) conducting a family session, (5) providing parent feedback through a summary/discussion session and corresponding letter, and (6) constructing and delivering child feedback through an individualized fable presented to the child and parents. We close by presenting research findings addressing pre-/postassessment change.

BACKGROUND AND ASSESSMENT QUESTIONS

David, a European American male, was 10 years old at the time of the TA, living with his biological mother, Karen, his stepfather, Carlos, his 14-year-old biological sister, and his maternal grandmother. David's mother and stepfather had been married one year. His biological father, John, and Karen divorced five years prior, and John lived in another state. John had numerous physical ailments and reportedly had significant difficulty managing his anger. Due to his ailments and emotional instability, John was frequently unemployed and was at times unable to financially support himself. David had infrequent contact with him. However, Karen reported that when John was particularly low on funds, he would call her, David, or David's sister to borrow money. These requests were very stressful, since David's family also was struggling financially.

Karen sought individual therapy for David from a community mental health agency due to concerns about his disrespectful behavior and poor emotional regulation. After Karen was informed about TAP through the agency, she expressed high interest in participating. David and Karen attended all of the TA sessions; Carlos attended only a few, due to work conflicts and a cycle of his disengaging and reengaging with the family. Questions for the assessment were coconstructed by Karen, Carlos, and the assessors during the first session, the initial interview. David was invited to develop questions during the second session and in the presence of his parents. The parents' questions were:

> How is David's emotional state? (Is he sad? Is his "heart torn up," like his school counselor said? Is he angry?)
> Why is David so aggressive and disrespectful?
> Why does David not connect with me (mother)?
> Why does it take a reward to get him to do something rather than just doing it out of love and respect (unless he's doing it for other people, like the neighbors)?
> How can I (mother) show my strength as a parent?
> How did what he saw in my marriage to his father affect him?
> How does he feel about his stepfather?

David posed one question:

> Why does everyone in the house accuse me of stuff, like if something is missing?

Teaching Point

Assessment questions are constructed in a collaborative fashion, engaging parents. They set the course for the testing and intervention sessions and provide the template for feedback to parents. If a child can provide questions, they also inform the process and are often very instructive to parents.

CHILD TESTING SESSIONS AND PARENTS' OBSERVATION/PROCESSING

The process of parents observing and processing testing sessions is unique to TA with children. Typically, in psychological assessment of children, the assessor interviews the parents and then proceeds to test the child while the parents are waiting in an adjoining room. Then, following an analysis of the findings, the assessor provides the parents with feedback and recommendations, typically a week or two later. Finn (2007) came to see this usual practice model as a missed opportunity to involve the parents and began to explore the utility of parents observing *during* the child testing process. Finn came to see that through observing their child's testing, parents are given a chance to discover answers to their questions about their child, are helped to feel less inadequate when they see the assessor struggling with the same problems they encounter with their child, and benefit from observing the assessor model new ways of dealing with their child's challenging behaviors, among other things. We also have found through the TAP that pre-adolescent children not only are willing to disclose with their parents observing but, having a strong alliance with their assessor, they use it as an opportunity to communicate directly with their parents.

In a one-assessor model of child TA, the assessor checks in with parents before and after they have observed the assessment from the corner of the room, or through a live video feed in an adjacent room. In a two-assessor model, the second assessor sits with parents behind a one-way mirror as they observe and process, or sits with them as they observe through a live video feed. This two-assessor model allows for constant discussion or dialogue with the parents, especially when the live video feed is used.

🔊 Teaching Point

Working with parents as they observe testing creates an opportunity for the child to communicate with their parents and allows the parents the opportunity to process information learned through the assessment with a clinician who guides them as they consider a new understanding of their child. This process prepares parents to really "hear" and internalize the accumulated findings summarized at the end. The clinician can also draw attention to the ways in which the assessor is building a relationship with their child, which allows the parents to see behaviors they can use to enhance their relationship with their child.

We now illustrate parent observation/processing in our case with David. His mother and stepfather, accompanied by Brad, observed the sessions over a live video feed in an adjoining room. We describe the testing process, findings, and reactions from the parent observation deck.

Human Figure Drawings

It is customary to begin the first session with the child by doing unstructured assessment activities, such as human figure drawings (Tharinger & Roberts, in press). David's first drawing (Draw-A-Person) was of his father, working in his workshop. David said his father was feeling tired, and he was sad because he missed his family. He also said his father was not well, and he needed help from a friend to get things done. When asked if his father had ever been hurt, David related a story that would come up again. He described how his father had almost been badly injured while rock climbing with David and his sister.

As his mother watched over the monitor from the other room, she commented that David might be feeling partially responsible for his father's sadness and might be worried about his father's poor health. This was an opportunity for Brad to help her connect with the strong emotions David was experiencing about his father. This was also a chance for

Karen to begin to feel more empathy for her son and better understand the existence and impact of past (and ongoing) stressors in his life.

Following this task, David completed a Kinetic Family Drawing (KFD). It included himself, his cousin, and his mother. He drew himself and his cousin playing video games together, while his mother brought them popcorn. He said his mother was feeling left out and that she was thinking, "I hope they like the popcorn I made by myself." David's response illustrated the disconnection he felt with his mother. Also, David's sister, grandmother, and stepfather were left out of the drawing, possibly reflecting the conflict or rejection David has experienced with each of those family members. After Brad and Karen noticed how David depicted his mother in the drawing, Brad used this as an opportunity to discuss the emotional distance between mother and son, which linked directly to an assessment question (Why does he not connect with me?). Thus, the work to help David's mother see the importance of repairing her bond with David was in motion.

When asked what he would like to change about his family, David said that he wished his family was more active and would do more things with him, like ride bikes. He also described a typical day in his family where all the family members did their own thing and rarely interacted with one another. David said he was usually the only one outside, and he would often go to a friend's house rather than stay home. After hearing this over the monitor, David's mother said she was often too busy or tired to play with him, and she noted that he spent a lot of time away from home. This comment provided an opportunity for Brad to bring up the need to spend time with David in order to strengthen their bond. Brad also highlighted the discrepancy between what the mother originally reported (David doesn't connect with us) and the idea that David may really want to connect with her and his stepfather, as he said he wished his mother and stepfather would do more things with him. This helped inform one of the parents' assessment questions.

Subsequently, David was asked to draw a picture of his house. He said the house was his grandmother's 30-year-old trailer house. He said the largest bedroom would be his and it would be filled with things. There were other bedrooms, but David did not want anyone to live with him in the house, so he designated them as guest bedrooms. David said it was a happy house, although it needed a garden and to be made of brick, instead of wood. His desire for sturdier building materials probably reflected his desire for a more sturdy foundation for his home life.

From their observation deck, Carlos said, "I think he drew that house because he feels that the family, though we live in a house now, our family, he feels that it's not a strong family, things could easily be blown away quick. I think, I think he wants a solid family, a solid foundation, a solid house, and he seems to be insecure of the house. . . . I think he feels . . . he probably feels insecure with us, I think. We're unstable." Karen said the house was "fragile" and she worried how it would weather storms. Carlos went on to discuss how, when he was growing up, his home had a "stable, strong foundation" and he didn't know what it had been like for David to move from place to place and not have that strong foundation. Brad used this discussion as another opportunity to help Karen and Carlos gain empathy for David's painful and unresolved emotional state.

Teaching Point

Drawings and related dialogue can be an excellent first activity for a child, as they are unstructured and open-ended. They also provide an excellent opportunity for parents to engage in the observation process, since they have face validity and encourage important discussion about the child and the family.

Self-Report Measure

After David completed the drawings, he completed the Beck Youth Inventories with Melissa. David did not endorse any sadness, irritability, aggressive behaviors, or anxiety. In the other room, Karen commented to Brad that David was not being truthful about his feelings and behaviors. Brad used this as another opportunity to explain how David could be feeling many things on the inside but seemed to be trying to hide those feelings on the outside. David's denial of the negative behaviors on the externalizing behavior section of the Beck started a dialog about

David's aggressive behavior at home that was central to one of his mother's assessment questions. Brad used this as an opportunity to learn more about the consequences for David's aggressive and disrespectful behaviors, which alerted the clinicians to how discipline was inconsistently applied in the home.

Teaching Point

Self-report measures provide a wealth of information. In this case, the child's propensity to underreport provided a window into his protective armor and an excellent opportunity to engage the parents and discuss their central concerns about their son not "telling the truth."

Sentence Completion Method

In the second testing session, David was asked to complete an incomplete sentences task, developed by the assessors and their supervisor, with the sentence stems designed to explore his and his parents' assessment questions. For most of the sentence stems, David gave straightforward, unveiled answers. His responses indicated a desire for less conflict and arguing at home, a desire for more fun activities with his mother and stepfather, and frustration at frequently being blamed for things. David also expressed his distress about losing his father ("My heart felt broken . . . *when my dad moved to South Carolina*"). He also informed one of his mother's assessment questions by saying, "It is easier to behave around teachers and friends than my parents because . . . *I know I'll get in really big trouble at school or at friends' houses, and my friends' parents might have big consequences for breaking the rules.*"

David's overt statement about why he behaved respectfully outside the home provided the ideal opening for Brad to talk with Karen and Carlos about the need for increased consistency in structure and rules in their home. This is an example of how, through the parents observing the testing sessions, the child was able to directly answer one of the parent's assessment questions. In our experience, this is much more salient than the assessor stating what he or she thinks the child is trying to say.

Because David was so direct about what helped him to behave, Brad seized the chance to introduce the idea that "rules without relationship equals rebellion." This idea captured what was missing from David's home: rules *and* a relationship with Karen and Carlos.

Teaching Point

The construction of idiographic sentence completion items allows for a direct exploration of assessment questions and demonstrates to the family that their questions are the focus of the assessment and guide the process.

Play as Part of Testing Sessions

We typically use play in TA with children, often at the end of many of the testing sessions (see Tharinger, Christopher, & Matson, 2011). After completing the testing in each session, often for the last 15 minutes, Melissa invited David to engage in play. David chose active games, usually a game involving catching a ball. He led the activity and made up the rules, which he explained and demonstrated for Melissa. As they played, David talked about his friends or things he had done over the week. He spoke openly and freely, and occasionally told stories and jokes. Melissa listened attentively, respectfully asked follow-up questions, and praised David's positive actions. David smiled often and seemed to enjoy the play and the attention. Melissa also enjoyed their play; David's games were creative and fun. From the observation deck, Carlos seemed most in tune with the synchrony between David and Melissa, and noted several times that their interactions could be a guide for their own with David. Again, we continued to appreciate Carlos's insights and connections.

Teaching Point

Play serves multiple purposes, including an opportunity for building the collaborative alliance with the child and encouraging the child's expression of thoughts and feelings germane to the process. Play also can be a fun break and model healthy interaction for the observing parents.

Stories Told to Apperception Cards

In the third testing session, Melissa invited David to tell stories to cards drawn from the Thematic Apperception Test, Family Apperception Test, and Roberts Apperception Test for Children. The cards were selected to activate schemes that would inform the assessment questions, including sadness, aggression, and David's perception of interpersonal relationships. One of David's stories allowed for a further discussion of rules and consequences between Brad and Karen. David told the story of a boy who was told to clean his room by his mother, but he ignored her and watched TV instead. When the boy heard his mother coming, he started to clean, but after his mother left, he went back to watching TV.

From the observation deck, Brad and Karen discussed how that was exactly what happened at home. David's story illustrated further how the lack of consistent consequences at home facilitated his noncompliance and encouraged him to test limits. Karen seemed to really understand this and expressed the desire to set better limits and boundaries for her son. David's other stories were permeated by themes of sadness, isolation, and hopelessness that he could not solve or resolve. This content provided an opportunity for Brad to again highlight David's vulnerable emotional state. By providing emotional support to Karen, Brad was able to help her connect with what David had been through and see how it affected him.

☞ Teaching Point

Including storytelling opportunities and using carefully chosen apperception cards related to the assessment questions provides an opportunity for the child to construct a narrative that can be examined for both content and form reflective of the child's current state of awareness and resolution. The stories often generate useful discussion with the parents "behind the mirror," and likely build upon earlier themes.

Rorschach

To further investigate David's emotional functioning, reality testing, and self-concept, the Rorschach was introduced in the fourth session. David's responses to the Rorschach supported Brad and

Melissa's hypotheses that David was experiencing feelings of isolation and ongoing emotional stress. The pattern of David's responses on the Rorschach also suggested an underlying and longstanding depression (*Depression Index* of 6), which was also underscored by the content in some of his responses to the cards. For example, David's responses to Card I and Card II were "an old rag" and "a stained rag," which he described as torn apart, ripped on all sides, with pieces coming off and full of holes. These images seemed like metaphors for the raw, painful emotion he was defending against, and his scores suggested that deep down, David did not feel worthwhile and valued. Being able to hear and discuss her son's own despondent responses seemed to get Karen in touch with the possibility that he was suffering with, and trying to cover up, some significant sadness. It is important to note that David reported no depression and high self-esteem on the self-report measures he completed. Finn (1996) has suggested that such discrepancies between the Rorschach and self-report testing indicate the relatively successful use of defenses to ward off underlying states of painful affect.

In discussing David's Rorschach responses with Brad from the observation deck, Karen indicated that it seemed like he might feel like he's not whole, be hurting inside, and feel torn apart. During the extended inquiry (Handler, 2007) of his Rorschach responses, David elaborated on many of his lonely and despondent feelings. Listening to the extended inquiry, Karen continued to express empathy for her son and hypothesized about why he felt the way he did. She commented that David felt like he didn't fit in with his family and friends; he felt left out. She was able to connect that all of the things David had experienced (e.g., painful divorce, domestic violence, conflict with his sister) had contributed to his feelings of hurt and loneliness.

Teaching Point

Similar to stories told to apperception cards, Rorschach responses typically are of great interest to observing parents. They may comment on how their own imagined responses are similar or different to responses their child gave, or they may ask for an understanding of the meaning of particular responses. Although content is only one aspect of scoring and interpreting the Rorschach, some content communicates strongly how children perceive themselves or their environment.

Early Memories Procedure (EMP)

To better understand David's early experiences, perceptions of himself and his family, and his ability to manage emotions, the EMP (Bruhn, 1990) was administered. David's clearest, most negatively rated memory was when he broke his arm while skateboarding. He said that he was skateboarding down a large hill, and one of his wheels got stuck in a crack in the sidewalk. Because he was going so fast, he flipped over and landed on his arm. David also stated that his arm still does not look right. As Karen listened to David's memory of the accident, she said that she worried about David skateboarding because he did not have any protective gear. However, despite her worries, she did not prevent him from skateboarding. Furthermore, David's primary solution for safety while skateboarding was for him to fend for himself (e.g., he should have used grip tape to help him stay on his skateboard). He also suggested that the environment could have been different (if the crack in the sidewalk was not so wide, his wheel would not have gotten stuck). To the assessors, this memory reflected David's sense that he could not count on his mother or anyone else to protect him, and he had to rely on himself. We wondered if his mother was able to consider this possibility.

When asked to describe memories of his mother, father, stepfather, and sister, David described memories that started as positive but then turned negative. David reported something hurtful or dangerous happening to him in each memory. From the observation deck, Karen noted to Brad how "dramatic" or stressful David's life has been and how he was remembering a lot of negative events. She noticed how David would begin to describe a good experience, but then something bad would happen to him. Brad saw this discussion as an opportunity to help Karen begin to change how she responds to David's negativity. Because Brad and Karen noticed that David seemed to get stuck on negative things,

Brad talked with Karen about how she could help him get unstuck. He encouraged her to listen to and accept David's negative feelings and not to push them away or discount them.

🔊 Teaching Point

Using the EMP with children provides insight into the child's state of mind, and similar to apperception cards and the Rorschach, the narratives are of high interest to the observing parents. The procedure tends to stimulate much discussion, especially because parents are often aware of some version of the memories.

ESTABLISHING RELATIONSHIPS WITH THE FAMILY MEMBERS

Following the testing/observing sessions, it is time to reflect on the test findings in relation to the assessment questions *and* to consider what one has learned from the relationships formed with the family members. We focus here on the assessors' experience of the family members and then highlight the findings in our description of the summary/discussion sessions. From the beginning and throughout the TA, Melissa felt positively about David. She found him to be bright, engaging, fun, and quite self-aware. She appreciated how he was responsive to questions and complied with every task he was given. Melissa also perceived David to be a survivor and fighter; someone who has encountered much adversity in his life but has demonstrated resiliency and self-sufficiency (perhaps, we thought, at a cost to him).

Brad and Melissa felt compassion for David's mother, because Karen revealed that she had experienced extensive trauma in her childhood in relation to her domineering father. By providing support and understanding for Karen, Brad and Melissa better understood the impact of Karen's childhood on her personal development and her parenting capacities. She seemed emotionally overwhelmed and frequently jumped from topic to topic; when the topics became too painful or emotionally overwhelming, she seemed to switch to talking about something else. Brad provided Karen with extensive emotional support when she was observing and discussing David's testing sessions, which seemed to help her center and gain empathy for her son. When Carlos attended the sessions, he served as a support and calming influence for her. We were cautiously optimistic that with support she could become a "saucer" for David when his emotional "cup" would overflow.

Brad and Melissa experienced Carlos as insightful and surprisingly psychologically minded; for example, he provided metaphors that Brad and Melissa wove into the parent feedback and the fable for David. Carlos also sometimes acted as an interpreter for David's mother, explaining ideas expressed by Brad or Melissa to her so she could understand them more fully. He also usually functioned as a calming experience for Karen, and we were disappointed that he attended fewer than half of the sessions.

The therapeutic relationship that developed between David and Melissa helped Karen see David in a different light. She noticed how David responded positively to Melissa and complied with her requests. Perhaps most importantly, Brad's therapeutic relationship with Karen facilitated their discussions about the themes that emerged from David's TA: the importance of the relationship (rules without relationship equals rebellion), the importance of structure and consistency, and the need for empathy for David, given his negative life experiences.

Teaching Point

Relationship building is a key tool in TA. Assessors need to give time and attention to developing strong relationships with the parents and the child. Building a relationship with the parents builds trust and comfort so they may share more of their background and life story, which helps the clinician better understand what has shaped their worldview. Building a relationship with the child eases the assessment process and demonstrates that the child can respond positively to someone.

FAMILY INTERVENTION SESSION

In a family intervention session, family members are asked to interact on a task or engage in an activity together. Through this method, the assessment team can test hypotheses and bring family patterns to light through the behaviors family members manifest (Tharinger, Finn, Austin, et al., 2008). This session also helps the assessment team consider how ready the parents are for systemic feedback that may include their role or influence in their child's problems, and thus informs the plan for the subsequent summary/discussion session.

In planning the family intervention session with David and his parents, we drew upon the hypothesis that David's problem behaviors were the result of inadequate structure, lack of consistency, and a lack of positive reinforcement. We thought David was experiencing feelings of rejection, as well as confusion and anxiety, and that these feelings manifested themselves in the angry, disrespectful behaviors Karen and Carlos reported. We hypothesized that if Karen and Carlos could demonstrate their willingness to spend time with David and show that they enjoyed being with him, it would help David feel loved, accepted, and safe. We also thought that David would be more responsive to consequences from his parents after he understood that the consequences were given out of love and concern. Based upon David's positive experience with nondirective play with Melissa over the course of the testing sessions, we thought that this might be a useful technique to teach to Karen and Carlos. In addition, we felt the use of the play techniques would allow Karen opportunities to interact with David without becoming overwhelmed or frustrated. The specific techniques Brad and Melissa focused on teaching Karen and Carlos were praising David's positive behaviors, allowing David to direct the activity, and teaching Carlos to support Karen as she played with David.

At the beginning of the family intervention session, Melissa asked David to create several games using the toys and materials in the room. He created three games, and after explaining the rules to Melissa, David and Melissa played the three games while Brad, Karen, and Carlos watched from the other room over the monitor. Next, David and his mother were asked to play, and Carlos was asked to support Karen as she played with David (e.g., "catch" her if she started to impose her own ideas on the game). Carlos had difficulty following this request and often tried to take over the interaction. Brad and Melissa blocked that behavior and emphasized the need for David's mother to be able to develop skills to play with David. Carlos caught on to the idea and began practicing being supportive of Karen as she played with David.

During the last part of the family session, David and Carlos played together, while David's mother supported Carlos. At first, Carlos had difficulty understanding David's rules, but Karen helped him understand when David explained the rules again. Carlos and David were able to play together well, but Karen had to frequently remind Carlos that it was "just a game" and that he did not have to take the play so seriously. After the session, David, Karen, and Carlos reported that they had enjoyed the play, and Carlos said he saw how he needed to change his behavior to support Karen, rather than take over for her.

Teaching Point

Family intervention sessions provide the opportunity for parents to implement the recommended interventions in a supportive environment. When planning the session, clinicians should select activities that provide in vivo experience of the positive parenting practices discussed "behind the mirror." This allows the parents to experience success through seeing positive child behaviors. This session also provides clinicians with the opportunity to test hypotheses, assess parents' capacity to relate effectively with their child, and evaluate their readiness for feedback.

SUMMARY/DISCUSSION SESSION AND PARENT FEEDBACK LETTER

For some cases, first presenting general findings and then addressing each assessment question in turn fits well. In other cases, all findings can be integrated under the assessment questions. In addition, Finn (2007) suggests organizing the findings by levels that are progressively more discrepant from the parents' view of their child. If the consultations with the parents as they observe their child's testing have been productive, we have found that the parents are ready to hear all or most findings.

Brad and Melissa provided extensive emotional support for David's mother during the summary/discussion session. Although they had already introduced the findings throughout, hearing the findings altogether was still challenging for Karen. Also, Carlos was not able to attend this session, and thus, his usual insight and support were not available to Karen. Brad and Melissa made the feedback as concrete as possible and referred to David's actual testing responses to prime Karen's memory of what she had experienced in earlier sessions. With this process, Karen was able to sit with the integrated findings and answers to her assessment questions. We believed that Karen was trying to reconcile her old perspective of David and his behavior with a new perspective, and it was a struggle for her. We were also optimistic that with some time, discussions with her husband, and attending the child feedback session, she would begin to absorb and act on the new story. Several weeks later, we sent a letter reflecting the findings and process of the summary/discussion session to Karen and Carlos. We include excerpts here to illustrate how we addressed several of their assessment questions.

How Is David's Emotional State?

From the testing we did, it seems like David is experiencing a lot of sadness and some anger. When we worked with David, he didn't seem sad on the outside, but his responses and stories had a lot of sadness in them. This may be one of the ways David copes with his sad feelings; rather than letting them out, he keeps them hidden inside. On the Rorschach, David's responses are similar to responses other children give who are depressed; according to the results and what you've told us, it seems like David has been experiencing a lot of sadness for awhile now. And, one thing we know about kids with depression is that their sadness comes out in different ways. Sometimes depression in children is more difficult to recognize because in addition to feeling sad, they may also be irritable and angry, have aggressive outbursts, or be withdrawn. . . .

Why Is David So Aggressive and Disrespectful?

Some of why David is disrespectful can definitely be tied to the things he saw between you and his father, which we know, Karen, is what you had partly acknowledged before. A lot of times kids model the behaviors they see from their parents, and you described that he saw a lot of anger from his father and also that his father was verbally abusive towards you. You talked a lot about how the kids "walked all over you" and that they felt you "didn't have your own mind." We think that David picked up on a lot of these things and has developed a pattern of feeling like he doesn't have to listen to what he is told. The wonderful thing is that you are aware of some of these things and have taken steps to begin resolving it by setting firmer limits and enforcing consequences for his disrespectful behavior. Because this might be different than what he has experienced earlier in his life, there will likely be some rebelling against it and frustration on his part because he has gotten used to wearing you down until he gets his way. It takes patience and time, but with some of the strategies we give you, hopefully you will see a change in his behavior.

In addition, some of David's disrespectful behavior may be tied to his depression as well. When kids have depression, they often may find it very hard to do things that require a lot of energy, such as cleaning their room and doing other chores. When you ask David to do these reasonable tasks, it may seem like too much to him, and instead of just doing them, he boils over and says ugly things to you. When kids are depressed, they are often quite irritable as well. This seems to be the case for David.

What Can We Do to Help David?

We talked a lot during the assessment about how you can help him become more respectful: spend time with him. This is what we were talking about in regards to the "Relationship without Rules equals Rebellion." What we learned from the testing is that David really values and enjoys the time he spends with both you and Carlos. I think we noted that the times you do spend with him you notice that he appears calmer and responds better to what you ask of him. This approach over time will hopefully help you see lasting changes in his ability to give you the respect you have been looking for. . . .

Teaching Point

Providing thoughtful oral and written answers to parents' initial assessment questions is intended to help them better understand their child and provides the reasoning for why specific recommendations are given. Answers to questions should include parents' own language or explanations they had given during observations to allow parents to better internalize the information.

FEEDBACK SESSION WITH DAVID, KAREN, AND CARLOS

We wrote a fable for David, based on the findings from the assessment and from our sense of what the parents had committed to in terms of changes in the family. A guide for constructing fables is available in Tharinger, Finn, Hersh, et al. (2008). David's fable began by describing a young boy, his mother, and his stepfather. There was a lot of fighting in the family, which made the boy feel bad. He discovered that skateboarding helped him feel better and took his mind off of his problems. The boy wished his family would skateboard with him so they could feel better too. Usually, his family didn't want to do anything fun with the boy, and this made him unhappy. The boy liked skateboarding more than doing his chores, his homework, or anything his mother and stepfather wanted him to do. The boy tried to get around doing his chores so he'd be able to skateboard more, which made his mother and stepfather angry.

The boy usually skateboarded at a community center, and there was going to be a show there for all of the kids to demonstrate stunts they had learned. The boy decided he was going to do a very dangerous trick that involved crossing a long, shaky bridge. One of the skateboarding instructors at the center talked to the boy about the trick he was going to perform and what he would need in order to be successful. The boy said he thought that if his family came and cheered for him he might feel more confident. The instructor and the boy discussed how he could ask his mother and stepfather to come and cheer for him, and the boy was glad he had talked with the instructor about what he needed. That night, after dinner, the boy talked to his mother and his stepfather about his skateboarding show and how he wanted them to come to it. He explained that skateboarding was something he was really good at, and it made him feel really good when he did it.

As the boy talked, he started to feel a lot of sadness and anger inside of him, and he started to cry. His mother and stepfather didn't understand why he was so upset, and he explained that he just wanted them to see him skate and to spend time with him. He said that sometimes it seemed as though they didn't want to be with him at all. The boy's mother and stepfather hadn't realized how much he enjoyed spending time with them. The boy's mother and stepfather were very busy and didn't have a lot of free time, but they decided that they needed to spend more time doing fun things with the boy. They knew the show was important to him, and they agreed to come. The boy asked if they would cheer for him, and they said they would. The boy's mother and stepfather also helped him practice his tricks, and his mother even tried skateboarding. The whole family was smiling more, and the boy was feeling closer to his mother and stepfather. He was even doing more of his chores. Then, the day of the show finally arrived. With his family cheering for him, the boy crossed the bridge and landed safely on the other side. The boy could really feel how much they cared for him, and it was a great day.

Brad and Melissa enjoyed sharing the fable with David, Karen, and Carlos. The atmosphere of the session was positive, and David seemed to enjoy the fable, as did Karen and Carlos. David paid a lot of attention to the events in the fable and seemed to know it was really about him. Karen cried a little during the story, and she seemed to understand the message in the fable. Interestingly, David seemed to think the story was missing something; the bad, painful thing that was supposed to happen to the main character didn't happen. Eventually he seemed to be able to accept the positive middle and ending to the story, despite not having experienced that kind of positive resolution in his own life. Carlos seemed to really connect with the fable, especially the metaphor of the wobbly bridge (a metaphor he had actually given to us in the initial interview). The fable showed Karen and Carlos in story form where they could be headed in real life and what the results of building a relationship and adding structure could look like.

◣ Teaching Point

In our experience, the fables are not only extremely meaningful to children but also summarize the findings and point to the next step for the parents.

RESEARCH FINDINGS

Our research findings indicated that the Therapeutic Assessment had a positive impact on David and his family. Both David and his mother reported that they were pleased with their experience of assessment. The assessment process helped his mother to see David's sadness and develop empathy for him, despite her anger toward him, and led to improvements in her relationship with her son. Specifically, Karen reported an increase in positive feelings toward David, a decrease in negative feelings, and improved overall family communication. On the BASC-2, she also indicated that David was showing significantly fewer overall behavioral problems, as well as fewer internalizing and externalizing symptoms. On the Parents' Experience of Assessment Survey (Finn, Tharinger, & Austin, 2008), David's mother indicated that she had a positive, collaborative relationship with the assessment team. She further stated that she had learned new ways to work with David, and that the assessment process had helped her develop an increased awareness of the systemic causes of David's behavior. She highlighted the importance of the live video feed as a component of comprehensive TA that contributed to her better understanding of David.

SUMMARY

In this chapter we described the comprehensive model of TA with children and provided a case study and teaching points to highlight each part of the process. The idiographic nature of this method of assessment requires clinical flexibility in order to meet each family where they are currently functioning. TA with children offers parents a unique opportunity to better understand their child through observation and ongoing clinical support. It also offers the child a way of communicating their struggles to their parents (both directly and indirectly) through a supportive and collaborative relationship with the assessor. Our experience is that TA offers a powerful method of identifying and understanding child difficulties, uncovering family dynamics, and providing intervention tailored to the unique needs of each family.

REFERENCES

Bruhn, A. R. (1990). *Earliest childhood memories: Vol. 1. Theory and application to clinical practice.* New York: Praeger.

Finn, S. E. (1996). *Manual for using the MMPI-2 as a therapeutic intervention.* Minneapolis: University of Minnesota Press.

Finn, S. E. (2007). *In our clients' shoes: Theory and techniques of therapeutic assessment.* Mahwah, NJ: Lawrence Erlbaum.

Finn, S. E., Tharinger, D. J., & Austin, C. (2008). Parent Experience of Assessment Survey (PEAS). Unpublished test (available from first author).

Hamilton, A. M., Fowler, J. L., Hersh, B., Hall, C., Finn, S. E., Tharinger, D. J., et al. (2009). Why won't my parents help me?: Therapeutic Assessment of a child and her family. *Journal of Personality Assessment, 90,* 108–120.

Handler, L. (2007). The use of therapeutic assessment with children and adolescents. In S. Smith & L. Handler (Eds.), *Clinical asssessment of children and adolescents: A practioner's guide* (53-72). Mahwah, NJ: Lawrence Erlbaum.

Tharinger, D. J., Christopher, G., & Matson, M. (2011). Play, playfulness, and creative expression in therapeutic assessment with children. In S. W. Russ & L. N. Niec (Eds.), *An evidence-based approach to play in intervention and prevention: Integrating developmental and clinical science* (pp. 109–148). New York, NY: Guilford Press.

Tharinger, D. J., Finn, S. E., Austin, C., Gentry, L., Bailey, E., Parton, V., & Fisher, M. (2008). Family sessions as part of child psychological assessment: Goals, techniques, clinical utility, and therapeutic value. *Journal of Personality Assessment, 90,* 547–558.

Tharinger, D. J., Finn, S. E., Gentry, L., Hamilton, A., Fowler, J., Matson, M., Krumholz, L., & Walkowiak, J. (2009). Therapeutic Assessment with children: A pilot study of treatment acceptability and outcome. *Journal of Personality Assessment, 91*(3), 238–244.

Tharinger, D. J., Finn, S. E., Hersh, B., Wilkinson, A., Christopher, G., & Tran, A. (2008). Assessment feedback with parents and pre-adolescent children: A collaborative approach. *Professional Psychology: Research and Practice, 39,* 600–609.

Tharinger, D. J., Krumholz, L., Austin, C., & Matson, M. (in press). The development and model of Therapeutic Assessment with children: Application to school-based assessment. In M. A. Bray & T. J. Kehle (Eds.), *Oxford Press handbook of school psychology.* New York, NY: Oxford University Press.

Tharinger, D. J., & Roberts, M. (in press). Human figure drawings in Therapeutic Assessment with children: Process, product, life context, and systemic impact. In L. Handler (Ed.), *Projective techniques: Research, innovative techniques, and case studies.* Mahwah, NJ: Lawrence Erlbaum.

CHAPTER

16

Collaborative Assessment on an Adolescent Psychiatric Ward: A Psychotic Teenage Girl

Heikki Toivakka

Collaborative assessment in an adolescent psychiatric hospital is challenging, because most of the clients suffer from severe disorders and their cooperation cannot be relied upon. This chapter describes a case from the late 1990s when I started to apply principles of collaborative assessment to my work on the adolescent psychiatric ward of Tampere University Hospital.

When a teenager is admitted to a psychiatric hospital, there is always an issue about the client's own will. Maybe the best starting point is when the adolescent can understand the situation and say, "I do not want to, but I do not see any other option." Some inner motivation in seeking help and cooperating in the assessment often exists from the beginning. Sometimes the parents' authority, often with support from health care or child protection professionals, is the outside force that brings the adolescent to us, saying, "I do not want to, but my parents made me."

At the far end of the continuum are those who are admitted to the hospital according to the Mental Health Act. In Finland, commitment to psychiatric care is allowed for minors in broader terms than for adults. Minors can be committed to and detained in involuntary psychiatric treatment if they suffer from a severe mental disorder (e.g., anorexia or major depression with suicidal risk) and fulfill the additional commitment criteria defined in the Mental Health Act. Adults can be committed to involuntary psychiatric care only if they are mentally ill and fulfill the additional criteria (Turunen, Välimäki, & Kaltiala-Heino, 2010).

Therapeutic/Collaborative Assessment can be problematic with unwilling or involuntary clients, but some techniques and basic principles may be useful in any assessment context (Finn, 2007, p. 263; Purves, 2002). When I get a referral, I contact the client and ask if we could have a little chat. When we meet, I ask if he or she has ever been psychologically assessed or tested, as it is usually called. If there are former experiences, I ask when, where, why, and by whom the assessment was made and what were the results. Quite often the memories of even the psychologist's gender are vague. Most say that nobody told them about the results. Then I tell them that, at least in this situation, things will now be different.

If there are no former assessments I use more time, but I tell everybody some basic facts about the assessment process:

> We have about four to five sessions; I will give you different tasks with instructions about how to do them. After that I have a pile of assessment data and I try to look at them to find answers to the referral questions that your doctor made and you might make. Then we will have a feedback session. Feedback means that I tell you what kind of answers the data give and you give me feedback by telling how my ideas sound to you. If you have any questions or feel unsure about anything, just ask me. I will answer you if it is possible, or tell you why it is not possible. It might be that I do not know or that I know but have to postpone the answer, or something else. After our final meeting I will write a formal report where I will describe what we did, what we found out and what are the answers or recommendations. The report just says the same things that we spoke about and what you thought of them.

It is quite usual that the adolescents see coming to the hospital as unjustified, and their motivation is based on the hope that the assessment will prove that there is nothing wrong with them. I try to find possibilities for collaboration by defining my position as follows:

> Unlike many people, the tests that I use have no personal prejudices; they just assess things as they come. If you are right and there is no reason to be worried about you, I should see it from the results. If that happens, I will tell your doctor and parents. I try to start with no opinion at all, but towards the end of the assessment I will have an opinion and I will tell it to you and others who need to know. But you can't order from me the results that you would like to have. Neither can anybody else.

The next phase of the initial meeting is maybe the most important. From the beginning I have, at least implicitly, expressed that participation is voluntary. Sometimes I get the question: "Do I have to?" My reply is usually something like, "I can't make you do anything. The only way for me is that we do this together. You can refuse, but what would be the probable consequences for you?" Usually, we have now achieved some kind of agreement about cooperation. My next question is: "If you would hire me to do the assessment, what would your questions be?" More often than not the immediate response is silence that seems to say, "Who, me? Nobody's ever asked me." Finding the client's own questions may take time. One solution is to settle for the "doctor's questions" or quite the opposite: "Everybody says that I'm depressed. Is it possible that I am depressed even though I do not feel I am?" Sometimes, though, the client finds an astonishingly relevant and well-focused question that, in itself, may have a therapeutic impact when said aloud.

Based on their earlier experiences, involuntary clients often have good reasons to be unwilling to speak their own worries. I accept these situations and try to use whatever possibilities I find for a therapeutic impact during the assessment process. One way to get the client's own questions is by giving the patient examples of some questions that others have asked. These may be about relationships to parents or friends, school, their own feelings, and so on. During the testing sessions I try to maintain a collaborative relationship and at the same time follow the standard procedures. A comprehensive assessment is usually needed to gain an understanding of complicated problems.

In the feedback summary discussion (Finn, 2007), I first ask how we should proceed, what would be the most important issues for the client? If I do not get a suggestion, I try to start with my own ideas of "Level 1" findings, those that verify the client's way of seeing him- or herself and that will probably be accepted easily (Finn, 2007). It seems that, at least with adolescents, it is useful to speak about the results using a modification of externalizing conversations (White & Epston, 1990; cf. Handler, this volume). In practice I might say, "Let's imagine that the person who provided the assessment data is sitting there on the empty seat in this room. I will tell you about that person, and you can listen. Sometimes I will ask you if there is something that sounds familiar to you and your experiences or feelings or ways of acting. Is that okay for you?" Most people, but especially adolescents in their search for identity, do not accept others saying, "You are like this . . . or like that." Probably, after the third such statement, they would say, at least in their minds, "No, I'm not." This is a way to give them room to listen and not feel that their identity is defined by someone else.

Toward the end of the session I ask some questions: "If there was one thing about this session that would be useful for you to remember, what would it be?" or "If you could remember only one thing about this conversation after you leave this room, what would you want to remember?" More questions include: "If I tell something about this assessment to your parents/doctor/social worker, what would be the most important thing for you, so that they could do what you really need?" This is a way to connect with the client's view and continue the collaboration to the larger context of the case.

FANTASY ANIMAL DRAWINGS WITH ADOLESCENTS

In my work, the referrals for psychological assessment are mostly about diagnoses and treatment planning. I use the usual methods: interview, self-reports, cognitive and neuropsychological tests, Rorschach, Thematic Apperception Tests (TAT), and graphic techniques.

The Fantasy Animal Drawing is usually the last task in the data-gathering phase. I learned the basic idea from Dr. Handler. His publications have mostly dealt with children (Handler, 2007, 2009; Handler & Hilsenroth, 1994). When I started using the method with adolescents, I first tried to imitate Handler's case illustrations. During the next years I adapted the method to my working style and context and eventually it developed into a loosely structured five-phase model (Toivakka, 2005, 2009). An outline of this procedure follows:

1. I give the client a sheet of paper and a pencil with the instruction, "Draw a make-believe animal, an animal that nobody's ever seen before" (Handler, 2007). At first the clients may need some encouragement to get started, but most of the time they start right away.

2. When the drawing is ready, I ask about the animal's name and ask the client to write it on the paper. If the client does not find a name easily, I try to offer some help by speaking generally about names: "Some names tell you something about the animal, for instance, how it looks, like 'bluebird'; some names are just names, like 'cat' or 'dog.' What would this be?"

3. Next I ask questions about the drawing, as if it were a real animal (e.g., the client was a zoologist who found it, and I was a reporter writing an article about it). I start with questions like, "What kind of an animal is this?" Then I continue "interviewing" the client about how it came about, where it lives, what are its eating habits, social habits, natural enemies, ways of protecting itself, and so on, letting the answers guide my interview forward.

4. Then I say, "Tell me a story about this animal. Once upon a time there was. . . . You tell it and I'll write it down." Often more encouragement is needed. Many adolescents start describing the "facts" they told before. In that case I say, "Okay, that's very good, go on. . . . One day . . . how would you go on . . ."

5. After the client's story I say, "Let's see if I have learned anything about this animal. Is it okay if I try to tell *you* a story about it?" As Handler (2007) recommends, I try to get hold of the

essential conflict in the client's story and offer a new solution to it. The story is based on the client's story, but by this time I have the background information and preliminary ideas from other assessment data that can help me in constructing the story. After this counter-story I ask the client's opinion of my story. If the client accepts my version or says that it was a better story, I see it as a positive indication for psychotherapy, the ability to consider another self-narrative. Sometimes the client's story ends in total destruction that gives no chance to find new openings. Then I might ask about any points in the story where something else could have happened and made a different ending possible.

If I get stuck in my story, I may ask the client to help me. Yet, if I get no idea, I don't force myself to make up a counter-story. Partly this happens because of time limitations.

I do not know about any published quantitative research about adolescents' fantasy animals. My experience has brought up some hypothetical ideas. The sequence starts from a relatively easy task, drawing. By this time the client has probably taken many other tests and even made some drawings. In my practice about 90% of clients agree to draw the fantasy animal. Total refusal usually reflects motivational problems and opposition that have already been seen all along the assessment process. Another possibility is that for some adolescents this task is a regressive pull that they can't cope with, and they refuse by saying that it is childish or stupid.

Naming seems to be more difficult. Of those who do the drawing, 90% find a name for their animal, with some assistance. Inability in this phase seems to reflect identity problems that also appear elsewhere in the material. Telling a story is the most difficult part. About two thirds can tell a story with a real plot, one fifth stick to a description of the picture or say several sentences, and the rest of the clients cannot provide anything, even with support. Often these difficulties seem to be related with constriction of affect or an insecure, avoidant attachment style.

The fantasy animal drawing can be used in an idiographic way to give information about the client's self-experience, interpersonal relating, readiness to engage in a psychotherapeutic relationship, prognosis, and attachment style.

THE CASE OF TEA

Presenting Issues

Tea, a 17-year-old girl, was referred to our outpatient clinic by a general practitioner because of depression, suicidality, self-cutting, and alcohol abuse. The resident adolescent psychiatrist's impression from the first appointment was that Tea might need antidepressant medication and hospital treatment. Tea wanted to get help and had a positive attitude toward the possibility of inpatient treatment. After waiting four weeks, she was admitted, voluntarily, to the adolescent psychiatric hospital ward.

Background Information

The outpatient clinic charts and initial interviews with Tea and her mother on the ward brought out the following account of Tea's life history: Tea is the younger of two children. Her sister is three years older and by Tea's description, flawless, "pure as the driven snow," and she herself was the "black sheep" of the family. Her father had retired 10 years ago after a brain infarct when Tea was 7 years old. When the incident happened, only Tea and her father were at home. He had the infarct in the yard, and when her mother came home she found her husband lying on the ground. Tea was close to him, skipping rope. She had been a "daddy's girl," but later their relationship deteriorated, partly because, despite rehabilitation, her father's right hand was paralyzed, he had dysphasic symptoms, and he was quite irritable. Tea and her father argued a lot, and her mother tried to calm them down. On the other hand, her mother explained that Tea seemed to have some guilty feelings concerning her father's illness, because she had not called an ambulance when he had the brain infarct. Tea and her mother were quite close to each other, and at home Tea was quite childishly dependent on her mother.

In primary school Tea's grades had been average, but in junior high school they dropped quite dramatically and she failed twice to graduate. She started self-cutting at the age of 13. She had attempted suicide twice, once by slashing her wrists and once by taking an overdose of diazepam. Supposedly those situations had been taken care of at home, between Tea and her mother. Her father heard about them only when Tea was in the hospital.

During the ongoing year, things had been getting more and more out of hand. Her alcohol consumption had increased; she was drunk almost every weekend. She drank a minimum of half a liter of hard liquor per night. Tea described herself as short-tempered, even while she was sober, but when she was drunk, she had assaulted unknown persons on the street several times. Sometimes the police interfered and had taken her to jail for the night. She was worried about her depression, suicidal thoughts, and lack of control of her drinking, aggressiveness, and self-injury.

During the first weeks in the hospital, Tea's behavior was often defiant and she tested the limits of the staff on the ward. On the other hand, she was regressive and fearful. She told the nurses about threatening figures she saw in the dark and voices she heard during the nights.

Assessment Referral

About two weeks after Tea's admission her resident adolescent psychiatrist made a referral for psychological assessment. I was asked to do a psychological assessment to support her diagnosis and treatment planning. Because I met with the resident daily, we could collaborate in clarifying her goals for the assessment (Finn, 2007). It turned out that the main goal was finding out if Tea was psychotic, maybe schizophrenic. Another hypothesis was that her hallucinations were of a dissociative nature.

Initial Session With Tea and Her Questions

I had previously met Tea in passing on the ward, but after getting the referral I contacted her and asked if we could have a chat about the referral. She was a sturdy girl, about 5 feet 6 inches tall and weighed 171 pounds. She had cropped hair, lots of earrings, her lower lip and tongue were pierced, and she wore hip-hop-style clothes. I told her how the assessment would proceed and asked if she had any questions about this information or any other things I did not mention. She had none. I read her the referral, sentence by sentence, and she confirmed the given facts. I asked if there was something missing that should have been there, but nothing was mentioned. Then I asked, "If you would hire me to do this assessment, what would be your own questions?" She said she hoped to get some clarification of her auditory and visual hallucinations. She seemed to be quite eager to tell me about them.

I probably missed a really important chance here since, according to my notes, I did not interview her more precisely about this issue. At least I could have asked some of the following questions: "Why do you want to get clarification?" or "If you got the answers, how could you use them?" or "What difference would it make to your depression, control problems, or other things?" or "What would be the worst possible outcome for you?" In hindsight I see at least two possibilities for my mistake, and both can be true. I was only starting to apply the Collaborative/Therapeutic Assessment principles in my work, and I might have been a little anxious about my own safety in her presence. Actually, if the latter was true I could have said it aloud: "I've heard that you can be quite dangerous, even to strangers. Should I be worried about my own safety with you?"

Assessment Sessions

During the assessment sessions Tea was cooperative most of the time and followed the instructions. However, when we had worked 50 minutes with the WAIS-R (Wechsler, 1992), she asked if we could have a break so that she could go smoke a cigarette. I saw this as kind of a test for me and decided to see what would happen if I did not give her permission. She took it quite easily, and we continued the testing for another hour. In following sessions she did not try to test the limits of the situation anymore.

Cognitive Assessment

Tea's cognitive performance was Low Average, Verbal IQ = 94, Performance IQ = 94, Full Scale IQ = 93. The range of the WAIS-R subtest standard scores was from 5 (Digit Span) to 11 (Picture Completion). She had some difficulties in finding accurate verbal expressions and at least twice she mixed words in a way that made me think about, at least, a mild dysphasic disorder. When I asked her about this, she told me about situations when she mixed up words in her early school years. Later I heard from her mother that Tea had difficulties in reading in the first and second grade and that she received some remedial instruction.

I could not do a more in-depth neuropsychological screening because at the time I did not have suitable tools, but I recommended that Tea should be referred for further assessment. For the referral question about possible schizophrenia, it would have been essential to get more information about her working memory, declarative memory, attention, and executive functions.

Personality Assessment

We continued with the Rorschach, Comprehensive System (Exner, 2003) and drawing tests: human figure drawing (DAP) and Fantasy Animal Drawing (Handler, 2007). Tea provided a Rorschach protocol of 28 responses with a very avoidant style (Lambda = 6.00). The basic indices pointed to a psychotic, maybe paranoid condition (Perceptual Thinking Index = 4, Hypervigilance Index = positive), and Ego Impairment Index = 1.77, pointing to a risk of relapse (Perry et al., 2003; Stokes et al., 2003). The Structural Summary (see Table 16.1) is rich with data, but I will focus here on the response contents.

After the Response Phase and Inquiry, we had a discussion about some of her responses (Handler, 2009):

> **Card III R8**: Two women who are arguing and who have a good heart. [INQ:] There are the women and there is the heart and there is what they are arguing about. (arguing?) They both touch it—pull it. (good heart?) It is good because it's red and otherwise they are black.

H. T.: If those women could talk, what would they say?
   T: Let it go, we'll split it in half.

Table 16.1 Comprehensive System 5th Edition Structural Summary

Location Features	Determinants	Contents	Approach

Approach

N	$FV + VF + V + FD > 2$
Y	Col-Shd Bl > 0
N	Ego, .31 or $>.44$
Y	MOR > 3
Y	Zd $> \pm 3.5$
Y	es $>$ EA
N	$CF + C >$ FC
Y	$X+\% < .70$
Y	S > 3
N	P < 3 or > 8
N	Pure H < 2
N	R < 17
5	TOTAL

Location Features

Zf	= 11
ZSum	= 40.5
ZEst	= 34.5
W	= 6
D	= 18
W + D	= 24
Dd	= 4
S	= 5

DQ

+	= 5
o	= 23
v/+	= 0
v	= 0

Form Quality

	FQx	MQual	W+D
+	= 0	= 0	= 0
o	= 9	= 1	= 7
u	= 9	= 0	= 8
−	= 10	= 1	= 9
none	= 0	= 0	= 0

Determinants

Blends: Ma.FC.FC′

Single

M	= 1
FM	= 2
m	= 0
FC	= 0
CF	= 0
C	= 0
Cn	= 0
FC′	= 0
C′F	= 0
C′	= 0
FT	= 0
TF	= 0
T	= 0
FV	= 0
VF	= 0
V	= 0
FY	= 0
YF	= 0
Y	= 0
Fr	= 0
Rf	= 0
FD	= 0
F	= 24
(2)	= 10

Contents

H	= 2	Hh	= 1
(H)	= 2	Ls	= 0
Hd	= 1	Na	= 1
(Hd)	= 3	Sc	= 2
Hx	= 0	Sx	= 0
A	= 12	Xy	= 0
(A)	= 0	Id	= 1
Ad	= 6		
(Ad)	= 0		
An	= 3		
Art	= 1		
Ay	= 0		
Bl	= 0		
Bt	= 1		
Cg	= 0		
Cl	= 0		
Ex	= 0		
Fd	= 0		
Fi	= 0		
Ge	= 0		

Special Scores

		Lv1	Lv2
DV = 0		0×1	0×2
INC = 2		2×2	1×4
DR = 0		0×3	0×6
FAB = 0		0×4	3×7
ALOG = 0		0×5	
CON = 0		0×7	

Raw Sum6 = 4
Wgtd Sum6 = 29

AB	= 0	GHR	= 4
AG	= 1	PHR	= 4
COP	= 0	MOR	= 4
CP	= 0	PER	= 0
		PSV	= 0

RATIOS, PERCENTAGES, AND DERIVATIONS

R = 28	L = 6.00

EB = 2:0.5	EA = 2.5	EBPer = NA
eb = 2:1	es = 3	D = −1
	Adj es = 3	Adj D = 0

FM = 2	SumC′ = 1	SumT = 0
m = 0	SumV = 0	SumY = 0

FC:CF+C	= 1:0	COP	= 0
Pure C	= 0	GHR:PHR	= 4:4
SmC′:WSmC	= 1:0.5	a:p	= 4:0
Afr	= 0.56	Food	= 0
S	= 5	SumT	= 0
Blends/R	= 1:28	Human Cont	= 8
CP	= 0	PureH	= 2
		PER	= 0
		Isol Indx	= 0.11

AG = 1

XA%	= 0.64	Zf	= 11	3r+(2)/R	= 0.36
WDA%	= 0.63	W:D:Dd	= 6:18:4	Fr+rF	= 0
X−%	= 0.35	W:M	= 6:2	SumV	= 0
S−	= 1	Zd	= +6.00	FD	= 0
P	= 6	PSV	= 0	An+Xy	= 3
X+%	= 0.32	DQ+	= 5	MOR	= 4
Xu%	= 0.32	DQv	= 0	H:(H)+Hd+(Hd)	= 2:6

		Sum6	= 6
		Lv2	= 4
a:p	= 4:0	WSum6	= 29
Ma:Mp	= 2:0	M−	= 1
2AB+Art + Ay	= 1	Mnone	= 0
MOR	= 4		

PTI = 4	DEPI = 4	CDI = 3	S-CON = 6	HVI = YES	OBS = NO

Card IV, R 11: A monster that's like coming towards you; it looks kinda like my hallucination. [INQ:] Hands, head, feet, tail. (monster?) Torn hands, big feet, small head, snout—nose.

H. T.:   If it could speak?

T: Be afraid of me!

To me this sounded like Tea wanted to tell me something about her feeling of threat, the monster, but also something about an inner conflict; did the women want to have it all or could they find a solution and share whatever they were arguing about. Again, I missed a point: I could have asked her to tell more about these responses: "Tell me a story about those women. How did they get into this situation? What are their other options?" Here the responses could be used like TAT stories (Handler, 2009).

Tea's Human Figure Drawing (Figure 16.1) was a clear-cut self-image, and she was well aware of it, as the following account shows:

T: It is a young woman, about 17 years old.

H. T.:   Who did you think about when you drew it?

T: Myself.

H. T.:   What is she thinking?

T: She's angry about something. She's in a bad temper.

H. T.:   Tell me more.

T: She thinks that I'm not afraid of anybody; just try me if you dare.

H. T.:   How is she feeling?

T: She is mad and bitter because of things that happened, like—somebody's taken her boyfriend, somebody hit her.

H. T.:   Of all the people that you know, who comes into your mind from that picture?

T: Me, the appearance, the defiant look.

H. T.:   What would this person need most?

T: Love and care, she has not got enough.

It was quite clear that Tea had conscious awareness concerning her conflict between needs of independence and those of care. I should have

Figure 16.1   Tea's Human Figure Drawing

asked more about "things that happened," because it sounded like she gave a hint to some traumatic experience, even though there was nothing of the kind in the background information, except for her father's brain infarct.

Fantasy Animal Drawing

Finally Tea drew the fantasy animal, "an animal that nobody has ever seen or heard of before." She took the crayons and started drawing immediately. Tea called her fantasy animal "Lollo." The word does not mean anything in Finnish, but it has connotations with something like jelly, fat, or being formless.

She told the following story:

> T.:   It is a meat-eater, it has those octopus hands that it uses for hunting. It takes cover, it lives in the sea and eats fish—and humans. It has those feelers. It sees, but is not seen. Bigger fish are its enemies.
>
> H. T.:   Tell me a story about Lollo. Once upon a time . . . ?
>
> T: Once upon a time there was Lollo; it was born from its mother's—mouth. Mom was Tollo, dad was Pollo. It ate, grew, learned to hunt, and became good at it. It wanted to have everything, wanted to control everything, but it really can't. It is big, but it is weak. One day a shark bit off one of its arms. It went to its mother. Mother said: Go and take yourself a new arm from somebody else. It got a new hand and was satisfied.

It is hard to say if Tea's way of telling the story was poetic or psychotic. Lollo's mother's response showed no love or care or empathy.

Figure 16.2   Tea's Fantasy Animal Drawing

Actually, it seemed to encourage aggressive action. The parent's names "Tollo" and "Pollo" may reflect Tea's tendency to perseveration. On the other hand, in Finnish, they have a connotation of stupidity. I decided to focus on Lollo's weakness and greed.

H. T.: That was a nice story. Now, is it okay if I try to tell a story about Lollo to see if I have learned anything about it?

T: Go ahead.

H. T.: Lollo was big, but weak, and that's why its life was hard. It had to hide in a safe place for a long time and think about a solution. Help me, Tea, what would happen next?

T: It grew a skin.

H. T.: Thank you. Okay, Lollo had a very thin skin and that made it feel vulnerable. Almost everything that touched it felt painful. It started to grow a thicker skin, and little by little it noticed that things were not so painful. And then it noticed that having everything and controlling everything was not so important anymore. And little by little it got new friends and it felt that they were reliable and caring. And it found out that sharing things with others could be as much fun as having it all to yourself. End of story. Well, how did that sound?

T: It was a good story.

As you see, I had some trouble with my plan, and I solved it by asking Tea, "What would happen next?" I hoped that the idea of "growing a skin" could be a metaphor for individuation and giving up the paranoid feeling of outside threat. On the other hand, Tea might see it as a permit to continue her tough role as a way of self-defense. So, maybe I should have asked more: "What made it a good story?" "How would Lollo begin to take the first steps to growing a skin?" "What would be the most difficult things for it?" "Who could help Lollo in its mission?" Bringing some benevolent animals into the part about the safe place might have triggered some response about Tea's readiness for a psychotherapeutic relationship.

Actually, this was probably the most therapeutic incident in our work together. After a couple of days we had a feedback session. I told Tea about my impressions, based on the assessment data, and asked what she thought about them. Remembering Tea's avoidant, "high Lambda" Rorschach protocol, I tried to express myself in simple terms. That did not help. We did not find a common understanding. Tea did not object to my ideas; it looked more that she did not perceive connections between things or link them to her own experience.

Feedback to Parents

About a week later, Tea made deep cuts again to her arms. She was anxious and delusional. Her behavior could not be contained without physical restraint, and she was committed to involuntary treatment. The crisis resolved in a couple of weeks, after the addition of antipsychotic medication and setting firm limits for Tea.

It was then possible to arrange a meeting where Tea, both of her parents, and the ward team discussed Tea's situation and the treatment plan. The atmosphere was quite stressed, Tea's mother was critical, and her attitude toward Tea and the treatment team was very hostile. She probably felt misunderstood when we tried to tell her about the strengths of her daughter. Unfortunately, this happens quite often: We try to find the good points, and the parents feel that we do not understand their worries.

The meeting seemed to arrive at a dead end. On an impulse I asked Tea if I could show her Fantasy Animal Drawing and tell her story about it. I got her permission and showed the picture to everybody and read aloud my notes about Lollo. Everybody was silent for a moment. Then the mother started to cry, silently. I probably grasped her feeling and said, "It was really a sad story, wasn't it?" After this the atmosphere changed; we could speak together and make a plan to help Tea.

This was the second situation where the fantasy animal seemed to have a therapeutic impact in Tea's assessment. Unfortunately, it does not work as a lockpick. Later I tried the same approach on another case. The parents, who did not seem to understand their child's problems, just laughed when I told the sad story about their daughter's fantasy animal. The parents' reaction might be an indication of their motivation, or rather, lack of motivation, to work for their child's benefit.

Follow-Up

Tea left the hospital about three months later. Her behavior on the ward had mostly been cooperative, but at times she was challenging and rebellious. The treatment plan included weekly sessions with her personal psychiatric nurse, family sessions, and participation in the ward's group activities. Antipsychotic medication had helped in reducing her psychotic symptoms. When her psychotic experiences subsided, she reported having a lack of energy and initiative and was depressed. An antidepressant was added to her medication. During the hospital treatment, she stopped cutting herself. She spent the weekends at home. Tea and her father had found better ways to get along and even give positive feedback to each other. The atmosphere at home was optimistic and much lighter. The relationship with her mother seemed more age-appropriate. Tea's functioning at home and with her friends was more controlled; she used alcohol only occasionally. She was referred to continue her therapy at our outpatient clinic.

From Tea's charts I saw that her contact with the adolescent outpatient clinic ended 10 months later. She was described as relatively well functioning. Anxiety, depression, and psychotic symptoms had almost totally disappeared. She did not harm herself, and her alcohol intake was moderate. This made me think that her psychotic-like experiences were expressions of high-level anxiety and searching for care and safety, rather than signs of schizophrenia.

SUMMARY

Creating a collaborative assessment relationship with adolescent psychiatric patients is challenging, but also rewarding. Even if the cooperation is good, we cannot be sure of the therapeutic gains of the assessment. One complicating problem is the continuing flow of client admissions and discharges that leave no time for systematically planned assessment intervention sessions. If I had more time, I would follow Finn's (2007) recommendations: Have a peaceful conversation with the adolescent and the parents before the assessment, and try to bring out the parents' questions and worries. After that I would speak privately with the client and ask about his or her thoughts about the parents' questions and then about his or her own assessment questions. Nowadays my interventions are mostly improvised, as in the feedback to Tea's parents, but I could use more time in planning how to use the data I have.

This being said, I must also state that bringing some principles and techniques of Collaborative/Therapeutic Assessment to an adolescent psychiatric ward's everyday practice during the last 10 years has probably brought out more useful assessment results, better treatment plans, better client satisfaction, and sometimes even a lasting psychotherapeutic effect. The self-critical points in the case description are an effort to describe what I have learned about Collaborative/Therapeutic Assessment after my early work with Tea.

Teaching Points

Some of the following points may have been implicitly included in the preceding text, but by listing them here I want to emphasize their importance in the assessment of hospitalized adolescents:

- Respect the autonomy of the adolescent client, especially an involuntary client. Support the client's sense of agency by giving freedom of choice, when it is possible.
- State explicitly that participation in the assessment is voluntary, that you do not take a refusal personally, and that you will help the client in assessing the consequences of refusing to participate.
- If there is a conflict between the adolescent and the parents, do not take sides and do not try to explain the parents' view to the client.
- Do not understand the client's ideas too easily. Adolescents often complain that nobody understands them. Almost as often, they do not want to be understood immediately. If you imagine that you understand something, make a question about it to the client and prepare yourself for a surprise. Accept the response and make another question.
- Do not overestimate the client's self-reflective capacity. If you ask about feelings or thoughts, "I don't know" may be the precisely correct answer.

- Invite the client to help you in building feedback for parents and other concerned adults.
- Update regularly your knowledge of adolescent development and the methods that you use. Administer the tests "by the book," but be ready to bend the rules and improvise if it is essential for the collaborative relationship.
- Maintain a stance of playful seriousness or serious playfulness to help your client in finding new self-narratives or solutions.

REFERENCES

Exner, J. E. (2003). *The Rorschach: A comprehensive system* (4th ed.). Hoboken, NJ: Wiley.

Finn, S. E. (2007). *In our clients' shoes: Theory and techniques of Therapeutic Assessment*. Mahwah, NJ: Erlbaum.

Handler, L. (2007). The use of therapeutic assessment with children and adolescents. In S. R. Smith & L. Handler (Eds.), *The clinical assessment of children and adolescents* (pp. 53–72). Mahwah, NJ: Erlbaum.

Handler, L. (2009). Empathic insights from the Rorschach: Paul Lerner's legacy. *Journal of Personality Assessment, 91,* 15–19.

Handler, L., & Hilsenroth, M. (1994, April). *The use of a fantasy animal drawing and storytelling technique in assessment and psychotherapy*. Paper presented at the Annual Meeting, Society for Personality Assessment, Chicago, IL.

Perry, W., Minassian, A., Cadenhead, J. S., & Braff, D. (2003). The use of the Ego Impairment Index across the schizophrenia spectrum. *Journal of Personality Assessment, 80,* 50–57.

Purves, C. (2002). Collaborative assessment with involuntary populations: Foster children and their mothers. *The Humanistic Psychologist, 30,* 164–174.

Stokes, J., Pogge, D., Powell-Lunder, J., Ward, A., Bilginer, L., & DeLuca, V. (2003). The Rorschach Ego-Impairment Index: Prediction of treatment outcome in a child psychiatric population. *Journal of Personality Assessment, 76,* 209–229.

Toivakka, H. (2005, July). *The Draw-A-Make-Believe-Animal technique in therapeutic assessment of hospitalized adolescents*. Paper presented at the XVIII International Congress of Rorschach and Projective Methods, Barcelona, Spain.

Toivakka, H. (2009, March). *Using assessment results as family interventions with hospitalized adolescents*. Paper presented at the Annual Meeting, Society for Personality Assessment, Chicago, IL.

Turunen, S., Välimäki, M., & Kaltiala-Heino, R. (2010). Psychiatrists' views of compulsory psychiatric care of minors. *International Journal of Law and Psychiatry, 33*, 35–42.

Wechsler, D. (1992). *WAIS-R*. Helsinki, Finland: Psykologien Kustannus.

White, M., & Epston, D. (1990). *Narrative means to therapeutic ends*. New York: W. W. Norton.

Special Applications

Therapeutic Assessment Alternative to Custody Evaluation: An Adolescent Whose Parents Could Not Stop Fighting[1]

F. BARTON EVANS

Therapeutic Assessment (TA; Finn, 2007) has increasingly become well known for powerfully validating and life-changing clinical feedback in an "experience-near" fashion (see Finn, 2007). A growing literature indicates that TA is an effective treatment approach in working with troubled children and their parents (Hamilton et al., 2009; Handler, 2007; Smith & Handler, 2009; Smith, Handler, & Nash, 2010; Smith et al., 2009; Tharinger et al., 2008, 2009) as well as adolescents and their parents (Tharinger, Finn, Gentry, & Matson, in press). This therapeutic approach has rarely been considered in the context of issues normally reserved for forensic psychology, although a successful

---

[1]Originally presented in part as a paper for the symposium *Life Validity of the Rorschach via Collaborative Assessment*, S. E. Finn (Chair), International Rorschach Congress, Leuven, Belgium, July 24, 2008.

court project through the Center for Therapeutic Assessment in Austin, TX (Finn, personal communication) demonstrated the utility of TA as an alternative child custody/parenting plan evaluation (CC/PPE). What is not well known is how TA can be used in legal or quasi-legal settings to accomplish similar goals, and perhaps in even more effective ways.

Although many forensic psychologists believe that treatment approaches such as TA run counter to forensic assessment (see Greenberg & Shuman, 1997), there are many opportunities where TA can help resolve contentious legal situations by empowering the parent litigants themselves. This hybrid approach is especially effective when a mastery of TA is blended with an understanding of legal principles, as well as forensic neutrality, which incorporates both compassion and skepticism as dual lenses of observation (see Evans, 2005). The purpose of this chapter is to present an adaptation of the TA model as an alternative to CC/PPE, providing a detailed case study illustrating its potential.

TA IN CC/PPE

Beginning with Schutz et al.'s (Schutz, Dixon, Lindenberger, & Ruther, 1989) seminal work, the field of CC/PPE has provided domestic courts with expert psychological consultation on very difficult decisions regarding determination of parents' time-sharing and decision-sharing in regard to their children in contentious divorce settlements. While the legal standard for this court matter is "the best interest of the child" (with "parenting capacity" as an important consideration), the adversarial nature of the legal system fuels contentious litigation. In turn, this can lead to a cascading pattern of increased parental conflict, which has been shown to be the most salient factor for poor long-term adjustment in children of divorce (see Baris et al., 2000; Garrity & Baris, 1997; Johnston, Roseby, & Kuehnle, 2009). Alternatives have been offered, such as parent coordination in the fields of psychology (Johnston et al., 2009; also see the *Journal of Child Custody*'s special issue on parenting coordination, Sullivan, 2008) and collaborative law in the legal arena (Tesler & Thompson, 2006; Webb & Ousky, 2006). Although they are valuable innovations, neither of these solutions fully addresses fundamental long-term problems for children in high-conflict divorce litigation, such as breaking the destructive pattern of parental conflict and replacing it with cooperative coparenting.

In CC/PPE, a comprehensive psychological assessment is conducted, but parental feedback and therapeutic intervention are under-emphasized, because the primary task is to provide consultation to the domestic court judge or domestic court master. The rules and dictates of the litigious legal system predominate, and it is understood that the Court is the psychologist's client. In my experience, both the grueling process and the outcome of highly contentious divorce proceedings de-emphasize the needs of children trapped between warring parents. Additionally, court-determined parenting arrangements frequently are followed by low compliance between the parents, leading to further destructive litigation, with children caught in the middle (Johnston et al., 2009).

For those in the legal profession who recognize this basic difficulty, the collaborative law approach (Tesler & Thompson, 2006; Webb & Ousky, 2006) provides mediation and legal services with the goal of settling the legal dispute without litigation. Before beginning a collaborative law process, the parties and their attorneys agree that the attorneys will cease to represent their clients if the case goes into litigation. This collaborative process goes forward unless the parties remain deadlocked and decide on litigation, at which point the collaborative attorneys are replaced by litigating attorneys. The collaborative law approach is a highly significant advancement in domestic matters in that it reduces conflict of interest. As a result, attorneys do not benefit from protracted litigation when negotiation of an agreement fails.

In my experience, a modified version of TA also offers a powerful and affirming alternative to CC/PPE by intervening directly with divorcing parents. TA employs psychological assessment as an "empathy magnifier" (Finn & Tonsager, 2002) for parents regarding the needs of their children, thereby accessing the most powerful motivation for parents to settle their dispute. TA focuses on helping parents resolve their differences in the care and time-sharing of their children, while also helping parents look to a future in which they can continue a long-term collaborative parental relationship for the benefit of their children. In order to do that, the TA assessor works on finding common interests as well as reducing, rather than increasing, parental splitting (e.g., seeing the other parent as "all bad") and projection (e.g., seeing aggression in the other parent and denying his or her own), which are so common in high-conflict divorce proceedings. Additionally, working with parents to develop a collaborative relationship provides a lasting benefit for children well beyond what could be accomplished in a protracted litigation. Court-appointed child custody evaluators commonly experience a powerful pull from parents and attorneys alike to take sides. By having everyone on the "same side of the table," the TA assessor is in a much better position to help parents negotiate a parenting plan based more on the children's needs and interests.

Although it is beyond the scope of this chapter to fully describe the many details involved in conducting TA as an alternative to CC/PPE (see Evans, 2009), I will briefly summarize the advantages of TA in this context before turning to a case illustration. First, this model is responsive to the needs and interests of parents and their children. Because it does not require the often voluminous and time-consuming review of legal records and other collateral information, TA is significantly less expensive to conduct than CC/PPE and has the strong potential for lowering legal bills. TA allows parents to have increased control over the outcome of their dispute. TA focuses on parents' and children's specific interests and emotional needs and can lead to resolutions that are far more responsive to children's needs than legal agreements, especially those imposed by judges or law masters.

Additionally, the process of TA is inherently likely to be less conflictual. After jointly identifying parents' underlying anxieties and emotional issues, the "good parent/bad parent" splitting and projection that is at the core of the difficulty of resolving disputes can be addressed, reframed, and changed. The adversarial, win/lose nature of litigation often found in domestic proceedings very often increases and even "sets in stone" splitting for both parents and children. Beyond deactivating splitting, TA teaches parental cooperation in regard to specific goals. One of the more interesting findings in studies of the long-term psychological outcomes for children of high-conflict divorce is the better adjustment rate of children from "high conflict, high cooperation" coparenting (Garrity &

Barris, 1997). When parents who do not get along well, and may actively dislike each other, learn to cooperate in a limited and specific way around the needs of their children, they send a powerful message to their children about their importance as people and about learning that negotiating with adversaries can have positive results.

Second, a TA alternative to CC/PPE is responsive to the interests of attorneys. It is my experience that most domestic attorneys are interested in positive, straightforward, and durable agreements that have good outcomes for children. TA offers a strong possibility of increased resolution of perhaps the most contentious aspects of many divorce proceedings. Many attorneys are well aware of what they can and cannot offer to the best interest of children under the limitation of the CC/PPE model. High-conflict divorces with suffering children who are stuck in the middle are often highly distressing to many domestic attorneys, keeping them up late at night more often than concerns about who gets the living room furniture or how much retirement goes to each party. Such attorneys frequently understand the damage done to children caused by protracted, high-conflict legal proceeding and are likely to embrace the possibility of less litigation involving children. Another potential positive outcome of successful resolution of parenting issues using TA is an increased capacity to negotiate and cooperate for property and other matters.

Last, a TA alternative to CC/PPE is responsive to the interests of psychologists. Simply put, TA utilizes what psychologists do best—that is, treatment and assessment for a positive therapeutic benefit—and as a result is more likely to be satisfying professionally. TA practitioners end up working on the behalf of children and parents instead of primarily for the court and are likely to experience greater effectiveness rather than the helplessness about negative outcomes that are all too common in domestic court. With this said, I caution practitioners not to enter lightly into practice of TA as an alternative to CC/PPE. The work requires at least a knowledge both of TA with difficult families and of the legal underpinnings of CC/PPE to avoid the many pitfalls associated with work so close to the legal issues. A third expertise is also needed in developing negotiation skills associated with domestic mediation

(Folberg, Milne, & Salem, 2004), if the TA practitioner wishes to also work with attorneys and their clients in fashioning agreements regarding parenting plans.

CASE STUDY

Context of Referral

This case describes a TA intervention with parents who had been divorced for more than 12 years and continually feuded over their 15-year-old son, leading to many cross-recriminations and multiple court appearances. I was originally contacted by a domestic attorney who requested that I conduct a parenting plan evaluation of this adolescent. As always, I asked to speak together with both attorneys, and a conference call was arranged. The attorneys told me that this was a high-conflict set of parents who had been divorced for many years, but who had been in court every year for the past 12 years, fighting over some point regarding the time-sharing or decision-making for their son. I offered to conduct a Therapeutic Assessment in lieu of a custody evaluation, explaining the purposes and advantages of TA. I described the process leading to a feedback session with the parties and attorneys where the results of the evaluation of the adolescent would be given to the parents. Hopefully, feedback could lead to a mediated agreement between the parents, which would be responsive to the adolescent's current needs. I established rules for my subsequent depositions and court testimony; that is, that I could be called only as a fact witness to describe the TA and not as an expert who would offer a specific parenting plan regarding time-sharing and decision-making responsibility. A written agreement to this effect would need to be signed by the attorneys and their clients before I would begin the TA.

The goal of resolving the parents' current dispute would be served by assessing the adolescent and assisting both of his parents in developing a mutually agreeable parenting plan focusing on his current needs and issues. Fortunately, both attorneys were looking for a way to stop the continual court actions, which they both agreed were unnecessary and difficult on the adolescent. The attorneys for the parents agreed to introduce the idea to their clients, and within several days they contacted me to say that the parents were interested.

Meeting With Attorneys and Parents

I initially met with both of the attorneys and the parents (whom I shall call Fred and Kim) together to describe the goals and methods of Therapeutic Assessment and to elicit what concerns the parents had about their son. Including the attorneys in the initial and feedback sessions with the parents is an important aspect of TA as an alternative to custody evaluation. Splitting and projection can occur between attorneys as well as parents, and many psychologists find that CC/PPE recommendations accepted by parents in a mutual meeting are frequently derailed when parents return to discuss them with their attorneys. At the end of this initial meeting, the parents signed a form agreeing to participation in the TA and to the rules of my future participation in court.

Rather than discussing the current time-sharing and decision-making issues, I first asked what general concerns Kim and Fred had about their son Ken, who was the only child from their brief and highly contentious marriage. They both agreed that Ken was not happy and doing poorly in school. Neither parent had remarried since their divorce, 12 years ago, and neither was currently involved in a dating relationship. The father worked in a blue-collar job with little social contact and was somewhat of a loner outside of work. The mother worked in a technical job with considerable supervisory responsibility.

During the interview, Kim was articulate and critical and usually the first to speak, whereas Fred struggled in expressing his beliefs and ideas and was quite reticent. I observed that there was a distinct mismatch in the dynamics between the parents and that Fred was easily overwhelmed by Kim's verbal quickness and obvious disdain for him. Fred would flood with anger, which he had trouble containing. The tension between the couple was palpable and intense. Rather than attempt to elicit a mutually agreed-upon list of questions to address in the TA at that time, I decided to have separate meetings with each parent to establish their respective concerns. I also decided to wait for the feedback session to integrate their questions into a common set of issues to be addressed in the TA.

Meeting With the Adolescent Son

The first step in a TA is to gather the questions each person wants addressed. I met with Ken, a tall, slender adolescent male who was initially aloof and uncommunicative. He was indeed shut down and obviously unhappy and seemed to me skeptical of the idea that talking about himself would be of any use to him whatsoever. I told him that I needed his help, if I was to understand how to help his parents settle their disagreements about him. I also shared that my job was not to decide which parent was right or wrong, but rather to help them understand what he needed. This intervention opened the door somewhat, and he increasingly, though haltingly and painfully, shared his worries.

Ken shared that he felt nervous and on edge most of the time, in large part because of arguments between his parents about his time with them. He said he was always sad and angry after these arguments. Ken related that, over the past school year, he rarely woke up rested, despite sleeping 8 to 9 hours a night. His concentration was poor in school, resulting in poor grades, and he dropped off the high school baseball team despite his past excellence in the sport. Ken was especially disappointed that his father refused to allow him to participate in tennis when he was "on his parenting time." Introduced to tennis by his mother, he won several international youth championships until his father's recent interference with his participation in tournaments.

Ken developed three questions for the TA:

1. What can I do, where can I go, what can I say, when my parents are arguing?
2. How can I learn to stand up for myself?
3. Why do I feel so helpless?

Assessment Findings With the Adolescent Son

I selected five psychological instruments: the Rorschach Comprehensive System (CS; Exner, 2003); the Roberts 2 (Roberts, 1994, formerly the Roberts Apperception Test for Children); the MMPI-A (Butcher et al., 1992), the Beck Depression Inventory II (Beck, Steer, & Brown, 1996); and the Beck Hopelessness Scale (BHS; Beck, 1988). The MMPI-A was administered to give the adolescent an opportunity to share his own view of his current inner world. The Rorschach CS and Roberts 2 were chosen because, as performance-based measures, they elicit implicit information about individuals, which in Ken's case was essential because of his difficulty articulating the internal sources of his distress and his view of others. The BDI and BHS were chosen because of my concern about possible depression and the depth of his feelings of hopelessness, a significant predictor of suicidal thoughts and behavior.

Not surprisingly, Ken's MMPI-A was valid and indicated no psychological concerns. Indeed all clinical scales were 50 or below, with the exception of Scale 2 (Depression), which was 55. On the Rorschach, Ken provided a 25-response protocol, a surprisingly productive protocol for adolescent males in general and for Ken in particular. Nevertheless, his *Lambda* (which measures openness to experience) of 3.17 indicated a young man who overly utilized an avoidant, "shutdown" style. Not surprisingly, his *Coping Deficit Index* (which measures social adeptness and maturity) of 4 and *Depression Index* (which measures painful emotional experience) of 5 together strongly suggested that he was socially inept and vulnerable to problems in social adjustment, about which he was understandably upset and depressed. Related to his social ineptness, his very low *Egocentricity Index* $[3r + (2)/R = .08]$ indicated poor self-concept and an inability to attend to his own needs. Illustrating his alienation from human interaction, Ken's Rorschach included only four human responses, none of the whole human, with three imaginary human contents and only one *Human Movement* (M) response, which was a highly telling M-response (indicating distorted perception of others) that will be described later.

His Rorschach pattern suggested that Ken's development of empathy and the capacity to understand others was developmentally arrested, making it difficult for him to form all-important peer relationships outside of his relationship with his parents. Additionally, Ken's combined scores on *Cooperative Movement* (tendency toward positive social relationships) and *Aggressive Movement* (perception of aggressiveness in relationship) strongly suggested a deep-seated belief that aggressiveness is a natural part of relationships ($COP = 0$, $AG = 2$). Furthermore, high scores on *Aggressive Content* ($AgC = 6$) indicated his belief that anger and aggressiveness are used regularly to control and dominate interpersonal relationships. Together, Ken's inner anger combined with his pervasively avoidant style (*Lambda*) and avoidance of affective expression and engagement (illustrated by his low *Affective Ratio* of .32), giving me the strong impression of buried rage.

Ken's Roberts 2 stories showed a similarly devitalized pattern of social relationships with recurrent thematic contents of rejection, depression, aggression, and anxiety. Very few of the 16 stories had resolved outcomes, reliance on others, or support from others, underscoring Ken's feelings of helplessness, disconnection, and nonresolution of important life problems. In Ken's stories, adults were viewed as arguing with each other or the child, and they were highly critical of the child's academic struggles with little in the way of constructive support. His Beck Depression Index, a frequently used self-report measure of depression, was 13, indicative of mild depression.

Perhaps most disturbing was a very troubling score of 12 on the Beck Hopelessness Scale, well above the cutoff score of 8, indicating a paralyzing level of hopelessness that was right at the core of Ken's question about feeling helpless and unable to protect himself. Frankly, I was deeply worried about this young man, who needed a powerful experience of being heard—and now! Yet, I found it difficult to connect with Ken and was worried about whether I was going to be up to this task of finding a way in with this young man who had such social ineptness, hopelessness, intense inner suffering, and buried rage, a volatile combination that elicited anxiety in me about his potential for suicide.

Assessment Intervention With the Adolescent Son

For the feedback session with Ken, I looked for a Rorschach response that might open the door to discussing the depth of his feelings of inadequacy, frozenness, and perhaps allow us to explore his buried rage. I wanted to find a Rorschach response that allowed us to enter his inner world in terms of his expressed concerns, in particular his distress about not being shielded from his parents' unrelenting conflict and verbal aggression. Given his extreme avoidant style and low affective engagement, finding such a response was not easy. Yet, Ken's response to Card II proved emblematic of his situation. "It looks like a face, a yelling face." On Inquiry, he stated, "It looks like a mouth and it's open, yelling. I used the whole thing. This is the nose and the eye holes." This was his only human movement response on the entire Rorschach.

When asked to reflect what his response meant in terms of his life, Ken was able to share, "This is how it has been with my parents as long as I remember. Whenever they are together, they fight. I have grown up frightened by them, of their anger at each other and their anger at me. First I tried to excel in sports and school, hoping they would stop, but now I just try to block everything out." We then focused on the meaning of his Rorschach scores, confirming and supporting that indeed Ken *did* feel powerless and overwhelmed by being caught in the middle of his parents' unrelenting arguments. We developed a metaphor for his experience: needing to stay low to the ground while the machine gun fire of his parents' conflict flew overhead. Lift your head to say something and you will get gunned down! It's way better to lay low and hope that it will stop, but there is nothing you personally can do about it.

Not surprisingly, he was adamantly opposed to talking directly with his parents about his feelings. When I commented that he seemed exhausted and really needed some help, we were able to negotiate an agreement that I would present his results to his parents for him with their attorneys present to lend their help to reduce conflict. Ken agreed to academic tutoring and individual psychotherapy (both of which he had heretofore refused), if his parents would agree not to argue in front of him and to support him in playing the sports he chose. I now had to face the difficult task of finding a way to lower the flames of this 15-year conflict between his parents, feeling that Ken's life literally was on the line.

Individual Meetings With the Parents and Assessment Findings for Each

Next I met individually with each of the parents to talk about their concerns, help them formulate the questions they wanted addressed by the assessment, and to conduct psychological testing. One important modification of standard TA procedure with couples suggested by Finn (personal communication) was to allow each parent to talk about the other parent. The usual TA approach with couples is to only allow each person to ask questions about herself or himself, as a way to interrupt the projection process and focus on inner change from the beginning. As part of formulating an intervention in TA as an alternative to CC/PPE, each parent is allowed to ask a question about the other parent as a way to assess the structure of projections and splitting. My modification in this particular case was to ask each parent to formulate questions about their son, but not about each other or themselves unless it specifically pertained to Ken. I was concerned that an intervention with the parents focusing on their inner issues would not be as helpful as focusing on their only real common issue, the well-being of their son.

I interviewed each parent individually and administered the Rorschach CS (Exner, 2003) and the MMPI-2 (Butcher, Dahlstrom, Graham, Tellegen, & Kaemmer, 1989). I chose the MMPI-2 because it is used in more than 90% of parenting evaluations and has a solid research base, with many normative studies on this population. I also very much like Alex Caldwell's Custody Report describing 26 interpersonal variables common in custody matters, such as awareness of potential for interpersonal provocation, potential for self-centered actions, externalizing/internalizing, and quality of parent–child bonding. The Rorschach also frequently is used in parenting evaluations, and there is a strong rationale for use with this population (Evans & Schutz, 2008), with significant, supportive empirical research. Indeed, Singer et al.'s (2008) normative data on parents in child custody evaluations found that Rorschach data better describes the CC/PPE population than the MMPI-2 does in regard to known parent characteristics in high-conflict divorcing couples.

With some assistance, Fred and Kim were each able to develop assessment questions. Both parents had a good grasp of Ken's issues and concerns, giving me hope that a resolution could be reached.

Kim's Questions
1. What's holding Ken back from learning to express himself?
2. Why is Ken not doing well in school?
3. How can I focus better on Ken's well-being instead of focusing on arguments?
4. Why are my concerns about Ken being dismissed?

Fred's Questions

1. Why does Ken seem so unhappy?
2. Why is Ken doing so poorly in school?
3. Why is he giving up?

When asked for their best guesses about the reasons for Ken's difficulties, not surprisingly each focused on the other parent's behavior as the cause of Ken's difficulties, and neither parent appeared aware that his or her conflict with the other might contribute to his distress. This parental blind spot also indicated to me that I would have important feedback for them that could easily skirt the deep conflicts they had with each other.

The parents' MMPI-2 scores were useful in getting a picture of their contributions to their conflict. Kim's approach to the test was self-favorable and moderately minimized her emotional problems. Even with this defensive approach, she had a spike 6 (Paranoid) profile ($T = 74$), indicating a tendency toward fixed projections, self-control, and self-righteousness. Her Caldwell Custody Report score suggested a tendency to be externalizing and to see things in terms of her own agenda, as well as severe problems with losing control of her temper and with "forgiving and forgetting" past perceived wrongs.

Fred's approach to the MMPI-2 also was self-favorable and moderately minimized his emotional problems. This validity pattern is common in child custody matters (Bagby, Nicholson, Buis, Radovanovic, & Fidler, 1999). He only had one scale elevated above $60T$, Scale 6, suggesting persecutory projections were likely under periods of stress. The overall pattern identified a distancing, insecure, and immature individual with a tendency to be interpersonally inappropriate or odd at times. His Caldwell Custody Report scores also suggested a tendency to externalize and to see things in terms of his own agenda, as well as to have problems with losing control of his temper and with "forgiving and forgetting" past wrongs. Unlike Kim, Fred tested average or above average in his ability to form adequate to good parent–child bonding.

It was not surprising that, on the Rorschach CS, both parents also had positive *Coping Deficit Indexes* with low *Affective Ratios* and *Egocentricity Indexes*, indicating respectively poor social skills, avoidance of emotionally charged situations, and poor self-regard. Both parents had elevated *Active:Passive* ratios, so both were likely to be rigid and entrenched in their beliefs. Fred had elevated *Space* and *Space Minus* responses with *Coping Capacity (D/AdjD)* equal -1, indicating that he was an individual who had a low tolerance for frustration and was vulnerable to angry outbursts. This pattern reinforced my clinical impression to move slowly and carefully with him. Kim's poor attention to detail ($Zd = -3.5$) and susceptibility to distorting reality ($X- = .29$) alerted me to address her vulnerability to misinterpretation and to make sure to be extra clear with her about the details of any parenting agreement.

Furthermore, Fred had a high number of Texture responses ($T = 3$) indicating strong, unfulfilled needs for closeness. Kim's responses indicated powerful conflict about closeness. She had no Texture responses, suggesting caution in creating close interpersonal relationships, but a high number of *Food Responses* ($Fd = 3$) and an elevated *Rorschach Oral Dependency Scale* score of .29, indicating high dependency needs. Clearly, Ken played a central role in both Fred's and Kim's depleted and conflicted inner emotional lives, but they had little capability to understand their deeper neediness as part of their conflict over him. I believed that I would have good use for a metaphor I developed with Ken that would activate his parents' desire to protect him, while allowing the parents to achieve détente.

Assessment Intervention With Both Parents

Because the ultimate goal of this TA was to develop a parenting agreement that would respond to, and be protective of, this highly vulnerable adolescent, I wanted all of the relevant adults to be in the room, so that I could deal with as much of the splitting and projection as possible. I was determined that the parents and the attorneys not leave the room without a detailed and well-formulated agreement. Initially, I thanked both parents for bringing Ken to the assessment and praised them for their awareness that he was in considerable distress, pointing out their similarities in the questions they asked about Ken. I emphasized that he was disturbingly filled with feelings of hopelessness, which, if not corrected, was a serious warning sign for possible self-harm down the road. Both parents were quiet and appeared deeply concerned about their son. I then shared with them the two most extreme findings on Ken's Rorschach, which were that he was very shut down and avoidant of experiencing life ("giving up") and that in giving up he could not develop a healthy sense of himself as someone whose actions in the world mattered ("holding back from learning to express himself"). The metaphor that I used was that Ken experienced the world in terms of being "caught in a powerful cross-fire," and hence the only way he could manage this situation was to stay as still and low to the ground as possible. In that situation, he could not develop the positive sense of himself he needed to grow and thrive emotionally.

As if on cue, Fred and Kim erupted, loudly blaming each other for Ken's difficulties. Waving their obviously distressed attorneys off, I then said to Fred and Kim that their explosive anger toward each other was exactly how Ken predicted they would respond and that this conflict between them was the cross-fire in which he felt trapped. Both parents fell silent. After a powerful moment of reflection, I shared the research findings about the very negative effects on children of ongoing parental conflict, but reassured them that I believed, now that they were aware of this, that they could work to find ways to keep Ken out of the middle. I also shared with them the positive outcomes for children from high-conflict/high-cooperation parenting. What ensued was a discussion in which several heretofore buried issues surfaced. Fred was able to articulate his concern about not having Ken during "his time." I was able to help Fred understand that time belonged to Ken, and, if Fred wanted Ken to shape his own life ("not give up"), then being flexible in regard to accommodating Ken's interests would help Ken learn to express and negotiate what he wanted in life.

As I gently worked with Fred, it became increasingly apparent that Kim became agitated. She stated rather intensely that she had tried to tell Fred that Ken needed to make his own choices and felt that Fred was paranoid and needed to control Ken. The rage, fear, and disdain in her voice was chilling. I told Kim that she had formed an interesting hypothesis about Fred's functioning that was very well suited for TA. I related that the MMPI-2 had a scale that was specifically focused on paranoia, and we could consult the testing to see what it might say about Kim's belief that Fred was paranoid. With Fred's permission I showed both of them his profile and pointed out that his MMPI-2 was not significant for paranoia. Pausing a moment for effect, I pulled out Kim's MMPI-2 and, pointing to her elevation on Scale 6, said, "On the other hand, your MMPI-2 shows significant paranoia." Before her shock wore off, I asked Kim if she knew why people became paranoid. Using Caldwell's (2001) adaptational model for the MMPI-2 as my guide, I asked her if she grew up in a family where anger and punishment were common. Kim grew tearful and shared that she grew up in a physically abusive family, where everyone walked on eggshells around her highly controlling father, who was unpredictably explosive and violent. I replied it was no wonder that she was so sensitive to even the slightest possibility that Fred would try to control or attack Ken. No wonder she was worried that her concerns about Ken were being dismissed (one of her assessment questions). She did not want what happened to her to happen to Ken!

Kim then tearfully admitted that she had had a bad temper with Ken growing up and always worried about how this had affected him. I pointed out that her third assessment question, "How can I focus better on Ken's well-being instead of focusing on arguments?" reflected her concern, which was a positive step in a productive direction. I suggested that a place to begin was to focus on how to disengage from the intense arguments she had with Fred. We then discussed in detail whether Fred had been violent with Ken. She acknowledged that he had not, although in their brief marriage she and Fred had been physically aggressive with each other. She acknowledged that her intense arguments and frequent legal battles with Fred could not help Ken's well-being, even though she had fought to be protective of Ken. I suggested that Fred was also trying to be protective of Ken in these fights, but that it was not helpful to have Ken in the middle any longer. At this point, I thought it best to move toward "fixing the problem instead of the blame." After a break, I suggested that we move toward negotiating a parent plan that was in Ken's best interest.

Summarizing: Negotiating a Parenting Plan With Parents and Attorneys

The next step of the process of the modified TA as an alternative to CC/PPE is to assist the parents *and* their attorneys in developing a parenting plan together. As I have repeatedly pointed out, if the attorneys are not in the process, parenting plans developed solely between the parents run a significant risk of unraveling, because points of law and issues of control and splitting inherent in litigation can easily derail an excellent plan. Whether TA practitioners are initially comfortable working with attorneys or not, attorneys are nonetheless important stakeholders in the process of resolving differences of parenting with legal ramifications. Backing away from working with the attorneys and the parents means that the attorneys do not get the benefit of the results of the TA. Fortunately, in this particular case, the two attorneys (both women with their own children) were primarily invested in settling this longstanding dispute and keeping these parents out of court for good.

One approach to settling custody disputes involves adapting Roger Fischer's "one-text procedure" (see Fischer, Ury, & Patton, 1991). Fischer developed this method while assisting President Carter to negotiate the 1978 Camp David Accords, the groundbreaking agreement between Anwar al-Sadat of Egypt and Menachem Begin of Israel. In summary, the negotiator (1) explores underlying interests and positions about the parenting plan; (2) proposes or writes a first draft outlining the negotiator's "best guess" at a resolution of these interests emphasizing that this is only a working document and not written in stone; (3) discusses with all parties any problems with the first draft; and (4) repeats the process of drafting until all parties do not believe that the agreement can be significantly improved. In addition to this procedure, the TA practitioner is sensitive to and works actively with disappointments, splitting, and projections that threaten to derail formulating a wise and positive agreement for the child or children.

We five adults spent the next 2 hours working out an agreement in which Ken was allowed to play tennis, would attend psychotherapy and tutoring, and, most importantly, the parents agreed not to argue in front of him. We worked through the detailed mechanics of the time-sharing arrangement when tennis fell on the weekend that Ken would spend with his father. His mother agreed that, when his father chose to attend tennis games on his weekend, it would be best for her not to be present. Their attorneys drew up an informal statement to this effect, and both parents signed the agreement. All parties agreed that no formal document would be necessary to enter into the court, since no major changes were made in the formal court child-parenting plan. As part of the agreement, all parties agreed to return to work with the assessor should there be problems with the plan, before any further legal action could be taken. Additionally, if any difficulties arose with Ken following through with his side of the bargain, the parents would then return with him to work with the assessor, to assist the three of them in resolving their disagreement. This meeting was the last time I met with the parents, though I would later have the opportunity to meet with Ken one more time.

Follow-up

My follow-up consisted of speaking with both attorneys separately a year and a half after this TA intervention. They revealed that, for the first time in 14 years, the parents had not initiated legal action against the other, and Ken was doing well in school and in sports. I spoke with one of the attorneys two years later and found out that there had been no further litigation between the parents. Additionally, she had not heard of any problems with Ken.

Last summer I received a call "out of the blue" from Ken, who asked to meet with me. He needed a letter as part of an application for work stating that he was not depressed nor had a chronic mental illness. We met and talked for several hours. He shared that his parents had stopped arguing in front of him (though they still intensely disliked each other) and that he followed through with his agreement, although counseling was not especially helpful to him. He was still a somewhat laconic young man, but with a much more assured sense of himself. His depression and feelings of hopelessness resolved within a year after the TA, and his academic performance improved. In fact, he was selected by his high school to receive a special merit award. He participated successfully in high school athletics, although he had voluntarily given up tennis several years before. We concluded, and I wrote, "At that time, Ken showed signs of depression common to children and adolescents involved in the middle of a high-conflict situation between parents. His depression was situation-based, and he has not been depressed in several years."

Personal Impact on the Assessor

I still become emotional, and even tearful, every time I share this case with others. I feel that, through this TA, I was able to harness and integrate powerfully diverse parts of my professional life and interests, melding forensic psychology and mediation with depth interpersonal psychotherapy and personality assessment. I feel that this case was part of healing several "vertical splits" within my own personality, integrating the skeptical side of myself with my compassion, and my caution with my creativity. In the process, I believe that, with the help of Steve Finn, I may have discovered the beginning of a powerful new way to use creative personality assessment to heal the splits between parents who are struggling to find ways to care for their children living with the pain of divorce, avoiding the powerful forces of division and aggression at the heart of litigation. I hope that others will use this beginning to launch a new way to keep children from being caught in the middle of high-conflict divorce.

Summary of Teaching Points

- A modified version of TA offers a powerful and affirming alternative to CC/PPE by intervening directly with divorcing parents. The ultimate goal of this TA was to develop a parenting agreement that would respond to, and be protective of, this highly vulnerable adolescent.
- TA can help resolve contentious legal situations in high-conflict divorce by empowering the parent litigants. TA allows parents to have increased control over the outcome of their dispute. The process of TA is inherently likely to be less conflictual.
- TA assists parents in developing a mutually agreeable parenting plan focusing on children's current needs and issues. TA focuses on parents' and children's specific interests and emotional needs and can lead to resolutions that are far more responsive to children's needs than legal agreements, especially those imposed by judges or law masters.
- TA utilizes what psychologists do best—that is, treatment and assessment for a positive therapeutic benefit—and as a result is more likely to be satisfying professionally.

- Practitioners are cautioned not to enter lightly into practice of TA as an alternative to CC/PPE, which requires knowledge of the legal system.
- Including the attorneys in the initial and feedback sessions with the parents is an important aspect of therapeutic assessment as an alternative to custody evaluation. Parents *and* their attorneys develop a parenting plan together.

REFERENCES

Bagby, R. M., Nicholson, R. A., Buis, T., Radovanovic, H., & Fidler, B. J. (1999). Defensive responding on the MMPI–2 in family custody and access evaluations. *Psychological Assessment, 11*, 24–48.

Baris, M. A., Coates, C. A., Duvall, B. B., Garrity, C. B., Johnson, E. T., & LaCrosse, E. R. (2000). *Working with high-conflict families of divorce: A guide for professionals*. Northvale, NJ: Jason Aronson.

Beck, A. T. (1988). *Manual for the Beck Hopelessness Scale*. San Antonio, TX: Psychological Corporation.

Beck, A. T., Steer, R. A., & Brown, G. K. (1996). *Manual for the Beck Depression Inventory–II*. San Antonio, TX: Psychological Corporation.

Butcher, J. N., Dahlstrom, W. G., Graham, J. R., Tellegen, A., & Kaemmer, B. (1989). *The Minnesota Multiphasic Personality Inventory–2 (MMPI-2): Manual for administration and scoring*. Minneapolis: University of Minnesota Press.

Butcher, J. N., Williams, C. L., Graham, J. R., Archer, R., Tellegen, A., Ben-Porath, Y. S., & Kaemmer, B. (1992). *MMPI: A manual for administration, scoring, and interpretation*. Minneapolis: University of Minnesota Press.

Caldwell, A. B. (2001). What do the MMPI scales fundamentally measure? Some hypotheses. *Journal of Personality Assessment, 76*, 1–17.

Evans, F. B. (2005). Trauma, torture, and transformation in the forensic assessor. *Journal of Personality Assessment, 84*(1), 25–28.

Evans, F. B. (2009). *Therapeutic assessment in domestic court*. Presented as a workshop for The Rorschach Institute, New York, NY, April 9, 2009.

Evans, F. B., & Schutz, B. M. (2008). The Rorschach in child custody and parenting plan evaluations: A new conceptualization. In C. B. Gacono & F. B. Evans (Eds.), *The handbook of forensic Rorschach assessment* (pp. 233–254). New York, NY: Routledge.

Exner, J. E. (2003). *The Rorschach: A comprehensive system, Vol. 1: Basic foundations* (4th ed.). Hoboken, NJ: Wiley.

Finn, S. E. (2007). *In our clients' shoes: Theory and techniques of Therapeutic Assessment.* Mahwah, NJ: Erlbaum.

Finn, S. E., & Tonsager, M. E. (2002). How Therapeutic Assessment became humanistic. *The Humanistic Psychologist, 30*(1-2), 10–22.

Fisher, R., Ury, W. L., & Patton, B. (1991). *Getting to yes: Negotiating agreement without giving in.* New York, NY: Penguin.

Folberg, J., Milne, A. L., & Salem, P. (2004). *Divorce and family mediation: Models, techniques, and applications.* New York, NY: Guilford Press.

Garrity, C. B., & Baris, M. A. (1997). *Caught in the middle: Protecting the children of high-conflict divorce.* San Francisco, CA: Jossey-Bass.

Greenberg, S. A., & Shuman, D. W. (1997). Irreconcilable conflict between therapeutic and forensic roles. *Professional Psychology: Research and Practice, 28*(1), 50–57.

Hamilton, A. M., Fowler, J. L., Hersh, B., Austin, C. A., Finn, S. E., Tharinger, D. J., . . . & Arora, P. (2009). Why won't my parents help me? Therapeutic Assessment of a child and her family. *Journal of Personality Assessment, 90,* 108–120.

Handler, L. (2007). The use of therapeutic assessment with children and adolescents. In S. R. Smith & L. Handler (Eds.), *The clinical assessment of children and adolescents: A practitioner's handbook* (pp. 53–72). Mahwah, NJ: Erlbaum.

Johnston, J. R., Roseby, V., & Kuehnle, K. (2009). *In the name of the child: A developmental approach to understanding and helping children of conflicted and violent divorce, second edition.* New York, NY: Springer.

Roberts, G. E. (1994). *Roberts 2.* Los Angeles, CA: Western Psychological Services.

Schutz, B. M., Dixon, E. B., Lindenberger, J. C., & Ruther, N. J. (1989). *Solomon's sword: A practical guide to conducting child custody evaluations.* San Francisco, CA: Jossey-Bass.

Singer, J., Hoppe, C. F., Lee, S. M., Olesen, N. W., & Walters, M. G. (2008). Child custody litigants: Rorschach data from a large sample. In C. B. Gacono & F. B. Evans (Eds.), *The handbook of forensic Rorschach assessment* (pp. 445–464). New York, NY: Routledge.

Smith, J. D., & Handler, L. (2009). "Why do I get in trouble so much?": A family Therapeutic Assessment case study. *Journal of Personality Assessment, 31*(3), 197–210.

Smith, J. D., Handler, L., & Nash, M. R. (2010). Therapeutic Assessment for preadolescent boys with oppositional-defiant disorder: A replicated single-case time-series design. *Psychological Assessment, 22*(3), 593–602.

Smith, J. D., Wolf, N. J., Handler, L., & Nash, M. R. (2009). Testing the effectiveness of family Therapeutic Assessment: A case study using a time-series design. *Journal of Personality Assessment, 91*(6), 518–536.

Sullivan, M. J. (2008). Introduction to the special issue on parenting coordination. *Journal of Child Custody: Research, Issues, and Practices*, Vol. 5 (1-2), 1–3.

Tharinger, D. J., Finn, S. E., Gentry, L., Hamilton, A., Fowler, J., Matson, M., Krumholz, L., & Walkowiak, J. (2009). *Therapeutic Assessment with children: A pilot study of treatment acceptability and outcome, 91*(3), 238–244.

Tharinger, D. J., Finn, S. E., Gentry, L., & Matson, M. (in press). Therapeutic Assessment with adolescents and their parents: A comprehensive model. In D. Sakllofske & V. Schwean (Eds.), *Oxford Press handbook of psychological assessment of children and adolescents*. New York, NY: Oxford University Press.

Tharinger, D. J., Finn, S. E., Hersh, B., Wilkinson, A., Chistopher, G., & Tran, A. (2008). Assessment feedback with parents and children: A collaborative approach. *Professional Psychology: Research and Practice, 39*, 600–609.

Tessler, P. H., & Thompson, P. (2006). *Collaborative divorce: The revolutionary new way to restructure your family, resolve legal issues, and move on with your life*. New York, NY: Regan Books/Harper Collins.

Webb, S., & Ousky, R. (2006). *The collaborative way to divorce: The revolutionary method that results in less stress, lower costs, and happier kids—without going to court*. New York, NY: Hudson Street Press.

18

❧

Therapeutic Assessment With a Couple in Crisis: Undoing Problematic Projective Identification via the Consensus Rorschach

STEPHEN E. FINN

Although my colleagues and I have practiced Therapeutic Assessment with couples for many years, I have written only a few pieces about this method (Finn, 2007), and there has been only one formal study (Durham-Fowler, 2010—summarized in Chapter 1). In this chapter, I write about a significant positive transformation that occurred in a couple I saw for a Therapeutic Assessment. I will describe the major events of the assessment and how I used the Consensus Rorschach as an assessment intervention. Then I will discuss the factors that led to the couple's positive changes.

REFERRAL

"Maria" was referred by her individual psychotherapist, Jane, because she was very concerned about Maria's being suicidal. Maria, age 44, suffered from chronic intense pelvic pain that had begun 4 years earlier and for which she had been unable to find any relief after seeing numerous physicians. Jane had been seeing Maria in supportive psychotherapy for 2 years and reported that many of Maria's physicians believed that her pain was psychogenic in origin. Maria, however, steadfastly refused to consider this possibility, saying that she "knew her body" and "was not crazy." Previously a successful high school teacher, Maria was now completely disabled by her pain and spent all of her time at home alone when her husband of 25 years and their two daughters, ages 21 and 13, were not with her. At the time of the referral, Maria was despondent about her pain and felt she was a burden on her family; she frequently said everyone would be happier if she just ended her life. Jane requested the assessment to evaluate Maria's risk for suicide and to get help in knowing how to work with Maria in regard to her pain.

FIRST IMPRESSIONS

Dr. Filippo Aschieri sat in on all the sessions and assisted me in conducting this assessment. When we went out to the waiting room to greet Maria, we saw an attractive, well-dressed, middle-aged woman sitting at one end of the waiting room and an unknown man sitting at the other end of the room, reading. The man looked up when we came into the room, but I assumed he was a client waiting for one of my colleagues in our office suite. We introduced ourselves, and Maria said hello to us in a quiet voice. She had dark circles under her eyes and gave a heavy sigh as she rose from the chair to accompany us down the hall to my office. I inquired whether she had had any trouble finding the office, and she replied that her husband was excellent with directions. At first this remark seemed like a non sequitur, until it dawned on me that she might be referring to the man I had seen in the waiting room. Their disconnected behavior had led me to see them as completely unrelated. I asked if that was her husband, and she replied, "Ah, yes. I don't drive, and he is very concerned about me too." On impulse, I then asked, "Would you like him to join us for our meeting?" She said she would like that very much. I asked for her husband's name (John) and went out to invite him into our session. John eagerly followed me into my office. He sat in a chair instead of joining Maria on the sofa.

INITIAL SESSION

Given that Maria was the person referred for the psychological assessment, Filippo and I began by asking her what she hoped to gain from the psychological assessment. She said, "Nothing. I'm only here because Jane and my husband want me to come. My problem is medical, but no one believes me. I just can't live with the pain anymore." She then launched into a long account of her pelvic pain and the various physicians she had seen to try to address it. John chimed in tentatively at several points to fill in certain details. We learned that the pain had begun 4 years earlier, around the same time that the couple's eldest daughter, Anna, had been hospitalized for anorexia. One gynecologist had assured Maria that he understood the cause of her pain and that it would be resolved if she had a hysterectomy and ovarectomy. Maria had followed his advice, only to find afterward that her pain was worse than before.

Maria described how the pain came and went, how sometimes it was a dull ache and other times a "stabbing" sensation, and how disabling it was when it was bad. She cried as she talked and said she blamed herself for going through with the surgery, and she now thought she would be better off dead. John looked up at us plaintively when she said this. I felt protective of them both, and after Maria stopped crying, I asked if I could say something. She nodded, and I said, "Maria, I hear that your pain is very real, and I don't want to suggest in any way that it is in your head. I don't presume to think we can help you with your physical pain, but perhaps we can help you live with it better while you keep looking for its medical cause. Would you be interested in working with us on that—seeing if there's anything that can help you make it through this incredibly difficult period of your life?" Maria dried her tears and nodded affirmatively; John looked relieved and grateful.

In the next 30 minutes, Maria posed the following questions for the assessment: "Will I be able to keep on living with my chronic pelvic pain?" "What will help me grieve the loss of my reproductive organs?" and "Will I be able to keep my marriage if I can't be intimate with my husband?" Regarding this last question, we learned that Maria and John had not had intercourse for over 2 years, and that Maria worried constantly that he would leave her. John denied this profusely, but Maria's question did give me the opportunity to ask how he was coping with Maria's pain and hopelessness. He admitted that he was struggling and said that he felt helpless to make her feel better. He then commented that when he tried to comfort Maria, he often seemed to "miss the mark." Maria nodded vigorously. John said he was worried about what to do, and he was very concerned about the effect of Maria's despondency on their daughters.

It was at this point that I made a crucial decision. I turned to the couple and said, "I certainly want to help, and Maria, I think you've come up with some very good questions for the assessment. But right now, I'm wondering about the possibility of expanding our focus to include both of you. John, would you also be interested in being tested and addressing some of your own questions? We could just meet with Maria, but it appears that you need help too. And I hear that you have questions about the best way for you to support Maria. Am I right?" John agreed and said that he very much wanted to take part in the assessment if it would help Maria. Maria seemed very excited about his being tested too; she said that he really didn't know how to support her. John and I then agreed on the following question: "If Maria's pain isn't well resolved, what can I do to help her not give up?" Filippo and I scheduled separate individual sessions with John and Maria as the next step of the assessment. They left and we shared our observations.

Teaching Point

Sometimes, individual clients seek a psychological assessment for issues that very much involve their spouses. In such instances, it sometimes is very useful to invite the spouse to participate in the assessment early on and to explore the possibility of doing a couples' rather than an individual assessment. The broader focus of a couples' assessment allows the referred client to feel less like the "identified patient." It also allows the assessor to assess the role of systemic factors in the client's problems in living.

INDIVIDUAL SESSIONS

As I have written about elsewhere (Finn, 2007), when conducting a full Therapeutic Assessment with a couple, the assessor generally meets with each partner individually after the initial conjoint session. The goal of these individual sessions is to continue gathering background information, administer relevant individual tests, and develop hypotheses about the contribution of each person to the couple's and each individual's difficulties. Also, the assessor tries to help each partner make individual shifts that might positively impact the couple.

Filippo and I had four individual sessions with John and Maria. During these sessions, each was interviewed extensively and given the Minnesota Multiphasic Personality Inventory–2 (MMPI-2; Butcher, Dahlstrom, Graham, Tellegen, & Kaemmer, 1989) and the Rorschach inkblots (Exner, 1993). As I will explain later, John but not Maria also completed the Early Memories Procedure (EMP; Bruhn, 1992).

Individual Meetings With Maria

Maria seemed to greatly appreciate the added support of the assessment sessions. Early in the assessment process, we listened carefully as she talked about the vicissitudes of her pain, and we rather quickly developed an understanding that while the physical pain was difficult, especially because of its unpredictability, what was most distressing to her was Maria's *feeling alone with the pain*. We jointly developed a distinction between "pain" and "suffering"—with the latter term including feelings of alienation, shame, and loneliness resulting from Maria's having little emotional support for her pain. Maria railed against her various physicians' refusal to believe that her pain was real. She also expounded more on John's unsuccessful attempts to comfort her, saying that he always tried to "fix her" or encourage her to look on the bright side of things. Maria knew that this optimistic style had long been characteristic of John (and of his whole family), but she confessed that she "hid it" when she felt physically better, because John would quickly assume that all was well and would (according to her) stop paying attention to her.

Around this time, Maria developed an additional assessment question: "What do I need from John so I can laugh with him when I am in pain, as I can with my sister?" Maria explained that she enjoyed getting together with her older sister (who lived several hours away) even when she was not feeling well, because the two of them would laugh and Maria would feel better. When I asked what was different with John, she explained, "My sister can listen to my pain. John can't." Maria agreed that this question would be shared with John.

Teaching Point

> During the individual sessions of a couples' assessment, partners some-times develop new assessment questions. These questions are always shared with the partner. This prevents the partners from feeling that the assessor is more allied with one of them than the other.

MMPI-2

Maria's MMPI-2 profile (Figure 18.1) showed how incredibly distressed she was. Without any validity scale elevations suggesting she had exaggerated her difficulties, her extremely high elevation on Scale 2 (Depression), combined with her extremely low score on Scale 9 (Hypomania), suggested Maria had a severe Major Depression with vegetative symptoms. The elevations on Scale 1 (Hypochondriasis) and Scale 3 (Hysteria) were expected and reflected her chronic pain and other bodily symptoms. Her score on Scale 8 (Schizophrenia) was mainly due to the scale content related to alienation, and the extremely high score on Scale 0 (Social Introversion) accurately reflected how isolated Maria was. She and John had admitted that they rarely saw other people, had few friends, and spent most of their time at home. One other interesting high score was on Scale 4 (Psychopathic Deviate); Filippo and I hypothesized that this score reflected the intense anger Maria felt about her situation and others' inability to comfort her. Although this anger was generally obscured by Maria's depression, she and John had reported that it did surface from time to time.

Rorschach

Maria's Rorschach was short but complex and exhausting to administer. There was a good deal of dysphoric and traumatic content in Maria's percepts. She saw a bleeding pelvis on Card II and a woman

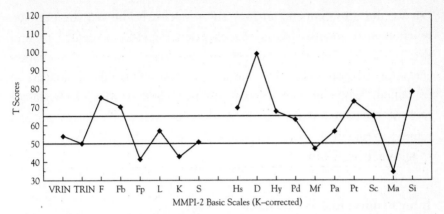

Figure 18.1   Maria's MMPI-2 Profile

Note: VRIN = Variable Response Inconsistency scale; TRIN = True-Response Inconsistency scale; F = Infrequency; Fb = Back F; Fp = Infrequency Psychopathology; L = Lie; K = Defensiveness; S = Superlative Self-Presentation; Hs = Scale 1, Hypochondriasis; D = Scale 2, Depression; Hy = Scale 3, Hysteria; Pd = Scale 4, Psychopathic Deviate; Mf = Scale 5, Masculinity-Femininity; Pa = Scale 6, Paranoia; Pt = Scale 7, Psychasthenia; Sc = Scale 8, Schizophrenia; Ma = Scale 9, Hypomania; Si = Scale 0, Social Introversion. Excerpted from the *MMPI®-2 (Minnesota Multiphasic Personality Inventory®-2) Manual for Administration, Scoring, and Interpretation, Revised Edition.* Copyright © 2001 by the Regents of the University of Minnesota. All rights reserved. Used by permission of the University of Minnesota Press. "MMPI" and "Minnesota Multiphasic Personality Inventory" are trademarks owned by the Regents of the University of Minnesota.

whose body was being devoured by squirrels on Card X. The Rorschach scoring confirmed the depression visible on the MMPI-2 (*DEPI* = 6), and the extremely high Trauma Content Index (*TCI* = .86; Armstrong & Loewenstein, 1990) suggested that Maria was severely traumatized by her chronic pain and past medical procedures. This score exceeded the range found in women with dissociative disorders (Kamphuis, Kugeares, & Finn, 2000), and it raised the question for Filippo and me of whether Maria had been traumatized earlier in her life. We broached the question in a later session with Maria, and she pointedly changed the topic. We ran into a similar situation earlier in the assessment, when we asked Maria to complete the Early Memories Procedure. As mentioned earlier, Maria refused this task, explaining that if she filled it out, everyone would try to convince her that her pelvic pain was related to her childhood, and she did not want this to happen.

Maria was in a great deal of physical pain by the end of the Rorschach administration, so we did not attempt an extended inquiry.

But we did all comment on how the test clearly showed the extreme psychological anguish Maria was experiencing. Maria seemed to find this acknowledgment comforting, and we found out later that when she returned home that day, she allowed herself to take a small dose of Valium, which gave her some relief. Several of Maria's physicians had prescribed Valium for pain (as a muscle relaxant), but Maria had refused to take it in the past because she insisted her pain "was not due to nerves."

John's Individual Assessment

John also came regularly for his individual sessions and seemed to appreciate the chance to talk about his experience of Maria's pelvic pain. Filippo and I quickly discovered that John "led" with his rationality and fine mind, and that he was not very fluent in discussing his emotions. However, he did tell us that he was feeling very worried and stressed by the tasks of attending to Maria and taking her to medical appointments, holding together the household, giving attention to his daughters, and meeting basic requirements at his job as a chemist. Over time, with a great deal of support from us, John disclosed that at times he felt extremely frustrated with Maria, but he was completely stymied about what to do with this anger. He knew that expressing it would likely plunge Maria into more shame and suicidal thoughts. We helped John form three more assessment questions: "How capable am I of managing this kind of stress over the long haul?", "What's the long-term prognosis for Maria, and how will it affect our relationship?", and "Is it ever appropriate for me to tell Maria, 'You need to keep going regardless of the pain!'?" These questions reflected a shift that John began to make during our individual sessions—from being a long-suffering caregiver to someone who began to recognize his own needs. In fact, one day when Maria refused to go to one of her medical appointments, he yelled at her, telling her it wasn't fair if she didn't take care of herself. In her next individual appointment, Maria said she didn't know "what had gotten into John" and that he seemed different lately—not as patient, but also "his hugs are better."

MMPI-2

John's MMPI-2 profile (Figure 18.2) showed very little distress. His slight elevation on Scale S (Superlative Self-Presentation) suggested that he was the type of person who put his best foot forward, looked like he could do everything, and generated envy in other people because he seemed to have it all together. His elevation on Scale 5 (Masculinity-Femininity) was associated with emotional sensitivity, difficulties expressing anger directly, passivity, and a tendency to let himself get pushed around in intimate relationships. His slight elevation on Scale 7 (Psychasthenia) likely reflected the worry and stress he felt about Maria's situation, as well as his tendency to be "up in his head." The moderate score on Scale 0 (Social Introversion) reflected his isolation; as mentioned earlier, neither he nor Maria had friends.

It was interesting to note the contrast between Maria's highly elevated MMPI-2 profile and John's largely normal-range profile. My colleagues and I not infrequently see these kinds of "complementary" MMPI-2 profiles in the couples we assess, and we have long pondered their meaning. We have reached an understanding that seems useful in many instances.

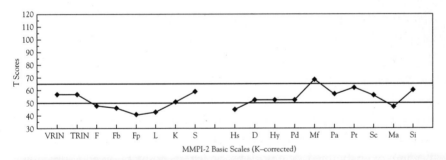

Figure 18.2   John's MMPI-2 Profile

Note: VRIN = Variable Response Inconsistency scale; TRIN = True-Response Inconsistency scale; F = Infrequency; Fb = Back F; Fp = Infrequency Psychopathology; L = Lie; K = Defensiveness; S = Superlative Self-Presentation; Hs = Scale 1, Hypochondriasis; D = Scale 2, Depression; Hy = Scale 3, Hysteria; Pd = Scale 4, Psychopathic Deviate; Mf = Scale 5, Masculinity-Femininity; Pa = Scale 6, Paranoia; Pt = Scale 7, Psychasthenia; Sc = Scale 8, Schizophrenia; Ma = Scale 9, Hypomania; Si = Scale 0, Social Introversion. Excerpted from the MMPI®-2 (*Minnesota Multiphasic Personality Inventory®-2*) *Manual for Administration, Scoring, and Interpretation, Revised Edition.* Copyright © 2001 by the Regents of the University of Minnesota. All rights reserved. Used by permission of the University of Minnesota Press. "MMPI" and "Minnesota Multiphasic Personality Inventory" are trademarks owned by the Regents of the University of Minnesota.

✍ Teaching Points

In couples experiencing marital difficulties, complementary profiles on self-report tests are not uncommon and appear to reflect the effects of "projective identification." Projective identification is a process that develops over time in couples, where partners gradually develop "opposing" personality styles and characteristic defense mechanisms. As partner X becomes more pessimistic, partner Y becomes more optimistic. As partner Y becomes more emotionally expressive, partner X becomes more emotionally constricted and rational. This systemic process grows out of each person's personality prior to entering the relationship and out of their interactions in the couple relationship.

Rorschach

John's Rorschach was above average in length ($R = 30$), and Filippo and I were interested and at first surprised that its content resembled that of Maria's Rorschach. For example, John also saw several pelvises, one of which was bloody. Also, as the administration went on, John seemed to become overwhelmed, and his responses involved more animals, aggressive animals in particular. In contrast to his MMPI-2 profile, the scoring of John's Rorschach showed a good deal of emotional distress [$DEPI = 5$; $S\text{-}CON = 7$; $3r + (2)/R = .20$]. He also had a great deal of color in his protocol ($WSUMC = 7.0$), which at first surprised us because John seemed so unemotional. As the assessment progressed, however, we came to see how this score fit. As the MMPI-2 had also indicated, John was in fact a highly emotionally sensitive man. However, he quickly became overwhelmed by emotions, at which point he would shut down and appear to operate only from his head. (This formulation helped us understand better the effects of Maria's emotional explosions on him.) And as John withdrew when Maria was emotionally aroused, this only made her feel more lonely and distressed. Last, it appeared that John was traumatized too ($TCI = .43$), although the couple had developed a story that Maria was the one who was suffering. Maria's role as the identified patient prevented John from getting attention for his needs, and it left Maria feeling alone with her pain.

Filippo and I discussed John's Rorschach responses with him after the standardized administration, and John too was struck by the many morbid and anatomy responses he had given. When we asked for his thoughts about this, John suddenly exclaimed, "I guess I'm being more affected by Maria's situation than I like to admit." We heartily agreed.

COUPLES' ASSESSMENT INTERVENTION SESSION

Teaching Point

> The role of a couples' assessment intervention session in Therapeutic Assessment is typically to help the partners see and understand systemic aspects of their problems in living. Because couples generally are unaware of how each other operates in outside relationships, partners frequently view cocreated problems in living as being the result of the other person alone. For example, "We have problems with fighting in our relationship. I never fight with other people. Therefore, you are the cause of our fights." This kind of attribution error is very common, and it is the main focus of many couples' assessment interventions.

Filippo and I decided to use the Consensus Rorschach (Handler, 1997) for the assessment intervention with John and Maria. Because I have described this technique fully elsewhere (Finn, 2007), I will not review the procedures here, but will go right to the session.

I should preface my account by relating that at the time of this session (several months after we had begun our work with Maria and John), Filippo and I sensed that important shifts were already taking place in the couple. Maria seemed calmer and less desperate, and John was warmer and taking care of himself better. Maria was having some relief from the chronic pelvic pain from very small doses of Valium, and the couple had even weathered a joint stressful event successfully. One week earlier, Maria and John had taken a trip out of state to consult with a physician who specialized in pelvic pain. Both felt the experience was not helpful, and at one point John even stood up for Maria with the physician, telling the man he was "talking down" to Maria.

Maria was ecstatic over John's being protective, and although the trip was not medically successful, they both came back reporting they had really enjoyed each other and felt as if they had been on a vacation. We hoped to build on this positive experience and to use the Consensus Rorschach to help them see how they "triggered" each other into painful places. We hoped to teach them what a helpful interaction would look like concerning Maria's pain, and to explore what got in the way of their having such interactions. As I have recommended (Finn, 2007), we videotaped the entire session.

Free Response Phase

Many interesting things happened during the free response phase of the Consensus Rorschach, in which the couple was asked to come up with responses "they both can see and both agree upon reporting." In instances where the couple has taken individual Rorschachs previously, it is common for partners to propose percepts they have seen before alone, and this is what Maria and John did. Overall, they worked together in a very collaborative manner, laughing at many points, and each seemed curious about the other's responses. They had few difficulties agreeing on conjoint responses, with one notable exception on Card II. Early on the couple agreed on a percept of two people with their hands pressed together. Then Maria suggested a second response:

Maria: All the grey is the pelvis, and this is bleeding, no?

John: Yes, and that's what that is (pointing to red spots on D1 area). It's blood.

M: (pointing to top D2 areas) And these would be the ovaries.

J: Yes, I see those. . . . And then I also see a butterfly here (pointing to D3 area).

M: In this woman with so much pain, I can't see beautiful things.

J: So you don't see a butterfly? (pointing to D3)

M: I don't see a butterfly in my pelvis.

J: You don't see a butterfly in your pelvis, I know. But does that look like a butterfly?

M: Hmmm . . .

J: You don't want to see a butterfly.

M: No, I don't see a butterfly. No.

J: Okay. (Takes the card and looks for something else, then hands it back to Maria.)

M: So you're giving up the butterfly?

J: Well, I see what looks like a butterfly to me, but if you don't see it, then you don't.

M: But we need to give an answer.

J: Do we need to agree on everything? We saw the one with the two people and the pelvis.

M: We need to agree.

J: Okay.

M: You'll see many butterflies outside. For now, give up the butterfly! (laughing)

J: (Laughing) We agreed on the pelvis and the weird guys giving the high-five. But you're not going to see a butterfly there? (laughing)

M: No.

J: Okay. I guess we won't agree on the appearance of a butterfly. (Starts to hand card back to Steve.)

M: (Takes the card.) You can give up the butterfly, come on! (laughing)

J: (Laughing) But do we need to agree on everything?

M: Yes, because this is just a butterfly. Come on, give up the butterfly! (laughing) It's the pelvis and the bleeding and the ovaries there.

J: I agree with that. But I'm also saying that I see a butterfly there.

M: (Shrugs and looks disappointed.)

J: So we can agree not to report it. (Hands back the card.)

Extended Inquiry

After the free response phase, Filippo and I gave Maria and John a 15-minute break, and we discussed what we had observed. We agreed the discussion on Card II was packed with meaning, and so we cued up that portion of the tape and invited Maria and John back in. We began by asking them about their reactions to the first part of the task. They said they enjoyed the task, found it pretty easy, and thought it reflected their lives at home and how they generally made joint decisions.

We then told them that we had cued up a portion of the tape to watch all together. Maria and John immediately laughed and knew we would be showing them the exchange on Card II. After viewing it again, we discussed that section of the tape:

S: Well, what did you see?

M: He is like this, you know. I am very emotional and people think I take advantage of him. But when he doesn't want something, he won't give up. I mean I can't take advantage of him. There are things he wants to do and he doesn't give up. He doesn't get angry or anything like that, but I cannot pressure him.

S: Okay, that's what you saw. John, what did you see?

J: I don't know. I wondered if what I saw was . . . I kind of felt that Maria saw a butterfly, or saw what could be a representation of a butterfly. But I guess in what I heard her say, it's that she was thinking about the pain in her pelvis and in that context she either could not see anything good about it and the butterfly could be considered something beautiful or good, or she didn't want to see it or she felt I was looking at her and her pelvis and her situation and either kind of ignoring it by saying "Here's a butterfly." You know, something serious is going on, and I'm saying like "Look, there's a butterfly." She thinks I'm either ignoring it or I'm refusing to see her situation.

S: (to Maria) Is that close? Is that what it felt like emotionally?

M: (nodding) And not just in this exercise, but in my situation now that I'm going through.

S: Maria, the message I saw you sending—let me see if I got it right—was "John, can't we just stick with the painful image without putting the happy thing on top? Do we always have to put the happy thing on top?" Is that right?

M: Yes.

I then moved on to bring up something I had noticed when they were working with this card.

S: I saw something interesting though. John, you seemed to notice fairly quickly that Maria didn't see the butterfly, and it looked like you were going to let it drop. But you, Maria, brought it back up again. You were the one who brought it back up when you said, "So are you letting go of the butterfly?"

M: Oh really, I don't remember that.

J: Can we see it again?

S: We can see it again, you bet.

And so we watched the tape one more time.

Steve: So what do you think about that?

M: Maybe I wanted him to see the butterfly. I don't know.

S: Do you have any ideas, John?

J: I guess I felt she could see a butterfly, but that it was important for her for me to say there wasn't a butterfly. It was important for her for me to acknowledge that it was hard for her to see something good right now.

S: I wonder. Maria, I wonder if it wasn't enough for him to go along with not seeing a butterfly. Maybe you wanted him to come over a little more to your side. Or maybe . . . I was remembering last week when we were talking about something and he didn't get optimistic. You were uncomfortable and said you needed him to hold the optimism. So maybe you were saying in a way. . . .

M: . . . Don't give up your butterfly. Yes, that's true. If he loses his optimism, I'm lost.

S: Unless . . . ?

M: Unless?

S: Unless you can find your own!

M: (nods)

S: It's a challenge though.

M: It's a challenge.

Maria then explained that when she had "good days" with less pain, John seemed to act as if everything was normal again.

Steve: I'm just putting myself in your shoes and imagining what you need at a time like that. My fantasy is that when you see the bloody pelvis, you need him first to go there with you. And you did, John. Maria gave the initial response and you not only agreed with it, but you added to it a bit, pointing out the places where the blood was. It was beautiful. Maria, he joined you right there. But then you need him to *not move away from that too quickly*.

M: Yes!

S: John, you can bring in your butterfly, but later. Maria, you said, "There are butterflies out there for later. But for now, can we stay with the bloody pelvis?!" (Both laugh.) But then what you also need, Maria, is for him to not get lost in the bloody pelvis, because if you're lost in it and he's lost in it, it's no good. John, she needs you to stay there a little while longer, and you'll have to watch her closely. When she starts to turn around a little bit herself, that would be the time to bring in the optimism. But you have to not bring in too much optimism, or you'll lose her. You need to bring in only a little bit. Maria, does that seem right?

M: Exactly.

S: And of course, John, this is a very difficult thing that we're asking you to do, and you're not going to be able to do it all the time because some times you'll be in your own emotional place.

M: Wow!

J: I see. When she said, "You can see butterflies out there" she meant there will be time for that later; that she'll get there.

S: Exactly, because Maria, what helps you is to not feel alone with the pain.

M: Yes, that's the worst.

At this point, the couple was sitting on the couch looking at each other; then, each seemed to get very curious, and they began wondering aloud about how they had developed the pattern we were discussing. This gave me a chance to describe how the notion of projective identification might characterize their interaction:

S: So can I run a theory by you, and you can tell me what you think? (Both nod.) John, you've been getting a little more emotional in the time we've known you. Of course, that's a mixed bag for you, Maria. You don't like him being angry, and it can hurt when he is. But, his hugs are better because he's more connected to himself emotionally, and you like that. And as this happens, Maria, I wonder if it isn't a little bit easier for you to keep control of your emotions.

M: Yes, yes, yes . . .

S: In a way, you're becoming slightly more logical as he becomes more emotional.

J: I've noticed that.

S: So I'm wondering if you came together in a relationship because in part you each had strengths the other didn't have. Maria, John tells us he was attracted to your vitality and your emotionality. My guess is you were attracted to his stability and ability to be calm.

M: Yes, that's what always caught me. (John nods.)

S: Exactly! You saw in each other the part you needed to balance your personality. (Both nod vigorously.) Now when things go well in a couple, they learn from each other the things they need to learn and they come closer together. But sometimes, things go awry and you become more like you're only holding one side. Maria, you become more emotional, which spurs John to become more rational. John, when you go up more in your head that spurs Maria to become highly emotional.

M: Yes, when we were happy, before the pain, we did a lot of things, and *he* was the clown, talking all the time, and doing risky things.

S: Exactly. And the thing that caused you to go apart more was this terrible trauma of the pain, and maybe other things too, like your older daughter's anorexia.

M: Yes, that was a difficult time.

S: Now, through the course of the assessment, you're starting to come back together again. John, you're learning about the importance of being able to go to the emotional side. Maria, you're feeling calmer and more rational and it's easier for you to take his point of view. And then the two of you experienced what you did on the recent trip. It was a very stressful situation, and it didn't go perfectly, but it didn't split the two of you apart. Does that seem right?

Both: Yes!

Trying Out New Behavior

We then shifted to the most touching part of the session. I handed the couple Card II and asked John to start by describing the painful image of the pelvis they had both seen. I asked him to "stay in the pain" with Maria as long as he could, unless he saw her shift out of it. I told Maria to just see what it was like for him to join her in the pain, and that if she had enough of it, and felt a shift inside herself, that *she* could bring in the butterfly. But that if she didn't shift, that was okay, and the butterfly could come in later.

J: (holding Card II) As we talked about, this looks like a pelvis. And these are the bloody spots. These could be the ovaries or some other part. And when I see this, I think about you, and the pain you're going through, and all the focus we're putting on this part.

M: (Starts to weep; John puts his arm around her and pulls her close.) Yes, and this all hurts (pointing), even though I don't have this. It hurts! (crying hard)

J: Yeah (soothingly). It really hurts.

M: I don't know what my future is going to be without the ovaries.

J: Yes, if you take the ovaries out, you still have the blood and all the pain.

M: And this still hurts. All of these red parts still hurt.

J: You said all of this still hurts. It makes me think about what Dr. A said about the neuropathic pain.

M: No. (upset) It's more than that. (starts to move away physically)

S: John, that was a bit of a butterfly. Don't put that in. Just stay with the pain.

M: You know, I won't have estrogen anymore. And they took all of this. They took all of this from me and it wasn't necessary!

J: Yes, it's a terrible, terrible loss. (Squeezes Maria close and kisses her lightly on the cheek.)

When we talked later, Filippo and I admitted that at that point we both felt like kissing John on the cheek! He was doing such an incredible job of staying with Maria's pain and supporting her. They continued in this way for about 15 minutes, with Maria crying hard at times as she talked about various aspects of her situation. A few times, John started to shift away from the pain, but each time, he accepted my encouragement to just stay in there. Eventually, Maria calmed down, said she was very tired, and they left. She never got to the place of bringing in the butterfly, and that seemed comfortable to everyone. We agreed to meet one week later for the summary/discussion session of the assessment.

SUMMARY/DISCUSSION SESSION

The summary/discussion session was held at the office of Jane, Maria's therapist, with Jane present. When Filippo and I walked into Jane's waiting room that day, the contrast was striking from what we had witnessed at the beginning of the assessment. Maria and John were sitting close together on a loveseat, with John's arm around Maria, and they were looking at a magazine and giggling. They seemed like young lovers. They told us they had had a very good week together, and this seemed to set the stage for a very productive session.

John volunteered to hear about his individual test results first, and as we talked about the stress and trauma he had been experiencing, and his underlying depression, Maria was very supportive. She expressed regret that she hadn't realized how much he was affected by her situation. John told her this was because he didn't know how to show anyone his pain, and he said he wanted to try to do more of this. When it was Maria's turn, John also was extremely supportive. He seemed to understand immediately the distinction Maria and we had made between "pain" and "suffering." John said he was so relieved now to know how to support Maria, and that he never wanted to leave her alone again with her pain.

In the latter half of the session, we discussed the systemic aspects of their relationship, which we had explored via the Consensus Rorschach. John and Maria took the lead here, explaining to Jane what they had learned about how they "triggered" each other, and they told of how they had already tried to "catch" and "change" their pattern in the last week. In effect, they explained projective identification to her. We parted, with plans to meet for a follow-up session in two months. They thanked us profusely, and just before we walked out the door, Maria handed us a manila envelope and said we should open it after we left.

Filippo and I went out to the car and opened the envelope. Inside was the Early Memory Procedure booklet that Maria had previously refused, completely filled out! Maria had attached a note: "I could fill this out now because I know you took my pain seriously. I also give you permission to share this with Jane." We began to read Maria's early memories, and as we had suspected, they were filled with trauma that she had never disclosed to Jane or us. Her most shocking memory was of being raped by an older cousin at a family gathering when she was 17. (This was the same age that Maria's daughter had developed anorexia and Maria had begun to have her pelvic pain.) Maria wrote about telling her mother about the rape, only to have her say, "Don't you ever say another word about this to anyone! Do you hear me? This never happened!" Maria wrote about being devastated by her mother's response and having never trusted her again.

FOLLOW-UP SESSION

Two months later, I met with Maria and John for the assessment follow-up session. (Dr. Aschieri had returned to Italy and was not able to attend.) I had heard from Jane previously that they were doing well, and I was astonished at how well they looked and how happy they seemed. One very important development was that Maria had found a new physician, who, she said, had successfully diagnosed her pain as being due to severe spasms in the pelvic floor. Maria had been getting physical therapy/massage for almost a month, and she reported that her pain was greatly decreased. Maria blushed and smiled as John let me know that they had recently had sexual intercourse again. And she blushed again and laughed when John asked her, "Aren't you going to show him? You have to show him!" He then beamed at me as Maria—to my surprise—began unbuttoning the top buttons of her blouse. She then folded back her collar and proudly showed me—on the top area of her breast—a small colorful tattoo of a butterfly! We all laughed together, and Maria said, "You said I could wait until it felt right to bring in the butterfly. Well, one day it felt right and so I did this!" John smiled and said it was the very best present anyone had ever given him, and they kissed. I teared up a bit, and thanked them for showing me. They expressed their appreciation and

Maria said, "You gave us back our marriage and gave me back my life. We can't thank you enough!" We hugged and said good-bye.

LONG-TERM FOLLOW-UP

I recently contacted Jane and learned that several years after the assessment, Maria and John are doing extremely well. Maria is now pain free and has returned to work. They recently bought a new house and moved. Their older daughter has moved into her own apartment and continues to go to college. Their younger daughter is doing well at school and has many friends. John and Maria also have developed friends, and Maria continues to see Jane twice a month for psychotherapy. Jane said she and Maria did a fair amount of work on Maria's traumatic childhood, but that what had healed Maria the most was her relationship with John. Maria often said that John had taken her pain seriously, which her family growing up had never done.

SUMMARY

Jane's comment leads to an important distinction I want to make between TA with individuals and TA with couples. As I have discussed elsewhere (Finn, 2007), TA with individual clients appears to be therapeutic in part because clients feel seen and recognized in new ways within the secure assessor–client relationship. This allows clients to see themselves in ways they have previously resisted and to try out new ways of being that help them meet their life goals. In contrast, in TA with couples, if all goes well, a new secure attachment is fostered *between members of the couple*. To be sure, the relationship the couple has with the assessor is important, but if each partner feels understood and supported by the assessor, this creates a kind of "positive triangulation" that can be used to help the couple heal. By using tests, the assessor helps each partner see the other more accurately and with more compassion. The assessor also helps name each individual's experiences in the relationship in new ways. Last, the assessor helps create a coherent story about the couple's relationship—why and how it developed, the source of its problems, and what it needs to continue to develop. This helps the couple find what Fischer (1985/1994) has called "personally viable options" about how to relate better. Equipped with this new set of options, couples leave the assessment and continue to grow and change as new life challenges occur. The assessment recedes into memory, but its impact continues and is interwoven with further insights and changes the couple develops on its own.

REFERENCES

Armstrong, J. G., & Loewenstein, R. J. (1990). Characteristics of patients with multiple personality and dissociative disorders on psychological testing. *The Journal of Nervous and Mental Disease, 178,* 448 454.

Bruhn, A. R. (1992). The Early Memories Procedure: A projective test of autobiographical memory: II. *Journal of Personality Assessment, 58,* 326–346.

Butcher, J. N., Dahlstrom, W. G., Graham, J. R., Tellegen, A., & Kaemmer, B. (1989). *Minnesota Multiphasic Personality Inventory–2 (MMPI-2): Manual for administration and scoring.* Minneapolis: University of Minnesota Press.

Durham-Fowler, J. A. (2010). *Therapeutic Assessment with couples.* Unpublished doctoral dissertation, University of Texas, Austin.

Exner, J. E. (2003). *The Rorschach: A comprehensive system, Vol. 1: Basic foundations* (4th ed.). Hoboken, NJ: Wiley.

Finn, S. E. (2007). *In our clients' shoes: Theory and techniques of Therapeutic Assessment.* Mahwah, NJ: Erlbaum.

Fischer, C. T. (1985/1994). *Individualizing psychological assessment.* Mahwah, NJ: Erlbaum.

Handler, L. (1997). He says, she says, they say: The Consensus Rorschach. In J. R. Meloy, M. W. Acklin, C. B. Gacono, J. F. Murray, & C. A. Peterson (Eds.), *Contemporary Rorschach interpretation* (pp. 499–533). Mahwah, NJ: Erlbaum.

Kamphuis, J. H., Kugeares, S. L., & Finn, S. E. (2000). Rorschach correlates of sexual abuse: Trauma content and aggression indices. *Journal of Personality Assessment, 75,* 212–224.

CHAPTER

19

Case Studies in Collaborative Neuropsychology: A Man With Brain Injury and a Child With Learning Problems

TAD T. GORSKE AND STEVEN R. SMITH

"The presentation of brain facts about specific damages is meaningless to patients unless they can begin to understand how the changes in their brains are lived out in everyday experiences and situations" (Varela, Thompson, & Rosch, 1991, as cited in McInerney & Walker, 2002).

The World Health Organization (WHO) estimates that approximately 1 billion people worldwide suffer from a neurological disorder (WHO, 2006). Neurological disorders include conditions such as epilepsy, stroke, dementia, Parkinson's disease, traumatic brain injury, and many others. Neurological disorders in childhood include developmental disorders such as autism, attention deficit disorder, dyslexia, and others (National Institute of Neurological Disorders and Stroke, 2009). Changes in cognitive functioning caused by a neurological illness can be a life-changing event that can significantly alter people's view of themselves and their world and can lead to lifelong changes in mood, thinking, behavior, work, social relationships, health, and overall outlook on life. In short, cognitive changes can negatively affect self-esteem, self-understanding, and family unity (Cosden, Elliot, Noble, & Kelemen, 1999).

A loss of cognitive function can be a frightening experience that can challenge an individual's personal view of themselves, their abilities, and their self-concept (Patterson & Staton, 2009). In many neurological injuries, individuals often have no memory of the event and may not remember the hours or months before or after the accident. Once they "wake up" and gain awareness, they realize that they have significantly changed physically, emotionally, and cognitively, but they may not understand why. Even when they are told about the terrible injury, it is difficult for them to believe what they are told because they have no conscious recollection of the event. They may feel as though someone robbed them of a part of their lives and left them alone and disabled.

Some of the existential challenges patients who suffer a loss of cognitive functioning face include (1) an awareness that they have changed and may never be the same; (2) emotional reactions to the change and loss of function; (3) the struggle to make sense of the changes; this often involves grappling with the question of "why?"; (4) grieving loss of function and a loss of self, with the hopes of moving toward some sense of (5) acceptance in order to begin the process of (6) creating a renewed sense of meaning and purpose in one's life (Howes, Benton, & Edwards, 2005; Parsons & Stanley, 2008; Patterson & Staton, 2009).

To begin the process of rehabilitation and recovery, an individual undergoes a comprehensive course of rehabilitation therapies designed to enhance his or her functional abilities. Psychological and neuropsychological care are important parts of rehabilitation. Psychological care may mean addressing the emotional needs of patients and their families. Neuropsychological care means addressing the short- and long-term cognitive deficits that may arise and how these deficits impact short- and long-term functioning (Taylor, Livingston, & Kreutzer, 2007).

The role of neuropsychological evaluation is changing, such that neuropsychologists are challenged to expand their roles from a purely technical consultant to a more holistic practitioner. A holistic neuropsychological perspective is a shift from viewing individuals from a purely brain-behavior perspective to viewing the person as a holistic emotional and relational being. A neuropsychologist operating from a holistic perspective (1) collaborates with and empowers patients and families to take an active role in the treatment process; (2) believes that people with neurological disabilities are more like people without neurological disabilities; (3) conveys honesty and caring in personal interactions to form a foundation for a strong therapeutic relationship; and thus (4) develops practical plans for rehabilitation while explaining rehabilitation techniques in understandable language. Neuropsychologists operating from within this framework help patients and families understand the neurobehavioral sequelae of neurological injury and recovery, while recognizing that change is inevitable, and they help families cope with change. All patients are important, and their existential issues are acknowledged and treated with respect (Taylor, Livingston, & Kreutzer, 2007).

COLLABORATIVE THERAPEUTIC NEUROPSYCHOLOGICAL ASSESSMENT (CTNA)

We have proposed a model that we call Collaborative Therapeutic Neuropsychological Assessment (CTNA; Gorske, 2008; Gorske & Smith, 2009) in which feedback from neuropsychological test results enlists the client and family members as active collaborators in the feedback process. The spirit of CTNA lies in therapeutic and collaborative models of assessment (Finn, 1996, 2007; Fischer, 1994) and uses the framework from Motivational Interviewing Principles for conducting client-centered feedback sessions (Miller & Rollnick, 1991/2001). CTNA is designed to demystify the neuropsychological assessment process by providing clients and families with objective feedback from test results, while facilitating collaboration and empathic understanding, answering client questions, and attempting to relate the results to the person's unique experience. In doing so, CTNA hopes to address important existential questions, look toward the future, and begin the process of creating new meaning for the individual and family members.

Specifically, CTNA has two phases: the collaborative interview and the therapeutic feedback session. The goal of the interview is not only to understand the magnitude and specifics of the patient's cognitive issues but also to understand the pragmatic and emotional consequences for the patient and/or his or her family. Although patients are referred for neuropsychological evaluations because of concerns about cognitive functioning, these issues have a real and powerful emotional consequence. The CTNA approach is designed to elicit the delicate interplay between cognitive issues and their emotional weight. For example, although many neuropsychologists might ask about Alzheimer's patients' memory problems and symptoms of disorientation, the CTNA clinician is equally concerned about those patients' embarrassment over their loss of function and stress in their relationships with their spouses/partners. CTNA recognizes that the emotional and relational consequences of an illness, disability, or injury are no less important than their primary symptoms.

The second main component of the CTNA approach is the feedback session (Gorske & Smith, 2009). As is the case for TA more broadly, CTNA recognizes the expertise of the patient and incorporates the perspective of the patient at each phase of the feedback process. Test results are presented and discussed with the patient in words that the patient (or the families) can understand. Consistent with Motivational Interviewing, patients are asked to provide information and real-world examples of how they see corollaries of the test results in their day-to-day lives. Both strengths and weaknesses are presented in a way that patients and/or their families can easily understand in the context of the patient's life. Last, rather than merely providing recommendations in a laundry list, patients and/or their families are asked to help generate accommodations and interventions that might be beneficial. That is, although they may not immediately recognize that occupational therapy is needed, for example, they might be able to recognize that they need some help with their loss of manual dexterity.

In sum, unlike the practice of traditional neuropsychology, the CTNA approach incorporates the lessons of therapeutic assessment to make the assessment process more patient-centered, sensitive, and holistic. Patients are seen as active collaborators, experts, and status-holders in the assessment. Although tests are administered and scored in a standardized fashion, the presentation of results is flexible and designed to answer the patient's and family's questions. The ultimate goal of CTNA is to relieve anxiety and give patients and their families a greater sense of personal agency and a realistic appraisal of their future possibilities.

THE CASE OF WALTER

I (Dr. Gorske) first met Walter at the University of Pittsburgh Medical Center Traumatic Brain Injury Rehabilitation Unit in early 2009. Walter was a European American gentleman in his mid-40s who had suffered a severe industrial accident, in which he fell and heavy equipment landed on him, causing a severe brain injury. When he came to the emergency room, Walter had a Glascow Coma Scale (a measure of an individual's level of consciousness following a head injury) score of 7, which suggests a severe head injury with a low level of consciousness. A CT scan of his head showed bleeding in his brain on both sides of the frontal lobes, a hematoma (a pocket or collection of blood underlying brain tissue) near the back of his brain, bilateral contusions to the temporal and frontal lobes, and a left occipital epidural hematoma. This means that there was a buildup of blood between the dura mater (the tough outer membrane of the brain) and the back part of the skull. Walter also sustained skull fractures in the left parietal bone and bilateral occipital bone. After being treated and stabilized in the emergency trauma unit, he was transferred to the brain injury rehabilitation unit about eight days later.

When I met Walter, he was suffering from severe head pain and was on multiple medications, so making an accurate assessment of his mental status was difficult. Based on the best assessment I could perform, and feedback from other staff, I determined that he was likely experiencing moderately severe posttraumatic amnesia (PTA, which is a state of confusion and memory deficits that occur following a traumatic brain injury) based on his score on the Galveston Orientation and Amnesia Test (Score = 39; 76 is normal)—a test that measures posttraumatic amnesia, cognition, and orientation following a brain injury (Levin, O'Donnell, & Grossman, 1979). When I saw Walter a few days later, his score improved to 79 and then to 85 a few days after that. Therefore, I determined that he was probably clear of PTA, and I commenced with inpatient neuropsychological testing.

In my experience, Walter's test results were fairly typical for patients in the rehabilitation unit. He was impaired on tests of oral and written information processing speed, letter fluency (the ability to generate words from letters), attention, visual tracking, and higher-level problem solving and logical reasoning (all scores were in the first percentile or less). Walter performed a little better, in the mild to moderately impaired range, on category fluency (the ability to generate words from categories such as animals), visuoconstructional ability (the ability to draw a complicated design), and visual memory (the ability to remember a series of designs). His verbal memory was moderately to severely impaired, although he scored normally in his ability to learn and retain verbal information. He was independent for most activities of daily living by the time of his discharge, about 25 days after the initial injury. However, because of his cognitive deficits, Walter was referred and accepted to a specialized residential brain injury rehabilitation program.

I met Walter for an outpatient neuropsychological examination a few months after his discharge from the hospital. He continued to reside at the residential rehabilitation program, and by all accounts was doing well in his therapies. However, when I interviewed Walter, he was much more pessimistic about his situation. He described himself as an "emotional train wreck," in part because he had severe sleeping problems and was also very anxious about getting back to his life and his work in construction. Overall, he denied any significant cognitive problems except for some mild word-finding difficulties. However, he was bitter about his situation because he felt that he had no control over his life in part because of chronic pain.

Walter had been attending active therapies, such as physical therapy and speech therapy, and the feedback he received was that he was making excellent progress. However, Walter expressed fears that he would never get out of the rehabilitation program, because every time he met a goal the rehabilitation staff kept adding new ones. (This was correct, but it was because Walter was accomplishing his goals, so the staff would develop new, more challenging goals.) When we discussed this further, it became obvious how concerned and anxious this made Walter feel, because he was convinced that he would never leave the program and other people would always see him as some sort of an "invalid."

When we started the testing, Walter's mental status was essentially normal, meaning he knew the correct date, day, month, year, and where he was at the time of testing. However, he missed one item in his ability to recall three words. Otherwise, he was alert and cooperative initially. He also denied any significant mood symptoms. However, as the testing progressed, Walter's frustration and anxiety increased dramatically. He expressed fears that the results of the testing would determine whether he could leave the rehabilitation program, which was not true and was made clear earlier. He became overly focused on "errors" he was making during testing and became more anxious and distracted as it progressed. In fact, however, Walter was doing quite well. For example, he completed one of the more complicated designs on the Block Design Subtest and became frustrated even though he was doing it correctly. After making several "errors," Walter became visibly upset and stopped cooperating, stating, "I'm never getting out." The neuropsychological technician stopped the testing and came into my office for a consultation. Walter was visibly upset and shaking, and I asked him what he was thinking and feeling.

Walter: They're [the rehabilitation program] never going to let me go. I'm never getting out of there.

Dr. Gorske: Walter, what makes you think that?

Walter: I'm failing these. I know I am. They're going to keep me there forever.

Dr. Gorske: You're very frightened that if you fail then that means there's something wrong with you and they'll keep you for a long time.

(Walter nodded and kept his head lowered.)

Dr. Gorske: Walter, can I share some information with you? People usually don't stay in rehabilitation because they don't do well on testing. All testing does is give a marker for progress and any other work that needs done. They will discharge you once they think you're ready.

Walter nodded in acknowledgment and was shaking a little less.

Dr. Gorske: Another thing, Walter, is that I'm looking at what you've done so far, and I can tell you that you're doing quite well, at least normal for everything. So I think you're doing better than you think.

Breaking standardization paid off because Walter looked up and his face seemed calmer. He was still shaking nervously. At that point, I asked him some mental status questions to make sure his thinking did not represent a delusional or psychotic process. I was comfortable that it was not, and no one had reported such symptoms in the rehabilitation program. I decided to discontinue testing at that point and reschedule it for the following week. I also was given written permission by Walter to consult with the rehabilitation psychologist (Dr. M) at the program. Walter agreed to come back the following week and in the meantime to discuss this situation with Dr. M.

I spoke with Dr. M that same day and explained the situation. We felt it would be good if, over the next week, he and Walter could work together discussing his thoughts and reactions to the testing in the context of his self-expectations. They would then work on test preparation in that Walter would learn cognitive and behavioral anxiety-reduction strategies to manage his own negative thoughts and expectations and learn to calm himself physically when he was anxious. Essentially, the following week's testing session would become a laboratory for helping Walter cope with anxiety, an issue I hypothesized he was going to have to deal with once he left the hospital.

About a week later, Walter came back and testing resumed. He was visibly more relaxed and was encouraged to participate fully in the examination by regularly giving the technician feedback about how he was feeling and any thoughts he had that were bothering him. During testing, he continued to perseverate on making "mistakes," but it was easier to divert his attention to the task at hand and let go of his performance anxiety. This was most evident on the Wisconsin Card Sorting Test (WCST). The WCST is a computerized test of problem solving, reasoning, and the ability to use one's judgment based on the feedback of the examiner (Heaton, Chelune, Talley, Kay, & Curtiss, 1993). Test takers complete several test trials and are told whether they are "right" or "wrong." The first time Walter heard the feedback "wrong," he became anxious and visibly uptight. With some encouragement, he was able to breathe, relax, and use self-talk, such as self-affirmations of his competency, to reduce his anxiety and continue with the test. Walter's test profile indicated that he was in the normal range on almost all neuropsychological tests with the exception of below average visual memory, letter fluency (word generation), and object naming (the ability to accurately name pictures he saw). He also demonstrated a mild deficit in category fluency (animal naming). He had clearly improved from his inpatient testing and was performing normally.

I met with Walter a few weeks later to review his test results. I provided him a graphic description of his test scores, and we reviewed his cognitive profile. Walter seemed rather surprised that he had done so well. We had a discussion about his expectation and perception of himself.

> Walter: I've always tried to do well at anything I did. I never liked to fail. I did well in high school and I tried college, but I wanted to work instead.
>
> Dr. Gorske: It seems that you think about failing as something that would be hard for you to handle.
>
> Walter: Yes, I've never liked it at all, but I don't remember ever reacting this way either. In the past, if I failed at something, I just fixed it, no problem.
>
> Dr. Gorske: But something is different now?
>
> Walter: Yes, when I'm anxious I get really on edge, like I can't control it.

What Walter was describing was consistent with observations in brain injury rehabilitation regarding the blend of a person's personality and the effects of a brain injury. Walter's personality style before his injury included high expectations of himself. Prior to his injury, this expectation would cause him some anxiety, but he was able to manage the anxiety and use it adaptively. However, his brain injury left him less able to manage the anxiety, so the symptoms seemed much worse to him. Additionally, the trauma of having gone through a brain injury can compound anxiety to where it feels unmanageable. Walter needed to relearn how to manage his anxiety while changing catastrophic thoughts that he was somehow permanently damaged and would never get better. We discussed ways to do this while in the safety of the residential program so that he and Dr. M could work together to apply this on a day-to-day basis.

The neuropsychological assessment results helped Walter see the discrepancy between his experience of himself and the actual quality of his performance. The collaborative approach allowed for a processing of Walter's reactions and helped him develop insight into how his expectations of himself were creating strong emotional reactions that were interfering with his brain injury recovery. The test scores were used as stimuli for exploring these deeper issues, and the examination itself served as a laboratory for testing out whether Walter could use the skills he learned. Walter and I agreed on recommendations that he would continue to learn anxiety-reduction strategies with Dr. M and would apply these strategies in day-to-day rehabilitation tasks to promote generalization.

When I consulted with Dr. M two days after our feedback session, he reported to me that Walter was more engaged and cooperative in the rehabilitation program than he had been prior to the testing and feedback session. Before testing, Walter had appeared anxious, irritable, agitated, and would often shut down and hastily quit at tasks. At one point, Walter had threatened to leave the rehabilitation program against medical advice. Most of these difficulties related to his anxieties and catastrophic thinking. With guided anxiety management strategies, he was able to change his catastrophic thinking, reduce his physiological response, and engage more in the rehabilitation process. This practice led to even quicker and more pronounced gains in his cognitive and functional abilities. The mingling of emotional and cognitive difficulties in Walter's case is therefore an exemplar of one of the primary challenges in brain injury rehabilitation (Bradbury et al., 2008; Hanna-Pladdy, Berry, Bennett, Phillips, & Gouvier, 2009).

The case of Walter demonstrates the strengths of a collaborative neuropsychological approach in brain injury rehabilitation. This approach:

> *Provides information on cognitive functioning and facilitates individual application:* Walter was able to see progress relative to his level of functioning while he was in the hospital. More importantly, he

was able to process his emotional reactions to the test results. In Walter's case, this meant challenging his thoughts of being disabled and feeling hopeless that things will ever get better.

Presents potential ameliorative strategies and discovers the individual's own resources for change: Walter was already in a cognitive rehabilitation program, so the issue for him was emotional management. The testing experience became a laboratory where Walter could examine his own reactions and resources for coping with anxiety in a safe and supportive environment.

Addresses a person's experience and reactions to information provided; balances education and the I-Thou interaction: Much of my interaction with Walter focused on his experience of the testing situation and the way in which this related to his life in the past and present. Such an approach allows for a holistic view of people versus compartmentalizing their struggles as purely a "brain injury issue" but rather a "human suffering from a brain injury issue."

Works to motivate individuals to personalize what they have learned in rehabilitation programs: Walter's anxiety and hopelessness interfered with his ability to integrate teachings from cognitive rehabilitation. Identifying and addressing his anxiety allowed this issue to be incorporated into his treatment and helped him to integrate the cognitive tasks.

Maintains a comprehensive, future-oriented perspective: Walter had a renewed sense that things could get better for him, giving him goals and direction. He was able to see past the rehabilitation experience and begin to think about how life could be in the future.

Most people will struggle with the aftereffects of a brain injury for a long time, possibly for the rest of their lives. This will likely be the case for Walter. However, the challenge is to become aware and acknowledge one's strengths and weaknesses and integrate them into one's life story (Finn, 2003). A collaborative neuropsychological approach goes beyond an analysis of the brain-behavior relationships and engages patients in an "I-thou" experience that can potentially allow them to use the neuropsychological information in a way that facilitates healing and growth.

✍ Teaching Points

1. When providing information on cognitive functioning, an emphasis should be placed on applying the information to the individual's personal experience. For example, when giving feedback on a patient's ability to solve a complex problem, important questions to ask include, "How does this fit with your own experience?" "Is this how you see yourself?" "What skills did you use to try and complete this test?" "How do you see those skills working in your daily life?" In this way you help the patient see the application of the test results to his or her personal life. This will allow for the development of personalized treatment interventions.

2. Giving feedback from neuropsychological tests should be accomplished without the use of complicated jargon. For example, instead of saying "verbal learning and memory," say "your ability to remember what you hear." This allows for the development of an egalitarian relationship within the feedback session that helps the patient feel empowered as part of the feedback and decision making process.

3. While the information during a feedback session is important, the client-centered interviewing skills are essential for maintaining collaboration. "Elicit–Provide–Elicit" from Motivational Interviewing is a helpful framework in this feedback process. First a therapist "elicits" information from the patient about his or her experience in the testing process. Second, the therapist "provides" information about the cognitive function being tested. Finally, the therapist "elicits" the patient's reaction to the feedback. All the while, the therapist uses client-centered verbal skills such as empathic statements, open-ended questions, affirmations, and reflective summaries to ensure that the client feels understood and that his or her opinions are heard and valued during the feedback process (Miller & Rollnick, 1991/2001).

4. Neuropsychological assessment results are viewed as snapshots of a person's cognition and must be considered from a holistic perspective. Although Walter had some cognitive difficulties, these difficulties were intertwined with his own negative self-concept, which contributed to increased anxiety. Brain-behavior relationships must be integrated

with life experiences that may contribute to patient's struggles but also provide strength for coping. Interventions must not only address the brain-behavior relationship but seek ways to help the person live life more fully.

CTNA WITH A CHILD: THE CASE OF ILYSSA

Ilyssa was a 10-year-old European American girl brought to my (Dr. Smith) Psychology Assessment Center on campus. Her pediatrician, Dr. N, expressed concerns regarding Ilyssa's cognitive functioning and her performance in school. Upon interview, Dr. N stated that Ilyssa had become increasingly distracted in her fifth-grade classroom, was frequently off-task, and had difficulty completing work on time. She wondered if Ilyssa might have a learning disability or other cognitive impairment that was resulting in these disruptive behaviors in school.

When I met with Ilyssa and her parents in our clinic, I experienced her as a pleasant child who was verbally precocious, energetic, and engaging. She was the older of two children, and her biological parents had been married for 12 years. Both parents were college-educated and had full-time professional jobs. Ilyssa was born full-term and was physically healthy with no history of birth complications, serious illness, falls, or academic difficulties prior to the present concerns. Her parents said that she had good friends but that she was becoming increasingly less social. There was no history of abuse, violence, or trauma in the home.

Ilyssa's mother reported that Ilyssa was generally an average student and that her behavior was usually unremarkable at home, but that she had become increasingly oppositional when doing homework. Her oppositional outbursts would often deteriorate into weeping and tearfulness. One incident was so bad that Ilyssa's parents had difficulty consoling her, and she threw a textbook at her 6-year-old brother. Both parents noted that Ilyssa was emotionally closer to her father and that she had always been "Daddy's little girl."

When I spoke with Ilyssa's parents, it became clear that they had different perspectives on her struggles. Her mother, like Dr. N, felt as though Ilyssa might be struggling with a learning disability or other cognitive issue. She stated, "You should see how much she struggles with the work. She just doesn't get it. My sister had dyslexia, and I worry that Ilyssa might have the same type of problem." Ilyssa's father had a different perspective, suggesting that "Ilyssa is just having problems with the harder classwork of fifth grade. She hasn't learned proper study skills. She's gonna need to learn to study at some point." When I spoke with Ilyssa, she noted that school was "hard," and that she felt "slow" compared to her peers.

As is outlined in the CNTA approach, I asked both parents and Ilyssa to generate questions that they would like to have addressed in the assessment. I had each do so separately without sharing or discussing these questions between them. The questions they posed were the following:

Ilyssa: "Why is school so hard for me?"
Mom: "Does Ilyssa have a learning disability? How can we better control her behavior at home? Does she need to be on medication?"
 Dad: "How can we teach Ilyssa better study skills so that she can be successful?"

Ilyssa was agreeable and eager to begin testing. As we settled into the WISC-IV, she began to talk more and more about life at home and at school. She stated that she felt "stupid" at school and was tired of her parents' pressure to do so much homework when it was so difficult. She said that she thought that her parents were tired of her and that they liked her younger brother because he did not cause the same trouble as she did.

When completing the Arithmetic subtest, she stated, "I'm not good at math," and she appeared to stop attending to the test. After testing was complete, I readministered portions of the Arithmetic subtest again, but this time I said, "I'd like for you to try a couple of these again, but here's the secret: This test really isn't about math, but really about your ability to listen carefully and think about what to do. The math part should be pretty easy for you." This time, Ilyssa had no difficulty attending to all of the items and was able to generate correct responses for many of them. Although this readministration could not be used formally, it was important in showing the change in Ilyssa's effort and quality of performance.

My assessment generally fell into four domains: cognitive and neuropsychological, achievement, emotional/personality, and behavioral.

The cognitive and neuropsychological assessments were generally unremarkable. Her performance was generally average apart from some deficits in processing speed and working memory that were in the lower average range. She had no remarkable scores on measures of auditory verbal memory, executive functions, or visuospatial processing. However, her Wechsler Individual Achievement Test (2nd ed., WIAT-II; Wechsler, Psychological Corporation, 2002) scores showed some scatter, with deficits in Pseudoword Decoding (i.e., a word-attack task) and single-word reading. Likewise, her oral reading (i.e., Gray Oral Reading Test, 4th ed.; GORT-4; Wiederholt & Bryant, 2001) scores were poor, both for fluency and comprehension.

Measures of emotional function and personality (i.e., Roberts-2, Roberts & Gruber, 2005; Rorschach, Exner, 2003; Personality Inventory for Youth [PIY], Lachar & Gruber, 1995) reflected a socially oriented young woman who had many psychological resources at her disposal. There were no signs of cognitive disruption or social concern, but she appeared to harbor an underlying sense of guilt and anxiety. Despite her ample resources, she appeared limited in her ability to take risks or express herself. Although there was some evidence of a depressive style (e.g., elevated *Psychological Discomfort* scores on the PIY, Rorschach MOR = 3), this did not appear to reach the level of clinical impairment.

As opposed to her self-report and performance-based scores, ratings of Ilyssa's behavior were quite striking. I asked her parents to complete the Personality Inventory for Children (PIC-2, Lachar & Gruber, 2001) separately and without discussion. Her mother's ratings reflected a child with several clinically significant problems, including depression, anxiety, and social ineptness. Her ratings suggested that Ilyssa had difficulty making and keeping friends, had a depressive style, and was unhappy at school. More concerning to me were elevated ratings of somatization issues and even some symptoms of thought disorder (i.e., PIC-2 *Somatic Concern* = 75T; *Reality Distortion* = 70T). However, her father's ratings were striking for their lack of elevation, with T-scores consistently within the average range for all scales and subscales.

I decided to provide feedback separately to Ilyssa and her parents. She was a bright child who was interested in the results of the tests, so I felt that she could use some of the information and integrate my feedback into her developing sense of self. I explained to her that she was a "really smart kid," who should be able to do well in school. In fact, she should be able to do as well as or even better than most of her friends.

Then I asked about what it was like for Ilyssa to read. She said that it was "pretty hard," and that it made her "brain hurt a little bit." I told her that I had seen that in the testing, and I described how even though she was really smart, reading might be more difficult for her than for other kids. I began discussing the idea with her that she had dyslexia, "when the part of the brain that makes sense of letters and words seems to work differently." It was at this point that I asked her if she knew who the cyclist Lance Armstrong was. She said that she did, and we both agreed that he wins a lot of bike races. "But you see," I said, "Lance Armstrong wins a lot of bike races, but he's not a very fast sprinter compared to lots of other racers. So, if a bike race comes down to the finish, he probably won't win in a big sprint. So what Lance has to do is think ahead, plan through his race, and make sure that he's way out ahead and by himself at the finish. He might have to work extra hard to get out ahead, but that's how he wins." I explained to Ilyssa that she would need to be like Lance and think ahead and work a little extra hard, but in the end, she will do great. She seemed pleased that there might be some extra help that she could get at school so that she wouldn't need to spend so much time doing homework each night.

I focused my feedback with Ilyssa's parents more on the emotional and relational aspects of her functioning. The diagnosis of dyslexia was not difficult or surprising for them to hear, and both parents understood this quite quickly. They seemed relieved to have a diagnosis that they could use within the school system to get Ilyssa the resources she needed to be successful. I emphasized that this diagnosis of dyslexia was quite mild and that they need not adjust their expectations for her performance once accommodations were in place.

Once the discussion of the cognitive and neuropsychological aspects was concluded, I called their attention to their PIC-2 scores. I brought out their two score profiles and showed these to Ilyssa's parents. I asked them what they made of the substantial difference in elevations. Her mother spoke first: "Well, I spend a lot more time with Ilyssa, and he

[Ilyssa's father] doesn't see all the things that I do. I think that this is just due to time spent with her." Ilyssa's father chimed in, "That might be true, but I think that some problems seem bigger to you than they do to me." Their tone was mutually respectful, and they agreed that they simply see things differently. I explained that this was not an uncommon situation for many parents and that, for one reason or another, they might have very different perspectives on their child.

At this point, I asked them to suspend their judgment about which one was "right" and to consider that these PIC-2 ratings were messages to Ilyssa. I asked them to imagine how different these messages were to Ilyssa. I said, "Mom, your ratings tell Ilyssa that she's really struggling and has a lot to overcome. They also tell her that her father is wrong. Dad, your ratings tell Ilyssa that her mother is wrong and might be crying wolf or thinking badly about her. And Dad, your ratings also tell Ilyssa that she shouldn't be struggling as much as she is." I emphasized that these ratings were not about truth, but rather different perspectives that then get communicated to the child; and two ratings this different are probably pretty confusing for a kid. I said that this confusion about her identity, abilities, and capacity probably "stall Ilyssa out," so that she feels uncertain of the strengths she has and the reality of her struggles.

From these discussions, Ilyssa's work in the schools was aided by a reduction in written assignments, additional tutoring, and untimed tests. Because her case was a mild one, her parents opted not to have note-taking accommodations at this point. However, in the weeks after the feedback, both parents contacted me to report that they were working together to present a "unified message" to Ilyssa regarding her strengths and challenges. And even more important than the appearance of synchrony, they reported that their views of Ilyssa were, in fact, growing more and more convergent.

Teaching Points

- First, there is always a connection between cognitive abilities/ functioning and their emotional consequence. With changes or deficits in our cognitive ability, we feel different, either from ourselves or from those around us. The emotional consequences are often more detrimental than the cognitive issues themselves.

- Second, although we all live and function in a social context, the relationship between parents and children is especially powerful in identity development. Children must look outside of themselves for messages of how well (or not well) they are doing. When those messages are confusing or mixed, the result can be fear or a loss of agency.
- The job of an assessment clinician is to "translate" a child to his or her parents. The principles of TA (broadly) and CTNA can help in this process of translation. The mingling of cognitive, social, systemic, and educational implications is complicated, but greater understanding leads to more clarity and consistency that will lead to better outcomes.

SUMMARY

The goal of this chapter was to demonstrate that the principles of Therapeutic Assessment (Finn, 2007) and Collaborative Assessment (Fischer, 1994, 2000) can be applied to neuropsychological assessment. Although we outline the full model elsewhere (Gorske & Smith, 2009), our Collaborative Therapeutic Neuropsychological Assessment gives clinicians a starting point from which to begin the process of collaborative assessment with neuropsychological assessment patients and their families. Not limited to those with brain injury or dementing conditions, the CTNA approach is also useful with such diverse referral questions as learning disabilities, ADHD, substance abuse, and serious psychiatric issues. Although the CNTA approach may not be useful for all settings, it can provide a theoretical foundation that can be adapted to multiple settings and situations. CTNA might help neuropsychologists with their goal of making neuropsychological assessment understandable, reachable, and personally relevant to all of their patients and their patients' families.

REFERENCES

Bradbury, C. L., Christenson, B. K., Lau, M. A., Ruttan, L. A., Arundine, A. L., & Green, R. E. (2008). The efficacy of cognitive behavior therapy in the treatment of emotional distress after acquired brain injury. *Archives of Physical Medicine and Rehabilitation, 89 (Supplement 2)*, S61–S68.

Cosden, M., Elliot, K., Noble, S., & Kelemen, E. (1999). Self-understanding and self-esteem in children with learning disabilities. *Learning Disability Quarterly, 22*, 279–290.

Exner, J. E. (2003). *Rorschach: A comprehensive system* (4th ed.). Hoboken, NJ: Wiley.

Finn, S. E. (1996). *Using the MMPI as a therapeutic intervention.* Minneapolis: University of Minnesota Press.

Finn, S. E. (2003). Therapeutic assessment of a man with "ADD." *Journal of Personality Assessment, 80*, 115–129.

Finn, S. E. (2007). *In our clients' shoes: Theory and techniques of therapeutic assessment.* Mahwah, NJ: Erlbaum.

Fischer, C. T. (1994). *Individualizing psychological assessment* (2nd ed.). Hillsdale, NJ: Erlbaum.

Fischer, C. T. (2000). Collaborative, individualized assessment. *Journal of Personality Assessment, 74*(1), 2–14.

Gorske, T. (2008). Therapeutic neuropsychological assessment: A humanistic model and case example. *Journal of Humanistic Psychology, 85*, 343–382.

Gorske, T., & Smith, S. (2009). *Collaborative therapeutic neuropsychological assessment.* New York, NY: Springer Science + Business Media.

Hanna-Pladdy, B., Berry, Z. M., Bennett, T., Phillips, H. L., & Gouvier, W. D. (2001). Stress as a diagnostic challenge for postconcussive symptoms: Sequelae of mild traumatic brain injury or physiological stress response. *The Clinical Neuropsychologist, 15*(3), 289–304.

Heaton, R. K., Chelune, G. J., Talley, J. L., Kay, G. G., & Curtiss, G. (1993). *Wisconsin Card Sorting Test manual: Revised and expanded.* Odessa, FL: Psychological Assessment Resources.

Howes, H., Benton, D., & Edwards, S. (2005). Women's experience of brain injury: An interpretive phenomenological analysis. *Psychology and Health, 20*(1), 129–142.

Lachar, D., & Gruber, C. (1995). *Personality Inventory for Youth.* Los Angeles, CA: Western Psychological Services.

Lachar, D., & Gruber, C. (2001). *Personality Inventory for Children* (2nd ed.). Los Angeles, CA: Western Psychological Services.

Levin, H. S., O'Donnell, V. M., & Grossman, R. G. (1979). The Galveston Orientation and Amnesia Test: A practical scale to assess cognition after head injury. *Journal of Nervous and Mental Disease, 167*(11), 675–684.

McInerney, R. G., & Walker, M. M. (2002). Toward a method of neurophenomenological assessment and intervention. *The Humanistic Psychologist, 30*(3), 180–193.

Miller, W. M., & Rollnick, S. (1991/2001). *Motivational Interviewing: Preparing people for change.* New York, NY: Guilford Press.

National Institute of Neurological Disorder and Stroke. (2009). *Pervasive developmental disorders information page.* Bethesda, MD: National Institutes of Health.

Parsons, L., & Stanley, M. (2008). The lived experience of occupational adaptation following acquired brain injury for people living in a rural area. *Australian Occupational Therapy Journal, 55,* 231–238.

Patterson, F. L., & Staton, A. R. (2009). Adult acquired traumatic brain injury: Existential implications and clinical considerations. *Journal of Mental Health Counseling, 31*(2), 149–163.

Psychological Corporation. (2002). *Wechsler Individual Achievement Test, second edition, Examiner's manual.* San Antonio, TX: Author.

Roberts, G. E., & Gruber, C. (2005). *Roberts 2.* Los Angeles, CA: Western Psychological Services.

Taylor, L. A., Livingston, L. A., & Kreutzer, J. S. (2007). Neuropsychological assessment and treatment of TBI. In N. D. Zasler, D. I. Katz, & R. D. Zafonte (Eds.), *Brain injury medicine: Principles and practice.* New York, NY: Demos Medical Publishing.

Varela, F., Thompson, E., & Rosch, E. (1991). *The embodied mind.* Cambridge, MA: MIT Press.

Wiederholt, J. L., & Bryant, B. R. (2001). *Gray Oral Reading Tests* (4th ed.). Austin, TX: Pro Ed.

World Health Organization. (2006). *Neurological disorders: Public health challenges.* Geneva, Switzerland: WHO Press.

Afterword: Forward!

Constance T. Fischer, Leonard Handler, and Stephen E. Finn

The inevitable labor of editing (and of coediting!) a book was repeatedly lightened as we found ourselves variously moved, impressed, and inspired by our authors' work. We enhanced our own understandings and practices. We discovered aspects of our own work that we had not made explicit before. We were impressed with the assessors' openness, caring, and creativity as they sought to understand and to be genuinely helpful to their clients. We were also impressed by their ways of accommodating clients' circumstances, sometimes being gently persistent in coming to mutual understandings. Beyond understanding the people with whom they were working, assessors explored ways to help clients to help themselves out of problematic ways of coping with life. No assessor followed a cookie-cutter format of conducting the assessment. Relative newcomers to Collaborative/Therapeutic Assessment (C/TA) were as successful as long-time practitioners. We were impressed by many aspects of each report. Here are examples from each chapter.

Part I concerns assessments with individual adults and, in the first chapter, *Judith Armstrong*'s traumatized and dissociating client's defenses were crumbling. Judith knew to assess the full range of trauma-related symptoms as well as earlier strengths in order to individualize treatment plans. Judith's openness to and with this woman was both collaborative and therapeutic throughout the assessment. *Marc Diener, Mark Hilsenroth, Thomas Cromer, Frank Pesale,* and *Jennelle Slavin-Mulford* reminded us of the usefulness for C/TA of the Brief Symptom Inventory and the Inventory of Interpersonal Problems. Their chart, "Summary of Clinician Activities Found to Be Significantly Related to Positive Therapeutic Alliance During the Initial Interview and Psychological

Assessment" (see Table 3.1), is useful for us all, as well as for giving context to their work with a depressed client. *Diane Engelman* used an array of neuropsychological instruments prior to collaboratively exploring their significance for a suicidal woman. Then she and *J. B. Allyn*, a freelance writer and dramatist, collaborated in constructing an allegorical story as their therapeutic report for this woman. Engelman and Allyn are among the first to create feedback fables for an adult.

Connie Fischer's collaboration with a man on his way to Officers' Candidate School began immediately following their review of his goals for the assessment. Their conversational, interpersonal explorations continued across two sessions, culminating in Jim's presenting his list of take-home points. *Chris Fowler's* perceptive attunement to his client's communications was evident throughout the assessment. His rapid analysis of Rorschach content scores brought him into close touch with the dynamics of a repeatedly suicidal woman's treatment crisis, and hence with the woman herself. *Jan Kamphuis* and *Hilde de Saeger* describe how Jan, in a persistent, caring way, helped a man to discover through C/TA that he could acknowledge his angry stance toward his father and recover his creativity. *Hale Martin* and *Erin Jacklin* describe the important role that a supervisor (Hale) can play in C/TA, in this case supporting Erin in taking risks with a young man who was confronted with problems of health, culture, and learning. Hale and Erin illustrated how an extended Rorschach inquiry deepened their understanding of the client, while providing rich images through which to communicate with the client. *Patrick McElfresh* described how a collaborative assessment approach prior to psychotherapy helped him to identify issues for case formulation, treatment planning, and likely therapeutic dynamics. Collaborative discussion of the Rorschach allowed the client, as well as Patrick, to track her progress throughout therapy. He helped the woman to move past feeling powerless and experiencing paralyzing self-criticism. *Carol Overton* made creative use of Ryle's Psychotherapy File, as well as carefully selected other material to help a severely abused woman to encounter her emotions. Carol used an extended Rorschach Inquiry to help the woman to learn that she could avoid finding herself flooded by emotion.

In Part II, assessments of children, adolescents, and young adults, *Marita Frackowiak's* chapter describes her use of the Adult Attachment Projective Picture System with a 14-year-old girl who had a history of abandonment. They came to use a metaphor of "catching on fire" for becoming angry. Marita added happy endings for the girl's stories to the Roberts Apperception Test, expanding her sense of what was possible. Engaging the mother, Marita helped her to "stay longer with the feelings," rather than erupting into emotional responses. *Len Handler* recounts his coming to know what it was like to be his unruly six-year-old client through the boy's requested drawing of an imaginary animal and his story about it. Len added to the story, showing the boy that he understood his situation. The story became their story as the boy found he could cope with his circumstances in new but personally viable ways. *Noriko Nakamura* described her use of repeated Rorschachs across psychotherapy with a young woman and in consultation with her mother. This account may be unique in showing how collaborative assessment can be used throughout ongoing therapy. *Caroline Purves* translates a Rorschach score $[3R + (2)/R]$ into a metaphor, "invisibilitis" in a compelling story for a 10-year-old girl, a story about a duckling named Matilda. The story of course contained many therapeutic messages for the girl.

Deborah Tharinger, *Melissa Fisher*, and *Bradley Gerber* arranged a family intervention session to help a 10-year-old boy. One assessor/therapist made use of a live video feed and consulted with the parents as the second team member worked collaboratively with the girl. All family members came to feel understood even as they developed revised understandings of one another. *Heikki Toivakka* has adapted Handler's Fantasy Animal Drawing Game and storytelling technique for use with hospitalized adolescents. He shared his experiences while developing the adaptation, and presented its use with a psychotic teenage girl, along with his use of other tests. At a family/staff meeting that seemed to have come to a dead end, Heikki asked the girl if he could show her picture to everyone and read aloud his notes from her story. The mother cried, the atmosphere changed, and cooperative plans were made to help the girl.

In Part III, special applications of C/TA, *Barton Evans* demonstrated that C/TA can be used in a custody situation. The divorced parents of an adolescent son regularly engaged in severe arguing. At one point, when the mother accused the father of being "paranoid," Barton presented the father's MMPI-2 profile, showing that his Paranoia scale was not elevated; then he presented the mother's MMPI-2 profile, which contained a spike on this very scale! The rest of the assessment was supportive to all three family members, as they shifted from their earlier entrenchments. *Tad Gorske* and *Steven Smith* have developed a model of Collaborative Therapeutic Neuropsychological Assessment. Tad drew on his experience with motivational interviewing and caringly empowered a brain-injured man to take an active role in his rehabilitation. Steven presented a case of a 10-year-old girl who turned out to be dyslexic. Facing that situation head-on, Steven asked her if she had heard of Lance Armstrong, and when she said that she had, he described how Armstrong wins a race by working slowly through it. The girl understood that Steven was suggesting that she could do the same. *Steve Finn* began work with a woman who had been referred for an individual assessment in regard to chronic pain. Soon he invited the woman and her husband to participate in a couples' Therapeutic Assessment, which Steve used as a systemic intervention. Steve's use of the Consensus Rorschach as an assessment intervention was a powerful turning point for the couple. The husband learned to support his wife emotionally, and she realized that he appreciated her pain. As the marital dynamics shifted, so the wife's pain lessened.

Returning to our impressions from across the chapters: We were not surprised that Collaborative/Therapeutic Assessment was very successfully implemented across four countries, across a range of settings, and across many kinds of client situations and reasons for the assessment. Nor were we surprised at the range of personal styles and theoretical orientations through which C/TA was successfully undertaken.

Although all assessors followed standardized procedures for administration and scoring, and were well versed in the literatures of personality and pathology, each assessor was attuned to the client as an individual. And each assessment became progressively individualized in light of what assessors and clients were learning. That process often led to a shift in choice of assessment materials as the assessment evolved across several sessions. In short, although assessors had planned ahead of the assessment, they revised their plan and approach when they anticipated that a shift might facilitate joint exploration of the issues that had been agreed upon. Although none of our authors said so explicitly, all were flexible.

The basic common ground, shared ground, was the world in which both client and assessor live. A sense of shared humanness often seemed to be jointly recognized. Many assessors made good use of their emotional connections with clients, most often in imagining "being in their shoes." Sometimes assessors' use of clients' language seemed to help to build common ground. Assessors' genuine interest in clients' life situations, and in how the clients—knowingly or unknowingly—were sustaining or trying to change them, helped clients to be curious about their ways of dealing with life.

Assessors collaborated at various points during the assessment, never just in the form of a feedback session at the end. The assessments were never unilateral, and they involved shared understandings and their implications for the client's life. Understandings and concerns were shared, clarified, and revised throughout the process. Clients were codiscoverers. Hence, clients seemed to feel genuinely understood, at least by the end of the assessment. Even clients who were initially resistant came to engage fully in the assessment.

Assessors made use of theory, research, diagnostic literature, and so on, but their focus was on individuals' lives, not on classification. Even though assessors sometimes drew on psychological constructs as organizing devices for diverse data, they did not reduce clients to types or explain them in terms of constructs. Instead, the focus, discussion, and recommendations were in terms of the client's life world. That is, throughout the assessment, assessors met their clients "where they lived." Assessors were keenly aware of contexts, past and present. Put differently, with their focus being clients' actual lives, assessors readily developed tailored—individualized—learning exercises during the assessments, followed by similar take-home suggestions.

Assessors did not feel compelled to share all that they had learned about the client. Rather, they shared what was relevant to the agreed-upon issues. However, they did not keep information "secret" that was also important for the client. During the assessment process, both clients and assessors sometimes shared gut senses for which they could not yet provide evidence. Often, both parties risked their earlier understandings in order to reach valid and more useful comprehensions. At various points, both parties found themselves personally affected by the assessment. C/TA certainly did not appear to be a dry, intellectual undertaking!

When third parties, such as parents, teachers, therapists, and so on, were involved, assessors not only gathered from them their impressions, reports of events, and concerns at the beginning, but also, with approval of the assessee, shared relevant joint findings with them at the end. This was important for helping the clients and their helpers to carry out the individualized suggestions that were developed during the assessment. These suggestions were always posed in terms of concrete life situations, and were ones that the client was ready to try out.

We should point out that although most of these chapters focused on the assessment process and outcomes and did not have room for related written reports, some C/TA reports are very brief, indicating the focal issues, and the joint understandings and suggestions that emerged. Some reports follow a more traditional format but describe the client much in the ways that appear in these chapters—that is, the findings and suggestions are described in terms of how they emerged through collaborative effort.

Some assessor/authors were not fully satisfied with their assessment work even though the assessed person and his or her involved others were satisfied. Many assessors, of varying years of C/TA practice, noted throughout the assessment what they were learning for later practice, knowing that each new assessment will challenge us differently. Across chapters we noted a high level of client and third-party satisfaction with the process and outcomes of the assessments. Nevertheless, many assessors were circumspect about the constraints that environments posed for their clients. All assessors "dared to care."

As we editors read these chapters, we noted that all of the assessments were therapeutic in process and outcome, whether or not they were formally referred to as therapeutic assessments. Clients experienced themselves as genuinely respected and eventually as deeply understood, and as making sense to themselves as well as to the assessor. Some clearly felt cared about. Some were pleased that now others, too, would understand them more personally. They all completed the assessment with a sense of greater agency, of being prepared to direct their lives more effectively and proudly.

We believe that psychologists in all areas of assessment, and at all levels of experience, can readily adapt aspects of C/TA to their own work. Most assessors find that they can readily expand what they are already doing in the way of collaborating with clients and engaging them in exploring and developing suggestions for their lives.

For assessors who have not yet attempted Collaborative/Therapeutic Assessment, let us suggest that the way to begin is to start. Our "afterword" is "forward"!

Author Index

Ackerman, S., 50, 54, 66
Ackerman, S. J., 8, 9, 113, 195, 196
Alden, L. E., 52
Allyn, J. B., 10, 11, 71, 84, 422
Almeida, A., 11
Altman, N., 244, 292
Armbruster, G., 289
Armstrong, J. G., 7, 33, 38, 39, 40, 207, 385, 421
Armstrong, L., 424
Aschieri, F., 13, 380
Austin, C., 311, 325, 331
Austin, C. A., 7, 17
Axline, V., 244
Axness, M. W., 239, 241

Bagby, R. M., 369
Baity, M. R., 8, 113, 196
Barends, A., 63, 65
Baris, M. A., 358, 361
Barker, P., 243
Beck, A. T., 137, 143, 364
Begin, M., 373
Bellak, L., 2, 295
Bellak, S. S., 295
Bender, L., 201, 295
Bennett, T., 410
Benton, D., 402
Berry, Z. M., 410
Bettelheim, B., 2, 243
Bieliauskas, L. A., 77
Blagys, M. D., 8, 113, 196
Blume, H., 73
Book, H., 50
Borckardt, J.J., 13
Borgen, F., 79
Bouchard, M., xviii
Bradbury, C. L., 410
Brand, B. L., 39
Brandon, M., 297
Braverman, S., 2
Breslau, N., 30
Brickman, A. S., 187
Briere, J., 33

Briggs, R., 244
Brown, G.K., 364
Brown, L. H., 73, 75
Bruhn, A., 202, 231
Bruhn, A. R., 75, 322, 383
Bryant, B. R., 415
Bucci, W., 243
Buck, J., 295
Budding, D. E., 73, 77
Buis, T., 369
Burns, D., 153
Burns, R., 295
Butcher, J., xiv
Butcher, J. N., 33, 75, 94, 137, 162, 201, 364, 368, 383

Caldwell, A., 368
Caldwell, A. B., 372
Carlson, E. B., 33
Carter, J., 373
Catell, R., 94
Chang, J., 40
Chelune, G. J., 408
Cho, D. W., 272
Christopher, G., 319
Cichetti, D. V., 36
Claiborn, C. D., 16
Clark, C., 29
Clemence, A. J., 8
Cohen, J., 65
Cosden, M., 402
Courtois, C. A., 29, 30, 77
Cox, M., 81
Crits-Christoph, P., 50, 243
Cromer, T. D., 8, 9, 421
Crowley, R., 243
Curtiss, G., 408

Dahlstrom, W. G., 75, 94, 137, 162, 201, 368, 383
Dalenberg, C. J., 30
Davis, D. A., xiv
Davis, M., 217
Dell, P. F., 77
Derogatis, L., 52

de Saeger, H., 6, 422
Diener, M. J., 9, 421
Dixon, E. B., 358
Durham-Fowler, J. A., 379
Dwivedi, K. N., 82

Edlis, G., 243
Edwards, S., 402
Elliot, K., 402
Engelman, D. H., 10, 11, 71, 84, 422
Epston, D., 243, 338
Erbauch, J. K., 137
Erdberg, S. P., 75
Erikson, E., 107
Evans, B., 423–424
Evans, F. B., 358, 360, 368
Exner, J., 201
Exner, J. E., 39, 75, 118, 137, 162, 182, 188, 201, 232, 281, 289, 295, 344, 364, 368, 383, 415
Exner, J. E. Jr., 298

Fanning, P., 217
Fidler, B. J., 369
Finn, S., 244, 261
Finn, S. E., xiv–xvi, xvii, xviii, xix, 1–2, 4, 5, 6, 7, 10, 11, 12, 13, 16, 17, 34, 40, 54, 56, 61, 75, 76, 78, 113, 114, 136, 138, 139, 144, 150, 154, 157, 170, 180, 187, 196–197, 207, 232, 237, 288, 311, 314, 321, 325, 326, 329, 331, 336, 338, 342, 351, 357, 358, 359, 367, 379, 383, 385, 389, 390, 399, 403, 411, 418, 424
Fischer, C. T., x–xiv, xv, xvi, xvii, xix, 2–4, 10, 11, 13, 54, 74, 93, 180, 187, 195, 400, 403, 422
Fisher, M., 7, 312, 423
Fisher, R., 373
Folberg, J., 362

427

Ford, J. D., 29, 77
Fowler, C., 50, 51, 422
Fowler, J. C., 7
Frackowiak, M., 7, 423
Frank, J. D., 196
Frankel, J., 244
Frankel, S. A., 10
Freud, S., 110
Freyd, J. J., 30
Fuchigami, Y., 273

Garbin, M. G., 143
Gardner, D., 82
Gardner, R., 243
Garrity, C. B., 358, 360
Gensler, D., 244
Gentry, L., 232, 261, 311, 357
Gentry, L. B., 7
George, C., 75, 232, 239
Gerber, B., 312, 423
Gold, L., 38
Goodyear, R.K., 16
Gorske, T., 403, 404, 418, 424
Gorske, T. T., 9
Gouvier, W. D., 410
Graham, J. R., 75, 94, 137, 138, 162, 201, 368, 383
Greenberg, S. A., 358
Greenway, P., 113
Grossman, R. G., 405
Gruber, C., 415
Guérette, L., xviii
Guerrero, B., 11

Hahn, E. D., 16
Hamilton, A., 261
Hamilton, A.M., 311, 357
Hammer, A., 79
Hampton, K., xiv
Handler, B., 243
Handler, L., xvi–xix, 5, 8, 17, 50, 71, 85, 113, 166, 167, 175, 208, 244, 245, 263, 321, 338, 339–340, 344, 346, 357, 389, 423
Hanna-Pladdy, B., 410
Hansen, J., 79
Hanson, W.M., 15–16
Harmon, L. W., 79, 86
Harrower, M., 2
Hatcher, R., 63, 65
Haydel, M. E., 11
Heaton, R. K., 408
Hegion, A., xiv
Herman, J. L., 77
Hersh, B., 7, 329

Hilsenroth, M., 8–9, 50, 66, 245, 339, 421
Hilsenroth, M. J., 54, 56, 113, 195
Hinings, D., 297
Holzheimer, P. E. III, 77
Horowitz, L. M., 52
Howe, D., 297
Howes, H., 402

Jacklin, E., 422
Jacobvitz, D., 239
Jacques, E., 2
Johnson, M., 83
Johnston, J. R., 358, 359
Josselson, R., 243
Jourard, A., 85
Jourard, M., 85
Jung, C. G., 179

Kaemmer, B., 75, 94, 137, 162, 201, 368, 383
Kaltiala-Heino, R., 336
Kamphaus, R. W., 237
Kamphuis, J., xviii, 422
Kamphuis, J. H., 6, 40, 75, 138, 139, 207, 385
Kashiwagi, Y., 272
Kaufman, S., 295
Kay, G. G., 408
Kelemen, E., 402
Kerber, K., 38
Kerr, B., 16
Kluft, R. P., 35
Kochinshi, S., 40
Kohut, H., 262
Kövecses, Z., 82
Koziol, L. F., 73, 77
Kreutzer, J. S., 402, 403
Krishnamurthy, R., 17, 81
Krumholz, L., 311
Kuehnle, K., 358
Kugeares, S. L., 40, 75, 207, 385

Lachar, D., 415
Lakoff, G., 83
Lance, B. R., 17, 81
Langenecker, S. A., 77
Lanius, R. A., 38
Lee, H. J., 77
Leiblich, A., 243
Lerner, H. D., 187
Lerner, Paul, 122
Levin, H. S., 405
Lindenberger, J. C., 358
Liotti, G., 37

Lipkind, J., 11
Livingston, L. A., 402, 403
Loewenstein, R. J., 39, 40, 207, 385
Lohr, N., 38
Lowman, M., 85
Luborsky, L., 2, 243
Lyons-Ruth, K., 239

Macdonald, H., 11
Machiavelli, Niccolò, 103
Machover, K., 229
Mahler, M., 246
Main, M., 239
Mankins, Jim, 94–110
Martin, H., 422
Martin, Hale, 6
Mather, N., 162
Matson, M., 7, 232, 311, 319, 357
Mayberg, H. S., 77
Mayman, M., 50
McAdams, D., 243
McArthur, D., 233
McCaulley, M. H., 94
McElfresh, P., 422
McElfresh, P. J., 4, 11
McGrew, K. S., 162
McInerney, R. G., 401
McKay, M., 217
McLeod, J., 243
McNary, S. W., 39
Meehl, P., xiv
Mendelson, M., 137
Mercer, B., 10, 11
Mercer, B. L., 11
Miller, W. M., 403, 412
Miller, W. R., 9
Mills, J., 243
Milne, A. L., 362
Mittman, B., 289
Mock, J. E., 137
Montgomery, L. M., 291
Morey, L., 52
Morey, L. C., 75, 182
Murray, H., 94
Murray, H. A., 2, 38, 118, 145, 170, 201, 295
Mutchnik, 8
Myers, I. B., 94

Nakamura, N., 10, 11, 270, 273, 423
Nakamura, S., 10, 270
Nash, M. R., 8, 17, 244, 357
Newman, M. L., 113

Nicholas, C., 244
Nicholas, C. R. N., 8, 17
Nicholson, R. A., 369
Nijenhuis, E. R. S., 29
Noble, S., 402
Nowinski, L. A., 40
Nylund, D., 243

O'Donnell, V. M., 405
Ohnuki, K., 269
O'Neil, J., 77
Ousky, R., 358, 359
Overton, C., 422
Overton, C. G., 7, 212

Paleg, K., 217
Pantone, P., 244
Parsons, L., 402
Pasquarelli, B.A., 2
Patterson, F. L., 402
Patton, B., 373
Patz, S., 40
Pearlman, L. A., 30
Perry, W., 344
Pesale, F. P., 9, 421
Peters, E., 50, 54, 66, 208
Peters, E. J., 8, 113, 195
Phillips, H. L., 410
Pilgrim, S., 17
Pincus, A. L., 52
Pollio, H. R., 243
Pollock, V., 272, 276
Poston, J. M., 15–16
Potash, H. M., 243
Purisch, A., 74
Purves, C., xvi, 10, 11,
   336, 423

Radovanovic, H., 369
Rauch, S. L., 77
Reitan, R. M., 295
Reker, D., 272
Reynolds, C. R., 237
Rhodes, R., 292
Roberts, G., 233
Roberts, G. E., 364, 415
Roberts, M., 315
Rogers, L. B., 16
Roid, G. H., 163
Rollnick, S., 9, 403, 412
Rorschach, H., 95, 162, 415

Rorschach, H. R., 212
Rosch, E., 401
Roseby, V., 358
Rosenberg, A., 11
Rosenblatt, E., 11
Rounsaville, B., 36
Ruther, N. J., 358
Ryle, A., 202–203, 422

Salem, P., 362
Schaber, P., 244
Schaber, P. M., 113
Schachtel, E. G., 212, 213
Schaufeli, W., 138
Scholfield, G., 297
Schroeder, D. G., 4, 16
Schutz, B. M., 358, 368
Sendak, M., 262
Shaber, 7
Shuman, D. W., 358
Siegel, D., 297
Silk, K., 38
Silverstein, M., 247
Singer, J., 368
Slavin-Mulford, J., 9, 421
Smith, C., 243
Smith, J. D., 8, 13, 17, 113, 243,
   244, 357
Smith, S., 9, 403, 404, 418, 424
Smith, S. R., 40
Solomon, J., 239
Solomon, M., 297
Sorai, K., 269
Spence, D., 243
Stanley, M., 402
Staton, A. R., 402
Steele, K., 29
Steer, R. A., 143, 364
Stein, D. J., 77
Steinberg, M., 36
Stelmachers, Ziegrieds, xiv
Stiles, W. B., 63
Stokes, J., 344
Strassle, C. G., 8
Sullivan, H. S., xiv, xv
Sullivan, M. J., 358
Swann, W. B. Jr., 4–5, 16

Talley, J. L., 408
Taylor, L. A., 402, 403
Teicher, M. H., 77

Tellegen, A., xiv, 75, 137, 138,
   162, 201, 368, 383
Tellegen, A. T., 94
Tesler, P. H., 358, 359
Tharinger, D., xvi, 244, 261, 423
Tharinger, D. J., 7, 17, 113, 232,
   241, 311, 312, 315, 319, 325,
   329, 331, 357
Theilgaard, A., 81
Thompson, E., 401
Thompson, P., 358, 359
Toivakka, H., 8, 11, 339, 423
Tonsager, M. E., xv, 1–2, 6, 7,
   13, 54, 113, 114, 154, 359
Tsugawa, R., 273
Turunen, S., 336

Uchida, Y., 269
Unger, M. A., 73, 75
Urist, J., 122
Ury, W. L., 373

Välimäki, M., 336
van der Hart, O., 29
van der Kolk, B.A., 29, 77
van Dierendonck, D., 138
Varela, F., 401
Verrier, N., 241
Volavka, J., 272

Walker, M. M., 401
Ward, C. H., 137
Webb, S., 358, 359
Wechsler, D., 118, 162, 201,
   236, 272, 295, 343
Weinstein, L., 243
Weissbecker, I., 29
Wertz, F. J., 4
West, M., 75, 232, 239
Westen, D., 38
White, K., 208
White, K. G., 8, 113
White, M., 243, 338
Wiederholt, J. L., 415
Wiggins, J. S., 52
Wilkinson, A., 7, 113, 244
Winkel, J., 208
Winkel, J. D., 8, 113
Winnicott, D., 243, 292
Wolf, N. J., 8, 244
Woodcock, R. W., 162

Subject Index

AAP. *See* Adult Attachment
Projective Picture System
(AAP)
Abuse:
developmentally based, 33
physical, 75, 76
severe (*see* Abuse, severe)
sexual, 28–29, 35–36, 38, 44
verbal, 49, 328
Abuse, severe:
assessment, current, 202–203
assessment, previous, 201–202
client's background, 199–201
client therapeutic assessment,
202–203
depression and, 200, 201, 202
diagnoses and, 200
"Julie," 199–212, 214–221
MMPI-2, 201, 202
moving past abuse, 218–221
personality template and,
216–217
Psychotherapy File, 202–203
Rorschach 1, 205–207, 208,
210–211, 212, 214–215
Rorschach 2, 209, 212
Rorschach as intervention
(*see* Rorschach as
therapeutic intervention)
self-creativity and, 215–217
TAT stories, 201, 218–220
teaching points, 203, 207,
208, 217
WAIS-R as therapeutic
intervention, 201,
203–205
Abusive parenting, 80
ADHD. *See* Attention Deficit
Hyperactivity Disorder
(ADHD)
Adolescents. *See also* Adopted
teenager; Psychotic teenage
girl
fantasy animal drawings with,
338–341

generally, 335–338
Adopted teenager:
assessment questions, 226
client's story, by client,
229–231
client's story, by mother,
227–229
coherent narrative on,
236–241
depression/poor self-esteem,
237–238
disorganized attachment,
239–240
Draw-A-Person (DAP), 229
early memories/EMP,
232–235
family session, 232–235
initial session, 225–227
Level 1 test results, 237
"Mary," 225–241
midassessment meeting, 235
"Ms. Smith," 226, 227–229,
232–235, 236–240, 241
neuropsychological test
results, 236
neuropsychologist and, 225,
235–236, 241
organic brain dysfunction, 236
personality/emotional test
results, 236–237
Roberts Apperception
Test, 233
Rorschach/BASC-2 results,
237, 238
summary/discussion session,
235–236, 240–241
teaching points, 241
thinking/emotional
dysregulation, 238–239
WISC-IV results, 236
Adult Attachment Projective
Picture System (AAP), 75,
76, 79, 232, 239, 423
Alcohol abuse, 49, 75, 77,
341, 342

"Alice," 245–246, 264
Allegorical story, 83
Allegory, 82–84
Alliance, compliance and, 9
"Amanda," 47–48, 58
American Orthopsychiatric
Association, 95
Amnesia, 36
Analyst in the Inner City, The
(Altman), 292
"Anna," 180–197
"Anne," 114–130
Anne of Green Gables
(Montgomery), 291
Anorexia, 336, 381, 395, 398.
See also Eating disorder
Anxiety, 405, 409–410
Approach-avoidance, 77
"Arnold," 133–155
Assessment:
as catalyst for psychotherapy,
63–66
collaboration throughout (*see*
Collaboration throughout
assessment)
collaborative (*see*
Collaborative
assessment(s);
Collaborative Therapeutic
Neuropsychological
Assessment (CTNA);
Collaborative/Therapeutic
Assessment (C/TA))
intervention session, couples'
(*see* Couples' assessment
intervention session)
neuropsychological (*see*
Neuropsychological
assessment)
questions, 5, 226
relational view of, 12
shift in materials for,
424–425
Assessment intervention
sessions, 5

Attachment:
  adopted teenager and,
    239–240, 241
  dismissing, 239
  disorganized, 76, 239–240
  insecure, 75, 76, 297
  intelligence and, 79–81
  problematic, 73
  roadmap metaphor and, 78,
    81–82
  secure, for couples, 399
  unresolved issues, 71, 73,
    76–77
Attachment theory, 6, 76
Attachment Theory, Child
  Maltreatment and Family
  Support (Howe, Brandon,
  Hinings & Scholfield),
  297
Attention Deficit Hyperactivity
  Disorder (ADHD), 70,
  236, 411
Autism, 262
Avoidant Personality Disorder,
  53, 200, 202

BASC-2, 331
BDI. *See* Beck Depression
  Inventory (BDI)
Beck Depression Inventory
  (BDI), 137, 143, 364, 365,
  366
Beck Hopelessness Scale (BHS),
  364, 365, 366
Beck Youth Inventories,
  317–318
Bender–Gestalt Test, 95, 201,
  295
BHS. *See* Beck Hopelessness
  Scale (BHS)
"Billy," 246–264
Biopsychosocial life history, 72
Bipolar disorder:
  appearance of, 39
  genetic risk factors, 80
  of parent, 70
Bisexuality, 55–56, 60, 64
Borderline personality disorder,
  207, 270
Boundaries/limits, for
  children, 247
Brain:
  dysfunction, organic, 236
  function, domains of, 74
  hemispheres of, 81
Brain-based functioning, 74

Brain injury:
  active role in therapy, 424
  aftereffects of, 411
  anxiety and, 409
  human suffering and, 411
  rehabilitation, 406, 409, 410
  test following, 405
  traumatic, 401, 405
  "Walter," 405–411, 412
Brief Symptom Inventory (BSI),
  52, 65, 421
BSI. *See* Brief Symptom
  Inventory (BSI)

Caldwell Custody Report,
  368, 369
Career decisions, 79, 81, 86–87
CASAR worker (child advocate
  for the court), 305
CASF-P. *See* Combined Alliance
  Short- Form Patient
  version (CASF- P)
CAT. *See* Children's
  Apperception Test (CAT)
Catholic University of Milan,
  Italy, xvi
CC/PPE. *See* Child custody/
  parenting plan evaluations
  (CC/PPE)
CCRT. *See* Core Conflictual
  Relational Themes
  (CCRT)
CDI. *See* Coping Deficit Index
  (CDI)
Center for Therapeutic
  Assessment, xv, 4, 6
Child custody/parenting plan
  evaluations (CC/PPE):
  assessment findings,
    adolescent, 364–366
  assessment intervention with
    adolescent, 366–367
  assessment intervention with
    both parents, 370–372
  assessment questions, by
    parents, 368–369
  Beck Depression Inventory
    (BDI), 364, 365, 366
  Beck Hopelessness Scale
    (BHS), 364, 365, 366
  collaborative law
    approach, 359
  divorce and, 358–359, 360,
    361, 362, 375
  follow-up, 374
  generally, 357–358

"Ken," 362–374
  meetings with parents/
    assessment findings,
    367–370
  meeting with adolescent,
    363–364
  meeting with attorneys/
    parents, 363
  MMPI-2, 368, 369, 371–372
  negotiation and, 359,
    361–362
  "one- text procedure," 373
  parenting plan, negotiation
    of, 372–374, 375
  personal impact on assessor,
    375
  psychological instruments,
    364–365
  referral and context, 362
  Roberts 2 stories, 364–365,
    366
  Rorschach test, 364–366, 368,
    369–370
  TA advantages, 375–376
  TA in, 358–362
  TA in lieu of custody
    evaluation, 362
  teaching points, 375–376
Childhood trauma, unresolved,
  75, 76
Child Protective Services, 293
Children. *See also* Child custody/
  parenting plan evaluations
  (CC/PPE); Collaborative
  storytelling with children;
  Foster care/bad behavior
  fables for (*see* Fables for
    children)
  family sessions with, 17
  feedback to parents via fables,
    17–18
Children's Apperception Test
  (CAT), 295
Chronic pain, 424
"Cinderella syndrome" passive
  style, 281–282
"Clarissa," 27–32, 33–44
Classification, 12
Client(s):
  helping directly, 12
  as individuals, 424
  life world of, 425
  respect for, 11
Cognitive difficulties, 70, 74–75,
  77, 78, 79, 81, 85, 86–87
Cognitive efficiency, 77

Cognitive functioning, loss of.
   See Learning problems
Cognitive-linguistic work, 83
Collaboration throughout
   assessment:
   bird guardians, 99, 100,
     102, 103
   client's summary, 107–108
   first session, 95–101
   generally, 93, 109
   inanimate movement
     responses, 100
   "Jim," 94–110
   MMPI-2, 94, 95, 96, 98–99
   Myers- Briggs ENTJ, 94, 96,
     97–98, 108
   OCS client, 94–95, 106,
     109, 110
   outcomes, 109–111
   post-inquiry discussion,
     101, 110
   readiness for movement, 107
   Rorschach card
     administration, 99–101
   Rorschach review, 101–104
   second session, 101–107
   table-flipping, 94, 99
   take-home themes, 107, 108
   TAT, 95, 101, 104–107
   teaching points, 96, 98,
     99, 101, 102, 104, 107,
     108, 110
   visual image, 96
Collaborative, individualized
   psychological assessment,
   2–4
Collaborative Assessment(s):
   benefits of, 196
   C/TA and, ix
   intake, 180, 195
Collaborative assessment(s):
   generally, 10–11
   major principles, 3
Collaborative storytelling with
   children:
   "Alice," 245–246, 264
   Bigger Animal, 258–259
   Billy's story, 246–260
   boundary and, 251, 254
   Circle Animal drawing, 252
   control and, 247, 249,
     252, 254, 259, 260, 261,
     262, 263
   discussion, 260–264
   embedded therapeutic
     messages, 260

entitlement and, 247
externalization, 264
family dynamics and, 261, 265
generally, 243–246
grandiosity and, 247, 257,
   261, 262
interpersonal theory, 244–245
Light Animal, 254–255,
   259–260, 262
Lightning Animal, 255–256,
   257
The Lion, 249–251, 252,
   253, 254, 255, 256–257,
   258, 260
make-believe animals,
   drawing, 244–264
mirroring, 247, 262
Mouth on Tummy Animal,
   252–254
mutual storytelling, 252
parents and, 244, 249, 250,
   251, 256, 257, 261,
   262–263, 265
playfulness and, 255, 262,
   264, 265
praise, need for, 247, 261, 262
protective defenses and, 247,
   249, 251, 262
relational theory, 244–245
resistance and, 250, 252
self-protection, 249, 250,
   256, 262
Sunshine and Moonshine
   Animal, 263–264
symbolization, 264
teaching points, 264–265
Three-headed animal,
   248–249, 251
trust and, 254
vulnerability and, 249, 252
Collaborative/Therapeutic
   Assessment (C/TA):
   adapting aspects of, 427
   burning question/feared
     answer and, 30–31
   closely related approaches, ix
   common features of, 11–13
   in custody situation, 423–424
     (*see also* Child custody/
     parenting plan evaluations
     (CC/PPE))
   history of (*see* History of C/
     TA)
   outcome research, 13–16
   process research, 16–18
   reports, 426

Collaborative/therapeutic
   neurological assessment,
   81, 82
Collaborative Therapeutic
   Neuropsychological
   Assessment (CTNA):
   case examples of, 9–10
   with a child, 413–417
   C/TA and, ix
   model of, developed, 424
   phases of, 403
   TA and, 418
   ultimate goal of, 404–405
Collaborative Therapeutic
   Neuropsychological
   Assessment (Gorske and
   Smith), 9
Combined Alliance Short-
   Form Patient version
   (CASF-P), 63
Common ground, 425
Compassion, 12
Competency benchmarks, 16
Compliance, alliance and, 9
Concentration problems, 74
Consensus Rorschach:
   couples' assessment (*see*
     Couples' assessment
     intervention session)
   first impressions, 380
   follow-up, long-term, 399
   follow-up session, 398–399
   generally, 379
   individual assessment -
     John, 386
   individual meetings with
     Maria, 383–384
   individual sessions, generally,
     383
   initial session, 381–382
   "John," 379, 381–382,
     383–384, 386–399
   "Maria," 379–386
   MMPI-2, 384, 385, 387, 388
   referral, 379–380
   Rorschach, 384, 385–386,
     388–389
   summary, 399–400
   summary/discussion session,
     397–398
   teaching points, 382, 388, 389
   Trauma Content Index
     (TCI), 385, 388
Consent, 30
Content (component)
   scales, 138

Control Mastery Theory, 6
Coping Deficit Index (CDI), 75, 298, 365, 369
Core Conflictual Relational Themes (CCRT), 50, 63
Counter-transference, 9
Couples' assessment
    intervention session. *See also* Consensus Rorschach
    extended inquiry, 391–395
    free response phase, 390–391
    generally, 389–390
    "identified patient," 382
    "personally viable options," 400
    secure attachment, 399
    teaching point, 389
    trying out new behavior, 396–397
Couples therapy, 15
"Creative". *See* Emotional constriction
C/TA. *See* Collaborative/ Therapeutic Assessment (C/TA)
CTNA. *See* Collaborative Therapeutic Neuropsychological Assessment (CTNA)
Cultural influences, 158, 163, 166
Culture(s), 11
Curiosity, 12
Custody evaluation. *See* Child custody/parenting plan evaluations (CC/PPE)

DAP. *See* Draw-A-Person (DAP)
"David," 312–313, 315–331
DDNOS. *See* Dissociative Disorder Not Otherwise Specified (DDNOS)
Department of Human Services, 304
DEPI. *See* Depression Index (DEPI)
Depression. *See also* Suicidality; Therapeutic assessment of depression
    abuse and, 200
    of adopted teenager, 237–238
    anxiety and, 75, 77, 85
    assessment as catalyst for psychotherapy, 63–66
    characterological, 201

dissociating client and, 28, 33
    indicators of, 183
    long-term, 76, 77, 237–238
    major, 77, 200, 201, 202, 336, 384
    parental conflict and, 374
    as presenting issue, 341
    reawakening of woman and, 180, 183
    symptoms of, 72, 80
Depression Index (DEPI), 75, 321
Derealization symptoms, 37
Developmental Coordination Disorder (dysgraphia), 236
DID. *See* Dissociative identity disorder (DID)
Disciplined thinking, 212, 215, 216, 217
Dismissing attachment, 239
Disorganized attachment, 76, 239–240
Disrespect/10-year-old boy:
    background/assessment questions, 312–313
    BASC-2, 331
    child testing sessions, parents' observation/processing, 314–323
    "David," 312–313, 315–331
    Early Memories Procedure (EMP), 322–323
    emotional state of child, 327
    fables and, 312, 324, 329, 330–331
    family intervention session, 324–326
    feedback session, 329–331
    generally, 311–312
    human figure drawings, 315–317
    parent feedback letter, 326–328
    Parents' Experience of Assessment Survey, 331
    play as part of testing sessions, 319
    reasons for disrespect/ aggressiveness, 327–328
    relationship building, 323–324, 328
    research findings, 331
    Rorschach test, 320–322, 327
    self-report measure, 317–318
    sentence completion method, 318–319

stories told to Apperception cards, 320
    summary/discussion session, 326–328, 331–332
    TAP assessments, 311, 312
    Teaching Points, 312, 314, 315, 317, 318, 319, 320, 321–322, 324, 326, 329, 331
    testing/observation, generally, 316–317
Dissociating client, therapeutic assessment:
    "Clarissa," 27–32, 33–44
    collaborative relationship, 30–32
    decline of client, 27–29
    "dissociation diary," 31–32
    feedback session - suicide barrier, 40–41
    followup: client's gift, 41–44
    MMPI-2 and, 33, 34, 42–43
    open-ended performance measures, 38–40
    reflections on client, 29–30
    Rorschach testing, 39–40, 43
    SCID-D-R and, 36–37, 44
    structured/semistructured performance tests, 32–37
    teaching points, 29, 30, 31, 32, 36, 39, 40
    Thematic Apperception Test (TAT), 38–39, 43
    VRIN, elevated, 33
Dissociation:
    attention control and, 43
    check-ins and, 35, 41–42
    as defense mechanism, 77
    emotional numbness and, 37
    traumatic, signs of, 31
Dissociation diary, 31–32
Dissociative Disorder Not Otherwise Specified (DDNOS), 37
Dissociative disorders, 37, 385
Dissociative Identity Disorder (DID), 31, 36, 37, 200
"Dissociative" lapses, 124
Dissociative obsessiveness, 44
Dissociative relational field, 32
Divorce:
    fueds following, 362
    high-conflict proceedings, 358–359, 360, 361, 375
Domains of brain function, 74

Draw-A-Person (DAP), 229,
315, 344, 347
Drawing. *See also* Fantasy
Animal Drawing Game
human figure drawings,
315–317
Kinetic Family Drawing
(KFD), 295, 297, 316
make-believe animals, xix,
244–264, 423
projective drawings, 272,
276, 295
Rorschach-based
psychotherapy and, 272,
276, 285, 285–286, 287
Drug use, 28
Duquesne University, 98
Dynamic assessment, ix
Dysgraphia, 236
Dysthymic Disorder, 53, 65,
200, 202

Early emotional deprivation,
75, 76
Early Memories Procedure
(EMP), 75, 231, 322–323,
383, 385, 398
Early Memories Test, 202
Early Memory protocol, 50–52
Eating disorder, 36, 53. *See also*
Anorexia
Effect size, 15
Egocentricity Index, 365, 369
Embedded therapeutic
messages, 260
Emotional attachment:
disorganized, 239–240
early trauma and, 241
Emotional constriction:
"Arnold," 133–155
assessment intervention
session, 145–148
Beck Depression Inventory
(BDI), 137, 143
concentration difficulties,
134, 136, 137, 143,
145, 151
follow-up, 153–154
impressions/hypotheses,
136–137
laziness, self-perceived, 135,
136, 137, 151
Maslach Burnout Inventory
(MBI), 138, 143
MMPI-2, 137, 138–139,
143, 145

passions/vitality, 135, 137,
143–144, 145, 146, 148,
150, 152–153
personal impact, 154–155
question generation/context,
133–136
referral and context, 133
reflections/hypotheses,
143–144
Rorschach Inkblot Method
(RIM), 137, 140–142, 143
standardized testing, 137–143
summary/discussion session,
148–150
teaching points, 136,
138, 148
written feedback for client,
150–153
Emotional deprivation, early,
75, 76
Emotional functioning. *See*
Rorschach tests
EMP. *See* Early Memories
Procedure (EMP)
Empathy, xviii
Empathy magnifiers, 13
Entitlement, 247
Essential human capacities, 212
Ethical decision making, 85
European Center for
Therapeutic Assessment,
xvi
Executive dysfunction, 77, 85
Executive function of brain,
74, 77
Existentialism, xiii
Externalization, 264

Fables for children. *See also*
Collaborative storytelling
with children; Therapeutic
letter/story
disrespect/10-year-old boy,
312, 324, 329, 330–331
individualized feedback via,
17–18
written, 4, 7, 12
"Factor analysis," 136
Family Apperception
Test, 320
Family dynamics, 261, 265
Family-of-origin, 85
Family sessions:
with adopted teenager,
232–235
with children, 17

disrespect/10-year-old boy,
324–326, 423
multiple life issues, 168–169
Family system, 236–237
Fantasy Animal Drawing Game.
See also Drawing
with adolescents, 338–341
with hospitalized adolescents,
423
"Tea," 344, 347–350
as widely used method, 8
Feedback. *See also* Test feedback
collaborative vs.
noncollaborative, 16
letter, 326–328
oral vs. written, 17
ordering of information in
session, 16–17
to parents, 7
sessions, 329–331
story, presenting, 304–306
story, writing, 300–304
written (*see* Therapeutic
letter/story)
"50/50" relationship, 159, 175,
176
Flexibility, 13
Flexible neuropsychological
battery, 74
Forensic psychology, 357–358
Forgetting, 36
Foster care/bad behavior:
assessment, team
involvement, 307–308
assessment sessions, 293–296
attachment theory/splitting,
297
A Duckling Named Matilda
story, 301–304
feedback story, presenting,
304–306
feedback story, writing,
300–304
generally, 291–292
outcomes, 306–307
referral, 293–294
Rorschach ink blot test, 295,
298, 300
Structural Summary, 299
"Tanisha," 293–308
teaching points, 307–308
testing instruments, 295
test results, 296–300
Thematic Apperception Test
(TAT), 295, 296, 297, 306
WISC-III, 295, 296

Galveston Orientation and
Amnesia Test, 405
GED. See General Educational
Development (GED) test
General Educational
Development (GED)
test, 159
Genetic disorder, 158, 160
Genetic risk factors, 80
Glasgow Coma Scale, 405
Grandiosity, 247, 257, 261, 262
Grief, 80

Harris Lingoes scales, 138
HCMSC. See Hennepin County
Medical Center (HCMC)
Healing Trauma: Attachment,
Mind, Body, and Brain
(Siegel & Solomon), 297
Hemispheres of brain, 81
Hennepin County Medical
Center (HCMC), xiv
History of C/TA:
collaborative assessment,
10–11
Collaborative Therapeutic
Neuropsychological
Assessment, 9–10
Finn's Therapeutic
Assessment (TA), 4–7
Fisher's collaborative,
individualized
assessment, 2–4
generally, 1–2
Handler's therapeutic
assessment with children, 8
Hilsenroth's Therapeutic
Model of Assessment,
8–9
therapeutic assessment, 7
Hole in the World: An American
Boyhood, A (Rhodes), 292
House-Tree-Person projective
drawings, 295
Human capacities, essential, 212
Human communications
system, 83
Human figure drawing. See
Draw-A-Person (DAP)
Humanistic psychology, 85–86
Human-science psychology, xiii
Hyperapnea, 270

Identified patient, 382
Identity development, 37, 181,
289, 338

Idiographic sentence
completion, 318–319
IIP. See Inventory of
Interpersonal Problems
(IIP)
"Ilyssa," 413–417
Impulsivity, 77
Inanimate movement responses,
100
Inborn trait, 250
Incomplete sentences task,
318–319
Individualized data sharing
method, 80
Individualized feedback fables,
17–18. See also Fables for
children
Individualized findings, 79
Individualized psychological
assessment, 2
Individualizing Psychological
Assessment (Fischer), xv, 93
Individuation process, 246
Information-gathering model of
assessment, 1–2
Informed Consent, 30
In Our Clients' Shoes: Theory and
Techniques of Therapeutic
Assessment (Finn), xiv,
xvi, xviii
Inpatients, 13
Intelligence, 79–81. See also
Wechsler test
Internal navigation. See
Dissociating client,
therapeutic assessment
International Society for
Rorschach and Projective
Methods, xvi
Interpersonal possibilities,
104–107
Interpersonal theory, 244–245
Intersubjectivity theory, 6
Intervention. See Family
intervention session
Intimacy, 70, 79, 87
Intimacy in Psychological
Assessment (Fischer), 4
Inventory of Interpersonal
Problems (IIP), 52, 65, 421
Involuntary psychiatric care, 336

"Jackie," 69–89
"Jim," 94–110
"John," 379, 381–382, 383–384,
386–399

Journal of Child Custody, 358
"Joy," 47–61, 62–66
Judgment, 12
"Julie," 199–212, 214–221

"Ken," 362–374
KFD. See Kinetic Family
Drawing (KFD)
Kinetic Family Drawing (KFD),
295, 297, 316
Kraepelin's Arithmetic Test, 277

Language process, 83
Learning disabilities, 70, 158,
159, 160, 163, 413–418
Learning problems:
CTNA and, 403–405
existential challenges, 402
neurological disorders and,
401–402
neurological evaluations and,
402–403
self-concept and, 402
Letter. See also Therapeutic
letter/story
to client, 173–175
parent feedback, 326–328
"Level 1, 2, and 3" schema, 5,
17, 34, 237, 338
Life issues. See Multiple life
issues
Life world, 425
Love, loss of. See Therapeutic
assessment of depression
Low motivation, 77
Low self-esteem, 75, 77, 85, 180,
184, 237–238

Machiavellian side, 100, 103
Major Depression, 200, 202
Make-believe animals. See under
Drawing
Managed care, 6, 16
Manual Assisted Cognitive
Therapy, 14
"Maria," 379–386
"Mariko," 270–276, 277–288
"Mary," 225–241
Maslach Burnout Inventory
(MBI), 138, 143
Mathematical Learning
Disability, 236
MBI. See Maslach Burnout
Inventory (MBI)
Mental Health Act, 336
Meta-analysis, 15

Metaphor:
  for becoming angry, 423
  in conceptual system, 83
  "Jackie," 69–89
  life story, changing, 79
  as linguistic expression, 82–83
  roadmap as, 71, 78, 81, 82
  "shoes," xviii
Metaphorical concepts, 83
Metaphorical story, 71, 79,
    82, 83
MI. See Motivational
    Interviewing (MI)
Minnesota Multiphasic
    Inventory (MMPI-2). See
    also Response Variability
    scale (VRIN)
Minnesota Multiphasic
    Personality Inventory–2
    (MMPI-2), 17, 75, 94,
    98–99, 137, 138–140,
    162, 166–166, 201, 217,
    368, 369, 371–372, 383,
    385, 387
Mirroring, 247, 262
MMPI-2, 424. See Minnesota
    Multiphasic Personality
    Inventory–2 (MMPI-2)
MMPI-A, 364, 365
Motivational Interviewing (MI),
    9, 412
"Ms. Smith," 226, 227–229,
    232–235, 236–240, 241
Multiple life issues:
  assessment intervention
    session, 170–172
  background on client,
    159–161
  cognitive testing, 163–165
  dilemma of change, 162
  family intervention session,
    168–169
  generally, 157–159
  growth in understanding,
    165–167
  letter to client, 173–175
  "Pouya," 157–176
  Rorschach extended inquiry,
    167–168
  summary/discussion
    session, 173
  teaching points, 162, 168,
    169, 172, 173, 175, 176
  testing plan/results, 162–168
  Thematic Apperception Test
    (TAT), 170

  value of supervision, 175–176
Multiple suicide attempts. See
    Suicidality
Mutuality of Autonomy
    Scale, 122
Myers-Briggs personality type,
    94, 96, 97–98, 108

Narrative therapy, 243
National Institute of
    Neurological Disorders and
    Stroke, 401
Negative self-view, 80, 86, 87
Neglect, 70, 75, 76
Negotiation, 359, 361–362
Neurobiology, 6
Neurodiversity, 73
Neuropathic pain, 396
Neuropsychological
    assessment:
  for adopted teenager, 225,
    235–236
  assessment process, 71–77
  career goals and, 79, 81,
    86–87
  childhood trauma and,
    75–76, 77
  cognitive functioning and,
    70, 74–75
  for complex trauma
    cases, 241
  creative shifts and, 85
  depression and, 72, 75, 76,
    77, 80, 85
  domains of brain function, 74
  dynamic flow of sessions,
    71–73
  findings: attachment/
    intelligence, 79–81
  generally, 69
  impact on client, 87
  impact on writer/assessor,
    88–89
  individualized findings, 79
  intervention: career decisions,
    86–87
  intervention: findings in story
    form, 84–86
  neuropsychological
    tests, tasks, and
    questionnaires, 72
  personality measures, 74–75
  ranking findings by levels, 78
  referral and context, 70–71
  suicidality/suicide attempt,
    69, 70, 72, 73, 75, 82

  summarizing, generally,
    77–79
  teaching points, 71, 72, 73,
    76, 78, 80, 82
  test data, 73–77
  therapeutic letter, 81–82
  therapeutic story: allegory,
    82–84
  transformation and, 71, 89
  WASI testing, 72, 74
Neuropsychological battery,
    flexible, 74
Neuropsychological evaluation,
    71–72
Neuropsychology, 74
Nomothetic comparisons, 2
Noncollaborative assessment,
    16, 18
Nonverbal Learning Disability
    (NVLD), 236
NVLD. See Nonverbal Learning
    Disability (NVLD)

Occupational Problem, 53
OCS. See Officers' Candidate
    School (OCS)
ODD. See Oppositional Defiant
    Disorder (ODD)
Officers' Candidate School
    (OCS), 94, 106, 109,
    110, 422
One-assessor model, 314
Oppositional Defiant Disorder
    (ODD), 15
Oral vs. written feedback, 17
Organic brain dysfunction, 236
Outcome research, 13–16
Overdosing, 270, 271, 342

PAI. See Personality Assessment
    Inventory (PAI)
Pain, 380, 424
Parent(s). See also Child
    custody/parenting plan
    evaluations (CC/PPE)
  collaborative storytelling and,
    244, 249, 250, 251, 256,
    257, 261, 262–263, 265
  fables as individualized
    feedback to, 17–18
  observation of child
    assessment sessions, 7
  parental splitting, 360,
    368, 370
  positive parenting practices,
    326

"Parenting capacity." *See* Child
    custody/parenting plan
    evaluations (CC/PPE)
Parents' Experience of
    Assessment Survey, 331
Partner Relational Problem, 53
Patient's Estimate of
    Improvement (PEI), 65–66
PEI. *See* Patient's Estimate of
    Improvement (PEI)
Perceptual Thinking Index
    (PTI), 300
Perfectionists, 14
Personality Assessment
    Inventory (PAI), 52, 53,
    75, 182
Personality template, basic:
    capacities/tensions between,
        212–213
    coartative types, 213–214
    dilation-coartation
        dimension, 213–214
    EB ratio, 213
Personal letter, 173–175
"Personally viable options," 400
Phenomenology, xiii
Play, as part of testing sessions,
    319
Playfulness, 255, 262, 264, 265
Play therapy, traditional, 244
POMS. *See* Profile of Mood
    States (POMS)
Positive triangulation, 399
Posttraumatic stress disorder
    (PTSD):
    cognitive therapy and, 27
    diagnostic criteria for, 33
    trauma-related symptoms, 29
"Pouya," 157–176
Praise, need for, 247, 261, 262
"Prideful satisfaction,"
    accomplishments
    and, 247
Prince, The (Machiavelli), 103
Privacy, protection of clients', ix
Processing speed, 74
Process research:
    collaborative vs.
        noncollaborative
        feedback, 16
    family sessions and, 17
    individualized feedback via
        fables, 17–18
    order of information in
        feedback session, 16–17
    written vs. oral feedback, 17

Profile of Mood States (POMS),
    272, 276, 288
Projection, 360, 368, 370
"Projective counseling," 2
Projective counseling, ix
Projective drawings, 2, 272, 276,
    285, 295
Projective identification:
    definition of, 388
    major, 394–395
Psychiatric inpatients, 13
Psychoanalytic psychology, 243
Psychodiagnostik, 269
Psychoeducation, 61–62
Psychogenic pain, 380
Psychological assessment. *See*
    Assessment
Psychological assessment
    instruments. *See* specific
    instrument
Psychosis, 207
Psychotherapy. *See also*
    Rorschach-based
    psychotherapy
    collaborative assessment prior
        to, 422
    early attachment experiences
        and, 76
    ethical decision-making in, 85
    stories and, 82
Psychotherapy File, The,
    202–203, 422
Psychotic teenage girl:
    alcohol abuse and, 342
    antipsychotic medication
        for, 350
    assessment referral, 342
    assessment sessions, 343
    background information,
        341–342
    cognitive assessment,
        343–344
    fantasy animal drawings with,
        338–341, 344, 347–350
    feedback to parents, 350
    follow-up, 351
    generally, 335–338
    Human Figure Drawing,
        346–347
    initial session/client's
        questions, 342–343
    personality assessment,
        344–347
    presenting issues, 341
    Rorschach tests, 344–345
    summary, 351–352

"Tea," 341–352
    teaching points, 352
PTI. *See Perceptual Thinking
    Index* (PTI)

Race(s), 11
RCs. *See* Reconstructed Clinical
    Scales (RCs)
Readiness for movement, 107
Reality testing. *See* Rorschach
    tests
Reawakening of woman:
    "Anna," 180–197
    depression and, 180, 183
    generally, 179–180
    intake collaborative
        assessment, 182–191
    Personality Assessment
        Inventory (PAI), 182, 183
    reawakening/dreams, 194–195
    recollections of assessment
        findings, 191–193
    referral and context, 180–181
    Rorschach tests and, 183–191
    self-criticism, 184–185,
        186, 192
    Sentence Completion, 181,
        184, 192
    summary/conclusion, 195–197
    teaching points, 181, 182,
        187, 191, 195
Reconstructed Clinical Scales
    (RCs), 138, 139–140
Relational theory, 244–245
Relational view of psychological
    assessment, 11–12
Relationship building, 323–324
Relationship seeking, 215, 216,
    217
Reports, 426
Repression, 29
Research on C/TA:
    outcome research, 13–16
    process research, 16–18
Research, process. *See* Process
    research
Resistance, 2, 9
Respect for clients, 11
Response Variability scale
    (VRIN), 33, 138
Retesting during psychotherapy,
    281–284, 288, 289
RIM. *See* Rorschach Inkblot
    Method (RIM)
Roadmap metaphor, 78, 81–82
Roberts 2 test, 364, 366

Roberts Apperception Test, 233, 320, 423

Rorschach as therapeutic intervention:
dilation-coartation dimension, 213–214
essential human capacities, 212, 216–217
generally, 205
personality template, 213, 216–217
Rorschach 1, 205–207, 208, 210–211, 212, 214–215
Rorschach 2, 208, 209, 212
Structural Summary, 206, 209
teaching points, 207

Rorschach-based psychotherapy:
background on client, 271–272
changes during therapy, 280–281
conclusion, 288
C/TA and, ix
drawings and, 272, 276, 285–286, 287
East meets West, 269–270
feedback, 273, 277, 285–288
"Mariko," 270–276, 277–288
POMS and, 272, 276, 277–278, 284, 288
presenting issues, 270
retest - first, 281–282
retest - second, 283–284
Rorschach test results, 273–276, 279, 280
structural summary, 273, 274
Suicide Constellation, 273, 283
teaching points, 277, 288–289
tests administered, 272
Uchida-Kraepelin (U-K) test, 272, 276–277, 279
WAIS-III and, 272, 276, 278, 284

Rorschach Extended Inquiry, 167–168

Rorschach indices:
Coping Deficit Index (CDI), 75, 298, 365, 369
Depression Index (DEPI), 237, 321, 365
Egocentricity Index, 365, 369
Suicide Index, 40–41
Traumatic Content Index (TCI), 77, 207, 385, 388

Traumatic Content Index (TC/R), 40, 41

Rorschach Inkblot Method (RIM), 137, 140–142, 162, 232, 295, 383

Rorschach Inquiry, extended, 422

Rorschach Structural Summary:
client feedback and, 101
Comprehensive System 5th Edition, 345
Coping Deficit Index (CDI), 298
Egocentricity Index, 300
FC:CF ratio (Form Color vs. Color Form), 298
for foster child, 299
Perceptual Thinking Index (PTI), 300
for reawakening of woman, 189
for suicidal client, 119–121
W:M ratio ("aspiration ratio"), 298

Rorschach tests. See also Consensus Rorschach
administration/responses, 99–101, 182, 183–191, 201
Comprehensive System (CS), 344, 364, 368, 370–371
content score analysis, 422
disrespect/10-year-old boy, 320–322
dissociative disorders and, 39–40
EB ratio, 213
first administration of, 205–207, 208, 210–211, 212, 214–215
Human Movement (M) response, 365, 367
personality template, 212–213, 216–217
post-inquiry discussion, 101
repeated, 423
review of, 101–104
second administration of, 208, 209, 212
"sign-in" response, 185
Structural Summary (see Rorschach Structural Summary)
Suicide Constellation, 273
as therapeutic intervention, 205–217

SB-5. See Stanford-Binet Intelligence Scales, fifth edition (SB-5)

Schema. See "Level 1, 2, and 3" schema; Self-schemas

Schizophrenia, 351

SCID-D-R. See Structured Clinical Interview for DSM-IV Dissociative Disorders–Revised (SCID-D-R)

Self-concept, 77, 84–85, 203, 402. See also Rorschach tests

Self-creativity, 215–217

Self-criticism, 59, 184–185, 186, 192, 422

Self-destructive behaviors, 129

Self-disclosure:
collaboration and, 88–89
ethical decision-making and, 85
judicious, 88

Self-esteem:
benefits to clients, 14, 15
low, 75, 77, 85, 180, 184, 237–238

Self-hatred, 80

Self-injury, 270, 271, 341, 351, 370

Self-loathing, 70

Self-perception, negative/critical, 183, 184–185, 186. See also Low self-esteem

Self-protection, 249, 250, 256, 262

Self-reflective capacity, 352

Self-report measures, 52–53, 317–318

Self-schemas, 5, 17

Self-verification theory, 5

Self-view, negative, 80, 86, 87

Sentence completion method, 318–319

Sentence Completion Series, 75

SEQ. See Session Evaluation Questionnaire (SEQ)

Session Evaluation Questionnaire (SEQ), 63

Sexual abuse. See under Abuse

Sexuality, 55–56, 60, 64

Sexual orientation, 64

Shared humanness, 425

"Sign-in" response, 185

Sixteen Personality Factor Test, 94

Social support system, 30
Society for Personality
    Assessment (SPA), xiii,
    xvi–xvii, 10
SPA. See Society for Personality
    Assessment (SPA)
Splitting, 297, 360, 368, 370
Stanford-Binet Intelligence
    Scales, fifth edition (SB-5),
    163, 164
Stories. See Collaborative
    storytelling with children;
    Feedback; Therapeutic
    letter/story
    externalization and, 264
    fables (see Fables for children)
    fantasy animal drawings and,
        338–341
    metaphor in (see Metaphor)
    symbolization and, 264
    told to Apperception
        cards, 320
Strong Interest Inventory, 86
Structural Summary. See
    Rorschach Structural
    Summary
Structured Clinical Interview
    for DSM- IV Dissociative
    Disorders–Revised (SCID-
    D-R), 36, 37, 44
Substance abuse, 418
Suicidality. See also Rorschach-
    based psychotherapy
    "Anne," 114–130
    comportment during testing
        sessions, 117–118
    dissociating client and, 28
    feedback session with client,
        126–128
    feedback to Dr. X, 125–126
    findings, formal, 118–124
    first session with client,
        116–117
    follow-up, 128–130
    generally, 113–114
    ideation/suicide attempt, 69,
        70, 72, 73, 75, 82
    involuntary psychiatric care,
        336
    "Jackie," 69–89
    "Mariko," 270–276, 277–288
    neuropsychological
        assessment, 69, 70, 72, 73,
        75, 82
    Rorschach tests/structural
        summary, 118, 119–124

therapist's request for
    consultation, 114–116
Suicide Index, 40–41
"Summary of Clinician
    Activities Found to Be
    Significantly Related
    to Positive Therapeutic
    Alliance During the
    Initial Interview and
    Psychological Assessment,"
    54–55, 421–422
Supervision, value of, 175–176

TA. See Therapeutic Assessment
    (TA)
TA-A. See Therapeutic
    Assessment with
    Adolescents (TA-A)
Table-flipping, 94, 99
TA-C. See Therapeutic
    Assessment with Children
    (TA-C)
Take-home themes, 107, 108
Tampere University Hospital,
    335
"Tanisha," 293–308
TAP. See Therapeutic
    Assessment Project
    (TAP)
TAT. See Thematic
    Apperception Test (TAT)
TCI. See Traumatic Content
    Index (TCI)
TC/R. See Traumatic Content
    Index (TC/R)
"Tea," 341–352
Teaching Points, x
Test feedback:
    interactive vs. delivered, 16
    written vs. oral, 17
Tests/testing sessions. See also
    specific test
    play as part of, 319
    special view of, 12–13
Thematic Apperception Test
    (TAT), 2, 38, 95, 104–107,
    118, 145–148, 170, 201,
    218–220, 295, 306, 320
Therapeutic assessment, ix
Therapeutic Assessment (TA):
    advantages of, 360–362
    C/TA and, ix
    emergence of model, xv
    generally, 4–7
    "Level 1, 2, and 3" findings,
        5, 338

in lieu of custody evaluation,
    362
modification, with couples,
    367–368
one-assessor model, 314
psychological assessment
    and, 359
training others in, xvi
two-assessor model, 314–315
Therapeutic assessment of
    depression. See also
    Depression
    "Amanda," 47–48, 58
    CASF-P and, 63, 66
    client affect/uncomfortable
        feelings, 60–61
    client initiation/exploration
        of issues, 58–59
    client's background, 48–49
    collaborative stance toward
        patient, 56–57
    Core Conflictual Relational
        Themes and, 50, 63
    distress sources/cyclical
        relational themes, 59–60
    Early Memory protocol,
        50–52
    "Joy," 47–61, 62–66
    longer, depth-oriented
        interviews, 55–56
    presented issues, 47–48
    reviewing assessment results,
        61–62
    self-report measures, 52–53
    sessions, dynamic flow of,
        49–63
    sexuality and, 55–56, 60, 64
    speaking/experience-near
        language, 57–58
    TMA and, 53–54, 56, 61
    treatment goals, collaboration
        in, 62–63
Therapeutic Assessment Project
    (TAP), 7, 311–312
Therapeutic Assessment
    with Adolescents (TA-A),
    6–7
Therapeutic Assessment with
    Children (TA-C), 6–7, 8
Therapeutic communication, 81
Therapeutic letter/story. See also
    Collaborative storytelling
    with children; Fables for
    children
    allegory/metaphorical stories,
        82–84

Therapeutic letter/story
(*continued*)
    assessment findings: story
        form, 84–86
    collaboration/self-disclosure,
        88–89
    data plus metaphor, 81–82
    messages through, 82, 83,
        84–85
Therapeutic messages,
    embedded, 260
Therapeutic Model of
    Assessment (TMA), ix,
    8–9, 53–54
Third parties, 426
Thought Stopping technique,
    217
Time-series analysis, 13, 17
TMA. *See* Therapeutic Model of
    Assessment (TMA)
TMT. *See* Trail Making Test A
    and B (TMT)
Toward the Structure of Privacy
    (Fischer), 4
Trail Making Test A and B
    (TMT), 295
Transformation, 10, 89
Trauma. *See also* Abuse; Abuse,
    severe
    adoption as, 241
    burning question/feared
        answer and, 30–31
    early childhood, 75, 76, 77
    family, extensive, 78
    "flooded" stage of, 29
    of foster care children, 292
    intergenerational, 292
    social support system and, 30
Trauma Index, 75
Trauma-related symptoms, 29
Trauma Symptom Inventory
    (TSI), 33
Traumatic Content Index
    (TCI), 77, 207, 385
Traumatic Content Index
    (TC/R), 40, 41
"Traumatic thought disorder," 38
Triangulation, positive, 399

Trust, 254, 256, 257, 261, 262,
    263
TSI. *See* Trauma Symptom
    Inventory (TSI)
Tubers and Zots toy, 258
Two-assessor model, 314–315

Uchida-Kraepelin (U-K) test,
    272, 276–277, 279
U-K. *See* Uchida-Kraepelin
    (U-K) test
University of Pittsburgh Medical
    Center Traumatic Brain
    Injury Rehabilitation
    Unit, 405
Unresolved childhood trauma,
    75, 76
Utrecht Burnout Scale, 138

Verbal abuse, 49, 328
Verbal intelligence (VIQ),
    74, 81
Veterans Administration
    hospitals, xvii
VIQ. *See* Verbal intelligence
    (VIQ)
Vocational planning, 79, 81,
    86–87
VRIN. *See* Response Variability
    scale (VRIN)
Vulnerability, 249, 252

WAIS-III. *See* Wechsler Adult
    Intelligence Scale–III
    (WAIS-III)
WAIS-IV. *See* Wechsler
    Adult Intelligence
    Scale, fourth edition
    (WAIS-IV)
WAIS-R. *See* Wechsler test
"Walter," 405–411, 412
WASI. *See* Wechsler
    Abbreviated Scale of
    Intelligence (WASI)
WCC. *See* WestCoast Children's
    Clinic (WCC)
WCST. *See* Wisconsin Card
    Sorting Test (WCST)

Wechsler Abbreviated Scale
    of Intelligence (WASI),
    72, 74
Wechsler Adult Intelligence
    Scale (WAIS) Similarities
    subtest, xvii
Wechsler Adult Intelligence
    Scale, fourth edition
    (WAIS-IV), 162, 163
Wechsler Adult Intelligence
    Scale–III (WAIS-III), 118,
    272, 276, 278
Wechsler Intelligence Scale for
    Children – Fourth Edition
    (WISC-IV), 236
Wechsler Intelligence Test for
    Children – III (WISC-III),
    295, 296
Wechsler test (WAIS-R), 202,
    203–205, 343
WestCoast Children's Clinic
    (WCC), 10
Where the Wild Things Are
    (Sendak), 262
WHO. *See* World Health
    Organization (WHO)
WISC-III. *See* Wechsler
    Intelligence Test for
    Children–III (WISC-III)
Wisconsin Card Sorting Test
    (WCST), 408
WJA-III. *See* Woodcock-
    Johnson Tests of
    Achievement–III
    (WJA-III)
W:M ratio ("aspiration ratio"),
    298
Woodcock- Johnson Tests of
    Achievement–III
    (WJA-III), 162
Working memory, 74
World Health Organization
    (WHO), 401
Written feedback. *See also*
    Feedback; Letter;
    Therapeutic letter/story
    vs. oral feedback, 17
    and verbal, 81